Lazy Learning

T0205645

Edited by

David W. Aha

Navy Center for Applied Research in Artificial Intelligence,
Naval Research Laboratory, Washington D.C., USA

Reprinted from *Artificial Intelligence Review*
Volume 11, Nos. 1–5, 1997

Kluwer Academic Publishers

Dordrecht / Boston / London

A C.I.P. catalogue record for this book is available from the Library of Congress.

ISBN 978-90-481-4860-8

Published by Kluwer Academic Publishers,
P.O. Box 17, 3300 AA Dordrecht, The Netherlands.

Sold and distributed in the U.S.A. and Canada
by Kluwer Academic Publishers,
101 Philip Drive, Norwell, MA 02061, U.S.A.

In all other countries, sold and distributed
by Kluwer Academic Publishers,
P.O. Box 322, 3300 AH Dordrecht, The Netherlands.

Printed on acid-free paper.

Table of Contents

Artificial Intelligence Review **11**: 1–6, 1997.

About the Authors

David W. Aha (UC Irvine 1990) joined the Naval Research Laboratory's Navy Center for Applied Research in Artificial Intelligence in 1993, having held post-doctoral fellowships at the Turing Institute, the Johns Hopkins University, and the University of Ottawa. His research interests lie at the intersection of machine learning (ML) and case-based reasoning (CBR). He serves both communities as a frequent conference program committee member, editing board member (*Machine Learning, Journal of Artificial Intelligence Research, Applied Intelligence*), workshop (co-)organizer (AAAI-94 Workshop on *CBR*, ICML-95 Workshop on *Applying ML in Practice*, AAAI-95 Fall Symposium on *Adaptation of Knowledge for Reuse*), and WWW page maintainer.

Ethem Alpaydin received his Ph.D. in Computer Science from the Swiss Federal Institute of Technology, Lausanne in 1990. He was a postdoc at the International Computer Science Institute, Berkeley in 1991 and a visiting scholar at the Department of Brain and Cognitive Sciences, MIT in 1994. Since 1991 he has been teaching at the Department of Computer Engineering, Bogazici University, Istanbul, Turkey. His research is on statistical techniques for machine learning and their application to pattern recognition, especially optical and pen-based handwritten character recognition.

Chris Atkeson recently joined the Georgia Tech College of Computing faculty. Previously, he was on the faculty of the MIT Brain and Cognitive Sciences Department and a member of the MIT Artificial Intelligence Laboratory. His research focuses on numerical approaches to machine learning, and uses robotics as a domain in which to explore the behavior of learning algorithms. His early work was on model-based learning. Recent work has explored task level learning and memory-based learning.

Daniel Borrajo is an Associate Professor of Computer Science at the Universidad Carlos III de Madrid. He received his Ph.D. in Computer Science from the Universidad Politécnica de Madrid in 1990. Dr. Borrajo leads several machine learning and problem solving projects at his research institution. His recent interests span across several areas, including machine learning, planning, game theory, and scientific discovery. His research explores, among other things, the integration of: analytical learning, inductive learning, and genetic programming; high-level planning and reactive planning; and search strategies and learning mechanisms. He is also interested in theory-based discovery, as well as the development of more efficient planners. Dr. Borrajo is the author of a book on Artificial Intelligence.

Antal van den Bosch received his (Dutch equivalent of the) M.A. degree in Computational Linguistics in 1992, from Tilburg University, The Netherlands. After having worked as a research assistant at the Institute for Language Technology and AI and at the department of Psychology at Tilburg University (1993), he is currently working on a four-year Ph.D. project on machine-learning of natural language, especially morpho-phonology, at the Department of Computer Science at the University of Limburg, Maastricht, The Netherlands (since 1994). His research interests include symbolic and connectionist inductive learning, and new methods in natural language processing.

Walter Daelemans (1960, Antwerp) studied linguistics and psycholinguistics at the Universities of Antwerp and Leuven. He worked as a research assistant at the University of Nijmegen in a project on the development of a dialogue system and author environment for Dutch, and at the Artificial Intelligence Laboratory in Brussels, where he was responsible for an ESPRIT project on office automation. In 1987 he earned a Ph.D. (University of Leuven) with an object-oriented model of Dutch morphology and phonology and its applications in language technology. He is presently affiliated as an associate professor to the Computational Linguistics group of Tilburg University and to the Linguistics Department of the University of Antwerp (UIA), teaching Computational Linguistics and Artificial Intelligence courses. His current research interests are in Machine Learning of Natural Language, and knowledge representation techniques for natural language processing. He has published on intelligent text processing, lexical database design, intelligent tutoring systems, speech synthesis, linguistic knowledge representation, machine learning of natural language, and office automation.

Pedro Domingos is a Ph.D. candidate in Information and Computer Science at the University of California, Irvine. He holds an M.S. in Information and Computer Science from U.C. Irvine, and an M.S. and B.S. in Electrical Engineering and Computer Science from the Techni-

cal University of Lisbon, where he has also been a teaching and research assistant. His main research interests are in machine learning and data mining. Previously, he has worked in real-time reasoning and computer graphics. He is the author of six journal articles and twenty conference publications.

Pat Langley has published widely on the topics of machine learning and scientific discovery, including the recent text *Elements of Machine Learning*. He is well known as an advocate of experimental studies in artificial intelligence, and his research crosses the areas of planning, natural language, diagnosis, vision, and control. Dr. Langley is an editor of the journal *Machine Learning* and edits the Morgan Kaufmann series on that topic. He holds a research position at Stanford University and serves as Director of the Institute for the Study of Learning and Expertise.

Charles X. Ling obtained his B.Sc. from Shanghai Jiao Tong University in China in 1985, and an M.Sc. and a Ph.D. from the University of Pennsylvania in 1989. Since 1989 he has been a faculty member in the Department of Computer Science at the University of Western Ontario (UWO). He is currently an Associate Professor. Currently he is also a faculty member at the University of Hong Kong. He has done extensive research in computational modeling of landmark cognitive learning tasks. He has also worked in several areas of machine learning, including Inductive Logic Programming (ILP), inductive learning from examples, artificial neural networks, and real-world application of machine learning. His Web home page, http://www.csd.uwo.ca/faculty/ling, contains details of his research areas and publications.

Oded Maron is a graduate student at the M.I.T. Artificial Intelligence Lab. He received his undergraduate degree from Brown University. He has done work in machine learning, model selection, and path planning. He has applied his research in the financial industry, creating several automated trading systems for an international investment firm.

Takao Mohri received his Ph.D. from the University of Tokyo in 1995 and spent a year there as a Postdoctoral Fellow. He is now a researcher at Fujitsu Laboratories Ltd. His interests lie mainly in artificial intelligence, especially in the areas of inductive reasoning, case-based and memory-based reasoning. Recently he is working on the application of artificial intelligence techniques to the Internet including WWW and netnews.

Andrew Moore has worked in the area of machine learning, locally weighted learning and reinforcement learning, for seven years. He has published over 25 papers in the area, and given invited talks at the International Conference on Machine Learning, the World Congress on Neural Nets, and numerous industrial and academic departments. His funding includes an NSF CAREER award, an NSF Research Initiation Award and gifts from the 3M corporation and a food processing company. He has applied these machine learning methods to processes in the power-distribution, automotive, food-manufacture, and textile industries. He is a co-founder of a Pittsburgh-based AI start-up company: Schenley Park Research, Inc.

Karl Pfleger is currently a Ph.D. student in Computer Science at Stanford University, having received a B.S.E. from Princeton University in 1992. He has done research in machine learning, neural networks, mobile robotics, and agent architectures. He has strong interdisciplinary interests in the long-term goals of artificial intelligence and cognitive science. His current research focuses on learning and abstraction, specifically on hierarchical compositional structure and chunking, learning in sequences, context effects in the integration of bottom-up and top-down processing, and lossless data compression.

Mehran Sahami is a doctoral candidate in the Computer Science Department at Stanford University. He received both his B.S. and M.S. in Computer Science from Stanford in 1992 and 1993, respectively. His research interests include machine learning, neural networks, adaptive agents, and probabilistic reasoning. He is currently completing a dissertation on probabilistic methods for information retrieval and data mining. He is also an instructor at Stanford, teaching classes on programming methodology and the ethical implications of technology, for which he received the George Forsythe Memorial Award for Excellence in student teaching.

Marcos Salganicoff received his B.S.E.E. from Case Western Reserve University in 1985, was a member of the technical staff at the Jet Propulsion Lab in the Applied Robotics Laboratory from 1985 to 1987, and received his Ph.D. in Computer and Information Science from the Moore School of the University of Pennsylvania in 1992. He is currently Director of Algorithm Research and Development for Sensar Inc., a subsidiary of the David Sarnoff Research Center, in Moorestown, New Jersey. His research interests include machine learning for vision and action, computational neuroscience, and real-time vision processing applications.

Steven Salzberg received the B.A.

degree in English and the M.S. and M.Phil. degrees in computer science from Yale University in 1980, 1982, and 1984 respectively. He received the Ph.D. degree in computer science from Harvard University. From 1985 to 1987, he was a research scientist with Applied Expert Systems of Cambridge, Massachusetts. In 1988 and 1989 he was a Research Associate at the Harvard Business School, where he worked on advanced manufacturing systems. In 1989 he joined the faculty of the Department of Computer Science at Johns Hopkins University in Baltimore, Maryland, where he is currently an Associate Professor. He holds joint faculty appointments in the Departments of Biomedical Information Sciences and Cognitive Science. His research interests include machine learning and computational biology, and he has authored more than 50 papers in these areas.

Stefan Schaal was a postdoctoral fellow at the Department of Brain and Cognitive Sciences and the Artificial Intelligence Laboratory at MIT, after receiving his Ph.D. from the Technical University of Munich in 1992. Currently, he is an Adjunct Assistant Professor at the Georgia Institute of Technology, the Head of the Computational Learning group of the ERATO Neural Computation Project, an Adjunct Assistant Professor at the Pennsylvania State University, and he holds a part-time affiliation with the ATR Human Information Processing Research Laboratories in Japan. Stefan's interests include topics such as statistical learning, neural networks, nonlinear dynamics, and nonlinear control theory, applied to research on artificial and biological motor control and motor learning. His research approach focuses on both theoretical investigations and experiments with human subjects and anthropomorphic robot equipment.

John Sheppard is a Principal Research Analyst with ARINC Incorporated. He holds a B.S. in Computer Science from Southern Methodist University and an M.S. in Computer Science from Johns Hopkins University. Currently, he is a Ph.D. candidate in Computer Science at Johns Hopkins where he is doing research in reinforcement learning and multiagent systems. At ARINC, he is responsible for research and development in intelligent diagnostic systems and holds a patent for a method and apparatus for intelligent diagnostic testing. He has published over 60 papers in test, diagnosis, artificial intelligence, and machine learning and is co-author of the first book on system test and diagnosis. In addition to his research activities, he is actively involved in IEEE and IEC standardization efforts in test and design automation.

Kai Ming Ting received his undergraduate degree in Electrical Engineering (1986) from the University of Technology, Malaysia, his master's degree in Computer Science (1992) from the University of Malaya, and his Ph.D. (1996) from the University of Sydney, Australia. He was a practicing engineer at the National Electricity Board, Malaysia from 1986 to 1992. He joined the Department of Computer Science at the University of Waikato, New Zealand in 1995, as a Post-Doctoral Fellow/Part-Time Lecturer. His main areas of research are Machine Learning and other aspects of Artificial Intelligence.

Manuela M. Veloso is Finmeccanica Assistant Professor of Computer Science at Carnegie Mellon University. She received her Ph.D. in Computer Science from Carnegie Mellon in 1992. Dr. Veloso's main research interest consists of the development of experience-based intelligent agents that combine high-level planning, low-level execution, and learning. She investigates different planning algorithms, analogical/case-based reasoning learning strategies, and the integration of analytical and inductive learning methods applied to planning. She also researches on methods in which perception and learning are combined to address jointly high-level and low-level reasoning tasks. Dr. Veloso is interested in strategy planning and learning in the context of multiple experience-based agents, in collaborative and adversarial environments, such as robotic soccer. She is the author of a book on *Planning and Analogical Reasoning*.

Handong Wang received the B.Sc. degree in precision machinery & instruments from the National University of Defense Science and Technology, China, in 1991, and the M.S. degree in computer science from the University of Electronic Science and Technology of China in 1994. From Oct. 1994 to Sept. 1995 he was a research associate in the Department of Computer Science at the University of Western Ontario, London, Canada. He is currently a graduate student in the Department of Computer Science at the University of Western Ontario. His research interests include software engineering, machine learning, and image processing.

Ton Weijters received his Ph.D. in Language Philosophy from the University of Nijmegen, The Netherlands, in 1989. In his Ph.D. thesis, entitled 'Denotation in Discourse: Analysis and Algorithm', a denotation resolution algorithm was developed, specifying how a discourse representation for a given text can be constructed. At present he is assistant professor at the Department of Computer Science at the University of Limburg in Maastricht, The Netherlands. He is involved in the research of the machine learning group of his department, focusing on the applicability of machine learning techniques to linguistic domains and the development of new machine-learning algorithms.

Dietrich Wettschereck received his M.Sc. and Ph.D. degrees in computer science from Oregon State University in 1990 and 1994, respectively. He has been a SYLFF (Sasakawa Young Leaders Fellowship Fund Program) fellow since 1993. He has been a Postdoctoral Fellow at the German National Research Center for Information Technology (GMD) since September 1994. He has published on the topics of neural networks, instance-based learning algorithms for propositional and relational representations, and data mining. He also participates in projects revolving around applied machine learning, data mining, and inductive logic programming.

Junming Yang obtained the B.S. degree in Mathematics from Shandong University in Jinan China in 1983 and a Ph.D. in Statistics from the Utah State University in 1996. His primary research interests are in statistical inference, statistical simulation, and machine learning. He is now a graduate student in Computer Science at the Utah State University.

Yeesat Yim completed her B.S. degree in Applied Mathematics from the National Chung Hsing University in Taiwan in 1988. She then worked for the Information Division of the National Museum of Natural Science as a System Programmer and Research Assistant for several years. She obtained her MS degree in Computer Science from Utah State University in 1995.

Jianping Zhang is Associate Professor of Computer Science at Utah State University. He received his Ph.D. in Computer Science from the Universi-

ty of Illinois at Urbana-Champaign in
1990. His research interests are Artificial
Intelligence, Machine Learning, Intelligent Computer-Assisted Instruction, and
Case-Based Reasoning. He has published
more than forty technical papers in these
areas.

Artificial Intelligence Review **11:** 7–10, 1997.

Editorial

Lazy Learning

DAVID W. AHA
Naval Research Laboratory, Navy Center for Applied Research in Artificial Intelligence, Washington, DC, USA.
E-mail: aha@aic.nrl.navy.mil (http://www.aic.nrl.navy.mil/~aha/)

Lazy learning algorithms exhibit three characteristics that distinguish them from other learning algorithms (i.e., algorithms that lead to performance improvement over time). First, they *defer* processing of their inputs until they receive requests for information; they simply store their inputs for future use. Next, they reply to information requests by *combining* their stored (e.g., training) data. Finally, they *discard* the constructed answer and any intermediate results. In contrast, *eager* learning algorithms greedily compile their inputs into an intensional concept description (e.g., represented by a rule set, decision tree, or neural network), and in this process discard the inputs. They reply to information requests using this a priori induced description, and retain it for future requests. This lazy/eager distinction exhibits many interesting tradeoffs. For example, while lazy algorithms have lower computational costs than eager algorithms during training, they typically have greater storage requirements and often have higher computational costs when answering requests. For the first time, this distinction, and its implications, are the focus of a (quintuple) special issue; *AI Review* has brought together 14 articles that review and/or investigate state-of-the-art learning algorithms that display lazy behaviors.

There is a risk involved in propagating jargon in any scientific discipline. To be useful, such jargon must clarify an important concept that is not otherwise easily described, and perhaps is also not well recognized. "Lazy learning" fulfills this requirement. It focuses attention on the lazy/eager distinction, which is often neglected. This is important; lazy algorithms offer a powerful alternative perspective on how to solve learning tasks. For example, lazy methods often use *local* approaches (Bottou and Vapnik 1992), which yield highly adaptive behavior not usually found in eager algorithms, and lazy algorithms are the basis of many industrial applications (e.g., Jabbour et al. 1987;

Creecy et al. 1992; Nguyen et al. 1993). Most previous jargon for describing lazy reasoning behavior is sadly lacking due to a focus on representation rather than on a combination of representation and processing (e.g., "case-based", "instance-based", "memory-based", "exemplar-based"). Lazy approaches do not derive their intelligent behaviors solely from their representation (i.e., *all* learning algorithms use "memory" and process "instances"), but rather from the flexibile manner in which specific stored information can be combined to answer queries. The terminology "lazy" serves to clarify by borrowing intuition from both common vernacular and, more importantly, previous scientific usage such as *lazy evaluation* in functional programming languages (e.g., delaying evaluation is used to process infinite data structures).

The papers in this special issue display three trends. First, they focus on *learning*. Thus, many use terminology most familiar in the machine learning literature, although several were inspired by earlier work in pattern recognition (Dasarathy 1991), cognitive psychology (Smith and Medin 1981; Nosofsky 1986), statistics (Friedman 1994; Dietterich et al. 1994), and, only more recently, case-based reasoning (Kolodner 1993; Aamodt and Plaza 1994) and machine learning (Aha et al. 1991). Second, almost all address *supervised* learning tasks. The exception is by Borrajo and Veloso, which is in the tradition of research on lazy *analytic* learning algorithms (e.g., Tadepalli 1989; Clark and Holte 1992; Bostrom 1992). Third, most of the articles focus on *partially* lazy learning algorithms (i.e., they compromise on some of the distinguishing characteristics of *purely* lazy algorithms noted above). While purely lazy algorithms are useful for some tasks, there are many ways in which lazy behaviors can be profitably compromised so as to decrease computational costs, enlarge the scope of applicability, or improve on some other performance measure(s). For example, compromises include a priori averaging of the input data, caching intermediate results (e.g., parameter settings for a similarity function), and tracking performance feedback to modify learning behavior.

Unlike many issues of *Artificial Intelligence Review*, this special issue focuses less on surveys and more on novel research contributions. However, it does begin with a review: Atkeson, Moore, and Schaal's article on *locally weighted learning*, which should be required reading in introductory classes on machine learning. Their topic has its roots in statistics. They detail how these methods can be applied to adaptive robotic control tasks in their second article.

The next four papers introduce extensions of k-nearest neighbor (kNN) algorithms on topics of particular interest in machine learning research. Thus, they provide useful departure points from Atkeson et al.'s survey. Alpaydin tackles the issue of voting among multiple (edited) kNN algorithms.

Salganicoff investigates how kNN can be enhanced in the contexts of concept and sample shift. Ting characterizes situations in which discretizing continuous features increases predictive accuracy. Finally, Zhang, Yim, and Yang evaluate an algorithm that intelligently selects a query's k nearest neighbors.

Purely lazy algorithms retain all their input data. When using feature-value representations to describe this data, kNN is highly susceptible to the curse of dimensionality, especially when many features are irrelevant to the performance task (Friedman 1994). Thus, many researchers have proposed methods for reducing the impact of irrelevant features. Four articles in this special issue address this topic; two eliminate features using feature selection techniques and two assign continuous weights to features. Thus, all four bias their similarity functions towards giving less (or no) influence for less relevant features. First, Maron and Moore describe parallel *racing* algorithms for both model and feature selection tasks. Racing algorithms have significant speed advantages compared with previous selection algorithms. Second, Domingos introduces a context-sensitive feature selection algorithm that allows the relevance of features to vary *locally*; feature relevance can differ depending on the region of the instance space. Third, Ling and Wang present a procedure that, for some classes of concept shapes, can be used to compute the optimal weights for each feature. This can be used to help validate the behavior of weighting algorithms. Fourth, Wettschereck, Aha, and Mohri review and empirically compare a subclass of feature weighting algorithms; they focus on distinguishing the task characteristics that favor using one weighting approach over others.

Finally, four articles describe applied research in which the authors also extend lazy learning algorithms in different directions. First, Langley, Pfleger, and Sahami use *evidence grids*, a probabilistic description of occupancy, to represent instances for a robotics place-learning task. Next, Sheppard and Salzberg use a genetic algorithm to generate examples for kNN, and show how this integration can be used to improve performance on a class of delayed reinforcement learning tasks (i.e., pursuit games). In their unique paper, Borrajo and Veloso's HAMLET system is shown to improve search efficiency and increase plan quality by using three lazy behaviors to incrementally learn control rules for nonlinear planning tasks. Finally, Daelemans, van den Bosch, and Weijters introduce modifications for using decision trees to compress the instance memory by removing feature-value redundancy. Their *IGTree* algorithm reduces storage requirements and response time for some linguistic tasks.

In summary, this collection broadly covers topics concerning the capabilities of learning algorithms that incorporate lazy behaviors; it serves as a snapshot of current research on lazy learning. Readers interested in pursuing this area are encouraged to supplement these articles with background publications from other disciplines, such as those mentioned earlier.

This special issue would not have been possible without the opportunity presented to me by Evangelos Simoudis, nor without the support of my colleagues here at NCARAI. Thanks also to Chris Atkeson, who has strongly encouraged me to create a collection like this, and to Diana Gordon, John Grefenstette, Pat Langley, and Len Breslow for their many consultations. Special thanks to the 28 reviewers, whose reviews greatly assisted the authors. Most importantly, thanks to the authors for their enjoyable contributions.

References

Aamodt, A., & Plaza, E. (1994). Case-based reasoning: Foundational issues, methodological variations, and system approaches. *AI Communications* **7**, 39–59.

Aha, D. W., Kibler, D., & Albert, M. K. (1991). Instance-based learning algorithms. *Machine Learning* **6**, 37–66.

Bostrom, H. (1992). Eliminating redundancy in explanation-based learning. In *Proceedings of the Ninth International Conference on Machine Learning* (pp. 38–42). Aberdeen, Scotland: Morgan Kaufmann.

Bottou, L., & Vapnik, V. (1992). Local learning algorithms. *Neural Computation* **4**, 888–900.

Clark, P., & Holte, R. (1992). Lazy partial evaluation: An integration of explanation-based generalisation and partial evaluation. In *Proceedings of the Ninth International Conference on Machine Learning* (pp. 82–91). Aberdeen, Scotland: Morgan Kaufmann.

Creecy, R. H., Masand, B. M., Smith, S. J., & Waltz, D. L. (1992). Trading MIPS and memory for knowledge engineering. *Communications of the ACM* **35**, 48–64.

Dasarathy, B. V. (Ed.). (1991). *Nearest neighbor(NN) norms: NN pattern classification techniques*. Los Alamitos, CA: IEEE Computer Society Press.

Dietterich, T. G., Wettschereck, D., Atkeson, C. G., & Moore, A. W. (1994). Memory-based methods for regression and classification. In J. Cowan, G. Tesauro, & J. Alspector (Eds.), *Neural Information Processing Systems 6*. Denver, CO: Morgan Kaufmann.

Friedman, J. H. (1994). Flexible metric nearest neighbor classification. Unpublished manuscript available by anonymous FTP from playfair.stanford.edu (see pub/friedman/README).

Jabbour, K., Riveros, J. F. V., Landsbergen, D., & Meyer W. (1987). ALFA: Automated load forecasting assistant. In *Proceedings of the 1987 IEEE Power Engineering Society Summer Meeting*. San Francisco, CA.

Kolodner, J. (1993). *Case-based reasoning*. San Mateo, CA: Morgan Kaufmann.

Nguyen, T., Czerwinsksi, M., & Lee, D. (1993). COMPAQ QuickSource: Providing the consumer with the power of artificial intelligence. In *Proceedings of the Fifth Annual Conference on Innovative Applications of Artificial Intelligence* (pp. 142–150). Washington, DC: AAAI Press.

Nosofsky, R. M. (1986). Attention, similarity, and the identification-categorization relationship. *Journal of Experimental Psychology: General* **15**, 39–57.

Smith, E. E., & Medin, D. L. (1981). *Categories and concepts*. Cambridge, MA: Harvard University Press.

Tadepalli, P. (1989). Lazy explanation-based learning: A solution to the intractable theory problem. In *Proceedings of the Eleventh International Joint Conference on Artificial Intelligence* (pp. 649–700). Detroit, MI: Morgan Kaufmann.

Artificial Intelligence Review **11**: 11–73, 1997.

Locally Weighted Learning

CHRISTOPHER G. ATKESON[1,3], ANDREW W. MOORE[2] and
STEFAN SCHAAL[1,3]

[1] *College of Computing, Georgia Institute of Technology, 801 Atlantic Drive, Atlanta,
GA 30332-0280*
E-mail: cga@cc.gatech.edu, sschaal@cc.gatech.edu
http://www.cc.gatech.edu/fac/Chris.Atkeson
http://www.cc.gatech.edu/fac/Stefan.Schaal
[2] *Carnegie Mellon University, 5000 Forbes Ave, Pittsburgh, PA 15213*
E-mail: awm@cs.cmu.edu
http://www.cs.cmu.edu/~awm/hp.html
[3] *ATR Human Information Processing Research Laboratories, 2-2 Hikaridai, Seika-cho,
Soraku-gun, Kyoto 619-02, Japan*

Abstract. This paper surveys locally weighted learning, a form of lazy learning and memory-based learning, and focuses on locally weighted linear regression. The survey discusses distance functions, smoothing parameters, weighting functions, local model structures, regularization of the estimates and bias, assessing predictions, handling noisy data and outliers, improving the quality of predictions by tuning fit parameters, interference between old and new data, implementing locally weighted learning efficiently, and applications of locally weighted learning. A companion paper surveys how locally weighted learning can be used in robot learning and control.

Key words: locally weighted regression, LOESS, LWR, lazy learning, memory-based learning, least commitment learning, distance functions, smoothing parameters, weighting functions, global tuning, local tuning, interference.

1. Introduction

Lazy learning methods defer processing of training data until a query needs to be answered. This usually involves storing the training data in memory, and finding relevant data in the database to answer a particular query. This type of learning is also referred to as *memory-based* learning. Relevance is often measured using a distance function, with nearby points having high relevance. One form of lazy learning finds a set of nearest neighbors and selects or votes on the predictions made by each of the stored points. This paper surveys another form of lazy learning, *locally weighted learning*, that uses locally weighted training to average, interpolate between, extrapolate from, or otherwise combine training data (Vapnik 1992; Bottou and Vapnik 1992; Vapnik and Bottou 1993).

In most learning methods a single global model is used to fit all of the training data. Since the query to be answered is known during processing of training data, training query-specific local models is possible in lazy learning. Local models attempt to fit the training data only in a region around the location of the query (the query point). Examples of types of local models include nearest neighbor, weighted average, and locally weighted regression (Figure 1). Each of these local models combine points near a query point to estimate the appropriate output. *Nearest neighbor* local models simply choose the closest point and use its output value. *Weighted average* local models average the outputs of nearby points, inversely weighted by their distance to the query point. *Locally weighted regression* fits a surface to nearby points using a distance weighted regression.

Weighted averages and locally weighted regression will be discussed in the following sections, and our survey focuses on locally weighted linear regression. The core of the survey discusses distance functions, smoothing parameters, weighting functions, and local model structures. Among the lessons learned from research on locally weighted learning are that practical implementations require dealing with locally inadequate amounts of training data, regularization of the estimates by deliberate introduction of bias, methods for predicting prediction quality, filtering of noise and identifying outliers, automatic tuning of the learning algorithm's parameters to specific tasks or data sets, and efficient implementation techniques. Our motivation for exploring locally weighted learning techniques came from their suitability for real time online robot learning because of their fast incremental learning and their avoidance of negative interference between old and new training data. We provide an example of interference to clarify this point. We briefly survey published applications of locally weighted learning. A companion paper (Atkeson et al. 1996) surveys how locally weighted learning can be used in robot learning and control. This review is augmented by a Web page (Atkeson 1996).

This review emphasizes a statistical view of learning, in which function approximation plays the central role. In order to be concrete, the review focuses on a narrow problem formulation, in which training data consists of input vectors of specific attribute values and the corresponding output values. Both the input and output values are assumed to be continuous. Alternative approaches for this problem formulation include other statistical nonparametric regression techniques, multi-layer sigmoidal neural networks, radial basis functions, regression trees, projection pursuit regression, and global regression techniques. The discussion section (Section 16) argues that

Nearest neighbor

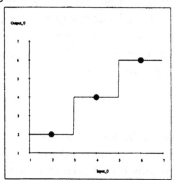
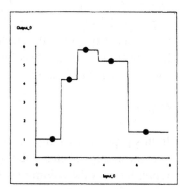

Weighted average

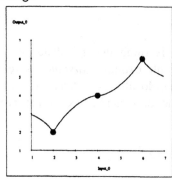
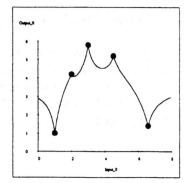

Locally weighted regression

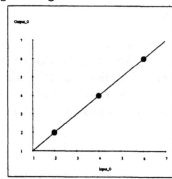
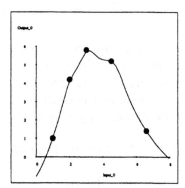

Figure 1. Fits using different types of local models for three and five data points.

locally weighted learning can be applied in a much broader context. Global learning methods can often be improved by localizing them using locally weighted training criteria (Vapnik 1992; Bottou and Vapnik 1992; Vapnik and Bottou 1993). Although this survey emphasizes regression applications (real valued outputs), the discussion section outlines how these techniques have been applied in classification (discrete outputs). We conclude with a short discussion of future research directions.

Notation

In this paper scalars are represented by italic lower case letters (y). Column vectors are represented as boldface lower case letters ($\mathbf{x}$) and row vectors are represented as the column vectors transposed ($\mathbf{x}^T$). Matrices are represented by bold face upper case letters ($\mathbf{X}$).

2. Distance Weighted Averaging

To illustrate how locally weighted learning using a distance function is applied, we will first consider a simple example, *distance weighted averaging*. This will turn out to be a form of locally weighted regression in which the local model is a constant. A prediction $\hat{y}$ can be based on an average of n training values $\{y_1, y_2, \ldots, y_n\}$:

$$\hat{y} = \frac{\sum y_i}{n} \tag{1}$$

This estimate minimizes a criterion:

$$C = \sum_i (\hat{y} - y_i)^2 \tag{2}$$

In the case where the training values $\{y_1, y_2, \ldots, y_n\}$ are taken under different conditions $\{\mathbf{x}_1, \mathbf{x}_2, \ldots, \mathbf{x}_n\}$, it makes sense to emphasize data that is similar to the query $\mathbf{q}$ and deemphasize dissimilar data, rather than treat all the training data equally. We can do this in two equivalent ways: weighting the data directly or weighting the error criterion used to choose $\hat{y}$.

2.1. *Weighting the Data Directly*

Weighting the data can be viewed as replicating relevant instances and discarding irrelevant instances. In our case an instance is represented as a data point $(\mathbf{x}, y)$. Relevance is measured by calculating a *distance* $d(\mathbf{x}_i, \mathbf{q})$ between the query point $\mathbf{q}$ and each data point input vector $\mathbf{x}_i$. A typical distance function is the Euclidean distance ($\mathbf{x}_i$ is the ith input vector, while $\mathbf{x}_j$ is the jth component of the vector $\mathbf{x}$):

$$d_E(\mathbf{x}, \mathbf{q}) = \sqrt{\sum_j (\mathbf{x}_j - \mathbf{q}_j)^2} = \sqrt{(\mathbf{x} - \mathbf{q})^T (\mathbf{x} - \mathbf{q})} \cdot \qquad (3)$$

A *weighting function* or *kernel function* $K(\ )$ is used to calculate a weight for that data point from the distance. A typical weighting function is a Gaussian (Figure 8):

$$K(d) = e^{-d^2} \qquad (4)$$

The weight is then used in a weighted average:

$$\hat{y}(\mathbf{q}) = \frac{\sum y_i K(d(\mathbf{x}_i, \mathbf{q}))}{\sum K(d(\mathbf{x}_i, \mathbf{q}))} \qquad (5)$$

Note that the estimate $\hat{y}$ depends on the location of the query point $\mathbf{q}$.

2.2. *Weighting the Error Criterion*

We are trying to find the best estimate for the outputs y_i, using a local model that is a constant, $\hat{y}$. Distance weighting the error criterion corresponds to requiring the local model to fit nearby points well, with less concern for distant points:

$$C(\mathbf{q}) = \sum_{i=1}^{n} [(\hat{y} - y_i)^2 K(d(\mathbf{x}_i, \mathbf{q}))] \qquad (6)$$

The best estimate $\hat{y}(\mathbf{q})$ will minimize the cost $C(\mathbf{q})$. For that value of $\hat{y}$, $\frac{\partial C}{\partial \hat{y}} = 0$. This is achieved by the $\hat{y}$ given in Equation 5, and so in this case weighting the error criterion and weighting the data are equivalent. Note that both the criterion $C(\mathbf{q})$ and the estimate $y(\mathbf{q})$ depend on the location of the query point $\mathbf{q}$.

This process has a physical interpretation. Figures 2 and 3 show the data points (black dots), which are fixed in space, pulling on a horizontal line (the constant model) with springs. The strength of the springs are equal in the unweighted case, and the position of the horizontal line minimizes the sum of the stored energy in the springs (Equation 2). We will ignore a factor of $\frac{1}{2}$ in all our energy calculations to simplify notation. In the weighted case, the springs are not equal, and the spring constant of each spring is given by $K(d(\mathbf{x}_i, \mathbf{q}))$. The stored energy in the springs in this case is C of Equation 6, which is minimized by the physical process. Note that the locally weighted average emphasizes points close to the query point, and produces an answer

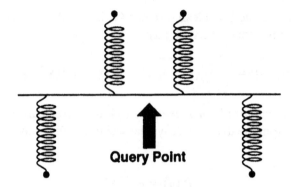

Figure 2. Unweighted averaging using springs.

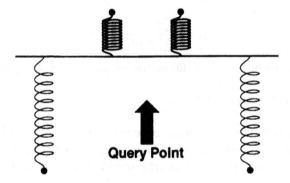

Figure 3. Locally weighted averaging using springs.

(the height of the horizontal line) that is closer to the height of points near the query point than the unweighted case.

2.3. *The Distance Weighted Averaging Literature*

In statistics the approach of fitting constants using a locally weighted training criterion is known as *kernel regression* and has a vast literature (Härdle 1990; Wand and Jones 1994). Nadaraya (1964) and Watson (1964) proposed using a weighted average of a set of nearest neighbors for regression. The approach was also independently reinvented in computer graphics (Shepard, 1968). Specht (1991) describes a memory-based neural network approach based on a probabilistic model that motivates using weighted averaging as the local model for regression. Connell and Utgoff (1987), Kibler et al. (1989) and Aha (1990) have applied weighted averaging to artificial intelligence problems.

3. Locally Weighted Regression

In *locally weighted regression* (LWR) local models are fit to nearby data. As described later in this section, this can be derived by either weighting the training criterion for the local model (in the general case) or by directly weighting the data (in the case that the local model is linear in the unknown parameters). LWR is derived from standard regression procedures for global models. We will start our exploration of LWR by reviewing regression procedures for global models.

3.1. *Nonlinear Local Models*

3.1.1. *Nonlinear Global Models*
A general global model can be trained to minimize the following unweighted training criterion:

$$C = \sum_i L(f(\mathbf{x}_i, \beta), y_i) \tag{7}$$

where the y_i are the output values corresponding to the input vectors $\mathbf{x}_i$, β is the parameter vector for the nonlinear model $\hat{y}_i = f(\mathbf{x}_i, \beta)$, and $L(\hat{y}_i, y_i)$ is a general loss function for predicting $\hat{y}_i$ when the training data is y_i. For example, if the model were a neural net, then β would be a vector of the synaptic weights. Often the least squares criterion is used for the loss function ($L(\hat{y}_i, y_i) = (\hat{y}_i - y_i)^2$), leading to the training criterion:

$$C = \sum_i (f(\mathbf{x}_i, \beta) - y_i)^2 \tag{8}$$

Sometimes no values of the parameters of a global model can provide a good approximation of the true function. There are two approaches to this problem. First, we could use a larger, more complex global model and hope that it can approximate the data sufficiently. The second approach, which we discuss here, is to fit the simple model to local patches instead of the whole region of interest.

3.1.2. *A Training Criterion For Nonlinear Local Models*
The data set can be tailored to the query point by emphasizing nearby points in the regression. We can do this by weighting the training criterion:

$$C(\mathbf{q}) = \sum_i [L(f(\mathbf{x}_i, \beta), y_i) K(d(\mathbf{x}_i, \mathbf{q}))] \tag{9}$$

where $K(\ )$ is the weighting or kernel function and $d(\mathbf{x}_i, \mathbf{q})$ is the distance between the data point $\mathbf{x}_i$ and the query $\mathbf{q}$. Using this training criterion,

$f(\mathbf{x}, \beta(\mathbf{q}))$ now becomes a *local* model, and can have a different set of parameters $\beta(\mathbf{q})$ for each query point $\mathbf{q}$.

3.2. *Linear Local Models*

Given that we are using local models, it seems advantageous to keep them simple, and to keep the training criterion simple as well. This leads us to explore local models that are linear in the unknown parameters, and to use the least squares training criterion. We derive least squares training algorithms for linear local models from regression procedures for linear global models.

3.2.1. *Linear Global Models*
A global model that is linear in the parameters β can be expressed as (Myers (1990):

$$\mathbf{x}_i^T \beta = y_i \tag{10}$$

In what follows we will assume that the constant 1 has been appended to all the input vectors $\mathbf{x}_i$ to include a constant term in the regression. The training examples can be collected in a matrix equation:

$$\mathbf{X}\beta = \mathbf{y} \tag{11}$$

where $\mathbf{X}$ is a matrix whose ith row is $\mathbf{x}_i^T$ and $\mathbf{y}$ is a vector whose ith element is y_i. Thus, the dimensionality of $\mathbf{X}$ is $n \times d$ where n is the number of data points and d is the dimensionality of $\mathbf{x}$. Estimating the parameters β using an unweighted regression minimizes the criterion

$$C = \sum_i (\mathbf{x}_i^T \beta - y_i)^2 \tag{12}$$

by solving the normal equations

$$(\mathbf{X}^T \mathbf{X})\beta = \mathbf{X}^T \mathbf{y} \tag{13}$$

for β:

$$\beta = (\mathbf{X}^T \mathbf{X})^{-1} \mathbf{X}^T \mathbf{y} \tag{14}$$

Inverting the matrix $\mathbf{X}^T \mathbf{X}$ is not the numerically best way to solve the normal equations from the point of view of efficiency or accuracy, and usually other matrix techniques are used to solve Equation 13 (Press et al. 1988).

3.2.2. *Weighting the Criterion: A Physical Interpretation*
In fitting a line or plane to a set of points, unweighted regression gives distant points equal influence with nearby points on the ultimate answer to the query,

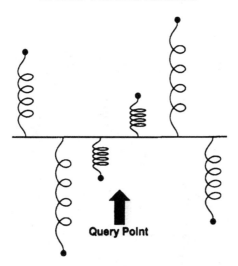

Figure 4. Unweighted springs.

for equally spaced data. The linear local model can be specialized to the query by emphasizing nearby points. As with the distance weighted average example we can either weight the error criterion that is minimized, or weight the data directly. The two approaches are equivalent for planar local models. Weighting the criterion is done in the following way

$$C(\mathbf{q}) = \sum_i [(\mathbf{x}_i^T \beta - y_i)^2 K(d(\mathbf{x}_i, \mathbf{q}))] \qquad (15)$$

We again have a physical interpretation for $C(\mathbf{q})$ of Equation 15. Much as thin plate splines minimize a bending energy of a plate and the energy of the constraints pulling on the plate, locally weighted regression can also be interpreted as a physical process. In LWR with a planar local model, the line in Figures 2 and 3 can now rotate as well as translate. The springs are forced to remain oriented vertically, rather than move to the smallest distance between the data points and the line. Figure 4 shows the fit (the line) produced by equally strong springs to a set of data points (the black dots), minimizing the criterion of Equation 12. Figure 5 shows what happens to the fit as the springs nearer to the query point are strengthened and the springs further away are weakened. The strengths of the springs are given by $K(d(\mathbf{x}_i, \mathbf{q}))$, and the fit minimizes the criterion of Equation 15.

3.2.3. *Direct Data Weighting*
Our version of directly weighting the data involves the following steps. For computational and analytical simplicity the origin of the input data is first

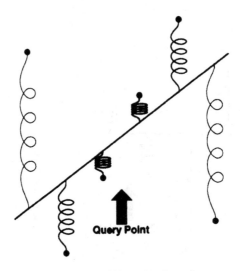

Figure 5. Weighted springs.

shifted by subtracting the query point from each data point (making the query point $\mathbf{q} = (0, \ldots, 0, 1)^{\mathrm{T}}$, where the 1 is appended for the constant term in the regression). A distance is calculated from each of the stored data points to the query point $\mathbf{q}$. The weight for each stored data point is the square root of the kernel function used in Equation 15, to simplify notation later:

$$w_i = \sqrt{K(d(\mathbf{x}_i, \mathbf{q}))} \qquad (16)$$

Each row i of $\mathbf{X}$ and $\mathbf{y}$ is multiplied by the corresponding weight w_i creating new variables $\mathbf{Z}$ and $\mathbf{v}$. This can be done using matrix notation by creating a diagonal matrix $\mathbf{W}$ with diagonal elements $\mathbf{W}_{ii} = w_i$ and zeros elsewhere and multiplying $\mathbf{W}$ times the original variables.

$$\mathbf{z}_i = w_i \mathbf{x}_i \qquad (17)$$

$$\mathbf{Z} = \mathbf{W}\mathbf{X} \qquad (18)$$

and

$$v_i = w_i y_i \qquad (19)$$

$$\mathbf{v} = \mathbf{W}\mathbf{y} \qquad (20)$$

Equation 13 is solved for β using the new variables:

$$(\mathbf{Z}^T\mathbf{Z})\beta = \mathbf{Z}^T\mathbf{v} \tag{21}$$

Formally, this gives us an estimator of the form

$$\hat{y}(\mathbf{q}) = \mathbf{q}^T(\mathbf{Z}^T\mathbf{Z})^{-1}\mathbf{Z}^T\mathbf{v} \tag{22}$$

3.3. *The Relationship of Kernel Regression and Locally Weighted Regression*

For data distributed on a regular grid away from any boundary locally weighted regression and kernel regression are equivalent (Lejeune 1985; Müller 1987). However, for irregular data distributions there is a significant difference, and LWR has many advantages over kernel regression (Hastie and Loader 1993; Jones et al. 1994). LWR with a planar local model is often preferred over kernel smoothing because it exactly reproduces a line (with any data distribution). The failure to reproduce a line, or any function used to generate the training data, indicates the bias of a function approximation method. LWR methods with a planar local model will fail to reproduce a quadratic function, reflecting the bias due to the planar local model. LWR methods with a quadratic local model will fail to reproduce a cubic function, and so on.

3.4. *The Locally Weighted Regression Literature*

Cleveland and Loader (1994a, c), Fan (1995) and Fan and Gijbels (1996) review the history of locally weighted regression and discuss current research trends. Barnhill (1977) and Sabin (1980) survey the use of distance weighted nearest neighbor interpolators to fit surfaces to arbitrarily spaced points, and Eubank (1988) surveys their use in nonparametric regression. Lancaster and Šalkauskas (1986) refer to nearest neighbor approaches as "moving least squares" and survey their use in fitting surfaces to data. Härdle (1990) surveys kernel and LWR approaches to nonparametric regression. Farmer and Sidorowich (1987, 1988a, b) survey the use of nearest neighbor and local model approaches in modeling chaotic dynamic systems.

Local models (often polynomials) have been used for over a century to smooth regularly sampled time series and interpolate and extrapolate from data arranged on rectangular grids. Crain and Bhattacharyya (1967), Falconer (1971) and McLain (1974) suggested using a weighted regression on irregularly spaced data to fit a local polynomial model at each point a function evaluation was desired. All of the available data points were used. Each data point was weighted by a function of its distance to the desired point in the regression. Many authors have suggested fitting a polynomial surface only to nearby points also using distance weighted regression (McIntyre et al. 1968; Pelto et al. 1968; Legg and Brent 1969; Palmer 1969; Walters 1969; Lodwick and Whittle 1970; Stone 1975, 1977; Benedetti 1977; Tukey 1977; Franke and Nielson 1980; Friedman 1984) Cleveland (1979) proposed using robust regression procedures to eliminate outlying or erroneous points in the regression process. Programs implementing a refined version of this approach (LOCFIT and LOESS) are available directly and also as part of the S+ package (Cleveland et al. 1992; Cleveland and Loader 1994a, b, c). Katkovnik (1979) also developed a robust locally weighted smoothing procedure. Cleveland et al. (1988) analyze the statistical properties of the LOESS algorithm and Cleveland and Devlin (1988) and Cleveland et al. (1993) show examples of its use. Stone (1977), Devroye (1981), Lancaster (1979), Lancaster and Šalkauskas (1981), Cheng (1984), Li (1984), Tsybakov (1986), and Farwig (1987) provide analyses of LWR approaches. Stone (1980, 1982) shows that LWR has an optimal rate of convergence in a minimax sense. Fan (1992) shows that local linear regression smoothers are the best smoothers, in that they are the asymptotic minimax linear smoother and have a high asymptotic efficiency (which can be 100% with a suitable choice of kernel and bandwidth) among all possible linear smoothers, including those produced by kernel, orthogonal series, and spline methods, when the unknown regression function is in the class of functions having bounded second derivatives. Fan (1993) extends this result to show that LWR has a high minimax efficiency among all possible estimators, including nonlinear smoothers such as median regression. Fan (1992), Fan and Gijbels (1992), Hastie and Loader (1993) and Jones et al. (1994) show that LWR handles a wide range of data distributions and avoids boundary and cluster effects. Ruppert and Wand (1994) derive asymptotic bias and variance formulas for multivariate LWR, while Cleveland and Loader (1994c) argue that asymptotic results have limited practical relevance. Fan and Gijbels (1992) explore the use of a variable bandwidth locally weighted regression. Vapnik and Bottou (1993) give error bounds for local learning algorithms.

Locally weighted regression was introduced into the domain of machine learning and robot learning by Atkeson (Atkeson and Reinkensmeyer 1988, 1989; Atkeson 1990, 1992), who also explored techniques for detecting irrelevant features, and Zografski (Zografski 1989, 1991, 1992; Zografski and Durrani 1995). Atkeson and Schaal (1995) explore locally weighted learning from the point of view of neural networks. Dietterich et al. (1994) report on a recent workshop on memory-based learning, including locally weighted learning.

4. Distance Functions

Locally weighted learning is critically dependent on the distance function. There are many different approaches to defining a distance function, and this section briefly surveys them. Distance functions in locally weighted learning do not need to satisfy the formal mathematical requirements for a distance metric. The relative importance of the input dimensions in generating the distance measurement depends on how the inputs are scaled (i.e., how much they are stretched or squashed). We use the term *scaling* for this purpose having reserved the term *weight* for the contribution of individual points (not dimensions) in a regression. We refer to the scaling factors as m_j in this paper. There are many ways to define and use distance functions (Scott 1992):

- **Global distance functions.** The same distance function is used at all parts of the input space.
- **Query-based local distance functions:** The form of $d(\ )$ or the distance function parameters are set on each query by an optimization process that typically minimizes cross validation error or a related criterion. This approach is referred to as a *uniform metric* by Stanfill (1987) and is discussed in Stanfill and Waltz (1986), Hastie and Tibshirani (1994) and Friedman (1994).
- **Point-based local distance functions:** Each stored data point has associated with it a distance function and the values of corresponding parameters. The training criterion uses a different $d_i(\ )$ for each point $\mathbf{x}_i$:

$$C(\mathbf{q}) = \sum_i [(f(\mathbf{x}_i, \beta) - y_i)^2 K(d_i(\mathbf{x}_i, \mathbf{q}))] \qquad (23)$$

The $d_i(\ )$ can be selected either by a direct computation or by minimizing cross validation error. Frequently, the $d_i(\ )$ are chosen in advance of the queries and are stored with the data points. This approach is referred to as a *variable metric* by Stanfill (1987). For classifiers, one version of a point-based local distance function is to have a different distance function for each class (Waltz 1987; Aha and McNulty 1989; Aha 1989, 1990). Aha and Goldstone (1990, 1992) explore the use of point-based distance functions by human subjects.

Distance functions can be asymmetric and nonlinear, so that a distance along a particular dimension can depend on whether the query point's value for the dimension is larger or smaller than the stored point's value for that dimension (Medin and Shoben 1988). The distance along a dimension can also depend on the values being compared (Nosofsky et al. 1989).

4.1. Feature Scaling

Altering the distance function can serve two purposes. If the feature scaling factors m_j are all nonzero, the input space is warped or distorted, which might lead to more accurate predictions. If some of the scaling factors are set to zero, those dimensions are ignored by the distance function, and the local model becomes global in those directions. Zeroing feature scaling factors can be used as a tool to combat the curse of dimensionality by reducing the locality of the function approximation process in this way.

Note that a feature scaling factor of zero does not mean the local model ignores that feature in locally weighted learning. Instead, all points aligned along that direction get the same weight, and the feature can affect the output of the local model. For example, fitting a global model using all features is equivalent to setting all feature scaling factors to zero and fitting the same model as a local model. Local model feature selection is a separate process from distance function feature scaling. Ignoring features using ridge regression, dimensionality reduction of the entire modeling process, and algorithms for feature scaling and selection are discussed in later sections.

Stanfill and Waltz (1986) describe a variant of feature selection ("predictor restriction") in which the scaling factor for a feature becomes so large that any difference from the query in that dimension causes the training point to be ignored. They also describe using an initial prediction of the output in an augmented distance function to select training data with similar or equal outputs ("goal restriction") (Jabbour et al 1978).

4.2. Distance Functions For Continuous Inputs

The functions discussed in this section are especially appropriate for ordered (vs. categorical, symbolic, or nominal) input values, which are either continuous or an ordered set of discrete values.

- **Unweighted Euclidean distance:**

$$d_E(\mathbf{x}, \mathbf{q}) = \sqrt{\sum_j (x_j - q_j)^2} = \sqrt{(\mathbf{x} - \mathbf{q})^T (\mathbf{x} - \mathbf{q})} \qquad (24)$$

- **Diagonally weighted Euclidean distance:**

$$d_m(\mathbf{x}, \mathbf{q}) = \sqrt{\sum_j (m_j(x_j - q_j))^2} = \sqrt{(\mathbf{x} - \mathbf{q})^T \mathbf{M}^T \mathbf{M}(\mathbf{x} - \mathbf{q})}$$
$$= d_E(\mathbf{M}\mathbf{x}, \mathbf{M}\mathbf{q}) \qquad (25)$$

where m_j is the feature scaling factor for the jth dimension and $\mathbf{M}$ is a diagonal matrix with $\mathbf{M}_{jj} = m_j$.

- **Fully weighted Euclidean distance:**

$$d_{\mathbf{M}}(\mathbf{x}, \mathbf{q}) = \sqrt{(\mathbf{x} - \mathbf{q})^{\mathrm{T}}\mathbf{M}^{\mathrm{T}}\mathbf{M}(\mathbf{x} - \mathbf{q})} = d_{\mathrm{E}}(\mathbf{M}\mathbf{x}, \mathbf{M}\mathbf{q}) \qquad (26)$$

where $\mathbf{M}$ is no longer diagonal but can be arbitrary. This is also known as the Mahalanobis distance (Tou and Gonzalez 1974; Weisberg 1985).

- **Unweighted L_p norm (Minkowski metric):**

$$d_p(\mathbf{x}, \mathbf{q}) = \left(\sum_i |\mathbf{x}_i - \mathbf{q}_i|^p \right)^{\frac{1}{p}} \qquad (27)$$

- **Diagonally weighted and fully weighted L_p norm:** The weighted L_p norm is $d_p(\mathbf{M}\mathbf{x}, \mathbf{M}\mathbf{q})$.

A diagonal distance function matrix $\mathbf{M}$ (1 coefficient for each dimension) can make a radially symmetric scaling function into an axis parallel ellipse (Figure 6 shows ellipses with the axes of symmetry aligned with the coordinate axes). Figure 7 shows an example of how a full distance function matrix $\mathbf{M}$ with cross terms can arbitrarily orient the ellipse (Ruppert and Wand 1994; Wand and Jones 1993). Cleveland and Grosse (1991), Cleveland et al. (1992) and Cleveland (1993a) point out that for distance functions with zero coefficients ($m_i = 0$, an entire column of $\mathbf{M}$ is zero, or $\mathbf{M}$ is singular), the model is global in the corresponding directions. They refer to this as a *conditionally parametric* model.

Fukunaga (1990), James (1985) and Tou and Gonzalez (1974) describe how to choose a distance function matrix to maximize the ratio of the variance between classes to the variance of all the cases in classification. Mohri and Tanaka (1994) extend this approach to symbolic input values. This approach uses an eigenvalue/eigenvector decomposition and can help distinguish relevant attributes from irrelevant attributes and filter out noisy data. This approach is localized by Hastie and Tibshirani (1994). Distance functions for symbolic inputs have been developed and are discussed in Atkeson (1996).

5. Smoothing Parameters

A smoothing or bandwidth parameter h defines the scale or range over which generalization is performed. There are several ways to use this parameter (Scott 1992; Cleveland and Loader 1994c):

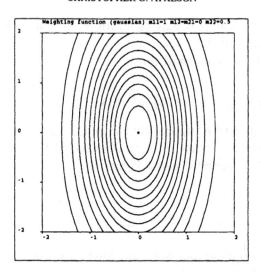

Figure 6. Contours of constant distance from the center with a diagonal **M** matrix.

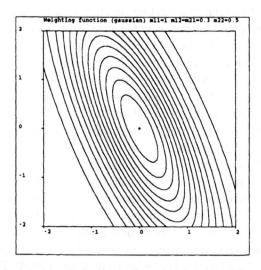

Figure 7. Contours of a constant distance from the center in which the **M** matrix has off-diagonal elements.

- **Fixed bandwidth selection:** h is a constant value (Fan and Marron 1993), and therefore volumes of data with constant size and shape are used. In this case h can appear implicitly in the distance function as the determinant of **M** for fully weighted distance functions ($h = |\mathbf{M}|$) or the magnitude of the vector **m** in diagonally weighted distance functions ($h = |\mathbf{m}|$) and/or explicitly in the weighting function:

$$K\left(\frac{d(\mathbf{x}_i, \mathbf{q})}{h}\right) \tag{28}$$

These parameters, although redundant in the explicit case, provide a convenient way to adjust the radius of the weighting function. The redundancy can be eliminated by requiring the determinant of the scaling factor matrix to be one ($|\mathbf{M}| = 1$), or fixing some element of $\mathbf{M}$.

- **Nearest neighbor bandwidth selection:** h is set to be the distance to the kth nearest data point (Stone 1977; Cleveland 1979; Farmer and Sidorowich 1988a, b; Townshend 1992; Hastie and Loader 1993; Fan and Gijbels 1994; Ge et al. 1994; Næs et al. 1990; Næs and Isaksson 1992; Wang et al. 1994; Cleveland and Loader 1994b). The data volume increases and decreases in size according to the density of nearby data. In this case changes in scale of the distance function are canceled by corresponding changes in h, giving a scale invariant weighting pattern to the data. However, h will not cancel changes in distance function coefficients that alter the shape of the weighting function, and the identity of the kth neighbor can change with distance function shape changes.
- **Global bandwidth selection:** h is set globally by an optimization process that typically minimizes cross validation error over all the data.
- **Query-based local bandwidth selection:** h is set on each query by an optimization process that typically minimizes cross validation error or a related criterion (Vapnik 1992).
- **Point-based local bandwidth selection:** Each stored data point has associated with it a bandwidth h. The weighted criterion uses a different h_i for each point $\mathbf{x}_i$:

$$C(\mathbf{q}) = \sum_i \left[(f(\mathbf{x}_i, \beta) - y_i)^2 K\left(\frac{d(\mathbf{x}_i, \mathbf{q})}{h_i}\right) \right] \tag{29}$$

The h_i can be set either by a direct computation or by an optimization process that typically minimizes cross validation error or a related criterion. Typically, the h_i are computed in advance of the queries and are stored with the data points.

Fan and Marron (1994b) argue that a fixed bandwidth is easy to interpret, but of limited use. Cleveland and Loader (1994a) argue in favor of nearest neighbor smoothing over fixed bandwidth smoothing. A fixed bandwidth and a weighting function that goes to zero at a finite distance can have large variance in regions of low data density. This problem is present at edges or between data clusters and gets worse in higher dimensions. In general, fixed bandwidth selection has much larger changes in variance than nearest neighbor bandwidth selection. A fixed bandwidth smoother can also not have any data within its span, leading to undefined estimates (Cleveland and Loader 1994b). Fan and Marron (1994b) describe three reasons to use variable local bandwidths: to adapt to the data distribution, to adapt for different levels of noise (*heteroscedasticity*), and to adapt to changes in the smoothness or curvature of the function. Fan and Gijbels (1992) argue for point-based in favor of query-based local bandwidth selection, explaining that having a bandwidth associated with each data point will allow rapid or asymmetric changes in the behavior of the data to be accommodated. Section 12 discusses global and local tuning of bandwidths.

6. Weighting Functions

The requirements on a weighting function (also known as a kernel function) are straightforward (Gasser and Muller 1979; Cleveland and Loader 1994c; Fedorov et al. 1993). The maximum value of the weighting function should be at zero distance, and the function should decay smoothly as the distance increases. Discontinuities in weighting functions lead to discontinuities in the predictions, since training points cross the discontinuity as the query changes. In general, the smoother the weight function, the smoother the estimated function. Weights that go to infinity when a query equals a stored data point allow exact interpolation of the stored data. Finite weights lead to smoothing of the data. Weight functions that go to zero at a finite distance allow faster implementations, since points further from the query than that distance can be ignored with no error. As mentioned previously, kernels with a fixed finite radius raise the possibility of not having enough or any points within the non-zero area, a possibility that must be handled by the locally weighted learning system. It is not necessary to normalize the kernel function, and the kernel function does not need to be unimodal. The kernel function should always be non-negative, since a negative value would lead to the training process increasing training error in order to decrease the training criterion. The weights (i.e., the square root of the kernel function) can be positive or negative. We have only used non-negative weights. Some of the kernel functions discussed in this section are shown in Figure 8.

A simple weighting function just raises the distance to a negative power (Shepard 1968; Atkeson 1992; Ruprecht et al. 1994; Ruprecht and Muller 1994a). The magnitude of the power determines how local the regression will be (i.e., the rate of dropoff of the weights with distance).

$$K(d) = \frac{1}{d^p} \tag{30}$$

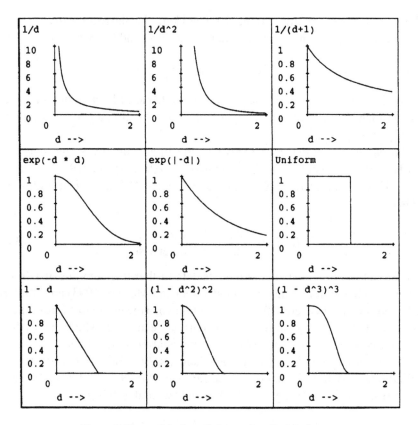

Figure 8. Some of the kernel shapes described in the text.

This type of weighting function goes to infinity as the query point approaches a stored data point and forces the locally weighted regression to exactly match that stored point. If the data is noisy, exact interpolation is not desirable, and a weighting scheme with limited magnitude is desired. The *inverse distance* (Wolberg 1990)

$$K(d) = \frac{1}{1 + d^p} \tag{31}$$

can be used to approximate functions like Equation 30 and the quadratic hyperbola kernel $1/(h^2 + d^2)$ with a well defined value at $d = 0$.

Another smoothing weight function is a *Gaussian kernel* (Deheuvels 1977; Wand and Schucany 1990; Schaal and Atkeson 1994):

$$K(d) = \exp(-d^2) \tag{32}$$

This kernel also has infinite extent. A related kernel is the *exponential kernel*, which has been used in psychological models (Aha and Goldstone 1992):

$$K(d) = \exp[-|d|] \tag{33}$$

These kernels have infinite extent, and can be truncated when they become smaller than a threshold value to ignore data further from a particular radius from the query.

The *quadratic kernel*, also known as the Epanechnikov kernel and the Bartlett-Priestley kernel, is (Epanechnikov 1969; Lejeune 1984; Altman 1992; Hastie and Loader 1993; Fan and Gijbels 1995a, b; Fan and Hall 1994):

$$K(d) = \begin{cases} (1 - d^2) & \text{if} |d| < 1 \\ 0 & \text{otherwise} \end{cases} \tag{34}$$

This kernel has finite extent and ignores data further than a radius of 1 from the query when building the local model. Fan and Marron (1993) and Muller (1993) argue that this kernel function is optimal in a mean squared error sense. However, there is a discontinuity in the derivative at $d = 1$, which makes this kernel less attractive in real applications and analytical treatments.

The *tricube kernel* is used by Cleveland (1979), Cleveland and Devlin (1988), Diebold and Nason (1990), LeBaron (1990), Næs et al. (1990), Næs and Isaksson (1992), Wang et al. (1994) and Ge et al. (1994):

$$K(d) = \begin{cases} (1 - |d|^3)^3 & \text{if} |d| < 1 \\ 0 & \text{otherwise} \end{cases} \tag{35}$$

This kernel also has finite extent and a continuous first and second derivative, which means the first and second derivative of the prediction will also be continuous.

For comparison, the *uniform weighting kernel* (or boxcar weighting kernel) is used by Stone (1977), Friedman (1984), Tsybakov (1986) and Muller (1987):

$$K(d) = \begin{cases} 1 & \text{if} |d| < 1 \\ 0 & \text{otherwise} \end{cases} \tag{36}$$

and the *triangular kernel* (used in locally weighted median regression) is:

$$K(d) = \begin{cases} 1 - |d| & \text{if} |d| < 1 \\ 0 & \text{otherwise} \end{cases} \tag{37}$$

A variant of the triangular kernel is the following (Franke and Nielson 1980; Ruprecht and Müller 1993, 1994, Ruprecht et al. 1994):

$$K(d) = \begin{cases} \frac{1-|d|}{|d|} & \text{if } |d| < 1 \\ 0 & \text{otherwise} \end{cases} \tag{38}$$

In general new kernel functions can be created by raising these kernel functions to a power. For example, the *biquadratic kernel* is the square of the quadratic kernel. The power can be non-integral, and also less than one. The triangular, biquadratic, and tricube kernels form a family. Ruprecht and Müller (1994b) generalize the distance function to a point-set metric.

In our view, there is no clear evidence that the choice of weighting function is critical (Scott 1992; Cleveland and Loader 1994a, c) However, there are examples where one can show differences (Fedorov et al. 1993). Cleveland and Loader (1994b) criticize the uniform kernel for similar reasons as are used in signal processing and spectrum estimation. Optimal kernels are discussed by Gasser and Muller (1984), Gasser et al. (1985), Scott (1992), Blyth (1993), Fedorov et al. (1993). Finite extent of the kernel function is useful, but other than that, the literature and our own work have not noted any substantial empirical difference in most cases.

7. Local Model Structures

So far we have discussed only a few kinds of local models, constant and linear local models. There are no limits on what model structure can be used as a local model. Models that are linear in the unknown parameters, such as local polynomials, train faster than more general models. Since a major component of the lookup cost is the training cost, this is an important benefit. Cleveland and Devlin (1988), Atkeson (1992), Farmer and Sidorowich (1988a, b), Cleveland and Loader (1994), Næs et al. (1990), Næs and Isaksson (1992) and Wang et al. (1994) have applied local quadratic and cubic models, which are analyzed by Ruppert and Wand (1994). Higher order polynomials reduce the bias but increase the variance of the estimates. Locally constant models handle flat regions well, while quadratics and cubics handle areas of high curvature such as peaks and valleys well.

Cleveland and Loader (1994a, c) present an approach to blending polynomial models, where a non-integral model order indicates a weighted blend between two integral model orders. They use cross validation to optimize the local model order on each query.

8. Regularization, Insufficient Data, and Prediction Bias

To uniquely interpolate between and extrapolate from the training data we must express a preference or learning bias. In function approximation that preference is typically expressed as a smoothness criterion to optimize. In the case of locally weighted learning the smoothness constraint is not explicit. However, there are several fit parameters that affect the smoothness of the predicted outputs. The smoothing bandwidth is an important control knob, as is a ridge regression parameter, to be described in the next section. The order of the local model also can serve as a smoothing parameter. The shape of the distance and weighting functions play a secondary role in smoothing the estimates, although in general the number of derivatives with respect to $\mathbf{x}$ of $K(d(\mathbf{x},\mathbf{q}))$ that exist determine the order of smoothness of the predicted outputs. There is an important link between smoothness control and overfitting. Seifert and Gasser (1994) explore a variety of approaches to handling insufficient data in local regression.

8.1. Ridge Regression

A potential problem is that the data points can be distributed in such a way as to make the regression matrix $\mathbf{Z}^T\mathbf{Z}$ in Equation 21 nearly singular. If there are not enough nearby points with non-zero weights in all directions, there are not enough different equations to solve for the unknown parameters β. *Ridge regression* (Draper and Smith 1981) is used to prevent problems due to a singular data matrix. The following equation, instead of Equation 21, is solved for β:

$$(\mathbf{Z}^T\mathbf{Z} + \Lambda)\beta = \mathbf{Z}^T\mathbf{v} + \Lambda\bar{\beta} \tag{39}$$

where Λ is a diagonal matrix with small positive diagonal elements λ_i^2:

$$\Lambda = \begin{pmatrix} \lambda_1^2 & 0 & \cdots & 0 \\ 0 & \lambda_2^2 & \cdots & 0 \\ \vdots & \vdots & \ddots & \vdots \\ 0 & 0 & \cdots & \lambda_n^2 \end{pmatrix} \tag{40}$$

and $\bar{\beta}$ is an apriori estimate or expectation of what the local model parameters will be (often $\bar{\beta}$ is taken to be a vector of all zeros). This is equivalent to adding n extra rows to $\mathbf{Z}$, each having a single non-zero element, λ_i, in the ith column. The equation $\mathbf{Z}\beta = \mathbf{v}$ becomes:

$$
\begin{bmatrix}
& & \mathbf{Z} & & \\
\lambda_1 & 0 & \cdots & 0 \\
0 & \lambda_2 & \cdots & 0 \\
\vdots & \vdots & \ddots & \vdots \\
0 & 0 & \cdots & \lambda_n
\end{bmatrix}
\beta =
\begin{bmatrix}
\mathbf{v} \\
\lambda_1 \bar{\beta}_1 \\
\lambda_2 \bar{\beta}_2 \\
\vdots \\
\lambda_n \bar{\beta}_n
\end{bmatrix}
\tag{41}
$$

Adding additional rows can be viewed as adding "fake" data, which, in the absence of sufficient real data, biases the parameter estimates to $\bar{\beta}$ (Draper and Smith 1981). Another view of ridge regression parameters is that they are the Bayesian assumptions about the apriori distributions of the estimated parameters (Seber 1977). As described in Section 12 on tuning, optimizing the ridge regression parameters using cross validation can identify irrelevant dimensions. These techniques also help combat overfitting.

8.2. *Dimensionality Reduction*

Principal components analysis (PCA) can also be used globally to eliminate directions in which there is no data (Wettschereck 1994). However, it is rarely the case that there is absolutely *no* data in a particular direction. A closely related technique, the singular value decomposition (SVD), is typically used in locally weighted regression to perform dimensionality reduction. Cleveland and Grosse (1991) compute the inverse of $\mathbf{Z}^T\mathbf{Z}$ using the singular value decomposition, and then set small singular values to zero in the calculated inverse. This corresponds to eliminating those directions from the local model. Principal components analysis can also be done locally on the weighted data, either around each stored data point, or in response to a query. Directions can be eliminated in either a hard fashion, explicitly setting the corresponding parameters to zero, or in a soft fashion (such as performing ridge regression in the coordinate system defined by the PCA or SVD).

In Bregler and Omohundro (1994) an interesting locally weighted learning approach is presented for identifying low-dimensional submanifolds on which data is lying. In Figure 9 the space has two dimensions, and yet each dot is locally embedded on a one dimensional curve. Bregler and Omohundro's method uses locally weighted principal component analysis (which performs a singular value decomposition of the $\mathbf{Z}$ matrix from Equation 18) to identify local manifolds. This is a useful analysis tool for identifying local dependencies between variables in a dataset. But it also has important consequences for

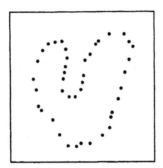

Figure 9. 2-dimensional input points scattered on a 1-dimensional non-linear manifold.

developing a local distance function: the principal component matrix reveals the directions in input space for which there is no data support.

These approaches only consider the input space (the space spanned by x_i). It is often important to also consider the outputs (the y_i) when performing distance function or smoothing parameter optimization. The outputs can provide more opportunities for dimensionality reduction if they are flat in some direction, or can be predicted by a local model. An alternative perspective is to consider the conditional probability $p(y|x)$. Perhaps one could do local principal components analysis in the joint density space $p(x, y)$ and eliminate the input directions that contribute least to predicting the outputs. A potential problem with dimensionality reduction in general is that the new dimensions, if not aligned with the previous dimensions, are not necessarily meaningful. Our focus is on reducing prediction error, ignoring comprehensibility of the local models.

9. Assessing the Predictions

An important aspect of locally weighted learning is that it is possible to estimate the prediction error, and derive confidence bounds on the predictions. Bottou and Vapnik (1992; Vapnik and Bottou, 1993) analyze confidence intervals for locally weighted classifiers. We start our analysis of locally weighted regression by pointing out that LWR is an estimator that is linear in the output data y (using Equations 20, 22, and 39):

$$\hat{y}(\mathbf{q}) = \mathbf{q}^T (\mathbf{Z}^T\mathbf{Z} + \Lambda)^{-1}\mathbf{Z}^T\mathbf{W}\mathbf{y} = \mathbf{s}_{\mathbf{q}}^T\mathbf{y} = \sum_{i=1}^{n} s_i(\mathbf{q})y_i \qquad (42)$$

The vector $\mathbf{s}_{\mathbf{q}}$, also written as $\mathbf{s}(\mathbf{q})$, will be useful for calculating the bias and variance of locally weighted learning.

9.1. *Estimating the Variance*

To calculate the variance of a prediction we assume the training data came from a sampling process that measures output values with additive random noise:

$$y_i = f(\mathbf{x}_i) + \epsilon_i \qquad (43)$$

where the ϵ_i are independent, have zero mean, and have variance $\sigma^2(\mathbf{x}_i)$. Under the assumption that $\sigma^2(\mathbf{x}_i) = \sigma^2$ (σ is a constant) and that the linear model correctly models the structure of the data, linear regression generates an unbiased estimate of the regression parameters. Additionally, if the error is normally distributed, $\epsilon_i = N(0, \sigma^2)$, the regression estimate becomes the best linear unbiased estimate in the maximum likelihood sense. However, unless stated explicitly, in this paper we will avoid any distributional assumption on the form of the noise.

Given this model of the additive noise (and dropping the assumption that a linear model correctly models the structure of the data), the expectation and variance of the estimate $\hat{y}$ is ($\mathbf{s}$ is from Equation 42):

$$\mathrm{E}(\hat{y}(\mathbf{q})) = \mathrm{E}(\mathbf{s}_\mathbf{q}^\mathsf{T}\mathbf{y}) = \mathbf{s}_\mathbf{q}^\mathsf{T}\mathrm{E}(\mathbf{y}) = \sum_i s_i(\mathbf{q})f(\mathbf{x}_i) \qquad (44)$$

$$\mathrm{Var}(\hat{y}(\mathbf{q})) = \mathrm{E}[\hat{y}(\mathbf{q}) - \mathrm{E}(\hat{y}(\mathbf{q}))]^2 = \sum_i s_i^2(\mathbf{q})\sigma^2(\mathbf{x}_i) \qquad (45)$$

One way to derive confidence intervals for the predictions from locally weighted learning is to assume a locally constant variance $\sigma^2(\mathbf{q})$ at the prediction point $\mathbf{q}$ and to use Equation 45. This equation has to be modified to reflect both the additive noise in sampling at the new point ($\sigma^2(\mathbf{q})$) and the prediction error of the estimator ($\sigma^2(\mathbf{q})\, \mathbf{s}_\mathbf{q}^\mathsf{T}\, \mathbf{s}_\mathbf{q}$).

$$\mathrm{Var}(y_{\mathrm{new}}(\mathbf{q})) = \sigma^2(\mathbf{q}) + \sigma^2(\mathbf{q})\mathbf{s}_\mathbf{q}^\mathsf{T}\mathbf{s}_\mathbf{q} \qquad (46)$$

This expression of the prediction intervals is independent of the output values of the training data y_i, and reflects how well the data is distributed in the input space. However, the variance only reflects the difference between the prediction and the mean prediction, and not the difference between the prediction and the true value, which requires knowledge of the predictor's bias. Only when the local model structure is correct will the bias be zero.

To conveniently derive an estimate of $\sigma^2(\mathbf{x})$ we will define some additional quantities in terms of the weighted variables. A locally weighted linear regression centered at a point $\mathbf{q}$ produces local model parameters $\beta(\mathbf{q})$. It also produces errors (*residuals*) at all training points. The weighted residual $r_i(\mathbf{q})$ is given by (v_i is defined in Equation 19):

$$r_i(\mathbf{q}) = \mathbf{z}_i^{\mathrm{T}}(\mathbf{q})\beta(\mathbf{q}) - v_i(\mathbf{q}) \tag{47}$$

The training criteria, which is the weighted sum of the squared errors, is given by:

$$C(\mathbf{q}) = \sum_i r_i^2(\mathbf{q}) \tag{48}$$

A reasonable estimator for the local value of the noise variance is

$$\hat{\sigma}^2(\mathbf{q}) = \frac{\sum r_i^2(\mathbf{q})}{n_{\mathrm{LWR}}(\mathbf{q})} = \frac{C(\mathbf{q})}{n_{\mathrm{LWR}}(\mathbf{q})} \tag{49}$$

where n_{LWR} is a modified measure of how many data points there are:

$$n_{\mathrm{LWR}}(\mathbf{q}) = \sum_{i=1}^{n} w_i^2 = \sum_{i=1}^{n} K\left(\frac{d(\mathbf{x}_i, \mathbf{q})}{h}\right) \tag{50}$$

In analogy to unweighted regression (Myers 1990), we can reduce the bias of the estimate $\hat{\sigma}^2(\mathbf{q})$ by taking into account the number of parameters in the locally weighted regression:

$$\hat{\sigma}^2(\mathbf{q}) = \frac{\sum r_i^2(\mathbf{q})}{n_{\mathrm{LWR}}(\mathbf{q}) - p_{\mathrm{LWR}}(\mathbf{q})} \tag{51}$$

where p_{LWR} is a measure of the local number of free parameters in the local model:

$$p_{\mathrm{LWR}}(\mathbf{q}) = \sum_i w_i^2 \mathbf{z}_i^{\mathrm{T}}(\mathbf{Z}^{\mathrm{T}}\mathbf{Z})^{-1}\mathbf{z}_i \tag{52}$$

We have described a variance estimator that uses only local information. An alternative way to obtain a variance estimate uses global information, i.e., information from more than one LWR fit, and assumes a single global value for the additive noise (Cleveland et al. 1988; Cleveland and Grosse 1991; Cleveland et al. 1992).

9.2. Estimating the Bias

Assessing the bias requires making assumptions about the underlying form of the true function, and the data distribution. In the case of locally weighted learning this is a weak assumption, since we need to know only the local behavior of the function and the local distribution of the data. Let us assume that the real function f is described locally by a quadratic model:

$$f(\mathbf{x}) = f(\mathbf{q}) + \mathbf{g}^T(\mathbf{x} - \mathbf{q}) + \frac{1}{2}(\mathbf{x} - \mathbf{q})^T]\mathbf{H}(\mathbf{x} - \mathbf{q}) \qquad (53)$$

where $\mathbf{q}$ is the query point, $\mathbf{g}$ is the true gradient at the query point, and $\mathbf{H}$ is the true Hessian (matrix of second derivatives) at the query point. The expected value of the estimate is given by Equation 44, which can be used to find the bias:

$$\text{bias} = \text{E}(\hat{y}(\mathbf{q})) - y_{\text{true}}(\mathbf{q}) = \sum[\mathbf{s}_i(\mathbf{q})f(\mathbf{x}_i)] - f(\mathbf{q}) \qquad (54)$$

This equation can be solved if we know the true function. For example, for the locally quadratic function, we can plug the quadratic function for $f(\mathbf{x})$ in Equation 53 into Equation 54 to get:

$$\begin{aligned} \text{bias} = &\ f(\mathbf{q})\sum[\mathbf{s}_i(\mathbf{q})] - f(\mathbf{q}) + \mathbf{g}^T\sum[\mathbf{s}_i(\mathbf{q})(\mathbf{x} - \mathbf{q})] \\ &+ \frac{1}{2}\sum[\mathbf{s}_i(\mathbf{q})(\mathbf{x} - \mathbf{q})^T\mathbf{H}(\mathbf{x} - \mathbf{q})] \end{aligned} \qquad (55)$$

The locally weighted regression process that generates $\mathbf{s_q}$ guarantees that $\sum \mathbf{s}_i(\mathbf{q}) = 1$, and since the linear local model exactly matches any linear trend in the data, $\sum \mathbf{s}_i(\mathbf{q})(\mathbf{x} - \mathbf{q}) = 0$. Therefore, the bias depends only on the quadratic term (Katkovnik 1979; Cleveland and Loader 1994a):

$$\text{bias} = \frac{1}{2}\sum_i \mathbf{s}_i(\mathbf{q})(\mathbf{x}_i - \mathbf{q})^T\mathbf{H}(\mathbf{x}_i - \mathbf{q}) \qquad (56)$$

assuming the ridge regression parameters λ_i have been set to zero. This formula raises the temptation to estimate and cancel the bias by estimating the second derivative matrix $\mathbf{H}$. It is not clear that this is better than simply using a quadratic local model instead of a linear local model. The quadratic local model would eliminate the local bias due to the quadratic term (and also remove the need for the distance metric to compensate for different curvature in different directions). Of course, if a quadratic local model is used, the bias will then be due to cubic terms in the Taylor series for the true function, whose elimination would require estimation of the cubic terms with a cubic local model, and so on. We have not yet found a principled termination of this cycle.

9.3. *Assessment Using Cross Validation*

We can assess how well locally weighted learning is doing by testing how well each experience $(\mathbf{x}_i, y_i)$ in the memory is predicted by the rest of the experiences. A simple measure of the ith prediction error is the difference between the predicted output of the input $\mathbf{x}_i$ and the observed value y_i. However, for non-parametric learners that are overfitting the data this measure may be deceptively small. For example, a nearest neighbor learner would always have an error measure of zero because $(\mathbf{x}_i, y_i)$ will be the closest neighbor to itself.

A more sophisticated measure of the ith prediction error is the *leave-one-out cross validation* error, in which the experience is first removed from the memory before prediction. Let $\hat{y}_i^{cv}$ be the output predicted for input $\mathbf{x}_i$ using the memory with the ith point removed:

$$\{(\mathbf{x}_1, y_1), (\mathbf{x}_2, y_2), \ldots, (\mathbf{x}_{i-1}, y_{i-1}), (\mathbf{x}_{i+1}, y_{i+1}), \ldots, (\mathbf{x}_n, y_n)\} \quad (57)$$

The ith leave-one-out cross validation error is $e_i^{cv} = (\hat{y}_i^{cv}\mathbf{r} - y_i)$. With the lazy learning formalism, in which most work takes place at prediction time, it is no more expensive to predict a value with one data point removed than with it included. This contrasts with the majority of learning methods that have an explicit training stage – in these cases it is not easy to pick an earlier experience and temporarily pretend we did not see it. Ignoring a training data point typically requires retraining from scratch with a modified training set, which can be fairly expensive with a nonlinear parametric model such as a neural network. In addition, the dependence of nonlinear parametric training on initial parameter values further complicates the analysis. To handle this effect correctly many training runs with different starting values must be undertaken for each different data set. All of this is avoided with locally weighted learning with local models that are linear in the unknown parameters, although tuning of fit parameters does reintroduce the problem. However, tuning of fit parameters can be a background process that operates on a slower time scale than adding new data and answering queries.

Cross validation can also be performed locally, i.e, from just fitting a locally linear model at one query point $\mathbf{q}$ (Cleveland and Loader 1994c). We first consider the locally weighted average of the squared cross validation error MSE^{cv} at each training point (Myers 1990):

$$MSE^{cv}(\mathbf{q}) = \frac{\sum (e_{i,\mathbf{x}_i}^{cv})^2 K(d(\mathbf{x}_i, \mathbf{q}))}{\sum K(d(\mathbf{x}_i, \mathbf{q}))} \quad (58)$$

This estimate requires a locally weighted regression to be performed at each training point with non-zero weight $K(d(\mathbf{x}_i, \mathbf{q}))$. One could imagine storing $e_{i,\mathbf{x}_i}^{cv}$ with each training point, but this value would have to be updated as new data was learned. We approximate $e_{i,\mathbf{x}_i}^{cv} \approx e_{i,\mathbf{q}}^{cv}$ to generate the following:

$$\text{MSE}^{\text{cv}}(\mathbf{q}) = \frac{\sum (e_{i,\mathbf{q}}^{\text{cv}})^2 K(d(\mathbf{x}_i, \mathbf{q}))}{\sum K(d(\mathbf{x}_i, \mathbf{q}))} = \frac{\sum (r_{i,\mathbf{q}}^{\text{cv}})^2}{n_{\text{LWR}}} \qquad (59)$$

where $r_{i,\mathbf{q}}^{\text{cv}}$ is the weighted cross validation error with point i removed from a locally weighted regression centered at $\mathbf{q}$. The weighted cross validation residual $r_{i,\mathbf{q}}^{\text{cv}}$ is related to the weighted residual ($r_i = w_i e_i$) by (Myers 1990):

$$r_i^{\text{cv}} = \frac{r_i}{1 - \mathbf{z}_i^{\text{T}}(\mathbf{Z}^{\text{T}}\mathbf{Z} + \Lambda)^{-1}\mathbf{z}_i} \qquad (60)$$

Thus, we obtain the final equation for MSE^{cv} as:

$$\text{MSE}^{\text{cv}}(\mathbf{q}) = \frac{1}{n_{\text{LWR}}} \sum_i \left(\frac{r_i}{1 - \mathbf{z}_i^{\text{T}}(\mathbf{Z}^{\text{T}}\mathbf{Z} + \Lambda)^{-1}\mathbf{z}_i} \right)^2 \qquad (61)$$

This equation is a local version of the PRESS statistic (Myers 1990). It allows us to perform leave-one-out cross validation without recalculating the regression parameters for every excluded point. Often, this is computationally very efficient.

10. Optimal Fit Parameters: An Example

In this section we will try to find optimal fit parameters (distance metric $d(\ )$, weighting function $K(\ )$, and smoothing bandwidth h) for a simple example. We will make the restrictive assumption that the data is uniformly spaced on a rectangular grid. We first approach this question by exploring kernel shapes in one dimension. We allow the weights w_i to be unknown, and numerically optimize them to minimize the mean squared error. We assume the underlying function is quadratic with second derivative $\mathbf{H}$ (Equation 53) and that there is additive independent identically distributed zero mean noise (Equation 43) with constance variance σ^2. The sampled data is regularly spaced with a distance of Δ between each data point (in Figure 10 $\Delta = 0.1$). Equation 42 is solved for $\mathbf{s}$, with the query at $\mathbf{x} = 0$. The mean squared error is the sum of the bias (Equation 54) squared and the variance (Equation 45). This quantity is minimized by adjusting the weights w_i. The resulting kernel shape $K(d) = w_i^2$ is shown in Figure 10. This kernel shape matches the quadratic kernel:

$$K(x) = \begin{cases} (1 - x^2) & if\ |x| < 1 \\ 0 & \text{otherwise} \end{cases} \qquad (62)$$

which has been described in Section 6.

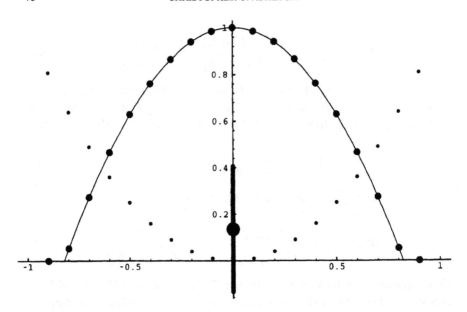

Figure 10. The kernel shape that minimizes mean squared error in one dimension. The large single dot is the predicted value, whose deviation from zero, the correct value, reveals the bias. The vertical bars show the standard deviation of the prediction (i.e., the square root of the variance), which is greatly reduced from the standard deviation of ±1 of the original data. The set of large dots have been optimized to minimize the mean squared error of the prediction, and reveal the optimal kernel shape for this criterion. The line through these points is a quadratic kernel with the appropriate bandwidth to match the optimized kernel values. The small dots are the value of the quadratic portion of the underlying function, for comparison.

Further numerical experimentation in one dimension revealed that the optimal scaling factor m for the one dimensional distance function is approximately:

$$m^2 \approx c\mathbf{H} \tag{63}$$

where c is a constant that takes into account issues such as data spacing Δ and the standard deviation of the additive noise:

$$c \propto \frac{\Delta^2}{\sigma} \tag{64}$$

The width of the resulting kernel is directly related to the optimal smoothing bandwidth.

In two dimensions we can explore optimization of the distance metric. Optimizing the values of the kernel at each of the data points is beyond our current computational resources, so we will assume the form of the kernel function is the quadratic kernel. We will choose a particular value for the

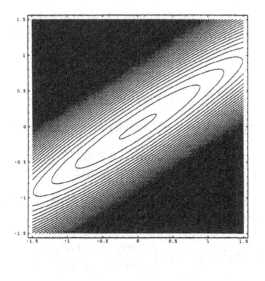

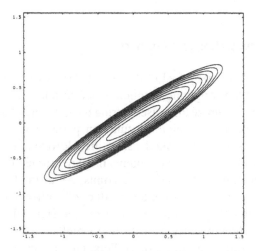

Figure 12. Contour plot of optimal kernel.

Hessian **H** in Equation 53, and then optimize the scaling matrix **M** for the multidimensional distance function to minimize the mean squared error. We found that the optimal **M** approximately satisfies the following equation:

$$\mathbf{M}^T\mathbf{M} \approx c\mathbf{H} \tag{65}$$

where c is the same as the one dimensional case. Figure 11 shows how the Hessian matrix **H** can orient the quadratic component in an arbitrary orientation. The distance function matrix $\mathbf{M}^T\mathbf{M}$ needs to be a full matrix in order to allow the optimal kernel (Figure 12) to match the orientation of the quadratic component of $f(\mathbf{x})$ (Figure 11). For this numerical experiment $\mathbf{H}$ was chosen to be:

$$\mathbf{H} = \begin{pmatrix} 1.23851 & -1.77313 \\ -1.77313 & 2.86149 \end{pmatrix} \tag{66}$$

The optimal scaling matrix $\mathbf{M}$ was found by numerical search to be:

$$\mathbf{M} = \begin{pmatrix} 2.32597 & -3.33005 \\ 0.0 & 1.18804 \end{pmatrix} \tag{67}$$

and Equation 65 is approximately satisfied, as $(\mathbf{M}^{\mathrm{T}}\mathbf{M})\mathbf{H}^{-1}$ is almost a multiple of the identity matrix for $c = 4.37$.

$$(\mathbf{M}^{\mathrm{T}}\mathbf{M})\mathbf{H}^{-1} = \begin{pmatrix} 0.99949 & -0.0001 \\ 0.0008 & 1.0002 \end{pmatrix} \tag{68}$$

11. Noisy Training Data and Outliers

The averaging performed by the locally weighted regression process naturally filters out noise if the weighting function is not infinite at zero distance. The tuning process can optimize the noise filtering by adjusting fit parameters such as smoothing parameters, weighting function parameters, ridge regression parameters, and choice of local model structure. However, it is often useful to explicitly identify *outliers*: training points that are erroneous or whose noise is much larger than that of neighboring points. An example of the effect of an outlier is given in Figure 13 and the effect of outlier rejection is shown in Figure 14. Robust regression (see, for example Hampel et al. 1986) and cross validation allow extensions to locally weighted learners in which we can identify or reduce the effects of outliers. Outliers can be identified and removed globally, or they can be identified and ignored on a query by query basis. Query-based outlier detection allows training points to be ignored for some queries and used for other queries. Other areas that have been explored are detecting discontinuities and nonstationarity in the training data.

11.1. *Global Weighting of Stored Points and Finding Outliers*

It is possible to attach weights to stored points during the training process and during lookup that downweight points that are suspected of being unreliable (Aha and Kibler 1989; Cost and Salzberg 1993). These weights can multiply the weight based on the weighting function. Totally unreliable points can be

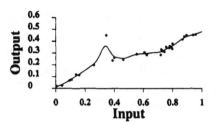

Figure 13. Locally weighted regression approximating a 1-dimensional dataset shown by the black dots. There is an outlier at $x \approx 0.33$.

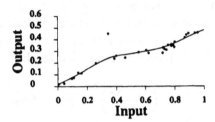

Figure 14. Locally weighted regression supplemented with outlier removal.

assigned a weight of zero, leading them to be ignored. The reliability weights can be based on cross validation: whether a stored point correctly predicts or classifies its neighbors. Another approach is to only utilize stored points that have shown that they can reduce the cross validation error (Aha 1990). Important issues are when the weighting decision is made and how often the decision is reevaluated. Global methods typically assign a weight to a point during training, in which case the decision is usually never reevaluated, or during an asynchronous database maintenance process, in which decisions are reevaluated each time the process cycles through the entire database.

11.2. *Local Weighting of Stored Points and Finding Outliers*

Local outlier detection methods do not label points as outliers for all queries, as do global methods. Points can be outliers for some queries and not outliers for others. We can generate weights for training data at query time based on cross validation using nearby points. The PRESS statistic (Myers 1990) can be modified to serve as a local outlier detector in locally weighted regression. For this, we need the standardized individual PRESS residual (also called the Studentized residual):

$$e_{\text{PRESS}} = \frac{r_i}{\hat{\sigma}\sqrt{1 - \mathbf{z}_i^{\mathrm{T}}(\mathbf{Z}^{\mathrm{T}}\mathbf{Z} + \Lambda)^{-1}\mathbf{z}_i}} \tag{69}$$

This measure has zero mean and unit variance and assumes a locally normal distribution of the error. If, for a given data point it deviates from zero more than a certain threshold, the point can be called an outlier. A conservative threshold would be 1.96, discarding all points lying outside the 95% area of the normal distribution. In our applications, we used 2.57, cutting off all data outside the 99% area of the normal distribution.

11.3. *Robust Regression Approaches*

Data with outliers can be viewed as having additive noise with long-tailed symmetric distributions. Robust regression is useful for both global and local detection of outliers (Cleveland 1979). A bisquare weighting function is used to additionally downweight points based on their residuals:

$$u_i = \begin{cases} \left(1 - \left(\frac{e_i}{6e_{\text{MED}}}\right)^2\right)^2 & \text{if } |e_i| < 6e_{\text{MED}} \\ 0 & \text{otherwise} \end{cases} \tag{70}$$

where e_{MED} is the median of the absolute value of the residuals e_i. The weights now become $w_i = u_i K(d(\mathbf{x}_i, \mathbf{q}))$. This process is repeated about 1–3 times to refine the estimates of u_i.

12. Tuning

Like most learning algorithms, locally weighted learning usually needs to be tuned to work well for a particular problem. Tuning means adjusting the parameters of the learning algorithm itself. The locally weighted fit criteria is

$$C(\mathbf{q}) = \sum_i \left[(f(\mathbf{x}_i, \beta) - y_i)^2 K\left(\frac{d(\mathbf{x}_i, \mathbf{q})}{h}\right) \right] \tag{71}$$

It includes several "fit" parameters: the bandwidth or smoothing parameter h, the distance metric $d(\ )$, and the weighting or kernel function $K(\ )$. There are additional fit parameters such as ridge regression parameters and outlier thresholds. There are several ways to tune these fit parameters.

- **Global tuning:** The fit parameters are set globally by an optimization process that typically minimizes cross validation error over all the data, and therefore constant size and shape volumes of data are used to answer queries.
- **Query-based local tuning:** The fit parameters are set on each query based on local information.

- **Point-based local tuning:** The weighted training criteria uses different fit parameters for each point x_i: a bandwidth h_i, a distance metric $d_i(\ )$, a weighting function $K_i(\ )$, and possibly a weight w_{x_i}:

$$C(\mathbf{q}) = \sum_i \left[(f(\mathbf{x}_i, \beta) - y_i)^2 w_{\mathbf{x}_i} K_i \left(\frac{d_i(\mathbf{x}_i, \mathbf{q})}{h_i} \right) \right] \qquad (72)$$

In typical implementations of this approach the fit parameters are computed in advance of the queries and are stored with the data points.

There are several approaches to computing the fit parameter values:

- **Plug-in approach:** The fit parameters can be set by a direct computation.
- **Optimization approaches:** The fit parameters can be set by an optimization process that either (Marron 1988):
  - minimizes the training set error,
  - minimizes the test or validation set error,
  - minimizes the cross validation error (CV),
  - minimizes the generalized cross validation error (GCV) (Myers 1990),
  - maximizes Akaike's information criterion (AIC),
  - or adjusts Mallow's C_p.

Fit parameters cannot be optimized in isolation. The combination of all fit parameters generates a particular fit quality. If one fit parameter is changed, typically the optimal values of other parameters change in response. If a locally constant model is used, then the smoothing parameter and distance function must reflect the flatness of the neighborhood in different directions. If the local model is a hyperplane, the smoothing parameter and distance function must reflect the second derivative of the neighborhood. If the local model is quadratic, it is the third spatial derivative of the data that must be dealt with.

For practical purposes it would be useful to have a clear understanding of how accurate the non-linear fit parameters should be for a good fit. Our intuition is that approximate values usually result in barely distinguishable performance from optimal parameters in practical use, although (Brockmann et al. 1993) states that this is not true for h in kernel regression.

The next section considers optimizing a single set of parameters for all possible future queries (global tuning). Section 12.2 considers optimizing multiple sets of parameters for specific queries (local tuning).

12.1. *Global Tuning*

Global cross-validation can be a particularly robust method for tuning parameters, because it does not make any special assumptions. Independent of the noise distribution, data distribution and underlying function, the cross-validation value is an unbiased estimate of how well a given set of parameters will perform on new data drawn from the same distribution as the old data. This robustness has lead to the use of global cross-validation in applications that attempt to achieve high autonomy by making few assumptions, such as the General Memory Based Learning (GMBL) system described in (Moore et al. 1992). GMBL performs large amounts of cross validation search to optimize feature subsets, the diagonal elements of the distance metric, the smoothing parameter, and the order of the regression.

12.1.1. *Continuous Search*
Continuous fit parameters make continuous search possible. Inevitably this is local hill climbing, with a large risk of getting stuck in local optima. The sum of the squared cross validation errors is minimized using a nonlinear parameter estimation procedure (e.g., MINPACK (More et al. 1980) or NL2SOL (Dennis et al. 1981)). As discussed in Section 9.3, in this locally weighted learning approach computing the cross validation error for a single point is no more computationally expensive than answering a query. This is quite different from parametric approaches such as a neural network, where a new model (network) must be trained for each cross validation training set with a particular point removed. In addition, if the local model is linear in the unknown parameters we can analytically take the derivative of the cross validation error with respect to the parameters to be estimated, which greatly speeds up the search process.

We can use the optimized distance metric to find which input variables are more or less important to the function being represented. Distance scaling factors that go to zero indicate directions that are irrelevant or are consistent with the local model structure, and that a global model will suffice for those directions. We can also interpret the ridge regression parameters. The ridge regression parameters for irrelevant terms in the local model become very large in the fit parameter optimization process. The effect of this is to force the corresponding estimated parameters β_i to the apriori values $\bar{\beta}_i$, which corresponds to a dimensionality reduction.

A relatively unexplored area is stochastic gradient descent approaches to optimizing fit parameters. Rather than use all the cross validation errors and their associated contributions to the derivative, why not use only a small random sample of the cross validation errors and their associated derivative contributions? Racine (1993) describes an approach to optimizing fit parameters based on partitioning the training data into subsets, calculating cross validation errors for each subset based only on data in the subset, and then averaging the results.

12.1.2. *Discrete Search*

Discrete search algorithms for good fit parameters is an active area of research. Maron and Moore (1996) describe "racing" techniques to find good fit parameter values. These techniques compare a wide range of different types of models simultaneously, and handle models with discrete parameters. Bad models are quickly dropped from the race, which focuses computational effort on distinguishing between the good models. Typically any continuous fit parameters are discretized (Maron and Moore 1996).

Techniques for selecting features in the distance metric and local model have been developed in statistics (Draper and Smith 1981; Miller 1990), including all subsets, forward regression, backwards regression, and stepwise regression. We have explored stepwise regression procedures to determine which terms of the local model are useful with similar results to the gradient based search described above. Feature selection is a hard problem because the features cannot be examined independently. The value of a feature depends on which other features are also selected. Thus the goal is to find a *set* of feature weights, not individual feature weights for each feature. In Maron and Moore (1996) a number of algorithms for doing this are described and compared, including methods based on Monte-Carlo sampling. Aha (1991) gives an algorithm that constructs new features, in addition to selecting features. Friedman (1994) gives techniques for query dependent feature construction.

12.1.3. *Continuous vs. Discrete Search*

Discrete search can explore settings for discrete fit parameters, and even select training algorithm features or function approximation methods (e.g., locally weighted regression, neural networks, rule-based systems). It would seem that continuous fit parameter optimization cannot make these choices. However, this is not the case. By blending the output of different approaches with a blending parameter α, continuous search can choose model order, algorithm features, and approximation method. For example, α could be optimized to blend two methods $f_1(\ )$ and $f_2(\ )$ in the following equation:

$$f(\mathbf{q}) = \alpha f_1(\mathbf{q}) + (1 - \alpha) f_2(\mathbf{q}) \tag{73}$$

Cleveland and Loader (1994a, c) present an approach to automatically choose the local model structure (i.e., order of the polynomial model) by blending polynomial models, where a non-integral model order indicates a weighted blend between two integral model orders. They use cross validation to optimize the local model order on each query.

12.2. *Local Tuning*

Local fit parameter optimization is referred to as "adaptive" or "variable" in the statistics literature, as in "adaptive bandwidth" or "variable bandwidth" smoothers. There are several reasons to consider local tuning, although it dramatically increases the number of degrees of freedom in the training process, leading to increased variance of the predictions and an increased risk of overfitting the data (Cleveland and Loader 1994c):

- **Adaptation to the data density and distribution:** This adaptation is in addition to the adaptation provided by the locally weighted regression procedure itself (Bottou and Vapnik 1992).
- **Adaptation to variations in the noise level in the training data.** These variations are known as *heteroscedasticity*.
- **Adaptation to variations in the behavior of the underlying function.** The function may be locally planar in some regions and have high curvature in others.

"Plug-in" estimators have been derived and local (locally weighted) training set error, cross validation, or validation (test) set error can drive an optimization of the local model.

13. Interference

Negative interference between old and new training data is one of the most important motivations for exploring locally weighted learning. To illustrate the differences between global parametric representations and a locally-weighted learning approach, a sigmoidal feedforward neural network approach was compared to a locally weighted learning approach on the same problem. The architecture for the sigmoidal feedforward neural network was taken from (Goldberg and Pearlmutter 1988, Section 6) who modeled arm inverse dynamics. The ability of each of these methods to predict the torques of the simulated two joint arm at 1000 random points was compared (Atkeson 1992). Figure 15 plots the normalized RMS prediction error. The points were sampled uniformly using ranges comparable to those used in Miller et al. (1978), which also looked at two joint arm inverse dynamics modeling. Initially, each method was trained on a training set of 1000 random samples, and then the predictions of the torques on a separate test set of 1000 random samples of the two joint arm dynamics function were assessed. The solid bar marked LWR at location 1 shows the test set error of a locally weighted regression with a quadratic local model. The light bar marked NN at location 2 shows the best test set error of the neural network. Both methods generalize well on this problem (bars 1 and 2 have low error).

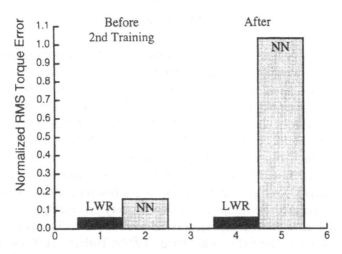

Figure 15. Performance of various methods on two joint arm dynamics.

Each method was then trained on ten attempts to make a particular desired movement. Each method successfully learned the desired movement. After this second round of training, performance on the random test set was again measured (bars at locations 4 and 5). The sigmoidal feedforward neural network lost its memory of the full dynamics (the light bar at location 5 has a large error), and represented only the dynamics of the particular movements being learned in the second training set. This interference between new and previously learned data was not prevented by increasing the number of hidden units in the single layer network from 10 up to 100. The locally weighted learning method did not show this interference effect (solid bar at location 4).

The interference is caused by the failure of the neural network model structure to match the arm inverse dynamics structure perfectly. There is no noise in the data, and no concept drift, so these causes are eliminated as possible sources of the interference. It can be argued that the sigmoidal neural network forgot the original training data because we did not include that data in the second training data set (learning a specific movement). That is exactly our point; if all past data is retained to combat interference, then the method becomes a lazy learning method. In that case we argue that one should take advantage of the opportunity to locally weight the training procedure, and get better performance (Vapnik 1992; Bottou and Vapnik 1992; Vapnik and Bottou 1993).

14. Implementing Locally Weighted Learning

There are several concerns about locally weighted learning systems, including whether locally weighted learning systems can answer queries fast enough and whether their speed will unacceptably degrade as the size of the database grows. This section explores these concerns. We discuss fast ways to find relevant data using either k-d trees in software, special purpose hardware, or massively parallel computers, and the current performance of our LWR implementation. Our goal is to minimize the need for compromises such as forgetting (discarding data) to keep the database size under a limit, instance averaging, which averages similar data, or maintaining an elaborate data structure of intermediate results to accelerate query processing. We will not discuss LWR acceleration approaches that are limited to low dimensional problems such as binning (Fan and Marron 1994a; Turlach and Wand 1995). Other discussions of fast implementations include Seifert et al. (1994) and Seifert and Gasser (1994).

14.1. *Retrieving Relevant Data*

The choice of method for storing experiences depends on what fraction of the experiences are used in each locally weighted regression and what computational technology is available. If all of the experiences are used in each locally weighted regression, then simply maintaining a list or array of experiences is sufficient. If only nearby experiences are included in the locally weighted regression, then an efficient method of finding nearest neighbors is required. Nearest neighbor lookup can be accelerated on a serial processor using the k-d tree data structure. Parallel processors and special purpose processors typically use parallel exhaustive search.

14.1.1. *K-d Trees*
Naively implemented search for a d dimensional nearest neighbor in a database of size n requires n distance computations. Nearest neighbor search can be implemented efficiently by means of a *k-d tree* (Bentley 1975; Friedman et al. 1977; Bentley and Friedman 1979; Bentley et al. 1980; Murphy and Selkow 1986; Ramasubramanian and Paliwal 1989; Broder 1990; Samet 1990; Sproull 1991). A k-d tree is a binary data structure that recursively splits a d-dimensional space into smaller subregions. The search for a nearest neighbor proceeds by initially searching the k-d tree in the branches nearest the query point. Frequently, distance constraints mean there is no need to explore further branches. Figure 16 shows a k-d tree segmenting a two dimensional space. The shaded regions correspond to areas of the k-d tree that were not searched.

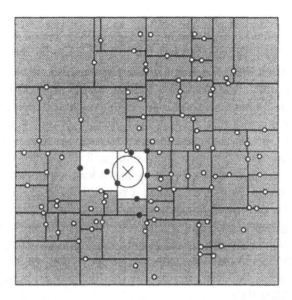

Figure 16. Generally during a nearest neighbor search only a few leaf nodes need to be inspected. The query point is marked by an × and the distance to the nearest neighbor is indicated by a circle. Black nodes are those inspected on the path to the leaf node.

The access time is asymptotically logarithmic in n, the size of the memory, although often overhead costs mean that nearly all the data points *will* be accessed in a supposed logarithmic search, for example, with eight dimensions or more and fewer than approximately 100,000 uniformly distributed data points. In fact, given uniformly distributed data points, the tree size for which logarithmic performance is noticeable increases exponentially with dimensionality. Two things can alleviate this problem. First, the data points are unlikely to be distributed uniformly. In fact, the less randomly distributed the training data is the better. Second, there are approximate algorithms that can find one or more nearby experiences, without guaranteeing they are the nearest, that *do* operate in logarithmic time. Empirically, these approximations do not greatly reduce prediction accuracy (Omohundro 1987; Moore 1990b). Bump trees (Omohundro 1991) are another promising efficient approximation. Cleveland et al. (1988), Farmer and Sidorowich (1988a, b), Renka (1988), Grosse (1989), Moore (1990a), Cleveland and Grosse (1991), Karalič (1992), Townshend (1992), Loader (1994), Wess et al. (1994), Deng and Moore (1995), Lowe (1995), and Smagt et al. (1994) have used trees in memory-based learning and locally weighted regression.

14.1.2. *Special Purpose Devices*

Special purpose hardware for finding nearest neighbors has a long history (Taylor 1959, 1960; Steinbuch 1961; Steinbuch and Piske 1963; Kazmierczak and Steinbuch 1963; Batchelor 1974). These machines calculated either a Manhattan or Euclidean distance for all stored points, and then did comparisons to pick the winning point. The current version of this technology is the wafer scale memory-based reasoning devices proposed by Yasunaga and Kitano (1993). The devices allocate one processor per data point, and can handle approximately 1.7 million data points per 8 inch wafer. The designers have exploited the properties of memory-based learning in two ways. First, the resolution of the computed distance is not critical, so analog adders and multipliers are used for weighting and distance calculations instead of digital circuits, saving much space on the silicon for other processors. Second, the device is robust to faulty processors, in that a faulty processor only causes the loss of a single data point. The authors advocate simply ignoring processor failures, although it would be possible to map the faulty processors and skip them when loading data.

14.1.3. *Massively Parallel Implementations*

Many nearest neighbor systems have been implemented on massively parallel Connection Machines (Waltz 1987). On a massively parallel computer, such as the CM1 and CM2 (Hillis 1985), exhaustive search is often faster than using k-d trees, due to the limited number of experiences allocated to each processor. The Connection Machine can have up to 2^{16} (65536) processors, and can simulate a parallel computer with many more processors. Experiences are stored in the local memory associated with each processor. An experience can be compared to the desired experience in each processor, with the processors running in parallel, and then a hardwired global-OR bus can be used to find the closest match in constant time independent of the number of stored experiences. The search time depends linearly on the number of dimensions in the distance metric, and the distance metric can be changed easily or made to depend on the current query point.

The critical feature of the massively parallel computer system IXM2 is the use of associative memories in addition to multiple processors (Higuchi et al. 1991). There are 64 processors (Transputers) in the IXM2, but each processor has 4K × 40 bits of associative memory, which increases the effective number of processors to 256K. This architecture is well suited for memory-based learning where the distance metric involves exact matches of symbolic fields, as that is the operation the associative memory chips can support. Future associative memories might implement Euclidean distance as a basic operation. There have been implementations of memory-based translation and parsing on the IXM2 (Kitano and Higuchi 1991a, b; Sumita et al. 1993; Kitano 1993a, b).

The current generic parallel computer seems to be on the order of 100 standard microprocessors tightly connected with a communication network. Examples of this design are the CM5 and the SNAP system (Kitano et al. 1991). The details of the communication network are not critical to locally weighted learning, since the time critical processing consists of broadcasting the query to the processors and determining which answer is the best, which can easily be done with a prespecified communication pattern. This form of communication is not difficult to implement. This machine does not have the thousands of processors that make exhaustive search the obvious nearest neighbor algorithm. The processors will probably maintain some sort of search data structure such as a k-d tree, although the local k-d trees may be too small for efficient search performance. Kitano et al. (1991) describe an implementation of memory-based reasoning on the SNAP system. This type of parallel computer is excellent for locally weighted learning, where the regression calculation dominates the lookup time if a large fraction of the points are used in each regression.

14.2. *Implementing Locally Weighted Regression*

Locally weighted learning minimizes the computational cost of training; new data points are simply stored in the memory. The price for trivial training costs is a more expensive lookup procedure. Locally weighted regression uses a relatively complex regression procedure to form the local model, and is thus more expensive than nearest neighbor and weighted average memory-based learning procedures. For each query a new local model is formed. The rate at which local models can be formed and evaluated limits the rate at which queries can be answered. We have implemented the locally weighted regression procedure on a 33MHz Intel i860 microprocessor. The peak computation rate of this processor is 66 MFlops. We have achieved effective computation rates of 15 MFlops on a learning problem with 10 input dimensions and 5 output dimensions, using a linear local model. This leads to a lookup time of approximately 15 milliseconds on a database of 1000 points, using exhaustive search. This time includes distance and weight calculation for all the stored points, forming the regression matrix, and solving the normal equations.

15. Applications of Locally Weighted Learning

The presence of the LOWESS and LOESS software in the S statistics package has lead to the use of locally weighted regression as a standard tool in many areas, including modeling biological motor control, feeding cycles in smokers and nonsmokers, lead-induced anemia, categories of tonal alignment in spoken English, and growth and sexual maturation during disease (Cleveland 1979; Cleveland et al. 1992).

Atkeson et al. (1996) survey our own work in applying locally weighted learning to robot control. Zografski has explored the use of locally weighted regression in robot control and modeling time series, and also compared LWR to neural networks and other methods (Zografski 1989, 1991, 1992; Zografski and Durrani 1995). Gorinevsky and Connolly (1994) compared several different approximation schemes (neural nets, Kohonen maps, radial basis functions, and local polynomical fits) on simulated robot inverse kinematics with added noise, and showed that local polynomial fits were more accurate than all other methods. van der Smagt et al. (1994) learned robot kinematics using local linear models at the leaves of a tree data structure. Tadepalli and Ok (1996) apply local linear regression to reinforcement learning. Baird and Klopf (1993) apply nearest neighbor techniques and weighted averaging to reinforcement learning and Thrun (1996) and Thrun and O'Sullivan (1996) apply similar techniques to robot learning. Connell and Utgoff (1987) interpolated a value function using locally weighted averaging to balance an inverted pendulum (a pole) on a moving cart. Peng (1995) performed the cart pole task using locally weighted regression to interpolate a value function. Aha and Salzberg (1993) explored nearest neighbor and locally weighted learning approaches to a tracking task in which a robot pursued and caught a ball. McCallum (1995) explored the use of lazy learning techniques in situations where states were not completely measured. Farmer and Sidorowich (1987, 1988a, b) apply locally weighted regression to modeling and prediction of chaotic dynamic systems. Huang (1996) uses nearest neighbor and weighted averaging techniques to cache simulation results and accelerate a movement planner.

Lawrence et al. (1996) compare neural networks and local regression methods on several benchmark problems. Local regression outperformed neural networks on half the benchmarks. Factors affecting performance included whether the data had differing density over the input space, noise level, dimensionality, and the nature of the function underlying the data.

Several researchers have applied locally weighted averaging and regression to free form 2D and 3D deformation, morphing, and image interpolation in computer graphics (Goshtasby 1988; Wolberg 1990; Ruprecht and Muller 1992; Ruprecht and Muller 1991; Ruprecht and Muller 1993; Ruprecht et al.

1994). Coughran and Grosse (1991) describe using locally weighted regression for scientific visualization and auralization of data.

Ge et al. (1994) apply locally weighted regression to predict cell density in a fermentation process. They used nearest neighbor weighting and a tricube weighting function. They also used principal components and cross validation to select features globally. Locally weighted regression outperformed other methods, including a global nonlinear regression. Hammond (1991) used LWR to model fermentation as well.

Næs et al. (1990), Næs and Isaksson (1992) and Wang et al. (1994) apply locally weighted regression to analytical chemistry. They use global principal components to reduce the dimensionality of the inputs, and they use cross validation to set the number of components to use. They also explore several weighted Euclidean distance metrics, including weighting depending on the range of the data in principal component coordinates, weighting depending on how good that dimension is in predicting the output, and a distance metric that includes the output value. They use a quadratic local model and the tricube weighting function. They use cross validation to select the number of points to include in the local regression. They make the important point that optimal experiment design is quite different when using locally weighted regression as compared to global linear regression.

Tamada et al. (1993) apply memory-based learning to water demand forecasting. They select features using Akaike's Information Criterion (AIC), and use locally weighted averaging within a neighborhood. They use a default temporally local regression scheme if no points are found in the neighborhood. They use error rates to set feature weights and to perform outlier removal.

Townshend (1992) applies locally weighted regression to the analysis, modeling, coding, and prediction of speech signals. He uses a singular value decomposition to reduce the dimensionality of the regression to a fixed value D, determined from other criteria. He uses the k closest points to form the local model. The distance to the nearest point is used as an estimate of the confidence in the prediction. A clustering process on the inputs and the outputs (x_i, y_i) is used to handle noise and one to many mapping problems. A k-d tree is used to speed up nearest neighbor search. This process lead to a significant improvement over a linear predictor.

Wijnberg and Johnson (1985) apply locally weighted regression to interpolating air quality measurements. They used cross validation to optimize the smoothing parameter globally, but did not find a well defined minimum for the smoothing parameter. Kozek (1992) describe using LWR to model automobile emissions.

Walden and Prescott (1983) use LWR to remove trends in time series involving climate data. Solow (1988) estimated the variance or noise level in time series climate data after having removed the mean using LWR.

Locally weighted regression has also been applied in economics and econometrics (Meese and Wallace 1991; LeBaron 1992). Meese and Rose (1990) used LWR to model exchange rates and conclude that no significant nonlinearity exists in the data. Diebold and Nason (1990) also used LWR to predict exchange rates, without any more success than other nonparametric regression techniques.

Turetsky et al. (1989) and Raz et al. (1989) use LWR to smooth biological evoked potential data, and explore approaches to choosing the smoothing parameter. Bottou and Vapnik (1992) apply locally weighted classification to optical character recognition (OCR). Rust and Bornman (1982) apply LWR to marketing data.

There have been a range of applications of locally weighted techniques in statistics (Cleveland 1993b, Cleveland and Loader 1995). The idea of local fitting was extended to likelihood-based regression models by Tibshirani and Hastie (1987) and Hastie and Tibshirani (1990) applied locally weighted techniques to many distributional settings such as logistic regression and developed general fitting algorithms. Lejeune and Sarda (1992) applied locally weighted regression to estimation of distribution and density functions. Cleveland et al. (1993) applied locally weighted regression to density estimation, spectrum estimation, and predicting binary variables. Fan and Kreutzberger (1995) applied locally weighted regression to spectral density estimation.

16. Discussion

16.1. *What Is A Local Learning Approach?*

To explore the idea of local learning, it is useful to first consider what a global learner is. A global/distributed representation is typically characterized by:
   1. Incrementally learning a single new training point affects many parameters.
   2. A prediction or answer to a query also depends on many parameters.
1 and 2 are characteristics of distributed representations. An additional criterion:
   3. There are many fewer parameters than data.
could serve as a definition of a global representation or model, and is a good predictor that 1 and 2 will be true for a particular method. However, it is also possible to have local methods with attribute 3, and not attributes 1 and 2,

such as a low resolution tabular representation with non-overlapping cells. A part of the design space that has not been explored are learning algorithms with huge numbers of parameters that use distributed representations (1 and 2, but not 3).

There are at least three different views of what constitutes local learning: local representations, local selection, and locally weighted learning. This has lead to some confusion and convoluted terminology. In a local representation, each new data point affects a small subset of the parameters and answering a query involves a small subset of the parameters as well. This view of local learning stems from the distinction between local and distributed representations in neuroscience (Thorpe 1995). Examples of local representations are lookup tables and exemplar/prototype based classifiers. It is not necessarily the case that the number of parameters in the representation be on the order of the number of data points (i.e., a considerable amount of local averaging can occur).

Local selection methods store all (or most) of the training data, and use a distance function to determine which stored points are relevant to the query. The function of local selection is to select a single output using nearest neighbor or using a distance-based voting scheme (k-nearest neighbor). Examples of these types of approaches are common, and include Stanfill and Waltz (1986) and Aha (1990).

Locally weighted learning stores the training data explicitly (as do local selection approaches), and only fits parameters to the training data when a query is known. The critical feature of locally weighted learning is that a criterion locally weighted with respect to the query location is used to fit some type of parametric model to the data (Vapnik 1992; Bottou and Vapnik 1992; Vapnik and Bottou 1993). We have the paradoxical situation that seemingly global model structures (e.g., polynomials, multilayer sigmoidal neural nets) are being called local models because of the locally weighted training criterion. All of the data can be involved in training the local model, as long as distant data matters less than nearby data.

This paper explores locally weighted training procedures, which involves deferring processing the training data until a query is present, leading to the use of the terms *lazy learning* and *least commitment learning*. There are many global approaches and representations such as: rules, decision trees, and parametric models (e.g., polynomials, sigmoidal neural nets, radial basis functions, projection pursuit networks). All of the above approaches can be transformed into locally weighted approaches by using a locally weighted training criterion (Vapnik 1992; Bottou and Vapnik 1992; Vapnik and Bottou 1993; Kozek 1992), so the scope of locally weighted learning is quite broad. We will discuss locally weighted classification as an example.

16.2. *Locally Weighted Classification*

In classification, there are several ways to incorporate distance weighting. In k-nearest neighbor approaches, the number of occurrences of each class in the k closest points to the query are counted, and the class with the most occurrences (or votes) is predicted. Distance weighting could be used to weight the votes, so that nearby data points receive more votes than distant points.

A second way to incorporate distance weighting in classifier training is to incorporate it into the cost criterion that is being minimized by training (Vapnik 1992; Bottou and Vapnik 1992; Vapnik and Bottou 1993):

$$C(\mathbf{q}) = \sum_i [L(\hat{c}_i, c_{\text{true}i}) K(d(\mathbf{x}_i, \mathbf{q}))] \tag{74}$$

C is the cost to be minimized and $L(\hat{c}_i, c_{\text{true}i})$ is the cost of predicting class $\hat{c}_i$ on training point $\mathbf{x}_i$ when the true class is $c_{\text{true}i}$. $K(\ )$ is the weighting or kernel function. A simple version of this approach is to select the k nearest points and just train a classifier on that data. In this case $K(\ )$ is a uniform or boxcar kernel. The form of the classifier is not constrained in any way. Locally weighted learning specifies the form of the training criterion only, and not the form of the performance algorithm.

A third way to incorporate distance weighting is to treat classification as a regression problem, where there are decision functions for each class, and the decision function with the largest value at the query point determines the class of the query. Training these decision functions can be distance weighted as well:

$$C(\mathbf{q}) = \sum_i \left[\left(\sum_j (g_j(\mathbf{x}_i) - t_{ij})^2 \right) K(d(\mathbf{x}_i, \mathbf{q})) \right] \tag{75}$$

where $g_j(\ )$ is the decision function for class j, and t_{ij} is the target for decision function $g_j(\ )$ on training point i. Hastie and Tibshirani (1994) describe an approach in which global approaches to finding discriminants are localized by locally weighting the algorithm directly, rather than the criterion.

In this paper we described fitting simple linear models using distance weighted fit criterion. One can imagine using distance weighted criterion to train linear decision functions and linear discriminants to create local classifiers. It is also possible to train general models, such as logistic regression, to perform classification in a locally weighted fashion.

16.3. *Requirements for Locally Weighted Learning*

Locally weighted learning has several requirements:

- **Distance function:** Locally weighted learning systems require a measure of relevance. The major assumption made by locally weighted learning is that relevance can be measured using a measure of distance. Nearby training points are more relevant. There are many other possible measures of relevance, and also more general notions of similarity. The distance function $d(a, b)$ needs to input two objects and produce a number. The distance function does not need to satisfy the formal requirements for a distance metric.

- **Separable criterion:** Locally weighted learning systems compute a weight for each training point. To apply this weight, the training criterion cannot be a general function of the predictions of the training points:

$$C = L(\hat{y}_1, y_1, \hat{y}_2, y_2, \ldots, \hat{y}_n, y_n,) \tag{76}$$

  but must be separable in some way. We use additive separability:

$$C = \sum_i [L(\hat{y}_i, y_i) K(d(\mathbf{x}_i, \mathbf{q}))] \tag{77}$$

  although there are other forms of separability.

- **Enough data:** There needs to be enough data to compute statistics, which is also true of other statistical learning approaches. How much is enough? We have run robot learning experiments where performance improvements started to occur with on the order of ten points in the training set, although we typically collect between 100 and 1000 points during an experiment. The amount of training data needed is highly problem dependent.

- **Labelled data:** Each training point needs to have an associated output y_i. For classification this is a label, and for regression (function approximation) it is a number.

- **Representations:** Although the above requirements are enough for a system using nearest neighbor techniques, locally weighted regression requires that each object produces a fixed length vector of the values (symbolic or numeric) for a list of specified features:

$$\mathbf{x} = \begin{pmatrix} x_1 \\ x_2 \\ \vdots \\ x_n \end{pmatrix} \tag{78}$$

However, more general representations can be handled by locally weighted learning approaches. For example, a more general training criterion is:

$$C = \sum_i \{L(f(X_i, \beta), Y_i) K(d(X_i, Q))\} \qquad (79)$$

The inputs X_i, outputs Y_i, and query Q can be complex objects such as entire semantic networks, with the distance functions being graph matching algorithms or graph difference measuring algorithms, and $f(\ )$ being a graph transformation with β as adjustable parameters (Elliot and Scott 1991). Or the objects can be text computer files, with the inputs X in Japanese and the outputs Y in English, the distance functions can be the number of characters in the output of a file difference program such as the UNIX diff, and the local model $f(\ )$ can be a machine translation program with adjustable parameters β. Typical parameters for an expert system might be strengths of rules, so changing β affects which rules are selected for application.

The input space distance $d(\ )$ can be generalized to take into account the output space distance between the output values of the training data and a predicted output:

$$C = \sum_i \left\{ L(f(X_i, \beta), Y_i) K \left(d \left(\begin{pmatrix} X_i \\ Y_i \end{pmatrix}, \begin{pmatrix} Q \\ Y_{pred} \end{pmatrix} \right) \right) \right\} \qquad (80)$$

This is useful when the function being approximated has several distinct outputs for similar inputs.

Although it has not yet been extensively explored by current research, it is possible for locally weighted learning systems to have stored objects that provide separate information to the query distance function (X_i) and to the local model $(\mathcal{X}_i)$ (Hammond 1991; Callan et al. 1991; Nguyen et al. 1993). In this case the training criterion might be:

$$C = \sum_i \{L(f(\mathcal{X}_i, \beta), Y_i) K(d(X_i, Q))\} \qquad (81)$$

One example of this is to use measures of volatility of the stock market to measure distance between data points and a query $d(X_i, Q)$, but use price histories and other factors to form local (with respect to volatility) predictive models for future prices $f(\mathcal{X}_i, \beta)$ (LeBaron 1990, 1992). Another example is to use nationality as the input to the distance function (requiring a distance calculation for symbolic values), and to use numeric features such as age, height, weight, and blood pressure to build a locally (with respect to the nationality distance) weighted regression to predict heart attack risk.

16.4. *Future Research Directions*

Our view of interesting areas of future research include:

- **Hybrid Tuning Algorithms:** We have developed independent continuous and discrete fit parameter optimization techniques. It is clear that a hybrid approach can do better than either approach alone. Parameters could initially be treated as discrete, and then more and more continuous optimization could be performed as optimal values were approached, for example. Another approach is for the racing algorithms to allow continuous tuning by each contestant during the race, rather than racing fixed sets of parameters.

- **New forms of local tuning:** So far research has focused on locally tuning bandwidth and smoothing parameters. More work needs to be done on locally tuning distance metrics, ridge regression parameters, outlier thresholds, etc., without overfitting.

- **Multiscale local tuning:** One dimensional fit parameters such as bandwidth and model order can be locally optimized using small neighborhoods. Multidimensional fit parameters such as the distance scale parameters in a distance matrix $\mathbf{M}$ or the set of ridge regression parameters need much larger neighborhoods and different kinds of regularization to be tuned locally. How should these different tuning processes interact?

- **Stochastic gradient approaches to continuous tuning:** Continuous optimization based on estimates of the gradient using small numbers of random queries rather than exhaustive query sets seems a promising approach to efficient tuning algorithms (Moore and Schneider 1995).

- **Properties of massive cross-validation:** We have discussed the use of cross-validation, and why locally weighted learning is particularly well suited to its use. Better understanding of how much cross validation can take place before it is in danger of overfitting (which must be guarded by an extra level of cross-validation) would be desirable.

- **Probabilistic approaches:** We would like to explore further the analogies between locally weighted learning and probabilistic models, including Bayesian models (Rachlin et al. 1994; Ting and Cameron 1994).

- **Forgetting:** So far, forgetting has not played an important role in our implementations of robot learning, as we have not run out of memory. However, we expect forgetting to play a more important role in the future, and expect it to be necessary to implement a principled approach to storage control.

- **Computational Techniques:** For enormous dataset sizes, new data management algorithms may be needed. They include principled ways to forget or coalesce old data, compactly represent high dimensional data clouds, ways of using samples of datasets instead of entire datasets, and, in the case of multi-gigabyte datasets, hardware and software techniques for managing data on secondary storage.

- **Less Lazy Learning:** This review has focussed on a pure form of lazy learning, in which only the data is stored between queries. This purist approach will be too extreme in some circumstances, and most tuning algorithms for fit parameters store the optimized fit parameters in between queries. Substantial amounts of data compression can be achieved by building a set of local models at fixed locations, using the techniques described in this paper. In addition to computational speedup in the presence of large datasets there may be statistical advantages to compressing data instead of merely storing it all (Fritzke 1995; Schaal and Atkeson 1995).

17. Summary

This paper has surveyed locally weighted learning. Local weighting, whether by weighting the data or the error criterion, can turn global function approximation into powerful alternative approaches. By means of local weighting, unnecessary bias of global function fitting is reduced, higher flexibility is obtained, but desirable properties like smoothness and statistical analyzability are retained. We have concentrated on how linear regression behaves under local weighting, and surveyed the ways in which tools from conventional regression analysis in global regression can be used in locally weighted regression. A major question has concerned the notion of locality: what is a good choice of distance metric, how close within that metric should points be and how can these decisions be automatically made from the data. The field of local learning is of large interest in the statistics community, and we have provided entry points into that literature. Locally weighted learning is also rapidly increasing in popularity in the machine learning community and the outlook is promising for interesting statistical, computational and application-oriented development.

18. Acknowledgments

Support for C. Atkeson and S. Schaal was provided by the ATR Human Information Processing Research Laboratories. Support for C. Atkeson was provided under Air Force Office of Scientific Research grant F49-6209410362, and by a National Science Foundation Presidential Young Investigator Award. Support for S. Schaal was provided by the German Scholarship Foundation and the Alexander von Humboldt Foundation. Support for A. Moore was provided by the U.K. Science and Engineering Research Council, NSF Research Initiation Award # IRI-9409912, and a Research Gift from the 3M Corporation.

References

AAAI-91 (1991). *Ninth National Conference on Artificial Intelligence*. AAAI Press/The MIT Press, Cambridge, MA.

Aha, D. W. (1989). Incremental, instance-based learning of independent and graded concept descriptions. In *Sixth International Machine Learning Workshop*, pp. 387–391. Morgan Kaufmann, San Mateo, CA.

Aha, D. W. (1990). *A Study of Instance-Based Algorithms for Supervised Learning Tasks: Mathematical, Empirical, and Psychological Observations*. PhD dissertation, University of California, Irvine, Department of Information and Computer Science.

Aha, D. W. (1991). Incremental constructive induction: An instance-based approach. In *Eighth International Machine Learning Workshop*, pp. 117–121. Morgan Kaufmann, San Mateo, CA.

Aha, D. W. & Goldstone, R. L. (1990). Learning attribute relevance in context in instance-based learning algorithms. In *12th Annual Conference of the Cognitive Science Society*, pp. 141–148. Lawrence Erlbaum, Cambridge, MA.

Aha, D. W. & Goldstone, R. L. (1992). Concept learning and flexible weighting. In *14th Annual Conference of the Cognitive Science Society*, pp. 534–539, Bloomington, IL. Lawrence Erlbaum Associates, Mahwah, NJ.

Aha, D. W. & Kibler, D. (1989). Noise-tolerant instance-based learning algorithms. In *Eleventh International Joint Conference on Artificial Intelligence*, pp 794–799. Morgan Kaufmann, San Mateo, CA.

Aha, D. W. & McNulty, D. M. (1989). Learning relative attribute weights for instance-based concept descriptions. In *11th Annual Conference of the Cognitive Science Society*, pp. 530–537. Lawrence Erlbaum Associates, Mahwah, NJ.

Aha, D. W. & Salzberg, S. L. (1993). Learning to catch: Applying nearest neighbor algorithms to dynamic control tasks. In *Proceedings of the Fourth International Workshop on Artificial Intelligence and Statistics*, pp. 363–368, Ft. Lauderdale, FL.

Altman, N. S. (1992). An introduction to kernel and nearest-neighbor nonparametric regression. *The American Statistician* **46**(3): 175–185.

Atkeson, C. G. (1990). Using local models to control movement. In Touretzky, D. S., editor, *Advances In Neural Information Processing Systems 2*, pp. 316–323. Morgan Kaufman, San Mateo, CA.

Atkeson, C. G. (1992). Memory-based approaches to approximating continuous functions. In Casdagli and Eubank (1992), pp. 503–521. Proceedings of a Workshop on Nonlinear Modeling and Forecasting September 17–21, 1990, Santa Fe, New Mexico.

Atkeson, C. G. (1996). Local learning. http://www.cc.gatech.edu/fac/Chris.Atkeson/local-learning/.

Atkeson, C. G., Moore, A. W. & Schaal, S. (1997). Locally weighted learning for control. *Artificial Intelligence Review*, this issue.

Atkeson, C. G. & Reinkensmeyer, D. J. (1988). Using associative content-addressable memories to control robots. In *Proceedings of the 27th IEEE Conference on Decision and Control*, volume 1, pp. 792–797, Austin, Texas. IEEE Cat. No.88CH2531-2.

Atkeson, C. G. & Reinkensmeyer, D. J. (1989). Using associative content-addressable memories to control robots. In *Proceedings, IEEE International Conference on Robotics and Automation*, Scottsdale, Arizona.

Atkeson, C. G. & Schaal, S. (1995). Memory-based neural networks for robot learning. *Neurocomputing* **9**: 243–269.

Baird, L. C. & Klopf, A. H. (1993). Reinforcement learning with high-dimensional, continuous actions. Technical Report WL-TR-93-1147, Wright Laboratory, Wright-Patterson Air Force Base Ohio. http://kirk.usafa.af.mil/~baird/papers/index.html.

Barnhill, R. E. (1977). Representation and approximation of surfaces. In Rice, J. R., editor, *Mathematical Software III*, pp. 69–120. Academic Press, New York, NY.

Batchelor, B. G. (1974). *Practical Approach To Pattern Classification*. Plenum Press, New York, NY.

Benedetti, J. K. (1977). On the nonparametric estimation of regression functions. *Journal of the Royal Statistical Society, Series B* **39**: 248–253.

Bentley, J. L. (1975). Multidimensional binary search trees used for associative searching. *Communications of the ACM* **18**(9): 509–517.

Bentley, J. L. & Friedman, J. H. (1979). Data structures for range searching. *ACM Comput. Surv.* **11**(4): 397–409.

Bentley, J. L., Weide, B. & Yao, A. (1980). Optimal expected time algorithms for closest point problems. *ACM Transactions on Mathematical Software* **6**: 563–580.

Blyth, S. (1993). Optimal kernel weights under a power criterion. *Journal of the American Statistical Association* **88**(424): 1284–1286.

Bottou, L. & Vapnik, V. (1992). Local learning algorithms. *Neural Computation* **4**(6): 888–900.

Bregler, C. & Omohundro, S. M. (1994). Surface learning with applications to lipreading. In Cowan et al. (1994), pp. 43–50.

Brockmann, M., Gasser, T. & Herrmann, E. (1993). Locally adaptive bandwidth choice for kernel regression estimators. *Journal of the American Statistical Association*, **88**(424): 1302–1309.

Broder, A. J. (1990). Strategies for efficient incremental nearest neighbor search. *Pattern Recognition* **23**: 171–178.

Callan, J. P., Fawcett, T. E. & Rissland, E. L. (1991). CABOT: An adaptive approach to case based search. In IJCAI 12 (1991), pp. 803–808.

Casdagli, M. & Eubank, S. (eds.) (1992). *Nonlinear Modeling and Forecasting*. Proceedings Volume XII in the Santa Fe Institute Studies in the Sciences of Complexity. Addison Wesley, New York, NY. Proceedings of a Workshop on Nonlinear Modeling and Forecasting September 17-21, 1990, Santa Fe, New Mexico.

Cheng, P. E. (1984). Strong consistency of nearest neighbor regression function estimators. *Journal of Multivariate Analysis* **15**: 63–72.

Cleveland, W. S. (1979). Robust locally weighted regression and smoothing scatterplots. *Journal of the American Statistical Association* **74**: 829–836.

Cleveland, W. S. (1993a). Coplots, nonparametric regression, and conditionally parametric fits. Technical Report 19, AT&T Bell Laboratories, Statistics Department, Murray Hill, NJ. http://netlib.att.com/netlib/att/stat/doc/.

Cleveland, W. S. (1993b). *Visualizing Data*. Hobart Press, Summit, NJ. books@hobart.com.

Cleveland, W. S. & Devlin, S. J. (1988). Locally weighted regression: An approach to regression analysis by local fitting. *Journal of the American Statistical Association* **83**: 596–610.

Cleveland, W. S., Devlin, S. J. & Grosse, E. (1988). Regression by local fitting: Methods, properties, and computational algorithms. *Journal of Econometrics* **37**: 87–114.

Cleveland, W. S. & Grosse, E. (1991). Computational methods for local regression. *Statistics and Computing* **1**(1): 47–62. ftp://cm.bell-labs.com/cm/cs/doc/91/4-04.ps.gz.

Cleveland, W. S., Grosse, E. & Shyu, W. M. (1992). Local regression models. In Chambers, J. M. & Hastie, T. J. (eds.), *Statistical Models in S*, pp. 309–376. Wadsworth, Pacific Grove, CA. http://netlib.att.com/netlib/a/cloess.ps.Z.

Cleveland, W. S. & Loader, C. (1994a). Computational methods for local regression. Technical Report 11, AT&T Bell Laboratories, Statistics Department, Murray Hill, NJ. http://netlib.att.com/netlib/att/stat/doc/.

Cleveland, W. S. & Loader, C. (1994b). Local fitting for semiparametric (nonparametric) regression: Comments on a paper of Fan and Marron. Technical Report 8, AT&T Bell Laboratories, Statistics Department, Murray Hill, NJ. http://netlib.att.com/netlib/att/stat/doc/, 94.8.ps, earlier version is 94.3.ps.

Cleveland, W. S. & Loader, C. (1994c). Smoothing by local regression: Principles and methods. Technical Report 95.3, AT&T Bell Laboratories, Statistics Department, Murray Hill, NJ. http://netlib.att.com/netlib/att/stat/doc/.

Cleveland, W. S., Mallows, C. L. & McRae, J. E. (1993). ATS methods: Nonparametric regression for non-Gaussian data. *Journal of the American Statistical Association* **88**(423): 821–835.

Connell, M. E. & Utgoff, P. E. (1987). Learning to control a dynamic physical system. In *Sixth National Conference on Artificial Intelligence*, pp. 456–460, Seattle, WA. Morgan Kaufmann, San Mateo, CA.

Cost, S. & Salzberg, S. (1993). A weighted nearest neighbor algorithm for learning with symbolic features. *Machine Learning* **10**(1): 57–78.

Coughran, Jr., W. M. & Grosse, E. (1991). Seeing and hearing dynamic loess surfaces. In *Interface'91 Proceedings*, pp. 224–228. Springer-Verlag. ftp://cm.bell-labs.com/cm/cs/doc/91/4-07.ps.gz or 4-07long.ps.gz.

Cowan, J. D., Tesauro, G. & Alspector, J. (eds.) (1994). *Advances In Neural Information Processing Systems 6*. Morgan Kaufman, San Mateo, CA.

Crain, I. K. & Bhattacharyya, B. K. (1967). Treatment of nonequispaced two dimensional data with a digital computer. *Geoexploration* **5**: 173–194.

Deheuvels, P. (1977). Estimation non-paramétrique del la densité par histogrammes généralisés. *Revue Statistique Appliqué* **25**: 5–42.

Deng, K. & Moore, A. W. (1995). Multiresolution instance-based learning. In *Fourteenth International Joint Conference on Artificial Intelligence*, pp. 1233–1239. Morgan Kaufmann, San Mateo, CA.

Dennis, J. E., Gay, D. M. & Welsch, R. E. (1981). An adaptive nonlinear least-squares algorithm. *ACM Transactions on Mathematical Software* **7**(3): 369–383.

Devroye, L. (1981). On the almost everywhere convergence of nonparametric regression function estimates. *The Annals of Statistics* **9**(6): 1310–1319.

Diebold, F. X. & Nason, J. A. (1990). Nonparametric exchange rate prediction? *Journal of International Economics* **28**: 315–332.

Dietterich, T. G., Wettschereck, D., Atkeson, C. G. & Moore, A. W. (1994). Memory-based methods for regression and classification. In Cowan et al. (1994), pp. 1165–1166.

Draper, N. R. & Smith, H. (1981). *Applied Regression Analysis*. John Wiley, New York, NY, 2nd edition.

Elliot, T. & Scott, P. D. (1991). Instance-based and generalization-based learning procedures applied to solving integration problems. In *Proceedings of the Eighth Conference of the Society for the Study of Artificial Intelligence*, pp. 256–265, Leeds, England. Springer Verlag.

Epanechnikov, V. A. (1969). Nonparametric estimation of a multivariate probability density. *Theory of Probability and Its Applications* **14**: 153–158.

Eubank, R. L. (1988). *Spline Smoothing and Nonparametric Regression*. Marcel Dekker, New York, NY.

Falconer, K. J. (1971). A general purpose algorithm for contouring over scattered data points. Technical Report NAC 6, National Physical Laboratory, Teddington, Middlesex, United Kingdon, TW11 0LW.

Fan, J. (1992). Design-adaptive nonparametric regression. *Journal of the American Statistical Association* **87**(420): 998–1004.

Fan, J. (1993). Local linear regression smoothers and their minimax efficiencies. *Annals of Statistics* **21**: 196–216.

Fan, J. (1995). Local modeling. EES Update: written for the Encyclopedia of Statistics Science, http://www.stat.unc.edu/faculty/fan/papers.html.

Fan, J. & Gijbels, I. (1992). Variable bandwidth and local linear regression smoothers. *The Annals of Statistics* **20**(4): 2008–2036.

Fan, J. & Gijbels, I. (1994). Censored regression: Local linear approximations and their applications. *Journal of the American Statistical Association* **89**: 560–570.

Fan, J. & Gijbels, I. (1995a). Adaptive order polynomial fitting: Bandwidth robustification and bias reduction. *J. Comp. Graph. Statist.* **4**: 213–227.

Fan, J. & Gijbels, I. (1995b). Data-driven bandwidth selection in local polynomial fitting: Variable bandwidth and spatial adaptation. *Journal of the Royal Statistical Society B* **57**: 371–394.

Fan, J. & Gijbels, I. (1996). *Local Polynomial Modeling and its Applications*. Chapman and Hall, London.

Fan, J. & Hall, P. (1994). On curve estimation by minimizing mean absolute deviation and its implications. *The Annals of Statistics* **22**(2): 867–885.

Fan, J. & Kreutzberger, E. (1995). Automatic local smoothing for spectral density estimation. ftp://stat.unc.edu/pub/fan/spec.ps.

Fan, J. & Marron, J. S. (1993). Comment on [Hastie and Loader, 1993]. *Statistical Science* **8**(2): 129–134.

Fan, J. & Marron, J. S. (1994a). Fast implementations of nonparametric curve estimators. *Journal of Computational and Statistical Graphics* **3**: 35–56.

Fan, J. & Marron, J. S. (1994b). Rejoinder to discussion of Cleveland and Loader.

Farmer, J. D. & Sidorowich, J. J. (1987). Predicting chaotic time series. *Physical Review Letters* **59**(8): 845–848.

Farmer, J. D. & Sidorowich, J. J. (1988a). Exploiting chaos to predict the future and reduce noise. In Lee, Y. C. (ed.), *Evolution, Learning, and Cognition*, pp. 277–??? World Scientific Press, NJ. also available as Technical Report LA-UR-88-901, Los Alamos National Laboratory, Los Alamos, New Mexico.

Farmer, J. D. & Sidorowich, J. J. (1988b). Predicting chaotic dynamics. In Kelso, J. A. S., Mandell, A. J. & Schlesinger, M. F. (eds.), *Dynamic Patterns in Complex Systems*, pp. 265–292. World Scientific, NJ.

Farwig, R. (1987). Multivariate interpolation of scattered data by moving least squares methods. In Mason, J. C. & Cox, M. G. (eds.), *Algorithms for Approximation*, pp. 193–211. Clarendon Press, Oxford.

Fedorov, V. V., Hackl, P. & Müller, W. G. (1993). Moving local regression: The weight function. *Nonparametric Statistics* **2**(4): 355–368.

Franke, R. & Nielson, G. (1980). Smooth interpolation of large sets of scattered data. *International Journal for Numerical Methods in Engineering* **15**: 1691–1704.

Friedman, J. H. (1984). A variable span smoother. Technical Report LCS 5, Stanford University, Statistics Department, Stanford, CA.

Friedman, J. H. (1994). Flexible metric nearest neighbor classification. http://playfair.stanford.edu/reports/friedman/.

Friedman, J. H., Bentley, J. L. & Finkel, R. A. (1977). An algorithm for finding best matches in logarithmic expected time. *ACM Transactions on Mathematical Software* **3**(3): 209–226.

Fritzke, B. (1995). Incremental learning of local linear mappings. In *Proceedings of the International Conference on Artificial Neural Networks ICANN '95*, pp. 217–222, Paris, France.

Fukunaga, K. (1990). *Introduction to Statistical Pattern Recognition*. Academic Press, New York, NY, second edition.

Gasser, T. & Müller, H. G. (1979). Kernel estimation of regression functions. In Gasser, T. & Rosenblatt, M. (eds.), *Smoothing Techniques for Curve Estimation*, number 757 in Lecture Notes in Mathematics, pp. 23–67. Springer-Verlag, Heidelberg.

Gasser, T. & Müller, H. G. (1984). Estimating regression functions and their derivatives by the kernel method. *Scandanavian Journal of Statistics* **11**: 171–185.

Gasser, T., Müller, H. G. & Mammitzsch, V. (1985). Kernels for nonparametric regression. *Journal of the Royal Statistical Society, Series B* **47**: 238–252.

Ge, Z., Cavinato, A. G. & Callis, J. B. (1994). Noninvasive spectroscopy for monitoring cell density in a fermentation process. *Analytical Chemistry* **66**: 1354–1362.

Goldberg, K. Y. & Pearlmutter, B. (1988). Using a neural network to learn the dynamics of the CMU Direct-Drive Arm II. Technical Report CMU-CS-88-160, Carnegie-Mellon University, Pittsburgh, PA.

Gorinevsky, D. & Connolly, T. H. (1994). Comparison of some neural network and scattered data approximations: The inverse manipulator kinematics example. *Neural Computation* 6: 521–542.

Goshtasby, A. (1988). Image registration by local approximation methods. *Image and Vision Computing* 6(4): 255–261.

Grosse, E. (1989). LOESS: Multivariate smoothing by moving least squares. In Chui, C. K., Schumaker, L. L. & Ward, J. D. (eds.), *Approximation Theory VI*, pp. 1–4. Academic Press, Boston, MA.

Hammond, S. V. (1991). Nir analysis of antibiotic fermentations. In Murray, I. & Cowe, I. A. (eds.), *Making Light Work: Advances in Near Infrared Spectroscopy*, pp. 584–589. VCH: New York, NY. Developed from the 4th International Conference on Near Infrared Spectroscopy, Aberdeen, Scotland, August 19–23, 1991.

Hampel, F. R., Ronchetti, E. M., Rousseeuw, P. J. & Stahel, W. A. (1986). *Robust Statistics: The Approach Based On Influence Functions*. John Wiley, New York, NY.

Härdle, W. (1990). *Applied Nonparametric Regression*. Cambridge University Press, New York, NY.

Hastie, T. & Loader, C. (1993). Local regression: Automatic kernel carpentry. *Statistical Science* 8(2): 120–143.

Hastie, T. J. & Tibshirani, R. J. (1990). *Generalized Additive Regression*. Chapman Hall, London.

Hastie, T. J. & Tibshirani, R. J. (1994). Discriminant adaptive nearest neighbor classification. ftp://playfair.Stanford.EDU/pub/hastie/dann.ps.Z.

Higuchi, T., Kitano, H., Furuya, T., ichi Handa, K., Takahashi, N. & Kokubu, A. (1991). IXM2: A parallel associative processor for knowledge processing. In AAAI-9 (1991), pp. 296–303.

Hillis, D. (1985). *The Connection Machine*. MIT Press, Cambridge, MA.

Huang, P. S. (1996). *Planning For Dynamic Motions Using A Search Tree*. MS thesis, University of Toronto, Graduate Department of Computer Science. http://www.dgp. utoronto.ca/people/psh/home.html.

IJCAI 12 (1991). *Twelfth International Joint Conference on Artificial Intelligence*. Morgan Kaufmann, San Mateo, CA.

IJCAI 13 (1993). *Thirteenth International Joint Conference on Artificial Intelligence*. Morgan Kaufmann, San Mateo, CA.

Jabbour, K., Riveros, J. F. W., Landsbergen, D. & Meyer, W. (1987). ALFA: Automated load forecasting assistant. In *Proceedings of the 1987 IEEE Power Engineering Society Summer Meeting*, San Francisco, CA.

James, M. (1985). *Classification Algorithms*. John Wiley and Sons, New York, NY.

Jones, M. C., Davies, S. J. & Park, B. U. (1994). Versions of kernel-type regression estimators. *Journal of the American Statistical Association* 89(427): 825–832.

Karalič, A. (1992). Employing linear regression in regression tree leaves. In Neumann, B. (ed.), *ECAI 92: 10th European Conference on Artificial Intelligence*, pp. 440–441, Vienna, Austria. John Wiley and Sons.

Katkovnik, V. Y. (1979). Linear and nonlinear methods of nonparametric regression analysis. *Soviet Automatic Control* 5: 25–34.

Kazmierczak, H. & Steinbuch, K. (1963). Adaptive systems in pattern recognition. *IEEE Transactions on Electronic Computers* EC-12: 822–835.

Kibler, D., Aha, D. W. & Albert, M. (1989). Instance-based prediction of real-valued attributes. *Computational Intelligence* 5: 51–57.

Kitano, H. (1993a). Challenges of massive parallelism. In IJCAI 13 (1993), pp. 813–834.

Kitano, H. (1993b). A comprehensive and practical model of memory-based machine translation. In IJCAI 13 (1993), pp. 1276–1282.

Kitano, H. & Higuchi, T. (1991a). High performance memory-based translation on IXM2 massively parallel associative memory processor. In AAAI-9 (1991), pp. 149–154.

Kitano, H. & Higuchi, T. (1991b). Massively parallel memory-based parsing. In IJCAI 12 (1991), pp. 918–924.

Kitano, H., Moldovan, D. & Cha, S. (1991). High performance natural language processing on semantic network array processor. In IJCAI 12 (1991), pp. 911–917.

Kozek, A. S. (1992). A new nonparametric estimation method: Local and nonlinear. *Interface* **24**: 389–393.

Lancaster, P. (1979). Moving weighted least-squares methods. In Sahney, B. N. (ed.), *Polynomial and Spline Approximation*, pp. 103–120. D. Reidel Publishing, Boston, MA.

Lancaster, P. & Šalkauskas, K. (1981). Surfaces generated by moving least squares methods. *Mathematics of Computation* **37**(155): 141–158.

Lancaster, P. & Šalkauskas, K. (1986). *Curve And Surface Fitting*. Academic Press, New York, NY.

Lawrence, S., Tsoi, A. C. & Black, A. D. (1996). Function approximation with neural networks and local methods: Bias, variance and smoothness. In *Australian Conference on Neural Networks, Canberra, Australia*, Canberra, Australia. available from http://www.neci.nj.nec.com/homepages/lawrence and http://www.elec.uq.edu.au/~lawrence.

LeBaron, B. (1990). Forecast improvements using a volatility index. Unpublished.

LeBaron, B. (1992). Nonlinear forecasts for the S&P stock index. In Casdagli and Eubank (1992), pp. 381–393. Proceedings of a Workshop on Nonlinear Modeling and Forecasting September 17–21, 1990, Santa Fe, New Mexico.

Legg, M. P. C. & Brent, R. P. (1969). Automatic contouring. In *4th Australian Computer Conference*, pp. 467–468.

Lejeune, M. (1984). Optimization in non-parametric regression. In *COMPSTAT 1984: Proceedings in Computational Statistics*, pp. 421–426, Prague. Physica-Verlag Wien.

Lejeune, M. (1985). Estimation non-paramétrique par noyaux: Régression polynômial mobile. *Revue de Statistique Appliquée* **23**(3): 43–67.

Lejeune, M. & Sarda, P. (1992). Smooth estimators of distribution and density functions. *Computational Statistics & Data Analysis* **14**: 457–471.

Li, K. C. (1984). Consistency for cross-validated nearest neighbor estimates in nonparametric regression. *The Annals of Statistics* **12**: 230–240.

Loader, C. (1994). Computing nonparametric function estimates. Technical Report 7, AT&T Bell Laboratories, Statistics Department, Murray Hill, NJ. Available by anonymous FTP from netlib.att.com in /netlib/att/stat/doc/94/7.ps.

Lodwick, G. D. & Whittle, J. (1970). A technique for automatic contouring field survey data. *Australian Computer Journal* **2**: 104–109.

Lowe, D. G. (1995). Similarity metric learning for a variable-kernel classifier. *Neural Computation* **7**: 72–85.

Maron, O. & Moore, A. W. (1997). The racing algorithm: Model selection for lazy learners. *Artificial Intelligence Review*, this issue.

Marron, J. S. (1988). Automatic smoothing parameter selection: A survey. *Empirical Economics* **13**: 187–208.

McCallum, R. A. (1995). Instance-based utile distinctions for reinforcement learning with hidden state. In Prieditis & Russell (eds.) (1995), pp. 387–395.

McIntyre, D. B., Pollard, D. D. & Smith, R. (1968). Computer programs for automatic contouring. Technical Report Kansas Geological Survey Computer Contributions 23, University of Kansas, Lawrence, KA.

McLain, D. H. (1974). Drawing contours from arbitrary data points. *The Computer Journal* **17**(4): 318–324.

Medin, D. L. & Shoben, E. J. (1988). Context and structure in conceptual combination. *Cognitive Psychology* **20**: 158–190.

Meese, R. & Wallace, N. (1991). Nonparametric estimation of dynamic hedonic price models and the construction of residential housing price indices. *American Real Estate and Urban Economics Association Journal* **19**(3): 308–332.

Meese, R. A. & Rose, A. K. (1990). Nonlinear, nonparametric, nonessential exchange rate estimation. *The American Economic Review* May: 192–196.

Miller, A. J. (1990). *Subset Selection in Regression*. Chapman and Hall, London.

Miller, W. T., Glanz, F. H. & Kraft, L. G. (1987). Application of a general learning algorithm to the control of robotic manipulators. *International Journal of Robotics Research* **6**: 84–98.

Mohri, T. & Tanaka, H. (1994). An optimal weighting criterion of case indexing for both numeric and symbolic attributes. In Aha, D. W. (ed.), *AAAI-94 Workshop Program: Case-Based Reasoning, Working Notes*, pp. 123–127. AAAI Press, Seattle, WA.

Moore, A. W. (1990a). Acquisition of Dynamic Control Knowledge for a Robotic Manipulator. In *Seventh International Machine Learning Workshop*. Morgan Kaufmann, San Mateo, CA.

Moore, A. W. (1990b). Efficient Memory-based Learning for Robot Control. PhD. Thesis; Technical Report No. 209, Computer Laboratory, University of Cambridge.

Moore, A. W., Hill, D. J. & Johnson, M. P. (1992). An empirical investigation of brute force to choose features, smoothers, and function approximators. In Hanson, S., Judd, S. & Petsche, T. (eds.), *Computational Learning Theory and Natural Learning Systems*, volume 3. MIT Press, Cambridge, MA.

Moore, A. W. & Schneider, J. (1995). Memory-based stochastic optimization. To appear in the proceedings of NIPS-95, Also available as Technical Report CMU-RI-TR-95-30, ftp://ftp.cs.cmu.edu/afs/cs.cmu.edu/project/reinforcement/papers/memstoch.ps.

More, J. J., Garbow, B. S. & Hillstrom, K. E. (1980). User guide for MINPACK-1. Technical Report ANL-80-74, Argonne National Laboratory, Argonne, Illinois.

Müller, H.-G. (1987). Weighted local regression and kernel methods for nonparametric curve fitting. *Journal of the American Statistical Association* **82**: 231–238.

Müller, H.-G. (1993). Comment on [Hastie and Loader, 1993]. *Statistical Science* **8**(2): 134–139.

Murphy, O. J. & Selkow, S. M. (1986). The efficiency of using k-d trees for finding nearest neighbors in discrete space. *Information Processing Letters* **23**: 215–218.

Myers, R. H. (1990). *Classical and Modern Regression With Applications*. PWS-KENT, Boston, MA.

Nadaraya, E. A. (1964). On estimating regression. *Theory of Probability and Its Applications* **9**: 141–142.

Næs, T. & Isaksson, T. (1992). Locally weighted regression in diffuse near-infrared transmittance spectroscopy. *Applied Spectroscopy* **46**(1): 34–43.

Næs, T., Isaksson, T. & Kowalski, B. R. (1990). Locally weighted regression and scatter correction for near-infrared reflectance data. *Analytical Chemistry* **62**(7): 664–673.

Nguyen, T., Czerwinsksi, M. & Lee, D. (1993). COMPAQ Quicksource: Providing the consumer with the power of artificial intelligence. In *Proceedings of the Fifth Annual Conference on Innovative Applications of Artificial Intelligence*, pp. 142–150, Washington, DC. AAAI Press.

Nosofsky, R. M., Clark, S. E. & Shin, H. J. (1989). Rules and exemplars in categorization, identification, and recognition. *Journal of Experimental Psychology: Learning, Memory, and Cognition* **15**: 282–304.

Omohundro, S. M. (1987). Efficient Algorithms with Neural Network Behaviour. *Journal of Complex Systems* **1**(2): 273–347.

Omohundro, S. M. (1991). Bumptrees for Efficient Function, Constraint, and Classification Learning. In Lippmann, R. P., Moody, J. E. & Touretzky, D. S. (eds.), *Advances in Neural Information Processing Systems 3*. Morgan Kaufmann.

Palmer, J. A. B. (1969). Automatic mapping. In *4th Australian Computer Conference*, pp. 463–466.

Pelto, C. R., Elkins, T. A. & Boyd, H. A. (1968). Automatic contouring of irregularly spaced data. *Geophysics* **33**: 424–430.

Peng, J. (1995). Efficient memory-based dynamic programming. In Prieditis & Russell (eds.) (1995), pp. 438–446.

Press, W. H., Teukolsky, S. A., Vetterling, W. T. & Flannery, B. P. (1988). *Numerical Recipes in C*. Cambridge University Press, New York, NY.

Prieditis, A. & Russell, S. (eds.) (1995). *Twelfth International Conference on Machine Learning*. Morgan Kaufmann, San Mateo, CA.

Rachlin, J., Kasif, S., Salzberg, S. & Aha, D. W. (1994). Towards a better understanding of memory-based reasoning systems. In *Eleventh International Conference on Machine Learning*, pp. 242–250. Morgan Kaufmann, San Mateo, CA.

Racine, J. (1993). An efficient cross-validation algorithm for window width selection for non-parametric kernel regression. *Communications in Statistics: Simulation and Computation* **22**(4): 1107–1114.

Ramasubramanian, V. & Paliwal, K. K. (1989). A generalized optimization of the k-d tree for fast nearest-neighbour search. In *International Conference on Acoustics, Speech, and Signal Processing*.

Raz, J., Turetsky, B. I. & Fein, G. (1989). Selecting the smoothing parameter for estimation of smoothly changing evoked potential signals. *Biometrics* **45**: 851–871.

Renka, R. J. (1988). Multivariate interpolation of large sets of scattered data. *ACM Transactions on Mathematical Software* **14**(2): 139–152.

Ruppert, D. & Wand, M. P. (1994). Multivariate locally weighted least squares regression. *The Annals of Statistics* **22**(3): 1346–1370.

Ruprecht, D. & Müller, H. (1992). Image warping with scattered data interpolation methods. Technical Report 443, Universität Dortmund, Fachbereich Informatik, D-44221 Dortmund, Germany. Available for anonymous FTP from ftp-ls7.informatik.uni-dortmund.de in pub/reports/ls7/rr-443.ps.Z.

Ruprecht, D. & Müller, H. (1993). Free form deformation with scattered data interpolation methods. In Farin, G., Hagen, H. & Noltemeier, H. (eds.), *Geometric Modelling (Computing Suppl. 8)*, pp. 267–281. Springer Verlag. Available for anonymous FTP from ftp-ls7.informatik.uni-dortmund.de in pub/reports/iif/rr-41.ps.Z.

Ruprecht, D. & Müller, H. (1994a). Deformed cross-dissolves for image interpolation in scientific visualization. *The Journal of Visualization and Computer Animation* **5**(3): 167–181. Available for anonymous FTP from ftp-ls7.informatik.uni-dortmund.de in pub/reports/ls7/rr-491.ps.Z.

Ruprecht, D. & Müller, H. (1994b). A framework for generalized scattered data interpolation. Technical Report 517, Universität Dortmund, Fachbereich Informatik, D-44221 Dortmund, Germany. Available for anonymous FTP from ftp-ls7.informatik.uni-dortmund.de in pub/reports/ls7/rr-517.ps.Z.

Ruprecht, D., Nagel, R. & Müller, H. (1994). Spatial free form deformation with scattered data interpolation methods. Technical Report 539, Fachbereich Informatik der Universität Dortmund, 44221 Dortmund, Germany. Accepted for publication by *Computers & Graphics*, Available for anonymous FTP from ftp-ls7.informatik.uni-dortmund.de in pub/reports/ls7/rr-539.ps.Z.

Rust, R. T. & Bornman, E. O. (1982). Distribution-free methods of approximating nonlinear marketing relationships. *Journal of Marketing Research* **XIX**: 372–374.

Sabin, M. A. (1980). Contouring – a review of methods for scattered data. In Brodlie, K. (ed.), *Mathematical Methods in Computer Graphics and Design*, pp. 63–86. Academic Press, New York, NY.

Saitta, L. (ed.) (1996). *Thirteenth International Conference on Machine Learning*. Morgan Kaufmann, San Mateo, CA.

Samet, H. (1990). *The Design and Analysis of Spatial Data Structures*. Addison-Wesley, Reading, MA.

Schaal, S. & Atkeson, C. G. (1994). Assessing the quality of learned local models. In Cowan et al. (1994), pp. 160–167.

Schaal, S. & Atkeson, C. G. (1995). From isolation to cooperation: An alternative view of a system of experts. NIPS95 proceedings, in press.

Scott, D. W. (1992). *Multivariate Density Estimation*. Wiley, New York, NY.

Seber, G. A. F. (1977). *Linear Regression Analysis*. John Wiley, New York, NY.

Seifert, B., Brockmann, M., Engel, J. & Gasser, T. (1994). Fast algorithms for nonparametric curve estimation. *Journal of Computational and Graphical Statistics* 3(2): 192–213.

Seifert, B. & Gasser, T. (1994). Variance properties of local polynomials. http://www.unizh.ch/biostat/manuscripts.html.

Shepard, D. (1968). A two-dimensional function for irregularly spaced data. In *23rd ACM National Conference*, pp. 517–524.

Solow, A. R. (1988). Detecting changes through time in the variance of a long-term hemispheric temperature record: An application of robust locally weighted regression. *Journal of Climate* 1: 290–296.

Specht, D. E. (1991). A general regression neural network. *IEEE Transactions on Neural Networks* 2(6): 568–576.

Sproull, R. F. (1991). Refinements to nearest-neighbor searching in k-d trees. *Algorithmica* 6: 579–589.

Stanfill, C. (1987). Memory-based reasoning applied to English pronunciation. In *Sixth National Conference on Artificial Intelligence*, pp. 577–581.

Stanfill, C. & Waltz, D. (1986). Toward memory-based reasoning. *Communications of the ACM* 29(12): 1213–1228.

Steinbuch, K. (1961). Die lernmatrix. *Kybernetik* 1: 36–45.

Steinbuch, K. & Piske, U. A. W. (1963). Learning matrices and their applications. *IEEE Transactions on Electronic Computers* EC-12: 846–862.

Stone, C. J. (1975). Nearest neighbor estimators of a nonlinear regression function. In *Computer Science and Statistics: 8th Annual Symposium on the Interface*, pp. 413–418.

Stone, C. J. (1977). Consistent nonparametric regression. *The Annals of Statistics* 5: 595–645.

Stone, C. J. (1980). Optimal rates of convergence for nonparametric estimators. *The Annals of Statistics* 8: 1348–1360.

Stone, C. J. (1982). Optimal global rates of convergence for nonparametric regression. *The Annals of Statistics* 10(4): 1040–1053.

Sumita, E., Oi, K., Furuse, O., Iida, H., Higuchi, T., Takahashi, N. & Kitano, H. (1993). Example-based machine translation on massively parallel processors. In IJCAI 13 (1993), pp. 1283–1288.

Tadepalli, P. & Ok, D. (1996). Scaling up average reward reinforcement learning by approximating the domain models and the value function. In Saitta (1996). http://www.cs.orst.edu:80/~tadepall/research/publications.html.

Tamada, T., Maruyama, M., Nakamura, Y., Abe, S. & Maeda, K. (1993). Water demand forecasting by memory based learning. *Water Science and Technology* 28(11–12): 133–140.

Taylor, W. K. (1959). Pattern recognition by means of automatic analogue apparatus. *Proceedings of The Institution of Electrical Engineers* 106B: 198–209.

Taylor, W. K. (1960). A parallel analogue reading machine. *Control* 3: 95–99.

Thorpe, S. (1995). Localized versus distributed representations. In Arbib, M. A. (ed.), *The Handbook of Brain Theory and Neural Networks*, pp. 549–552. The MIT Press, Cambridge, MA.

Thrun, S. (1996). Is learning the n-th thing any easier than learning the first? In *Advances in Neural Information Processing Systems (NIPS)* 8. http://www.cs.cmu.edu/afs/cs.cmu.edu/Web/People/thrun/publications.html.

Thrun, S. & O'Sullivan, J. (1996). Discovering structure in multiple learning tasks: The TC algorithm. In Saitta (1996). http://www.cs.cmu.edu/afs/cs.cmu.edu/Web/People/thrun/publications.html.

Tibshirani, R. & Hastie, T. (1987). Local likelihood estimation. *Journal of the American Statistical Association* 82: 559–567.

Ting, K. M. & Cameron-Jones, R. M. (1994). Exploring a framework for instance based learning and naive Bayesian classifiers. In *Proceedings of the Seventh Australian Joint Conference on Artificial Intelligence*, Armidale, Australia. World Scientific.

Tou, J. T. & Gonzalez, R. C. (1974). *Pattern Recognition Principles*. Addison-Wesley, Reading, MA.

Townshend, B. (1992). Nonlinear prediction of speech signals. In Casdagli and Eubank (1992), pp. 433–453. Proceedings of a Workshop on Nonlinear Modeling and Forecasting September 17–21, 1990, Santa Fe, New Mexico.

Tsybakov, A. B. (1986). Robust reconstruction of functions by the local approximation method. *Problems of Information Transmission* 22: 133–146.

Tukey, J. (1977). *Exploratory Data Analysis*. Addison-Wesley, Reading, MA.

Turetsky, B. I., Raz, J. & Fein, G. (1989). Estimation of trial-to-trial variation in evoked potential signals by smoothing across trials. *Psychophysiology* 26(6): 700–712.

Turlach, B. A. & Wand, M. P. (1995). Fast computation of auxiliary quantities in local polynomial regression. http://netec.wustl.edu/~adnetec/WoPEc/agsmst/agsmst95009.html.

van der Smagt, P., Groen, F. & van het Groenewoud, F. (1994). The locally linear nested network for robot manipulation. In *Proceedings of the IEEE International Conference on Neural Networks*, pp. 2787–2792. ftp://ftp.fwi.uva.nl/pub/computer-systems/autsys/reports/SmaGroGro94b.ps.gz.

Vapnik, V. (1992). Principles of risk minimization for learning theory. In Moody, J. E., Hanson, S. J. & Lippmann, R. P. (eds.), *Advances In Neural Information Processing Systems 4*, pp. 831–838. Morgan Kaufman, San Mateo, CA.

Vapnik, V. & Bottou, L. (1993). Local algorithms for pattern recognition and dependencies estimation. *Neural Computation* 5(6): 893–909.

Walden, A. T. & Prescott, P. (1983). Identification of trends in annual maximum sea levels using robust locally weighted regression. *Estuarine, Coastal and Shelf Science* 16: 17–26.

Walters, R. F. (1969). Contouring by machine: A user's guide. *American Association of Petroleum Geologists Bulletin* 53(11): 2324–2340.

Waltz, D. L. (1987). Applications of the Connection Machine. *Computer* 20(1): 85–97.

Wand, M. P. & Jones, M. C. (1993). Comparison of smoothing parameterizations in bivariate kernel density estimation. *Journal of the American Statistical Association* 88: 520–528.

Wand, M. P. & Jones, M. C. (1994). *Kernel Smoothing*. Chapman and Hall, London.

Wand, M. P. & Schucany, W. R. (1990). Gaussian-based kernels for curve estimation and window width selection. *Canadian Journal of Statistics* 18: 197–204.

Wang, Z., Isaksson, T. & Kowalski, B. R. (1994). New approach for distance measurement in locally weighted regression. *Analytical Chemistry* 66(2): 249–260.

Watson, G. S. (1964). Smooth regression analysis. Sankhyā: *The Indian Journal of Statistics*, Series A, 26: 359–372.

Weisberg, S. (1985). *Applied Linear Regression*. John Wiley and Sons.

Wess, S., Althoff, K.-D. & Derwand, G. (1994). Using k-d trees to improve the retrieval step in case-based reasoning. In Wess, S., Althoff, K.-D. & Richter, M. M. (eds.), *Topics in Case-Based Reasoning*, pp. 167–181. Springer-Verlag, New York, NY. Proceedings of the First European Workshop, EWCBR-93.

Wettschereck, D. (1994). *A Study Of Distance-Based Machine Learning Algorithms*. PhD dissertation, Oregon State University, Department of Computer Science, Corvalis, OR.

Wijnberg, L. & Johnson, T. (1985). Estimation of missing values in lead air quality data sets. In Johnson, T. R. & Penkala, S. J. (eds.), *Quality Assurance in Air Pollution Measurements*. Air Pollution Control Association, Pittsburgh, PA. TR-3: Transactions: An APCA International Specialty Conference.

Wolberg, G. (1990). *Digital Image Warping*. IEEE Computer Society Press, Los Alamitos, CA.

Yasunaga, M. & Kitano, H. (1993). Robustness of the memory-based reasoning implemented by wafer scale integration. *IEICE Transactions on Information and Systems* E76-D(3): 336–344.

Zografski, Z. (1989). *Neuromorphic, Algorithmic, and Logical Models for the Automatic Synthesis of Robot Action.* PhD dissertation, University of Ljubljana, Ljubljana, Slovenia, Yugoslavia.

Zografski, Z. (1991). New methods of machine learning for the construction of integrated neuromorphic and associative-memory knowledge bases. In Zajc, B. & Solina, F. (eds.), *Proceedings, 6th Mediterranean Electrotechnical Conference*, volume II, pp. 1150–1153, Ljubljana, Slovenia, Yugoslavia. IEEE catalog number 91CH2964-5.

Zografski, Z. (1992). Geometric and neuromorphic learning for nonlinear modeling, control and forecasting. In *Proceedings of the 1992 IEEE International Symposium on Intelligent Control*, pp. 158–163, Glasgow, Scotland. IEEE catalog number 92CH3110-4.

Zografski, Z. & Durrani, T. (1995). Comparing predictions from neural networks and memory-based learning. In *Proceedings, ICANN '95/NEURONIMES '95: International Conference on Artificial Neural Networks*, pp. 221–226, Paris, France.

Artificial Intelligence Review **11**: 75–113, 1997.   75
© 1997 *Kluwer Academic Publishers.*

Locally Weighted Learning for Control

CHRISTOPHER G. ATKESON[1,3], ANDREW W. MOORE[2] and
STEFAN SCHAAL[1,3]
[1] *College of Computing, Georgia Institute of Technology, 801 Atlantic Drive, Atlanta,
GA 30332-0280*
E-mail: cga@cc.gatech.edu, sschaal@cc.gatech.edu
http://www.cc.gatech.edu/fac/Chris.Atkeson
http://www.cc.gatech.edu/fac/Stefan.Schaal
[2] *Carnegie Mellon University, 5000 Forbes Ave, Pittsburgh, PA 15213*
E-mail: awm@cs.cmu.edu
http://www.cs.cmu.edu/~awm/hp.html
[3] *ATR Human Information Processing Research Laboratories, 2-2 Hikaridai, Seika-cho,
Soraku-gun, Kyoto 619-02, Japan*

Abstract. Lazy learning methods provide useful representations and training algorithms for
learning about complex phenomena during autonomous adaptive control of complex systems.
This paper surveys ways in which locally weighted learning, a type of lazy learning, has been
applied by us to control tasks. We explain various forms that control tasks can take, and how
this affects the choice of learning paradigm. The discussion section explores the interesting
impact that explicitly remembering all previous experiences has on the problem of learning to
control.

Key words: locally weighted regression, LOESS, LWR, lazy learning, memory-based learning,
least commitment learning, forward models, inverse models, linear quadratic regulation (LQR),
shifting setpoint algorithm, dynamic programming.

1. Introduction

The necessity for self improvement in control systems is becoming more
apparent as fields such as robotics, factory automation, and autonomous
vehicles become impeded by the complexity of inventing and programming
satisfactory control laws. Learned models of complex tasks can aid the design
of appropriate control laws for these tasks, which often involve decisions
based on streams of information from sensors and actuators, where data is
relatively plentiful. The tasks may change over time, or multiple tasks may
need to be performed. Lazy learning methods provide an approach to learning
models of complex phenomena, dealing with large amounts of data, training
quickly, and avoiding interference between multiple tasks during control of

complex systems (Atkeson et al. 1997). This paper describes five ways in which lazy learning techniques have been applied by us to control tasks.

In learning control, there is an important distinction between *representational tools*, such as lookup tables, neural networks, databases of experiences, or structured representations, and what we will call *learning paradigms*, which define what the representation is used for, where training data comes from, how the training data is used to modify the representation, whether exploratory actions are performed, and other related issues. It is difficult to evaluate a representational tool independently of the paradigm in which it is used, and vice versa. A successful robot learning algorithm typically is composed of sophisticated representational tools and learning paradigms. We will describe using the same representational tool, *locally weighted learning* (Atkeson et al. 1997), in different tasks with different learning paradigms and with different results.

In defining paradigms for learning to control complex systems it is useful to identify three separate components of an indirect (model-based) adaptive control system: modeling, exploration, and policy design. The first component, *modeling*, is the process of forming explicit models of the task and the environment. All of the approaches we will describe will form explicit world models. Moore and Atkeson (1993) explore some of the advantages and disadvantages of approaches that form explicit models versus those that avoid forming models. Often the modeling process is equated with *function approximation*, in which a representational tool is used to fit a training data set. Focusing only on the modeling component leaves several important questions unanswered. For example, "where does the training data come from?" and "what new training data should be collected?" are addressed by the *exploration* component. The question "how should the identified model be used to select actions?" is addressed by the *policy design* or *control law design* component.

The aim of this paper is to survey the implications of using locally weighted regression, a lazy learning technique, as the modeling component of our three part control system. Lazy modeling techniques cannot be implemented or discussed without exploring related issues in exploration and policy design. Although the policy design and exploration components are not "lazy" in the same sense as the modeling component, they should exploit the capabilities of lazy modeling, and make a lazy modeler's job easier.

1.1. *Why Focus on Lazy Learning For Learning to Control?*

We will not review lazy learning here, but expect that our reader has already read the companion paper in this collection (Atkeson et al. 1997), from which we will borrow both terminology and notation. In the form of lazy learning we will focus on, *locally weighted learning,* experiences are explicitly remembered, and predictions and generalizations are performed in real time by building a local model to answer any particular query (an input for which the function's output is desired). The motivation for focussing on locally weighted learning was not that it is a more accurate function approximator than other methods such as multi-layer sigmoidal neural networks, radial basis functions, regression trees, projection pursuit regression, other statistical nonparametric regression techniques, and global regression techniques, but that lazy learning techniques avoid negative interference. One of the primary characteristics of learning to control a robot is that data comes in continuously, and the distribution of the data changes as the robot learns and changes its performance task. Locally weighted learning easily learns in real time from the continuous stream of training data. It also avoids the negative interference exhibited by other modeling approaches, because locally weighted learning retains all the training data, as do many lazy learning methods (Atkeson et al. 1997).

Our approach to modeling the complex functions found in typical task or process dynamics is to use a collection of simple local models. One benefit of local modeling is that it avoids the difficult problem of finding an appropriate structure for a global model. A key idea in lazy learning is to form a training set for the local model after a query is given. This approach allows us to select from the training set only relevant experiences (nearby samples) and to weight those experiences according to their relevance to the query. We form a local model of the function at the query point, much as a Taylor series models a function in the neighborhood of a point. This local model is then used to predict the output of the function for that query. After answering the query, the local model is discarded. A new local model is created to answer each query. This leads to another benefit of lazy modeling for control: we can delay the choice of local model structure and structural parameters until a query must be answered, and we can make different choices for subsequent queries (Atkeson et al. 1997).

Locally weighted learning can represent nonlinear functions, yet has simple training rules with a single global optimum for building a local model in response to a query. This allows complex nonlinear models to be identified (trained) quickly. Currently we are using polynomials as the local models. Since the polynomial local models are linear in the parameters to be estimated, we can calculate these parameters using a linear regression. Fast training makes continuous learning from a stream of new input data possible. It is true that lazy learning transfers the computational load onto the lookup process, but our experience is that the linear parameter estimation process during lookup in locally weighted learning is still fast enough for real time robot learning (Atkeson et al. 1997).

We use cross validation to choose an appropriate distance metric and weighting function, and to help find irrelevant input variables and terms in the local model. In fact, performing one cross validation evaluation in lazy learning is no more expensive than processing a single query (Atkeson et al. 1997). Cheap cross validation makes search for model parameters routine, and we have explored procedures that take advantage of this (Atkeson et al. 1997; Maron and Moore 1994; Moore et al. 1992; Moore and Lee 1994).

We have extended the locally weighted learning approach to give information about the reliability of the predictions and local linearizations generated, based on the local density and distribution of the data and an estimate of the local variance (Atkeson et al. 1997; Schaal and Atkeson 1994a; Schaal and Atkeson 1994b). This allows a robot to monitor its own skill level, protect itself from its ignorance by designing robust policies, and guide its exploratory behavior.

Another attractive feature of locally weighted learning is flexibility. There are explicit parameters to control smoothing, outlier rejection, forgetting, and other processes. The modeling process is easy to understand, and therefore easy to adjust or control (Atkeson et al. 1997).

We will see how the explicit representation of specific memories can speed up convergence and improve the robustness and autonomy of optimization and control algorithms (Atkeson et al. 1997; Moore and Schneider 1995). It is frustrating to watch a robot repeat its mistakes, with only a slight improvement on each attempt. The goal of the learning algorithms described here is to improve performance as rapidly as possible, using as little training data as possible (data efficiency).

1.2. *Related Work*

Locally weighted learning is being increasingly used in control. (Connell and Utgoff 1987) interpolated a value function using locally weighted averaging to balance an inverted pendulum (a pole) on a moving cart. (Peng 1995) performed the cart pole task using locally weighted regression to interpolate a value function. (Zografski 1992) used locally weighted averaging to learn a model of the dynamics of a robot arm, and used that model to predict the forces necessary to drive the arm along a trajectory. (Aha and Salzberg 1993) explored nearest neighbor and locally weighted learning approaches to a tracking task in which a robot pursued and caught a ball. (McCallum 1995) explored the use of lazy learning techniques in situations where states were not completely measured.

Table 1. The control tasks explored in this paper. Symbols and mathematics described in some of the entries will be explained in the corresponding sections.

Task	Task Specification	Goal	Example	Sec.
Temporally Independent	y_d : the desired output	Choose u such that $E[y] = y_d$	Billiards	2
Deadbeat Control	x_d or trajectory $\{x_d(t)\}$	Choose $u(t)$ such that $E[x(t+1)] = x_d(t+1)$	Devil Sticking I	3.1
Dynamic Regulation	x_d and matrices Q and R	Minimize future cost $C = \sum_{t=0}^{\infty} \left(\delta x(t)^T Q \delta x(t) + u(t)^T R u(t) \right)$	Devil Sticking II	3.2
Dynamic Regulation, unspecified setpoint	Q and R	Choose setpoint to minimize future cost C	Devil Sticking III	3.4
Nonlinear Optimal Control	Cost function $G(x(t), u(t), t)$	Find a control policy to minimize the sum of future costs	Puck	3.6

1.3. *Outline*

This article is organized by types of control tasks, and in the next sections we will examine a progression of control tasks of increasing complexity. We have chosen these tasks because we have implemented lazy learning as part of a learning controller for each of them. For each type of task we will show how lazy learning of models interacts with other parts of the learning control paradigm being described. For several tasks we also provide implementation details. The progression of control tasks is outlined in Table 1. Temporally independent tasks include many forms of setpoint based process control, and are of economic importance. We describe several versions of temporally dependent tasks, which include trajectory following tasks such as process control transients and vehicle maneuvers. We conclude with a discussion of some of the benefits and drawbacks of lazy learning in this context.

2. Temporally Independent Tasks

In the simplest class of tasks we will consider, the environment provides an outcome represented with a vector **y** as a function of an action vector **u**, which we can choose, a state vector **x**, which we can observe but not choose, and random noise.

$$y = f(x, u) + \text{noise} \qquad (1)$$

The task is to choose **u** so that the expected outcome **y** is $\mathbf{y_d}$: $E[\mathbf{y}] = \mathbf{y_d}$, where E is the expectation operator from probability theory. The function $\mathbf{f}()$ is not known at the beginning of the task. Section 2.2 will describe how lazy learning can be used to learn a model of $\mathbf{f}()$: $\widehat{\mathbf{f}}()$.

Several relationships could be modeled using lazy learning techniques including forward models, inverse models, policies, and value functions. We will discuss policies and value functions in the context of temporally dependent tasks in later sections. The next sections describe inverse and forward models.

2.1. *Control Using Inverse Models*

An *inverse model* uses states and outcomes to predict the necessary action (Atkeson 1990; Miller 1989):

$$\mathbf{u} = \widehat{\mathbf{f}}^{-1}(\mathbf{x}, \mathbf{y}) \tag{2}$$

This function specifies directly what action to take in each state, but does not specify what would happen given a state and an action. A lazy learner can represent an inverse model using a database of experiences, arranged so that the input vectors of each experience are the concatenation of state and outcome vectors (Figure 1). The corresponding output is the action needed to produce the given outcome from the given state. The database is trained by adding new observed states, actions, and outcomes: $(\mathbf{x}, \mathbf{u}, \mathbf{y})$.

A learned inverse model can provide a conceptually simple controller for temporally independent tasks. An action is chosen by using the current state and desired outcome as an index into the database. The closest match in the database can be found or an interpolation of nearby experiences (i.e., a weighted average or locally weighted regression approach) can be used. If there are no stored experiences close enough to the current situation, another method, such as choosing actions randomly, can be used to select an action. This distance threshold is task dependent and can be set by the user.

The strength of an inverse model controller in conjunction with lazy learning is that the learning is *aggressive*: during repeated attempts to achieve the same goal the action that is applied is not an incrementally adjusted version of the previous action, but is instead the action that the lazy learner predicts will directly achieve the required outcome. Given a monotonic relationship between **u** and **y**, the sequence of actions that are chosen are closely related to the Secant method (Conte and De Boor 1980) for numerically finding the zero of a function. See (Ortega and Rheinboldt 1970) for a good discussion of the multidimensional generalization of the Secant method. An inverse

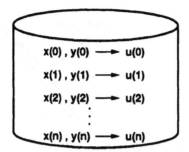

Figure 1. A database implementing an inverse model.

model, represented using locally weighted regression and trained initially with a feedback learner, has been used by (Atkeson 1990).

A commonly observed problem with the inverse model is that, if the vector space of actions has a different dimensionality than that of outcomes, then the inverse model is not well defined. Problems also result if the mapping is not one to one, or if there are misleading noisy observations. Learning can become stuck in permanent pockets of inaccuracy that are not reduced with experience. Figure 2 illustrates a problem where a non-monotonic relation between actions and outcomes is misinterpreted by the inverse model. Even if the inverse model had interpreted the data correctly, any locally weighted averaging on **u** would have led to incorrect actions (Moore 1991a; Jordan and Rumelhart 1992). In subsequent sections on temporally dependent tasks, we will discuss how sometimes the action selected by the inverse function is too aggressive.

2.2. *Control Using Forward Models*

The *forward model* uses states and actions to predict outcomes (Miller 1989; Mel 1989; Moore 1990; Jordan and Rumelhart 1992):

$$\mathbf{y} = \widehat{\mathbf{f}}(\mathbf{x}, \mathbf{u}) \tag{3}$$

This allows prediction of the effects of various actions (mental simulation) but does not prescribe the correct action to take.

We now arrange the memory-base so that the input vectors of each data point are the concatenation of state and action vectors (Figure 3). The corresponding output is the actual outcome that was observed when the state-action pair was executed in the real world. The forward model can be trained from observations of states, actions, and outcomes: $(\mathbf{x}, \mathbf{u}, \mathbf{y})$.

To use this model for control requires more than a single lookup. Actions are chosen by on-line numerical inversion of the forward model, that requires

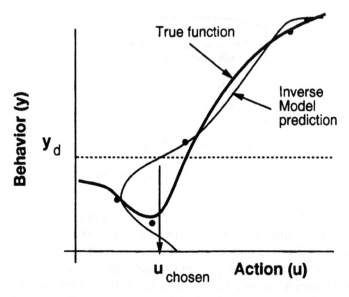

Figure 2. The true relation (shown as the thick black line) is non-monotonic. When an outcome is desired at the shown value y_d, the action that is suggested produces an outcome that differs from the desired one. Worse, the new data point that is added (at the intersection of the thick black line and the vertical arrow) will not change the inverse model near y_d, and the same mistake will be repeated indefinitely.

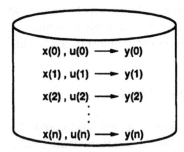

Figure 3. A database implementing a forward model.

searching a set of actions to find one that is predicted to achieve the desired output. This computation is identical to numerical root finding over the empirical model. A number of root-finding schemes are applicable, with desirability depending on the dimensionality of the actions, the complexity of the function and the amount of time available in which to perform the search:

- *Grid Search:* Generate all available actions sampled from a uniform grid over action space. Take the action that is predicted to produce the closest outcome to y_d.

- *Random Search:* Generate random actions, and again use the action which is predicted to produce the closest outcome to y_d.
- *First Order Gradient Search:* Perform a steepest-ascent search from an initial candidate action toward an action that will give the desired output (Press et al. 1988). Finding the local gradient of the empirical model is easy if locally weighted regression is used (Atkeson et al. 1997). Part of the computation of the locally weighted regression model forms the local linear map, so it is already available. We may write the prediction local to x and u as

$$\widehat{\mathbf{f}}(\mathbf{x} + \delta\mathbf{x}, \mathbf{u} + \delta\mathbf{u}) \approx \mathbf{c} + \mathbf{A}\delta\mathbf{x} + \mathbf{B}\delta\mathbf{u} + \textbf{2nd order terms} \qquad (4)$$

where **c** is a vector and **A** and **B** are matrices obtained from the regression, such that

$$\mathbf{c} = \widehat{\mathbf{f}}(\mathbf{x}, \mathbf{u}) \quad \mathbf{A}_{ij} = \frac{\partial \widehat{f}_i}{\partial x_j} \quad \mathbf{B}_{ij} = \frac{\partial \widehat{f}_i}{\partial u_j} \qquad (5)$$

The gradient ascent iteration is:

$$\mathbf{u}_{k+1} = \mathbf{u}_k + \mathbf{B}^{\mathrm{T}}(\mathbf{y}_d - \mathbf{c}) \qquad (6)$$

with **B** and **c** as defined in Equation 5. This approach may become stuck in local minima, so an initial grid search or random search may provide a set of good starting points for gradient searches.
- *Second Order Gradient Search:* Use Newton's method to iterate towards an action with the desired output (Press et al. 1988). If $\mathbf{u}_k$ is an approximate solution, Newton's method gives $\mathbf{u}_{k+1}$ as a better solution where

$$\mathbf{u}_{k+1} = \mathbf{u}_k + \mathbf{B}^{-1}(\mathbf{y}_d - \mathbf{c}) \qquad (7)$$

with **B** and **c** as defined in Equation 5. Newton's method is less stable than first order gradient search, but if a good approximate solution is available, perhaps from one of the other search methods, and the local linear model structure is correct in a region including the current action and the best action, it produces a good estimate of the best action in only two or three iterations.

If the partial derivative matrix **B** is singular, or the action space and state space differ in dimensionality, then robust matrix techniques based on the pseudo-inverse can be applied to invert **B** (Press et al. 1988). The forward model can be used to minimize a criterion C that penalizes large commands as well as errors, which also makes this search more robust:

$$C = (\mathbf{y}_d - \mathbf{c})^{\mathrm{T}}\mathbf{Q}(\mathbf{y}_d - \mathbf{c}) + \mathbf{u}^{\mathrm{T}}\mathbf{R}\mathbf{u} \qquad (8)$$

The matrices $\mathbf{Q}$ and $\mathbf{R}$ allow the user to control which components of the error are most important.

2.3. Combining Forward and Inverse models

The inverse model can provide a good initial starting point for a search using the forward model:

$$\mathbf{u}_0 = \widehat{\mathbf{f}}^{-1}(\mathbf{x}, \mathbf{y}_d)$$

$\mathbf{u}_0$ can be evaluated using a lazy forward model with the same data:

$$\widehat{\mathbf{y}} = \widehat{\mathbf{f}}(\mathbf{x}, \mathbf{u}_0)$$

Provided $\widehat{\mathbf{y}}$ is close to $\mathbf{y}_d$, Newton's method can then be used for further refinement. If $\widehat{\mathbf{y}}$ is not close to $\mathbf{y}_d$, the local linear model may not be a good fit, and the aggressive Newton step may move away from the goal.

2.4. Exploration in Temporally Independent Learning

A nice feature of the approaches described so far is that in normal operation they perform their own exploration, reducing the need for human supervision or external guidance. The experiments are chosen greedily at the exact points where the desired output is predicted to be, which for the forward model is guaranteed to provide useful data. If an action is wrongly predicted to succeed, the resulting new data point will change the prediction of the forward model for that state and action, helping to prevent the error from being repeated.

In the early stages of learning, however, there may be no action that is predicted to give the desired outcome. A simple experiment design strategy is to choose actions at random. It is more effective to choose data points which, given the uncertainty inherent in the prediction, are considered most likely to achieve the desired outcome. This can considerably reduce the exploration required (Moore 1991a; Cohn et al. 1995).

2.5. A Temporally Independent Task: Billiards

In order to explore the efficacy of lazy learning methods for the control of temporally independent tasks, the previously described approaches were implemented on the billiards robot shown in Figure 4 (Moore 1992; Moore et al. 1992). The equipment consists of a small ($1.5m \times 0.75m$) pool table, a spring actuated cue with a rotary joint under the control of a stepper motor, and two cameras attached to a Datacube image processing system. All sensing is visual: one camera looks along the cue stick and the other looks down at the

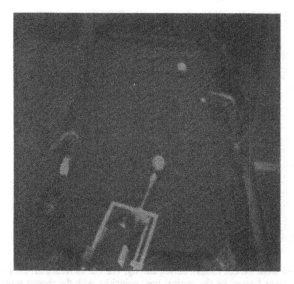

Figure 4. The billiards robot. In the foreground is the cue stick, which attempts to sink balls in the far pockets.

table. The cue stick swivels around the cue ball, which, in this implementation, has to start each shot at the same position. A shot proceeds as follows:

1. At the start of each attempt the *object ball* (i.e., the ball we want to sink in a pocket) is placed at a random position in the half of the table opposite the cue stick. This random position is selected by the computer to avoid human bias.

2. The camera above the table obtains the centroid image coordinates of the object ball $(x_{object}^{above}, y_{object}^{above})$, which constitute the state $\mathbf{x}$.

3. The controller then uses an inverse model followed by search over a forward model to find an action, $\mathbf{u}$, that is predicted to sink the object ball into the nearer of the two pockets at the far end of the table. The action is specified by what we wish the view from the cue to be just prior to shooting. Figure 5 shows a view from the cue camera during this process. The cue swivels until the centroid of the object ball's image (shown by the vertical line) coincides with the chosen action, x_{object}^{cue}, shown by the cross.

4. The shot is then performed and observed by the overhead camera. The image after a shot, overlaid with the tracking of both balls, is shown in Figure 6. The outcome is defined as the cushion and position on the cushion where the object ball first collides. In Figure 6 it is the point b.

5. Independent of success or failure, the memory-base is updated with the new observation $(x_{object}^{above}, y_{object}^{above}, x_{object}^{cue}) \rightarrow b$.

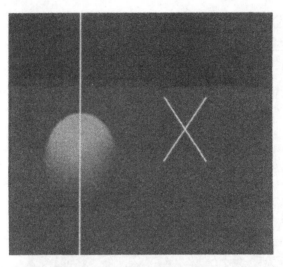

Figure 5. The view from the cue camera during aiming. The cue swivels until the centroid of the object ball's image (shown by the vertical line) coincides with the chosen action, x^{cue}_{object}, shown by the cross.

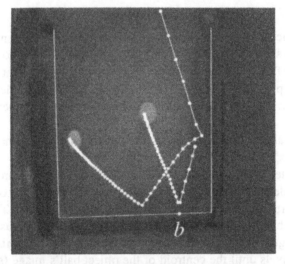

Figure 6. The trajectory of both balls is tracked using the overhead camera. b indicates the cushion and position on the cushion where the object ball first collides.

As time progresses, the database of experiences increases, hopefully converging to expertise in the two-dimensional manifold of state-space corresponding to sinking balls placed in arbitrary positions. Before learning

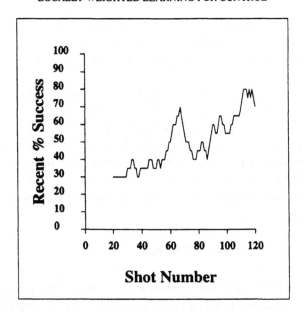

Figure 7. Frequency of successes versus control cycle for the billiards task. The number of successes, averaged over the twenty previous shots, is shown.

begins there is no explicit knowledge or calibration of the robot, pool table, or cameras, beyond having the object ball in view of the overhead camera, and the assumption that the relationship between state, action and outcome is reasonably repeatable.

In this implementation the representation used for both forward and inverse models was locally weighted regression using outlier removal and cross validation for choosing the kernel width (Atkeson et al. 1997). Inverse and forward models were used together; the forward model was searched with steepest ascent. Early shots (when no success was predicted) were uncertainty-based (Moore 1991a). After 100 shots, control choice running on a Sun-4 was taking 0.8 seconds.

This implementation demonstrates several important points. The first is the precision required of the modeling component. The cue-action must be extremely precise for success. Locally weighted regression provided the needed precision. A graph of the number of successes against trial number (Figure 7) shows the performance of the robot against time. Sinking the ball requires better than 1% accuracy in the choice of action, the world contains discontinuities and there are random outliers in the data due to visual tracking errors, and so it is encouraging that within less than 100 experiences the robot had reached a 75% success rate. An informal assessment of this performance is that its success rate is as high as possible (given that the ball is placed at random positions, some of which are virtually impossibly difficult). Unfortunately, the only evidence for this is anecdotal: the students who built the robot (one of whom was an MIT billiards champion) could not do any better.

A second point is the non-uniformity of the training data distribution due to the implicit exploration process. Although the function being learned is only 3 inputs → 1 output, it is perhaps surprising that it achieved sufficient accuracy in only 100 data points. The reason is the aggressive non-uniformity of the training data distribution – almost all the training data was clustered around state-action pairs which get the ball in or close to a pocket. The lazy learner did not expend many resources on exploring or representing how to make bad shots.

2.6. *Optimizing a Performance Criterion*

Often a goal in temporally independent learning is to optimize a particular criterion, rather than achieve a particular outcome. Lazy learning can be used to represent the cost function directly and to speed the search for maxima or minima (Moore and Schneider 1995). A linear local model can be used to estimate the first derivatives (gradient) and a quadratic local model can be used to estimate the second derivatives (Hessian) of the cost function at the current point in the optimization procedure. These estimates can be used in first order gradient search, or in a Newton search that uses estimates of second derivatives. Constraints on the output can be included in this optimization process.

2.7. *Temporal Dependence in Temporally Independent Tasks*

It is considerably easier to choose actions for temporally independent than temporally dependent tasks because the choice of action has no effect on future states. There is no need to consider the effects of the current action on future states and indirectly on future performance. In Section 3 we will consider temporally dependent tasks where there is an opportunity to choose suboptimal actions in the short-term to obtain more desirable states and thereby improve performance in the long-term.

However, temporally independent tasks do provide an opportunity to increase the knowledge available to the controller in order to improve future performance. They differ from batch learning tasks, because new training data becomes available after each action, and the choice of action, which depends on inferences from earlier training data, affects the training data available to future decisions. Modifying actions to increase knowledge rather than greedily pursue a desired outcome is the responsibility of the exploration component of the controller.

3. Temporally Dependent Tasks

A more complex class of learning control tasks occur when the assumption of temporal independence is removed: $x(t + 1)$ may now be influenced by $x(t)$. A useful case to explore is when the outcome is the next state:

$$x(t + 1) = f(x(t), u(t)) \qquad (9)$$

The task may be to regulate the state to a predefined desired value called a *setpoint* x_d or to a sequence or trajectory of states: $x_d(1)$, $x_d(2)$, $x_d(3) \ldots$

3.1. *Deadbeat Control*

One approach to performing temporally dependent tasks is to use the successful techniques from the previous section, and ignore the temporal dependence. One-step *deadbeat* control chooses actions to (in expectation) cause the immediate next state to be the desired next state (Stengel 1986). Assuming the next state is always attainable in one step, the action may be chosen without paying attention to future states, decisions, or performance.

3.1.1. *An Implementation of Deadbeat Control: Devil Sticking I*
Deadbeat control using lazy learning models was explored by implementing it for a juggling task known as *devil sticking* (Schaal and Atkeson 1994a, b). A center stick is batted back and forth between two handsticks. Figure 8 shows a sketch of our devil sticking robot. The juggling robot uses its top two joints to perform planar devil sticking. Hand sticks are mounted on the robot with springs and dampers. This implements a passive catch. The center stick does not bounce when it hits the hand stick, and therefore requires an active throwing motion by the robot. To simplify the problem the center stick is constrained by a boom to move on the surface of a sphere. For small movements the center stick movements are approximately planar. The boom also provides a way to measure the current state of the center stick. The task state is the predicted location of the center stick when it hits the hand stick held in a nominal position. Standard ballistics equations for the flight of the center stick are used to map flight trajectory measurements into a task state. The dynamics of throwing the devil stick are parameterized by five state and five action variables, resulting in a 10/5-dimensional input/output model for each hand.

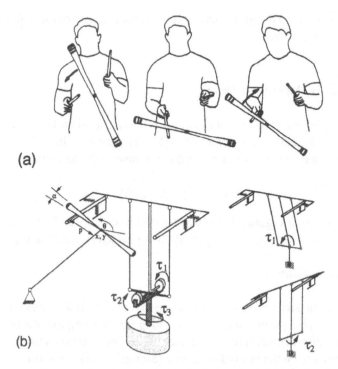

Figure 8. (a) An illustration of devil sticking, (b) A sketch of our devil sticking robot. A position change due to movement of joint 1 and 2, respectively, is indicated in the small sketches.

Every time the robot catches and throws the devil stick it generates an experience of the form $(\mathbf{x}_k, \mathbf{u}_k, \mathbf{x}_{k+1})$ where $\mathbf{x}_k$ is the current state, $\mathbf{u}_k$ is the action performed by the robot, and $\mathbf{x}_{k+1}$ is the state of the center stick that results.

Initially we explored learning an inverse model of the task, using deadbeat control to attempt to eliminate all error on each hit. Each hand had its own inverse model of the form:

$$\widehat{\mathbf{u}}_k = \widehat{\mathbf{f}}^{-1}(\mathbf{x}_k, \mathbf{x}_{k+1}) \tag{10}$$

Before each hit the system looked up a command with the predicted nominal impact state and the desired result state $\mathbf{x}_d$:

$$\widehat{\mathbf{u}}_k = \widehat{\mathbf{f}}^{-1}(\mathbf{x}_k, \mathbf{x}_d) \tag{11}$$

Inverse model learning using lazy learning (locally weighted regression) was successfully used to train the system to perform the devil sticking task.

Juggling runs up to 100 hits were achieved. The system incorporated new data in real time, and used databases of several hundred hits. Lookups took less than 15 milliseconds, and therefore several lookups could be performed before the end of the flight of the center stick (the flight duration was approximately 0.4s). Later queries incorporated more measurements of the flight of the center stick and therefore more accurate predictions of the state of the task.

However, the system required substantial structure in the initial training to achieve this performance. The system was started with a manually generated command that was appropriate for open loop performance of the task. Each control parameter was varied systematically to explore the space near the default command. A global linear model was made of this initial data, and a linear controller based on this model was used to generate an initial training set for the locally weighted system (of approximately 100 hits). Learning with small amounts of initial data was not possible. Furthermore, learning based on just an inverse model was prone to get stuck at poor levels of performance and to repeat the same mistakes for reasons discussed in the previous section.

To eliminate these problems, we also experimented with learning based on both inverse and forward models. After a command is generated by the inverse model, it can be evaluated using a forward model based on the same data.

$$\widehat{\mathbf{x}}_{k+1} = \widehat{\mathbf{f}}(\mathbf{x}_k, \widehat{\mathbf{u}}_k) \tag{12}$$

Because it produces a local linear model, the locally weighted regression procedure will produce estimates of the derivatives of the forward model with respect to the commands as part of the estimated parameter vector. These derivatives can be used to find a correction to the command vector that reduces errors in the predicted outcome based on the forward model.

$$\frac{\partial \widehat{\mathbf{f}}}{\partial \mathbf{u}} \Delta \widehat{\mathbf{u}}_k = \widehat{\mathbf{x}}_{k+1} - \mathbf{x}_d \tag{13}$$

This process of command refinement can be repeated until the forward model no longer produces accurate predictions of the outcome, which will happen when the query to the forward model requires significant extrapolation from the current database. The distance to the nearest stored data point can be used as a crude measure of the validity of the forward model estimate.

We investigated this method for incremental learning of devil sticking in simulations. However, the outcome did not meet expectations: without sufficient initial data around the setpoint, the algorithm did not work. We see two reasons for this. First, similar to the pure inverse model approach, the inverse-forward model acts as a one-step deadbeat controller in that it tries to eliminate all error in one time step. One-step deadbeat control applies large commands to correct for deviations from the setpoint, especially in the presence of state measurement errors. The workspace bounds and command bounds of our devil sticking robot limit the size of allowable commands. Large control actions may also be less accurate or robust. This was the case in devil sticking, where a large control action tended to cause the center stick to fly in a random direction, and nothing was learned from that hit. Second, the ten dimensional input space is large, and even if experiences are uniformly randomly distributed in the space there is often not enough data near a particular point to make a robust inverse or forward model.

Thus, two ingredients had to be added to the devil sticking controller. First, the controller should not be deadbeat. It should plan to attain the goal using multiple control actions. We discuss control approaches that keep commands small in the next section. Second, the control must increase the data density in the current region of the state-action space in order to arrive at the desired goal state. We discuss control approaches that are more tightly coupled to exploration in a Section 3.4.

3.2. *Dynamic Regulation*

In this section we discuss a reformulation of temporally dependent control tasks to avoid the problems encountered by the first implementation of a lazy learner for robot control, which used deadbeat control. From a theoretical point of view, it is often not possible to return to the desired setpoint or trajectory in one step: an attempt to do so would require actions of infinite magnitude or cause the size of the required actions to grow without limit. One step deadbeat control will fail on some non-minimum phase systems, of which pole balancing is one example (Cannon 1967). In these systems, one must move away from the goal to approach it later. In the case of the cart-pole system the cart must initially move away from the target position so that the pole leans in the direction of future cart motion towards the target. This maneuvering avoids having the pole fall backwards as the cart moves toward the target.

A controller can perform more robustly if it uses smaller magnitude actions and returns to the correct state or trajectory in a larger number of steps. This idea is posed precisely in the language of *linear quadratic regulation* (LQR), in which a long term quadratic cost criterion C is minimized that penalizes both state-errors and action magnitudes (Stengel 1986):

$$C = \sum_{t=0}^{\infty} \left((\mathbf{x}(t) - \mathbf{x_d})^T \mathbf{Q}(\mathbf{x}(t) - \mathbf{x_d}) + \mathbf{u}^T(t)\mathbf{R}\mathbf{u}(t) \right)$$

$$= \sum_{t=0}^{\infty} \left(\delta\mathbf{x}^T(t)\mathbf{Q}\delta\mathbf{x}(t) + \mathbf{u}^T(t)\mathbf{R}\mathbf{u}(t) \right) \tag{14}$$

where $\mathbf{Q}$ and $\mathbf{R}$ are matrices whose elements set the tradeoff between the size of the action components and the error components. If, for example, $\mathbf{Q}$ and $\mathbf{R}$ were identity matrices, then the sum of squared state errors and the sum of the squared action components would be minimized.

Not using deadbeat control laws implies some amount of lookahead. LQR control assumes a time invariant task and performs an infinite amount of lookahead. *Predictive* or *Receding Horizon* control design techniques look N steps ahead every time an action is chosen. All of these techniques will allow larger state errors to reduce the size of the control signals, when compared to deadbeat methods.

The *Linear* part of the LQR approach is a local linearization of the forward dynamics of the task. We can take advantage of the locally linear state-transition function provided by locally weighted regression (Equation 4):

$$\mathbf{x}(t+1) = \mathbf{x_d} + \delta\mathbf{x}(t+1) \approx \widehat{\mathbf{f}}(\mathbf{x_d} + \delta\mathbf{x}(t), \mathbf{u}(t))$$

$$\approx \widehat{\mathbf{f}}(\mathbf{x_d}, 0) + \mathbf{A}\delta\mathbf{x}(t) + \mathbf{B}\mathbf{u}(t) \tag{15}$$

We will assume that $(\mathbf{x_d}, 0)$ is an equilibrium point, so $\mathbf{x_d} = \widehat{\mathbf{f}}(\mathbf{x_d}, 0)$, and we have the following linear dynamics:

$$\delta\mathbf{x}(t+1) = \mathbf{A}\delta\mathbf{x}(t) + \mathbf{B}\mathbf{u}(t) \tag{16}$$

The optimal action with respect to the criteria in Equation 14 and linear dynamics in Equation 16 can be obtained by solution of a matrix equation called the *Ricatti equation* (Stengel 1986). Assuming the locally linear model provided by the locally weighted regression is correct, the optimal action $\mathbf{u}$ is

$$\mathbf{u} = -(\mathbf{R} + \mathbf{B}^T\mathbf{P}\mathbf{B})^{-1}\mathbf{B}^T\mathbf{P}\mathbf{A}\delta\mathbf{x} \tag{17}$$

where $\mathbf{P}$ is obtained by initially setting $\mathbf{P} := \mathbf{Q}$ and then running the following iteration to convergence:

$$\mathbf{P} := \mathbf{Q} + \mathbf{A}^T\mathbf{P}[\mathbf{I} - \mathbf{B}\mathbf{R}^{-1}\mathbf{B}^T\mathbf{P}]^{-1}\mathbf{A} \tag{18}$$

This rather inscrutable result is not obvious from visual inspection but follows from reasonably elementary algebra and calculus that can be found in almost any introductory controls text. We recommend (Stengel 1986). We also provide a very simplified self-contained derivation in Appendix A. The long term cost starting from state $\mathbf{x}_d + \delta\mathbf{x}$ turns out to be $\delta\mathbf{x}^T \mathbf{P} \, \delta\mathbf{x}$. Note that $\mathbf{u}$ is a linear function of the state $\mathbf{x}$ in Equation 17:

$$\mathbf{u} = -\mathbf{K}\delta\mathbf{x} \qquad (19)$$

Linear quadratic regulation has useful robustness when compared to deadbeat controllers even if the underlying linear models are imprecise (Stengel 1986).

3.3. Implementation of Dynamic Regulation: Devil Sticking II

Linear quadratic regulation controller design permitted successful devil sticking. It did require manual generation of training data to estimate the matrices of the local linear model: $\mathbf{A}$ and $\mathbf{B}$. However, once the local linear model was reliable the robot had a complete *policy* (i.e., a control law) for the vicinity of the local linear model. The aggressiveness of the control law could be controlled by choosing $\mathbf{Q}$ and $\mathbf{R}$. These matrices were set once by us, and then not adjusted during learning.

One drawback of our LQR implementation was the need for the manual search for an equilibrium point. The robot needed to be told a nominal hit that would actually send the devil stick to the other hand. There is a continuum of reasonable equilibrium points, but our formulation required the arbitrary selection of only one. Furthermore, the experimenter did not know in advance where the set of equilibrium points were for the actual machine, so manual search for equilibrium points was a difficult task, given the five dimensional action space. The next section describes a new procedure to search for equilibrium points.

3.4. Dynamic Regulation With An Unspecified Setpoint

The learning task is considerably harder if the desired setpoint is not known in advance, and instead must itself be optimized to achieve some higher level task description. However, the setpoint of the task can be manipulated during learning to improve exploration. This is done by the *shifting setpoint algorithm* (SSA) (Schaal and Atkeson 1994a).

SSA attempts to decompose the control problem into two separate control tasks on different time scales. At the fast time scale, it acts as a dynamic regulator by trying to keep the controlled system at a chosen setpoint. On a slower time scale, the setpoint is shifted to accomplish a desired goal. SSA uses local models from lazy learning and can be viewed as an approach to exploration in these regulation tasks, based on information on the quality of predictions provided by lazy learning.

3.4.1. *Experiment Design with Shifting Setpoints*

The major ingredient of the SSA is a statistical self-monitoring process. Whenever the current location in input space has obtained a sufficient amount of experience such that a measure of confidence rises above a threshold, the setpoint is shifted in the direction of the goal until the confidence falls below a minimum confidence level. At this new setpoint location, the learning system collects new experiences. The shifting process is repeated until the goal is reached. In this way, the SSA builds a narrow tube of data support in which it knows the world. This data builds the basis for the first success of the regulator controller. Subsequently, the learned model can be used for more sophisticated control algorithms, for planning, or for further exploration.

3.5. *Dynamic Regulation With An Unspecified Setpoint: Devil Sticking III*

The SSA method was tested on the devil sticking juggling task (Schaal and Atkeson 1994a, b). In this case it had the following steps.

1. Regardless of the poor juggling quality of the robot (i.e., at most two or three hits per trial), the SSA made the robot repeat these initial actions with small random perturbations until a cloud of data was collected somewhere in the state-action space for each hand. An abstract illustration for this is given in Figure 9a.
2. Each point in the data cloud of each hand was used as a candidate for a setpoint of the corresponding hand by trying to predict its output from its input with locally weighted regression. The point achieving the narrowest local confidence interval became the setpoint of the hand and a linear quadratic regulator was calculated for its local linear model, estimated using locally weighted regression. By means of these controllers, the amount of data around the setpoints could quickly be increased until the quality of the local models exceeded a statistical threshold (Figure 9b) (Atkeson et al. 1997).
3. At this point, the setpoints were gradually shifted towards the goal setpoints until the statistical confidence in the predictions made by the local model again fell below a threshold (Figure 9c).
4. The SSA iterated by collecting data in the new regions of the workspace until the setpoints could be shifted again. The procedure terminated when the goal was reached, leaving a ridge of data in the state-action space (Figure 9d).

The SSA was tested in a noise corrupted simulation and on the real robot. Each attempt to juggle the devil stick is called a *trial*, which consists of a series of left and right handed hits. Each series of trials that begins with the lazy learning system in its initial state is referred to as a *run*. Our measure of performance is the number of hits per trial. In the simulation it takes on

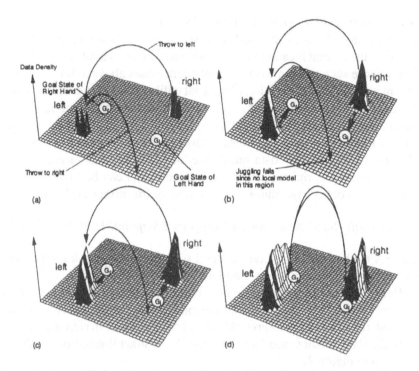

Figure 9. Abstract illustration on how the SSA algorithm collects data in space: (a) sparse data after the first few hits; (b) high local data density due to local control in this region; (c) increased data density on the way to the goals due to shifting the setpoints; (d) ridge of data density after the goal was reached.

average 40 trials before the setpoint of each hand has moved close enough to the other hand's setpoint. This is slightly better performance than with the real robot.

At that point, a breakthrough occurs and, afterwards the simulated robot rarely drops the devilstick. At this time, about 400 data points (hits) have been collected in memory. The real robot's learning performance is qualitatively the same as that of the simulated robot. Due to stronger nonlinearities and unknown noise sources the actual robot takes more trials to accomplish a steady juggling pattern. We show three typical learning runs for the actual robot in Figure 10. We do not show averages of these learning runs because averaged runs show a gradual increase in performance, which is unlike any individual learning run, which show sudden increases in performance. Peak performance of the robot was more than 2000 consecutive hits (15 minutes of continuous juggling).

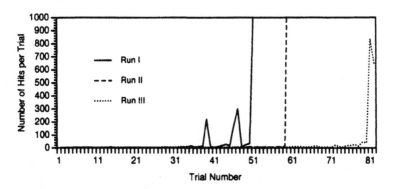

Figure 10. Learning curves of devil sticking for three runs.

3.5.1. *Limits For Linear Quadratic Regulation*

Control laws based on linear quadratic regulator designs are not useful if the task requires operation outside a locally linear region. The LQR controller may actually be unstable. For example, the following one dimensional system with a one dimensional action

$$x_{k+1} = 2x_k + u_k + x_k^2 u_k \qquad (20)$$

has a local linear model at the origin ($x = 0$) of $\mathbf{A} = \mathbf{2}$ and $\mathbf{B} = \mathbf{1}$ (all matrices are 1×1 for this one dimensional problem). For the optimization criteria $\mathbf{Q} = \mathbf{1}$ and $\mathbf{R} = \mathbf{1}$, and the Ricatti equation (Equations 17 and 19) gives $\mathbf{K} = \mathbf{1.618}$. For a goal of moving to the origin ($\mathbf{x_d} = 0$), this linear control law is unstable for x larger than 0.95, because the actions u are too large. This means that the LQR "optimal" action actually increases the error x if the error is already larger than 0.95. This limitation of linear quadratic regulation motivates us to explore full dynamic programming based policy design approaches, which are described in the next section. Figure 11 compares the LQR based control law and the control law based on full dynamic programming using the same model and optimization criteria. Note that the shifting setpoint algorithm can provide the initial training data for these more complex approaches.

3.6. *Nonlinear Optimal Control*

In more general control design we must accommodate a more general formulation of the cost function or criterion to optimize and also move from local control laws based on a small number of local models to more global control laws based on many local models. We now need to learn not just a local model

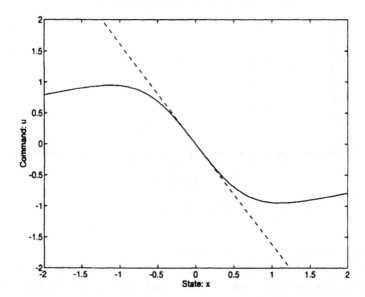

Figure 11. Solid line: optimal action based on dynamic programming (DP) using the nonlinear model; dashed line: optimal command based on a LQR design using a single linear forward model at the origin. Although in both cases the optimization criterion is the same and the LQR and DP-based control laws agree for small x, the LQR control law is linear and does not take into account the nonlinear dynamics of the task for large x.

of the task, but many local models of the task distributed throughout the task space. We will first discuss a more general formulation of cost functions.

We are given a cost function for each step, which is known by the controller:

$$g(t) = G(\mathbf{x}(t), \mathbf{u}(t), t) \tag{21}$$

The task is to minimize one of the following expressions:

$$\sum_{t=0}^{\infty} g(t) \text{ or } \sum_{t=0}^{t_{\max}} g(t) \text{ or } \sum_{t=0}^{\infty} \gamma^t g(t) \text{ where } 0 < \gamma < 1 \text{ or } \lim_{n \to \infty} \frac{1}{n} \sum_{t=0}^{n} g(t)$$

The attractive aspect of these formulations is their generality. All of the previously described control formulations are special cases of at least one of these. For example, the quadratic one step cost defined by $\mathbf{Q}$ and $\mathbf{R}$ can be viewed as a local quadratic model of $g(t)$.

The delayed rewards nature of these tasks means that actions we choose at time t do not only affect the quality of the immediate reward but also affect the next, and all subsequent states, and in so doing affect the future rewards attainable. This leads to computational difficulties in the general case. A large literature on such learning control problems has sprung up in recent years, with the general name of *reinforcement learning*. Overviews may be found in (Sutton 1988; Barto et al. 1990; Watkins 1989; Barto et al. 1995; Moore and Atkeson 1993). In this paper we will restrict discussion to the applications of lazy learning to these problems.

Again, we proceed by learning an empirical forward model $\widehat{x}_{k+1} = \widehat{f}(x_k, \widehat{u}_k)$. A general-purpose solution can be obtained by discretizing state-space into a multidimensional array of small cells, and performing a dynamic programming method (Bellman 1957; Bertsekas and Tsitsiklis 1989) such as value iteration or policy iteration to produce two things:

1. A *value function*, $V(x)$, mapping cells onto the minimum possible sum of future costs if one starts in that cell.
2. A *policy*, $u(x)$, mapping cells onto the optimal action to take in that cell.

Value iteration can be used in conjunction with learning a world model. However, it is extremely computationally expensive. For a fixed quantization level, the cost is exponential in the dimensionality of the state variables. For a D dimensional state space and action space, and a grid resolution of R for both states and actions, one value iteration pass would require R^{2D} evaluations of the forward model. The most computationally intensive version would perform several cycles of value iteration after every update of the memory base. Less expensive forms of dynamic programming would normally perform value iteration only at the end of each trial (as we do in the example in Section 3.6.1), or as an incremental parallel process (Sutton 1990; Moore and Atkeson 1993; Peng and Williams 1993).

3.6.1. *A Simulation Example: The Puck*

We illustrate this form of learning by means of a simple simulated example. Figure 12 depicts a frictionless puck on a bumpy surface, whose objective is to drive itself up the hill to a goal region in the minimum number of time steps. The state, $x = (x, \dot{x})$, is two-dimensional and must lie in the region $-1 \leq x \leq 1$, $-2 \leq \dot{x} \leq 2$. x denotes the horizontal position of the puck in Figure 12. The action $u = a$ is one-dimensional and represents the horizontal force applied to the puck. Actions are constrained such that $-4 \leq a \leq 4$. The goal region is the rectangle $0.5 \leq x \leq 0.7$, $-0.1 \leq \dot{x} \leq 0.1$. The surface upon which the puck slides has the following height as a function of x:

$$H(x) = \begin{cases} x^2 + x & \text{if } x < 0 \\ x/\sqrt{1 + 5x^2} & \text{if } x \geq 0 \end{cases} \tag{22}$$

The puck's dynamics are given by:

$$\ddot{x} = \frac{a}{M\sqrt{1 + (H'(x))^2}} - \frac{gH'(x)}{1 + (H'(x))^2} \tag{23}$$

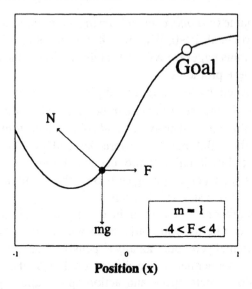

Figure 12. A frictionless puck acted on by gravity and a horizontal thruster. The puck must get to the goal as quickly as possible. There are bounds on the maximum thrust.

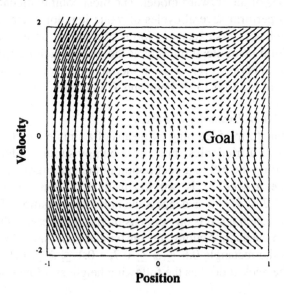

Figure 13. The state transition diagram for a puck that constantly thrusts right with maximum thrust.

where $M = 1$ and $g = 9.81$. This equation is integrated using:

$$x(t + 1) = x(t) + h\dot{x}(t) + \tfrac{1}{2}h^2\ddot{x}(t)$$
$$\dot{x}(t + 1) = \dot{x}(t) + h\ddot{x}(t)$$

(24)

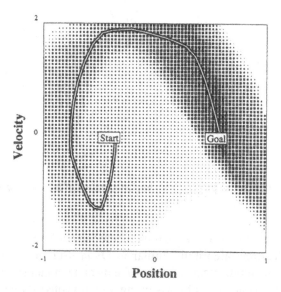

Figure 14. The minimum-time path from start to goal for the puck on the hill. The optimal value function is shown by the background dots. The shorter the time to goal, the larger the black dot. Notice the discontinuity at the escape velocity.

where $h = 0.01$ is the simulation time step.

Because of gravity, there is a region near the center of the hill at which the maximum rightward thrust is insufficient to accelerate up the slope. If the goal region is at the hill-top, a strategy that proceeded by greedily choosing actions to thrust towards the goal would get stuck. This is made clearer in Figure 13, a *state transition diagram*. The puck's state has two components, the position and velocity. The hairs show the next state of the puck if it were to thrust rightwards with the maximum legal force of 4 Newtons for 0.01s. At the center of state-space, even when this thrust is applied, the puck velocity decreases and it eventually slides leftwards. The optimal solution for the puck task, depicted in Figure 14, is to initially thrust away from the goal, gaining negative velocity, until it is on the far left of the diagram. Then it thrusts hard right, to build up sufficient energy to reach the top of the hill.

We explored two implementations of adaptive controllers, one of which used lazy learning techniques.

- **Implementation 1 (Grid Based): Conventional Discretization.** This used the conventional reinforcement learning strategy of discretizing state space into a grid of 60×60 cells for the forward model and value function. The reinforcement learning algorithm was chosen to be as efficient as possible (i.e., in terms of data needed for convergence) given that we were working with a fixed discretization. All transitions between cells

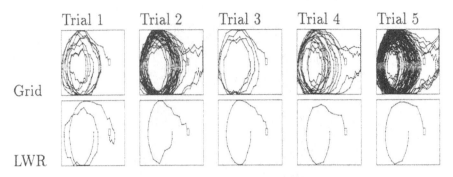

Figure 15. The first five trials for both implementations of the puck controller.

experienced by the system were remembered in a discrete state transition model. A learning algorithm similar to Dyna (Sutton 1990) was used with full value iteration carried out on the discrete model every time-step. Exploration was achieved by assuming any unvisited state had a future cost of zero. The action, which is one-dimensional, was discretized to five levels: $\{-4N, -2N, 0N, 2N, 4N\}$.

- **Implementation 2 (LWR): Lazy Forward Model.** The second implementation was the same as the first, except that transitions between cells were filled in by predictions from a locally weighted regression forward model $\mathbf{x}(t+1) = \hat{\mathbf{f}}(\mathbf{x}(t), \mathbf{u}(t))$. Thus, unlike implementation 1, many discrete transitions that had not been physically experienced were stored in the transition table by extrapolation from the actual experiences. Also, the lazy model supported a higher resolution representation in areas where many experiences had been collected. The value function was represented by a table in both implementations.

The experimental domain is a simple one, but its empirical behavior demonstrates an important point. A lazy forward model in combination with value iteration can dramatically reduce the amount of actual data needed during learning. The graphs of the first five trajectories of the two experiments are shown in Figure 15. The steps per trial for both implementations are shown in Figure 16. The best possible number of steps per trial is 23. The implementation using the locally weighted regression forward model learns much faster in terms of trials than the implementation using the grid. The lazy model based implementation also requires approximately two orders of magnitude fewer steps in order to reach optimal performance. For example, after trial 150 the grid based implementation has executed 26297 total steps more than the optimal required when all trials are combined, while the lazy forward model based implementation has executed only 260 suboptimal steps.

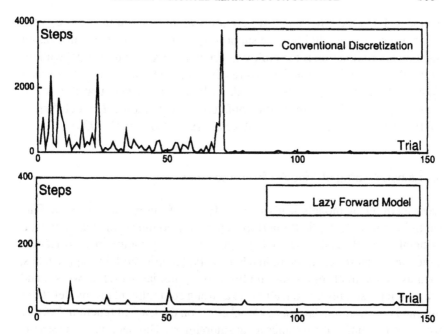

Figure 16. Top: Steps per trial for a grid based forward model. Bottom: Steps per trial for an LWR based forward model. Note the difference in vertical scales.

Since we did not include any random noise in this simulation these numbers are deterministic. The spikes in Figure 16 are due to the severe nonlinearity of this problem, where small errors in the policy may lead to the puck failing to have enough energy to get to the goal. In this case the puck slides back down and must perform another "orbit" of the start point in state space before reaching the goal. The lack of random sensor or actuator noise makes the problem unrealistically easy for both approaches. We expect the benefits of a lazy model over the standard grid model to carry over to the stochastic case.

The computational costs of this kind of control are considerable. Although it is not necessary to gather data from every part of the state space when generalization occurs with a model, the simple form of value iteration requires a multidimensional discretization for computing the value function. Several researchers are investigating methods for reducing the cost of value iteration when a model has been learned (e.g. (Moore 1991b; Mahadevan 1992; Atkeson 1994)).

3.6.2. *Exploration*
The approach we have described does not explicitly explore. If the learned model contains serious errors, a part of state space that wrongly looks unrewarding will never be visited by the real system, so the model will never

be updated. On the other hand, we do not want the system to explore every part of state space explicitly – the supposed advantage of lazy learning based function approximation is the ability to generalize parts of the model without explicitly performing an action. To resolve this dilemma, a number of useful exploration heuristics can be used, all based on the idea that it is worth exploring only where there is little confidence in the empirical model (Sutton 1990; Kaelbling 1993; Moore and Atkeson 1993; Cohn et al. 1995).

4. Lazy Learning of Models: Pros and Cons

Lazy learning of models leads to new forms of autonomous control. The control algorithms explicitly perform empirical nonlinear modeling as well as simultaneously designing policies, without a strong commitment to a model structure or controller structure in advance. Parametric modeling approaches, such as polynomial regression, multi-layer sigmoidal neural networks, and projection pursuit regression, all make a strong commitment to a model structure, and new training data has a global effect on the learned function. Locally weighted learning only assumes local smoothness. This section discusses the strengths and weaknesses of a local and lazy modeling approach in the context of control. (Stanfill and Waltz 1986) provide a similar discussion for lazy approaches to classification.

4.1. *Benefits of Lazy Learning of Models*

- **Automatic, empirical, local linear models.** Locally weighted linear regression returns a local linear map. It performs the job of an engineer who is trying to empirically linearize the system around a region of interest. It is not difficult for neural net representations to provide a local linear map too, but other approximators such as straightforward nearest neighbor or the original version of CMAC (Albus 1981; Miller 1989) are less reliable in their estimation of local gradients because predicted surfaces are not smooth. Additionally, if the input data distribution is not too non-uniform, it can be shown that the linearizations returned by locally weighted learning accomplish a low-bias estimate of the true gradient with fewer data points than required for a low-bias prediction of a query (Hastie and Loader 1993).
- **Automatic confidence estimations.** Locally weighted regression can also be modified to return a confidence interval along with its prediction. This can be done heuristically with the local density of the data providing an uncertainty estimate (Moore 1991a) or by making sensible statistical assumptions (Schaal and Atkeson 1994b; Cohn et al. 1995).

In either case, this has been shown empirically to dramatically reduce the amount of exploration needed when the uncertainty estimates guide the experiment design. The cost of estimating uncertainty with locally weighted methods is small. Nonlinear parametric representations such as multi-layer sigmoidal neural networks can also be adapted to return confidence intervals (MacKay 1992; Pomerleau 1994), but approximations are required, and the computational cost is larger. Worse, parametric models (e.g., global polynomial regression) that predict confidence statistically are typically assuming that the true world can be perfectly modeled by at least one set of parameter values. If this assumption is violated, then the confidence intervals are difficult to interpret.

- **Adding new data to a lazy model is cheap.** For a lazy model adding a new data point means simply inserting it into the data base.

- **One-shot learning.** Lazy models do not need to be repeatedly exposed to the same data to learn it. A consequence of this rapid learning is that errors are not repeated and can be eliminated much more quickly than approaches that incrementally update parameters. Nonlinear parametric models can be trained by 1) exposing the model to a new data point only once (e.g., (Jordan and Jacobs 1990; Kuperstein 1988)), or 2) by storing the data in a database and cycling through the training data repeatedly. In case 1, much more data must be collected, since the training effect of each data point is small. This leads to slower learning, since real robot movements take time, and to increased wear-and-tear on the robot or industrial process that is to be controlled. In case 2, a lazy learning approach has been adopted, and one must then evaluate the relative benefits of complex and simple local models.

- **Non-linear, yet no danger of local minima in function approximation.** Locally weighted regression can fit a wide range of complex non-linear functions, and finds the best fit directly, without requiring any gradient descent. There are no dangers of the model learner becoming stuck in a local optimum. In contrast, training nonlinear parametric models can get stuck in local minima.

However, some of the control law design algorithms we have surveyed can become stuck (Moore 1992; Jordan and Rumelhart 1992). The inverse-model method can become stuck with non-monotonic or highly noisy systems. The shifting setpoint algorithm can become stuck in principle, although this has not yet occurred in practice.

- **Avoids interference.** Lazy modeling is insensitive to what task it is currently learning or if the data distribution changes. In contrast, nonlinear parametric models trained incrementally with gradient descent eventually forget old experiences and concentrate representational power on new experiences.

4.2. *Drawbacks of Lazy Learning of Models*

Here we consider the disadvantages of lazy learning that may be encountered under some circumstances, and we also point out promising directions for addressing them.

- **Lookup costs increase with the amount of training data.** Memory and computation costs increase with the amount of data. Memory costs increase linearly with the amount of data, and are not generally a problem. Any algorithm that avoids storing redundant data would greatly reduce the amount of memory needed, and one can also discard data, perhaps selected according to predictive usefulness, redundancy, or age (Atkeson et al. 1997).

  Computational costs are more serious. For a fixed amount of computation, a single processor can process a limited number of training data points. There are several solutions to this problem (Atkeson et al. 1997): The database can be structured so that the most relevant data points are accessed first, or so that close approximations to the output predicted by locally weighted regression can be obtained without explicitly visiting every point in the database. There are a surprisingly large number of algorithms available for doing this, mostly based on k-d trees (Preparata and Shamos 1985; Omohundro 1987; Moore 1990; Grosse 1989; Quinlan 1993; Omohundro 1991; Deng and Moore 1995).

- **Is the curse of dimensionality a problem for lazy learning for control?** The curse of dimensionality is the exponential dependence of needed resources on dimensionality found in many learning and planning approaches. The methods we have discussed so far can handle a wide class of problems. On the other hand, it is well known that, without strong constraints on the class of functions being approximated, learning with many input dimensions will not successfully approximate a particular function over the entire space of potential inputs unless the data set is unrealistically large.

  This is an apparently serious problem for multivariate control using locally weighted learning, and raises the question as to why the examples given in this paper worked. Happily, it is actually quite difficult to think of useful tasks that *require* the system to have an accurate model over the entire input space (Albus 1981). Indeed, for a robot of more than, say, eight degrees of freedom, it will not be possible for it to get into every significantly different configuration even once in its entire lifetime.

Many tasks require high accuracy only in low-dimensional manifolds of input space or thin slices around those manifolds. In some cases these may be clumps around the desired goal value of stationary tasks. For example, in devil sticking the robot needs to gain highly accurate expertise only in the vicinity of stable juggling patterns. Another common task involves the system spending most of its life traveling along a number of important trajectories, "highways", through state space, in which case expertise need only be clustered in these regions. In general, the curse of dimensionality may not be dangerous for *tasks* whose solutions lie in a low-dimensional manifold or a thin slice, even if the number of state variables and control inputs is several times larger.

In any event we expect the performance of locally weighted regression to be as good as any other method as the dimensionality of the problem increases, as locally weighted learning can become global if necessary to emulate global models, and can become global or local in particular directions to emulate projection pursuit models (e.g., the distance function can be set to choose a projection direction, for example, but for multiple projection directions multiple distance functions must be used in additive locally weighted fits) (Friedman and Stuetzle 1981). We expect locally weighted learning to degrade gracefully as the problem dimensionality increases.

- **Lazy learning depends on having good representations already selected.** Good representational choices (i.e., choices of the elements of the state and control vectors, etc.) can dramatically speed up learning or make learning possible at all. Feature selection and scaling algorithms are a crude form of choosing new representations (Atkeson et al. 1997). However, we have not solved the representation problem, and locally weighted learning and all other machine learning approaches depend on prior representational decisions.

5. Conclusions

This paper has explored methods for using lazy learning to learn task models for control, emphasizing how forward and inverse learned models can be used. The implementations all used lazy models. The last section discussed in more detail the pros and cons of lazy learning as the specific choice of model learner.

There is little doubt that these advances can be converted into general purpose software packages for the benefit of robotics and process control. But it should also be understood that we are still a considerable way from full autonomy. A human programmer has to decide what the state and action variables are for a problem, how the task should be specified, and what class of control task it is. The engineering of real-time systems, sensors and actuators is still required. A human must take responsibility for safety and supervision of the system. Thus, at this stage, if we are given a problem, the relative effectiveness of learning control, measured as the proportion of human effort eliminated, is heavily dependent on problem-specific issues.

Appendix A: Simple Linear Quadratic Regulator derivation

This appendix provides a simplified, self-contained introduction to LQR control for readers who wish to understand the ideas behind Equations 17 and 18. Assume a scalar state and action, and assume that the desired state and action are zero ($x_d = u_d = 0$). Assume linear dynamics:

$$x_{k+1} = ax_k + bu_k \tag{25}$$

where a and b are constants. Define $V_k^*(x)$ to be the minimum possible sum of future costs, starting from state x, assuming we are at time-step k. Assume the system stops at time $k = N$, and the stopping cost is qx_N^2. For all other steps (i.e., $k < N$) the cost is $qx_k^2 + ru_k^2$.

$$V_k^*(x) = \sum_{j=k}^{N-1} \left(qx_j^2 + ru_j^2\right) + qx_N^2 \tag{26}$$

assuming $u_k, u_{k+1}, \ldots, u_{N-1}$ chosen optimally. $V_k^*(x)$ can be defined inductively:

$$V_N^*(x) = qx_N^2 \tag{27}$$

$$V_k^*(x) = \operatorname*{argmin}_{u_k} \left(qx_k^2 + ru_k^2 + V_{k+1}^*(x_{k+1})\right) \tag{28}$$

by the principal of optimality, which says that your best bet for minimal costs is to minimize over your first step for the cost of that step plus the minimum possible costs of future steps. We will now prove by induction that $V_k^*(x)$ is a quadratic in x, with the quadratic coefficient dependent on k: $V_k^*(x) = p_k x^2$ for some $p_0, p_1, \ldots, p_N$.

- **Base case:** $p_N = q$ from Equation 27.
- **Inductive step:** Assume $V_{k+1}^*(x) = p_{k+1}x^2$; we'll prove $V_k^*(x) = p_k x^2$ for some p_k.

From here on, all that remains is algebra. We begin with Equation 28, in which we replace x_{k+1} with $ax_k + bu_k$ from Equation 25:

$$V_k^*(x) = \operatorname*{argmin}_{u_k} \left(qx_k^2 + ru_k^2 + V_{k+1}^*(ax_k + bu_k) \right) \tag{29}$$

Then we use the inductive assumption $V_{k+1}^*(x) = p_{k+1}x^2$

$$V_k^*(x) = \operatorname*{argmin}_{u_k} \left(qx_k^2 + ru_k^2 + p_{k+1}(ax_k + bu_k)^2 \right) \tag{30}$$

Next we simplify with three new variables, α, β, γ:

$$V_k^*(x) = \operatorname*{argmin}_{u_k} \left(\alpha x_k^2 + 2\beta x_k u_k + \gamma u_k^2 \right) \qquad \text{where} \tag{31}$$

$$\alpha = q + p_{k+1}a^2 \tag{32}$$
$$\beta = p_{k+1}ab \tag{33}$$
$$\gamma = r + p_{k+1}b^2 \tag{34}$$

To minimize Equation 31 with respect to u we differentiate and set to zero the bracketed expression giving:

$$2\beta x + 2\gamma u_k^* = 0 \tag{35}$$

where u_k^* is the optimal action. Thus

$$u_k^* = -(\beta/\gamma)x_k \tag{36}$$

Since u_k^* minimizes Equation 31 we have

$$V_k^*(x) = \alpha x^2 + 2\beta x u_k^* + \gamma (u_k^*)^2 \tag{37}$$

So from Equation 36

$$
\begin{aligned}
V_k^*(x) &= \alpha x^2 + 2\beta x(-\beta/\gamma)x + \gamma(-\beta/\gamma)^2 x^2 \\
&= \left(\alpha - 2\beta^2/\gamma + \beta^2/\gamma \right) x^2 = \left(\alpha - \beta^2/\gamma \right) x^2
\end{aligned} \tag{38}
$$

so that we have shown $V_k^*(x) = p_k x^2$ where

$$p_k = \left(\alpha - \beta^2/\gamma \right) \qquad (39)$$

Inserting back the substitutions of Equations 32, 33, 34 into Equations 36 and 39:

$$u_k^* = \left(\frac{-p_{k+1}ab}{r + p_{k+1}b^2} \right) x_k \qquad (40)$$

$$V_k^*(x) = p_k x^2 \ \text{ where } p_k = q + a^2 p_{k+1} \left(1 - \frac{p_{k+1}b^2}{r + p_{k+1}b^2} \right) \qquad (41)$$

Assuming that there are $N-k$ steps remaining, to compute the cost-to-go from state x we set $p := q$ and then iterate the assignment $p := q + a^2 p(1 - \frac{pb^2}{r+pb^2})$ a total of $N-k$ times. As $N-k$ becomes large p converges to a constant value (not proven here). This gives the cost-to-go value function of px^2, assuming that the system will run forever.

6. Acknowledgments

Support for C. Atkeson and S. Schaal was provided by the ATR Human Information Processing Research Laboratories. Support for C. Atkeson was provided under Air Force Office of Scientific Research grant F49-6209410362, and by a National Science Foundation Presidential Young Investigator Award. Support for S. Schaal was provided by the German Scholarship Foundation and the Alexander von Humboldt Foundation. Support for A. Moore was provided by the U.K. Science and Engineering Research Council, NSF Research Initiation Award # IRI-9409912, and a Research Gift from the 3M Corporation.

References

Aha, D. W. & Salzberg, S. L. (1993). Learning to catch: Applying nearest neighbor algorithms to dynamic control tasks. In *Proceedings of the Fourth International Workshop on Artificial Intelligence and Statistics*, pp. 363–368, Ft. Lauderdale, FL.

Albus, J. S. (1981). *Brains, Behaviour and Robotics*. BYTE Books, McGraw-Hill.

Atkeson, C. G. (1990). Using local models to control movement. In Touretzky, D. S. (ed.), *Advances in Neural Information Processing Systems 2*, pp. 316–323. Morgan Kaufmann, San Mateo, CA.

Atkeson, C. G. (1994). Using local trajectory optimizers to speed up global optimization in dynamic programming. In Hanson, S. J., Cowan, J. D. & Giles, C. L. (eds.), *Advances in Neural Information Processing Systems 6*, pp. 663–670. Morgan Kaufmann, San Mateo, CA.

Atkeson, C. G., Moore, A. W. & Schaal, S. (1997). Locally weighted learning. *Artificial Intelligence Review*, this issue.

Barto, A. G., Sutton, R. S. & Watkins, C. J. C. H. (1990). Learning and Sequential Decision Making. In Gabriel, M. & Moore, J. W. (eds.), *Learning and Computational Neuroscience*, pp. 539–602. MIT Press, Cambridge, MA.

Barto, A. G., Bradtke, S. J. & Singh, S. P. (1995). Learning to act using real-time dynamic programming. *Artificial Intelligence* **72**(1): 81–138.

Bellman, R. E. (1957). *Dynamic Programming*. Princeton University Press, Princeton, NJ.

Bertsekas, D. P. & Tsitsiklis, J. N. (1989). *Parallel and Distributed Computation*. Prentice Hall.

Cannon, R. H. (1967). *Dynamics of Physical Systems*. McGraw-Hill.

Cohn, D. A., Ghahramani, Z. & Jordan, M. I. (1995). Active learning with statistical models. In Tesauro, G., Touretzky, D. & Leen, T. (eds.), *Advances in Neural Information Processing Systems 7*. MIT Press.

Connell, M. E. & Utgoff, P. E. (1987). Learning to control a dynamic physical system. In *Sixth National Conference on Artificial Intelligence*, pp. 456–460, Seattle, WA. Morgan Kaufmann, San Mateo, CA.

Conte, S. D. & De Boor, C. (1980). *Elementary Numerical Analysis*, McGraw Hill.

Deng, K. & Moore, A. W. (1995). Multiresolution Instance-based Learning. In *Proceedings of the International Joint Conference on Artificial Intelligence*, pp. 1233–1239. Morgan Kaufmann.

Friedman, J. H. & Stuetzle, W. (1981). Projection Pursuit Regression. *Journal of the American Statistical Association*, **76**(376): 817–823.

Grosse, E. (1989). LOESS: Multivariate Smoothing by Moving Least Squares. In C. K. Chul, L. L. S. & Ward, J. D. (eds.), *Approximation Theory VI*. Academic Press.

Hastie, T. & Loader, C. (1993). Local regression: Automatic kernel carpentry. *Statistical Science* **8**(2): 120–143.

Jordan, M. I. & Jacobs, R. A. (1990). Learning to control an unstable system with forward modeling. In Touretzky, D. (ed.), *Advances in Neural Information Processing Systems 2*, pp. 324–331. Morgan Kaufmann, San Mateo, CA.

Jordan, M. I. & Rumelhart, D. E. (1992). Forward Models: Supervised Learning with a Distal Teacher. *Cognitive Science* **16**: 307–354.

Kaelbling, L. P. (1993). *Learning in Embedded Systems*. MIT Press, Cambridge, MA.

Kuperstein, M. (1988). Neural Model of Adaptive Hand-Eye Coordination for Single Postures. *Science* **239**: 1308–3111.

MacKay, D. J. C. (1992). Bayesian Model Comparison and Backprop Nets. In Moody, J. E., Hanson, S. J. & Lippman, R. P. (eds.), *Advances in Neural Information Processing Systems 4*, pp. 839–846. Morgan Kaufmann, San Mateo, CA.

Mahadevan, S. (1992). Enhancing Transfer in Reinforcement Learning by Building Stochastic Models of Robot Actions. In *Machine Learning: Proceedings of the Ninth International Conference*, pp. 290–299. Morgan Kaufmann.

Maron, O. & Moore, A. (1994). Hoeffding Races: Accelerating Model Selection Search for Classification and Function Approximation. In *Advances in Neural Information Processing Systems 6*, pp. 59–66. Morgan Kaufmann, San Mateo, CA.

McCallum, R. A. (1995). Instance-based utile distinctions for reinforcement learning with hidden state. In Prieditis and Russell (1995), pp. 387–395.

Mel, B. W. (1989). MURPHY: A Connectionist Approach to Vision-Based Robot Motion Planning. Technical Report CCSR-89-17A, University of Illinois at Urbana-Champaign.

Miller, W. T. (1989). Real-Time Application of Neural Networks for Sensor-Based Control of Robots with Vision. *IEEE Transactions on Systems, Man and Cybernetics* **19**(4): 825–831.

Moore, A. W. (1990). Acquisition of Dynamic Control Knowledge for a Robotic Manipulator. In *Proceedings of the 7th International Conference on Machine Learning*, pp. 244–252. Morgan Kaufmann.

Moore, A. W. (1991a). Knowledge of Knowledge and Intelligent Experimentation for Learning Control. In *Proceedings of the 1991 Seattle International Joint Conference on Neural Networks.*

Moore, A. W. (1991b). Variable Resolution Dynamic Programming: Efficiently Learning Action Maps in Multivariate Real-valued State-spaces. In Birnbaum, L. & Collins, G. (eds.), *Machine Learning: Proceedings of the Eighth International Workshop*, pp. 333–337. Morgan Kaufmann.

Moore, A. W. (1992). Fast, Robust Adaptive Control by Learning only Forward Models. In Moody, J. E., Hanson, S. J. & Lippman, R. P. (eds.), *Advances in Neural Information Processing Systems 4*, pp. 571–578. Morgan Kaufmann, San Mateo, CA.

Moore, A. W. & Atkeson, C. G. (1993). Prioritized Sweeping: Reinforcement Learning with Less Data and Less Real Time. *Machine Learning* **13**: 103–130.

Moore, A. W., Hill, D. J. & Johnson, M. P. (1992). An Empirical Investigation of Brute Force to Choose Features, Smoothers and Function Approximators. In Hanson, S., Judd, S. & Petsche, T. (eds.), *Computational Learning Theory and Natural Learning Systems, Volume 3*. MIT Press.

Moore, A. W. & Lee, M. S. (1994). Efficient Algorithms for Minimizing Cross Validation Error. In *Proceedings of the 11th International Conference on Machine Learning*, pp. 190–198. Morgan Kaufmann.

Moore, A. W. & Schneider, J. (1995). Memory-Based Stochastic Optimization. In *Proceedings of Neural Information Processing Systems Conference.*

Omohundro, S. M. (1987). Efficient Algorithms with Neural Network Behaviour. *Journal of Complex Systems* **1**(2): 273–347.

Omohundro, S. M. (1991). Bumptrees for Efficient Function, Constraint, and Classification Learning. In Lippmann, R. P., Moody, J. E. & Touretzky, D. S. (eds.), *Advances in Neural Information Processing Systems 3*, pp. 693–699. Morgan Kaufmann, San Mateo, CA.

Ortega, J. M. & Rheinboldt, W. C. (1970). *Iterative Solution of Nonlinear Equations in Several Variables.* Academic Press.

Peng, J. (1995). Efficient memory-based dynamic programming. In Prieditis and Russell (1995), pp. 438–446.

Peng, J. & Williams, R. J. (1993). Efficient Learning and Planning Within the Dyna Framework. In *Proceedings of the Second International Conference on Simulation of Adaptive Behavior.* MIT Press.

Pomerleau, D. (1994). Reliability estimation for neural network based autonomous driving. *Robotics and Autonomous Systems*, 12.

Preparata, F. P. & Shamos, M. (1985). *Computational Geometry.* Springer-Verlag.

Press, W. H., Teukolsky, S. A., Vetterling, W. T. & Flannery, B. P. (1988). *Numerical Recipes in C.* Cambridge University Press, New York, NY.

Prieditis, A. & Russell, S. (eds.) (1995). *Twelfth International Conference on Machine Learning*, Tahoe City, CA. Morgan Kaufmann, San Mateo, CA.

Quinlan, J. R. (1993). Combining Instance-Based and Model-Based Learning. In *Machine Learning: Proceedings of the Tenth International Conference*, pp. 236–243. Morgan Kaufmann.

Schaal, S. & Atkeson, C. (1994a). Robot Juggling: An Implementation of Memory-based Learning. *Control Systems Magazine* **14**(1): 57–71.

Schaal, S. & Atkeson, C. G. (1994b). Assessing the Quality of Local Linear Models. In Cowan, J. D., Tesauro, G. & Alspector, J. (eds.), *Advances in Neural Information Processing Systems 6*, pp. 160–167. Morgan Kaufmann.

Stanfill, C. & Waltz, D. (1986). Towards Memory-Based Reasoning. *Communications of the ACM* **29**(12): 1213–1228.

Stengel, R. F. (1986). *Stochastic Optimal Control.* John Wiley and Sons.

Sutton, R. S. (1988). Learning to Predict by the Methods of Temporal Differences. *Machine Learning* **3**: 9–44.

Sutton, R. S. (1990). Integrated Architecture for Learning, Planning, and Reacting Based on Approximating Dynamic Programming. In *Proceedings of the 7th International Conference on Machine Learning*, pp. 216–224. Morgan Kaufmann.

Watkins, C. J. C. H. (1989). Learning from Delayed Rewards. PhD. Thesis, King's College, University of Cambridge.

Zografski, Z. (1992). Geometric and neuromorphic learning for nonlinear modeling, control and forecasting. In *Proceedings of the 1992 IEEE International Symposium on Intelligent Control*, pp. 158–163. Glasgow, Scotland. IEEE catalog number 92CH3110-4.

Artificial Intelligence Review **11**: 115–132, 1997.

Voting over Multiple Condensed Nearest Neighbors

ETHEM ALPAYDIN
Department of Computer Engineering, Boğaziçi University, TR-80815 Istanbul, Turkey
E-mail: alpaydin@boun.edu.tr

Abstract. Lazy learning methods like the k-nearest neighbor classifier require storing the whole training set and may be too costly when this set is large. The condensed nearest neighbor classifier incrementally stores a subset of the sample, thus decreasing storage and computation requirements. We propose to train multiple such subsets and take a vote over them, thus combining predictions from a set of concept descriptions. We investigate two voting schemes: simple voting where voters have equal weight and weighted voting where weights depend on classifiers' confidences in their predictions. We consider ways to form such subsets for improved performance: When the training set is small, voting improves performance considerably. If the training set is not small, then voters converge to similar solutions and we do not gain anything by voting. To alleviate this, when the training set is of intermediate size, we use bootstrapping to generate smaller training sets over which we train the voters. When the training set is large, we partition it into smaller, mutually exclusive subsets and then train the voters. Simulation results on six datasets are reported with good results. We give a review of methods for combining multiple learners. The idea of taking a vote over multiple learners can be applied with any type of learning scheme.

Key words: lazy learning, nonparametric estimation, k-nearest neighbor, condensed nearest neighbor, voting

1. Introduction

Lazy learning methods like the k-nearest neighbor classifier estimate directly from a given labelled sample (Duda and Hart 1973). In statistical estimation theory, such techniques are named *nonparametric*. This differs from the *parametric* approaches where a given model is assumed whose parameters are estimated from the given sample (e.g., using maximum likelihood). In many situations, no appropriate parametric model is known or the estimation of parameters may be too costly or not optimal. In such cases, one opts for the nonparametric approach where particular instances or examples are stored as opposed to abstracting general rules.

Methods where response is computed by interpolating from a table of stored patterns is called *instance-based* (Aha et al. 1991) or *memory-based* (Stanfill and Waltz 1986) in the machine learning literature. In statistics, this approach is called *kernel-based density estimation* (Silverman 1986) when one estimates the class-conditional densities for classification and *locally-weighted regression* (Härdle 1990) when one estimates a continuous function. The assumption is that the real world is smooth and that similar inputs give similar outputs or belong to the same class. Thus when giving an output, closest patterns with known outputs are the ones that should be taken into account; see (Hastie and Tibshirani 1990; Chapter 2) for a review of smoothing models.

In this paper, we concentrate on classification where a given input is to be assigned to one of several mutually exclusive classes; extension to continuous function approximation is straightforward. In Section 2, we explain the condensed nearest neighbor classifier that incrementally forms a "sufficient" subset of the training sample. Section 3 advocates forming multiple such subsets and taking a vote over their responses. This approach is empirically justified in Section 4 on six datasets with varying characteristics. In Section 5, a review of related literature on combining multiple learners is given. The final section concludes by pointing out the implications of the current work in a more general setting.

2. Condensed Nearest Neighbor Rule

A main disadvantage of a lazy learner like the k-nearest neighbor classifier is the large memory requirement to store the whole sample. When the sample is large, response time on a sequential computer is also large. To get rid of the redundancy and decrease the number of free parameters, an alternative to abstract, parametric models is an editing procedure that selectively discards the redundant part of the training set. Hart (1968) proposed to minimize the number of stored patterns by storing only a subset of the training set. The basic idea is that patterns in the training set may be very similar and some do not add extra information and thus may be discarded.

We want to find a subset of the sample S that is small and accurate. To choose the best subset $\mathcal{Z}^*$, out of the $2^{|S|}$ possible subsets, we define the error measure given in Equation (1) using regularization theory:

$$\mathcal{Z}^* = \arg\min_{\mathcal{Z}} E(\mathcal{Z})$$

$$E(\mathcal{Z}) = \sum_{x \in S} L(x|\mathcal{Z}) + \gamma |\mathcal{Z}| \qquad (1)$$

$$L(x|\mathcal{Z}) = \begin{cases} 1, & \text{if } \mathcal{D}(z_c, x) = \min_j \mathcal{D}(z_j, x) \text{ and} \\ & \text{class}(x) \neq \text{class}(z_c); \\ 0, & \text{otherwise.} \end{cases}$$

$z_c \in Z$ is the closest stored pattern to $x \in S$ using the distance measure $\mathcal{D}(\cdot)$. $L(x|Z)$ is non-zero when the labels of x and z_c do not match.

According to regularization theory (Vapnik 1995), the solution to a problem can be obtained by combining the data and prior smoothness information. The first term in Equation (1) measures the data-misfit that is due to the error in classification using the 1-NN rule. The second term measures the size of the subset stored and as such defines the smoothness of the class boundary. The nearest neighbor classifier divides the input space in the form of a Voronoi tesselation and the class boundaries are piecewise linear (Preparata and Shamos 1985). As we have more examples, this boundary becomes more ragged and less smooth. The smoothest case is when we have only one example per class where we have linear boundaries between classes. γ is the regularization parameter that indicates the trade-off between these two terms. Equivalently, this is a Bayesian approach that attributes higher prior probabilities to simpler models.

Minimizing Equation (1) is a combinatorial problem and no known polynomial time procedure can solve it to optimality. Though no formal proof is known, we believe this problem to be NP-complete. A computationally simple local search method has been proposed first as Condensed Nearest Neighbor (CNN) (Hart 1968) and then later independently as IB2 (Aha et al. 1991) and Grow and Learn (GAL) (Alpaydın1990). The *consistent subset*, Z, of a sample S, is the set of patterns that can classify all the elements of S correctly using the 1-NN rule. There are usually many consistent subsets – one trivial consistent subset is the set itself. One normally is interested in the *minimal* consistent subset (i.e., the subset with the minimum cardinality) to minimize the cost of storage and computation.

The CNN algorithm is given in Table 1. Starting from an empty stored subset, we pass one by one over the patterns and add a pattern to the subset if it cannot be classified correctly with the already stored subset. This implies that error is more important than size (i.e., $\gamma < 1$ in Equation 1). This method, being a local search, does not guarantee finding the minimal subset and furthermore, different subsets are found when the training set order is changed. Generally passing over the sample a few times is sufficient until no more additions are made when the stored subset classifies all the patterns in the training set. At each pass, on the average, classification accuracy increases and fewer patterns are added to the subset. To make learning even faster, one can stop if the number of added patterns in the last pass is fewer than say, 5%, of the training set.

The classification rule is 1-NN but other nonparametric variants are also possible at the expense of more computation. If the sample is noisy, there is also the possibility of using k-CNN but this may be costlier (Gates 1972). If

Table 1. The Condensed Nearest Neighbor Algorithm (CNN).

```
PROCEDURE CNN(S,D,Z)
BEGIN
Z := {};
REPEAT
        additions:=FALSE;
        FOR all patterns in the training set DO
                Randomly pick x from training set, S
                Find z_c ∈ Z such that D(x, z_c) = min_j D(x, z_j)
                IF class(x) ≠ class(z_c) THEN
                        Z := Z ∪ x;
                        additions:=TRUE
                END IF
        END FOR
UNTIL NOT(additions);
END CNN;
```

$k = 2i + 1$, then for the correct classification of a new pattern, at least $i + 1$ of its nearest neighbors must be from the correct pattern class and if this is not true, in the worst case, it would have to be added $i + 1$ times to Z.

Gates (1972) proposed the reduced nearest neighbor (RNN) rule that aims to further reduce the stored subset. With RNN, after having applied CNN, for each element of the subset we check if its removal causes an error in the training set and we accept the removal if it does not. GAL (Alpaydın 1990) also has a "sleep" mode where an element of the stored subset is removed if the closest stored element is also of the same class. In both approaches, it is concluded that the small saving in memory is not worth the extra computation.

3. Voting over Multiple Learners

The problem with this approach to determining a consistent subset is that when the order of the training set is changed, the search trajectory changes and one can converge to a different local minimum storing a different subset. These subsets, although they all classify all the patterns in the training set correctly, perform differently on the test set. A method proposed previously (Alpaydın 1991) is to train multiple such subsets and then take a vote over their responses. This method is not limited to lazy learning methods but can be generalized to any kind of learning scheme. A review of methods for combining multiple learners is given in Section 5.

Let us say we have m classifiers and n classes. We denote by d_{ji}, the estimate of classifier j for class i, computed for example using a lazy learning method. In voting, we combine votes for classes through a weighted sum and then assign the input to the class c receiving the maximum vote:

$$r_i = \sum_{j=1}^{m} d_{ji}\beta_j \tag{2}$$

$$c = \arg \max_{i=1}^{n} [r_i] \tag{3}$$

The weights are nonnegative and sum up to unity: $\beta_j \geq 0$, $\sum_{j=1}^{m} \beta_j = 1$. Unless there is any a priori reason to favor one voter over another, weights are taken as equal: $\beta_j = 1/m$. This is *simple voting*.

There is a method that can be used to determine the weights β_j easily for *weighted voting*: the outputs of most classifiers can be converted to probabilities. Then if, for classifier j, e is the most probable class and f is the next most probable, one can compute:

$$\alpha_j = p_j(e|x) - p_j(f|x) \tag{4}$$

which, after normalization can be used as weights: $\beta_j = \alpha_j / \sum_{l=1}^{m} \alpha_l$. If $\alpha_j \approx 1$, classifier j is very "certain"; as x gets closer to the boundary then $p_j(e|x) \approx p_j(f|x)$ and the difference gets closer to zero and classifier j is less certain. Thus certain classifiers will have more say in the final output than the classifiers who are not that sure.

In the case of CNN, we use a simple method to compute α_j by just looking at two neighbors. If $z_{j,[1]}$ is the closest pattern to x in $\mathcal{Z}_j$ and $z_{j,[2]}$ is the second closest, we have:

$$\alpha_j = \begin{cases} 1, & \text{if } \text{class}(x_{j,[1]}) = \text{class}(x_{j,[2]}); \\ \frac{\mathcal{D}(x,z_{j,[2]}) - \mathcal{D}(x,z_{j,[1]})}{\mathcal{D}(x,z_{j,[2]})}, & \text{otherwise.} \end{cases} \tag{5}$$

where $\mathcal{D}(\cdot)$ is the distance measure. If the two neighbors both belong to the same class, the classifier is very certain. Otherwise its certainty decreases as the input gets closer to the boundary which is halfway between them.

We show in the Appendix that error decreases through voting with an increasing number of uncorrelated voters. Intuitively what is happening is that each particular subset is generating a different noisy approximation to the real class boundary and the averaging process is smoothing over the noise (Figure 1). Each particular learner falls into a different (local) minimum and they perform poorly in different regions of the input space and their error terms will not be strongly correlated. As the number of voters increase, this

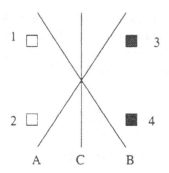

Figure 1. Patterns 1 and 2 belong to one class and 3 and 4 to the second one. One run of CNN can choose 1 and 4 which define the discriminant A and another CNN can choose 2 and 3 that define the discriminant B. Both are minimal consistent subsets. C is the average of A and B and is the right discriminant. Adapted from (Perrone 1993).

assumption of independence breaks down and voters become more similar and there is nothing to be gained by combining learners unless measures are taken to force them to be dissimilar.

4. Simulation Results

4.1 *Datasets*

To validate the advantage of voting over multiple CNN, we have compared it on six datasets with CNN and 1-NN. The properties of the datasets are given in Table 2. OCR is a handwritten digit database (Guyon et al. 1989). Others are available from the UCI Repository (Murphy 1994). In the OCR, VOWEL, and THYROID datasets, the training and test sets are separated. In others, we chose small training set sizes to prevent NN from having too large accuracy, thus leaving space for improvement. Euclidean distance is used as the distance metric; the WINE and THYROID databases are z-transformed before training (i.e., to normalize the numeric attributes such that all have zero mean and unit variance). 1-NN and 1-CNN are used in all datasets except VOWEL, where 7-NN and 7-CNN are used. This optimal k is chosen by 2-fold cross validation from among $\{1, 3, 5, 7, 9\}$. At each run of the CNN, the training set is scanned in a different order to get a new subset. Reported values are average and standard deviations of ten independent runs.

4.2 *First comparison*

We applied nearest neighbor (NN), condensed nearest neighbor (CNN) and voting to all six datasets. Both simple and weighted voting are used with

Table 2. Properties of the datasets used.

	Number of features	Number of classes	Number of training examples	Number of test examples
OCR	256	10	600	600
IRIS	4	3	15	135
WINE	13	3	100	78
VOWEL	10	11	528	462
THYROID	21	3	3,772	3,428
GLASS	9	7	100	114

Table 3. Accuracy results of applying nearest neighbor (NN), condensed nearest neighbor (CNN) and simple and weighted voting over three voters are given. Percentage of training stored by CNN is also given to show the gain in memory.

	NN	CNN (% of training set stored by CNN)	Voting		NN on union
			Simple	Weighted	
OCR	93.17	90.08 (0.20)	91.95	93.67	92.42
IRIS	91.85	91.41 (0.29)	92.67	94.00	92.22
WINE	94.87	93.21 (0.14)	93.85	95.00	93.97
VOWEL	60.17	51.62 (0.67)	56.56	55.97	57.14
THYROID	93.14	90.95 (0.17)	91.63	92.23	92.55
GLASS	71.93	69.82 (0.57)	70.00	71.67	71.40

various numbers of voters. Another way to combine the subsets found by multiple CNN is by applying NN to the union of subsets chosen by multiple CNN. Comparing the results of voting with the performance on the union allows us to highlight whether it is the voting process or the number of instances that increase the performance. However, this union approach can still be considered a multiple learner scheme because we run CNN multiple times as opposed to just once. This can only be used with a method like k-NN where effects are local; one cannot for example train multiple multi-layer perceptrons and combine all hidden units together as one big hidden layer and accept any improvement.

By taking a vote over as few as three CNN subsets, in three out of six datasets, although one collectively stores a *subset* of the training set, one achieves higher classification accuracy than the nearest neighbor, where the whole training set is stored (Table 3). In GLASS and THYROID, with three voters we also get better results by partitioning the dataset, as described in Section 4.3. We also note that voting is better than using NN on the union, showing that the performance benefit is not due to the larger number of stored

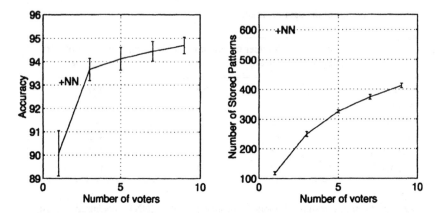

Figure 2. Average classification accuracy on the OCR dataset with weighted voting and the number of stored patterns stored as a function of the number of voters. For comparison, classification accuracy and the number of stored patterns are marked when NN is used over the whole training set.

patterns but rather to *the way predictions are combined* from a set of concept descriptions. Generally, weighted voting is better than simple voting.

As can be seen in Figure 2 for the case of weighted voting on the OCR database, when the number of voters increase, not only the average classification accuracy goes higher but the variance also decreases. This indicates better generalization and is the clear advantage of voting. Complete results are given in Table 4. Results for the IRIS and WINE datasets are similar and are omitted.

When one increases the number of voting subsets, after a certain number, new subsets do not contribute much. Whether an additional subset pays off the additional complexity and memory is a trade-off that needs to be resolved depending on the particular application at hand.

In three datasets, VOWEL, THYROID, and GLASS, we do not seem to gain anything by voting. The VOWEL database defines a quite difficult problem and is very noisy; the optimal k is 7. The result with 7-NN is the highest achieved and is better than all reported in the UCI Repository for that dataset (e.g., the multi layer perceptron gives 51.0). This is most probably due to the fact that each vowel sound is coded using only ten attributes and much information is lost in the process.

4.3 *Multiple training subsets*

In the case of the THYROID and GLASS datasets, the problem seems to be the large training set. It has been pointed out before that voting averages over noisy discriminants. As the training set gets larger, the variance of an

Table 4. Results on the OCR dataset with nearest neighbor classifier (NN) and condensed nearest neighbor classifier (CNN). Values are average, standard deviation over ten independent runs. Results with simple and weighted voting over multiple condensed 2-nearest neighbor classifiers are also given. Results on the IRIS and WINE datasets are similar.

Method	Accuracy	Patterns	Epochs
NN	93.17, 0.00	600.00, 0.00	1.00, 0.00
CNN	90.08, 0.97	117.70, 5.25	2.80, 0.63

| Number of voters | Accuracy | | | Patterns |
	Simple	Weighted	Union	
3	91.95, 0.78	93.67, 0.48	92.42, 0.64	250.40, 8.54
5	93.23, 0.55	94.12, 0.49	92.77, 0.53	325.50, 5.02
7	93.38, 0.50	94.45, 0.42	93.02, 0.30	373.50, 8.07
9	93.53, 0.53	94.70, 0.35	93.05, 0.16	412.10, 7.48

estimator decreases and the voters become more similar. This has been shown empirically for the case of linear regression by Meir (1994). To test this, we ran CNN on mutually exclusive subsets of the THYROID dataset while always testing on the same test set. As can be seen in Figure 3, as the training set gets larger, although classification accuracy on the test set increases, variance decreases indicating that the subsets become more similar.

Having multiple learners only make sense when they differ so that they fail under *different* circumstances. So with m voters, the training set is *partitioned* into m and a separate CNN is trained on each part. Subset sizes are as given in Figure 3. Voting over these we get better results than what we get when all are trained on the same large training set. The large difference is noticeable in the comparitive results given in Figure 4. The complete results with partitioning are given in Table 5.

We also use this approach on the GLASS dataset where the training set contains 100 patterns. When we use three voters, each voter has 33 patterns to be trained on and, with simple voting, we get 72.2%, which is higher than that achieved by the previous scheme and 1-NN on the whole training set. However if we partition the training set for example into five, each subset contains only 20 patterns and classification accuracy is low and gets lower as the number of voters is increased.

If the training set is not large enough to allow partitioning, one can use *bootstrap* which involves generating new datasets from one original dataset by sampling randomly *with* replacement (Perrone 1993) (LeBlanc and Tibshirani

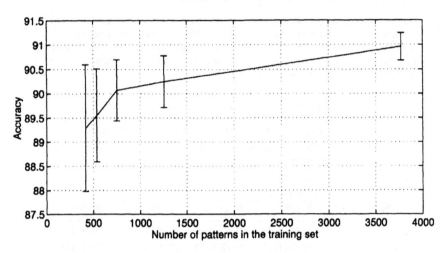

Figure 3. Average classification accuracy on the THYROID dataset with CNN as a function of the number of the training samples. The partitioning is into 9, 7, 5, 3, and 1.

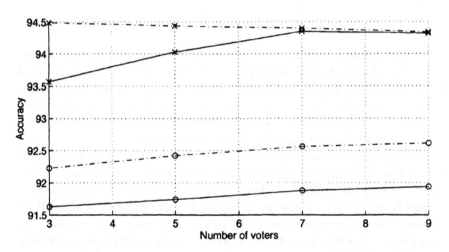

Figure 4. Comparison of averages on the THYROID dataset when the voters are trained on the entire training set ('o') vs. its partitions ('x') with simple (continuous) and weighted (dashed) voting.

1994). These new datasets can then be used to generate multiple CNN subsets. With the GLASS dataset, we used bootstrapping to generate samples of size 50 from a training set of 100 patterns. For more than three voters, bootstrapping worked better than partitioning. Results are given in Table 6. Especially with 7 and 9 voters, these results are higher than those achieved by applying CNN on the entire training set and also on its partitions.

Table 5. Complete results on the THYROID dataset. Partitioning is used when taking a vote.

Method	Accuracy	Patterns	Epochs
NN	93.14, 0.00	3,772.00, 0.00	1.00, 0.00
CNN	90.95, 0.24	625.30, 7.69	3.60, 0.70

| | Accuracy | | | |
Number of voters	Simple	Weighted	Union	Patterns
3	93.57, 0.19	94.49, 0.13	90.25, 0.53	708.70, 14.36
5	94.03, 0.29	94.44, 0.09	89.48, 0.44	738.50, 10.84
7	94.35, 0.15	94.40, 0.11	89.11, 0.28	776.30, 14.88
9	94.32, 0.14	94.34, 0.07	89.13, 0.36	792.50, 13.85

Table 6. Results on the GLASS dataset.

Method	Accuracy	Patterns	Epochs
NN	71.93, 0.00	100.00, 0.00	1.00, 0.00
CNN	69.82, 0.94	57.10, 3.11	2.30, 0.48

| | Accuracy | | | |
Number of voters	Simple	Weighted	Union	Patterns
3 (partition)	72.19, 1.31	70.53, 2.16	70.00, 1.93	64.30, 1.49
5 (bootstrap)	72.02, 1.96	72.11, 2.44	71.84, 1.52	74.60, 2.12
7 (bootstrap)	74.56, 1.89	73.25, 2.04	71.32, 1.24	84.50, 1.72
9 (bootstrap)	74.12, 1.39	74.30, 1.66	71.67, 0.59	88.60, 1.90

We thus conclude that if the training set is small, the voters converge to sufficiently different solutions, then voting helps. When the training set is of intermediate size, one can use bootstrapping to generate smaller training sets. When the training set is large, each voter can use a separate training set. What makes a training set "small" or "large" is the difficulty of the underlying task depending on several factors (e.g., the variance of noise, the dimensionality of the input, number of classes).

5. Combining Multiple Learners

The simplest way to combine multiple learners is by *voting*, which corresponds to taking a linear combination of the learners. If each voter just indicates the class it thinks the input belongs to, then one can only have *simple voting* where all voters have equal weight. If the voters can also supply information on how much they vote for each class, then these can be converted to certainties and used as weights in a *weighted voting* scheme.

In Section 3, we discussed one way to compute these weights in the case of lazy learning based on distances. A *belief* measure (Xu et al. 1992) or Dempster-Schafer theory can be used for the same purpose (Xu et al. 1992; Rogova 1994). Lincoln and Skrzypek (1990) propose a way to learn the weights in a voting scheme. Model complexities can also be taken into account in a Bayesian framework to make sure that complex models are not given very large weights (Alpaydın 1993). Perrone (1993) gives a number of didactic examples that depict the advantage of voting. He also shows that for minimum square error, when the learners are unbiased and uncorrelated, weights should be inversely proportional to variances (see Appendix). Benediktsson and Swain (1992) propose to use a voting scheme for multisource sensing where data from different sources are integrated based on consensus theory.

It has been shown by Hansen and Salamon (1990) that given independent classifiers with classification accuracy probability higher than 1/2, by taking a majority vote, classification accuracy increases as the number of voting classifiers increase. Mani (1991) has shown that in the case of simple voting, variance decreases as the number of voters increase (see Appendix).

Adapting what Perrone (1993) stated for regression to classification, if we view each learner as a random noise function added to the true class discriminant function and if these noise functions are uncorrelated with zero mean, then the averaging of the individual estimates is like averaging over the noise. In this sense, the voting method is smoothing in the functional space and can be thought of as a regularizer with a smoothness assumption on the true discriminant function.

Wolpert (1992) proposed a method called *stacked generalization* that extends voting. In stacking, the output of the learners is combined through a combiner system which is also trained and is not restricted to be linear. The learners are called level 0 generalizers and the combiner is the level 1 generalizer. The level 1 generalizer learns what the correct output is when level 0 generalizers give a certain output combination. Thus level 1 needs be trained on data unused in training the level 0 generalizers. Wolpert proposes to use leave-one-out though this is too costly and n-fold cross validation seems to be better. Zhang et al. (1992) use stacking for protein secondary structure prediction with significant improvement in accuracy. In their study, the level 0 generalizers are a statistical model, a lazy learner and a one hidden layer neural network. The level 1 generalizer is another neural network with one hidden layer. Breiman (1992) discusses stacking from a statistical perspective.

Boosting (Drucker et al. 1993) trains the learners serially. After having trained the first, they train the second learner with the data on which the first fails (and as many data on which the first succeeds) thus making sure that that the two learners complement one another. Then a third learner is trained with the data on which the two learners disagree. During testing, if the first two learners agree then that is taken as the output, otherwise the third learner is consulted. Large training samples are required for boosting as a learner is trained only with the data on which the previous learners fail.

The boosting approach makes sense because when we have a second learner, we do not care about its overall performance but we just want it to perform well on cases where the first one fails and an intelligent switch to choose between the two. In the *adaptive mixtures of local experts* (Jacobs et al. 1991), there are a set of local experts that partition the input space among themselves and a separate gating expert that, given an input, decides which expert to use. The local experts and the gating expert are trained all in parallel as opposed to the serial approach taken by boosting.

Krogh and Vedelsby (1995) measure "ambiguity" as the variation of the output of voters averaged over unlabelled data to quantify the disagreement among the voters. They define:

$$E = \overline{E} - \overline{A}$$

where E is the error after voting, $\overline{E}$ is the average of the generalization errors of the individual voters and $\overline{A}$ is the average of ambiguities. Thus for minimum error, we need to maximize the ambiguity. They show that if the voters are strongly biased, the ambiguity will be small because the voters implement very similar functions and thus agree on inputs even outside the training set. If on the other hand there is a large variation, the ambiguity is high and in this case the generalization error will be smaller than the average generalization error. They also note that one way to increase the ambiguity is to train the voters on different datasets. Our results given in Section 4 are in accordance with theirs.

Tresp and Taniguchi (1995) propose to use a "competence" measure to determine the weights in a voting scheme. This uses $\hat{p}(x|j)$, an estimate of the distribution of input data used to train voter j.

Although much work has been done on how to combine learners, the question of what to choose as the learners is an open problem. Wolpert (1992) stated that one wants level 0 generalizers to "span the space of generalizers" and be "mutually orthogonal." Generally this is done by biasing the learners in different ways (e.g., by using different learning methods or different initial conditions). For example because CNN is a local search method, we get different subsets by reordering the training set. A better idea seems to have rather different learners as opposed to variants of one method.

6. Conclusions

Many lazy learning techniques require storing the complete sample. They generalize well indicating that they are serious competitors to more complex, gradient-descent methods. Much of the functionality of neural networks (i.e., parallel structures for pattern recognition) can be obtained from closely related but simpler techniques (e.g., distance-based classifiers) without needing complex network structures, learning rules nor precise weights (Alpaydın and Gürgen 1995). Actually the distinction between a neural network and a lazy learning method is quite hazy. Omohundro (1987) shows how simple lazy learners can be implemented as a neural network. The neural network implementation of CNN is given in (Alpaydın1990). Most neural networks whose hidden units implement a local activation function like the gaussian can be recast as a lazy learner and vice versa.

To decrease storage requirements and speed-up processing, one can incrementally select a subset of the sample by making just a few passes over the sample. Most of the time, the gain in memory is worth the cost of this extra training time, which is much smaller than the time it takes to do gradient-descent. A method like CNN is promising when very rapid adaptation is necessary (e.g., in real-time systems such as robotics) and when memory space is a premium. Examples of its usage in a robotics domain is given in (Reignier et al. 1995) and in industrial measurement in (Hines et al. 1993).

Generalization can be improved by training a number of such subsets and combining their predictions. It is generally accepted that there is not one optimal learning method to do anything (Schaffer 1994). If we do not know a priori which learning method is the best, we can train a number of different learners and combine their predictions (e.g., by voting). This approach of voting is not limited to lazy learners but can be generalized to any estimation method. Recent advances in parallel processing technology allow separate voters to be implemented on separate processors thus leading to considerable increases in computational speed.

Acknowledgments

This work is supported by Grant EEEAG–143 from Tübitak, Turkish Scientific and Technical Research Council. The handwritten digit dataset (OCR) is provided by Isabelle Guyon of AT&T Bell Labs. The other datasets are from the UC Irvine Repository maintained by P. Murphy. Thanks to the two anonymous reviewers for constructive comments. Special thanks to David Aha for prompt feedback and many suggestions during the revision that significantly improved the content and the presentation of the paper.

Appendix. Effect of Voting on Estimation Error

Let us denote the output of learner j as d_j and the output after voting as r where

$$r = \sum_{j=1}^{m} d_j \beta_j$$

where $\beta_j \geq 0$ and $\sum_{j=1}^{m} \beta_j = 1$. We assume that $d_j, j = 1 \ldots m$ are independent and identically distributed. When b is an estimator of the parameter θ,

$$b_\theta(d) = E[d] - \theta$$

is the *bias* of d as an estimator of θ. If $b_\theta(d) = 0$ for all θ, then d is an *unbiased* estimator. In other words, an estimator is unbiased if its expected value equals the value of the parameter it is attempting to estimate. If we compute the expected value of r, we see that it is equal to the expected value of d_j:

$$E[r] = E\left[\sum_{j=1}^{m} d_j \beta_j\right] = \sum_j \beta_j E[d_j] = E[d_j] \sum_j \beta_j$$
$$= E[d_j] \tag{6}$$

Thus voting does not change the bias; if the voters are unbiased so is the combined estimator. The *variance* of estimator d measures how much d deviates from its expected value:

$$\text{Var}(d) = E[(d - E[d])^2]$$

Let us compute the variance of r in the case of simple voting where $\beta_j = 1/m$. We see that it decreases as the number of voters m increases:

$$\text{Var}(r) = \text{Var}\left(\sum_{j=1}^{m} d_j \beta_j\right) = \text{Var}\left(\sum_j \frac{d_j}{m}\right) = \frac{1}{m^2} \sum_j \text{Var}(d_j)$$

$$= \frac{1}{m} \text{Var}(d_j) \tag{7}$$

The mean square error of an estimator is equal to the sum of its variance and the square of its bias:

$$r(d, \theta) = \text{Var}(d) + (b_\theta(d))^2$$

Thus variance and mean square error decreases with increasing m. Note that this assumes independence of d_j which may not always be true. It can also be shown that for minimum variance, the optimal weight to give an estimator is inversely proportional to its variance. We want to minimize:

$$E(\beta) = \text{Var}\left(\sum_j d_j \beta_j\right) = \sum_j \beta_j^2 \text{Var}(d_j)$$

Taking $\sigma_j^2 \equiv \text{Var}(d_j)$ and using the method of Lagrange multipliers, we look for σ_j^2 that minimize:

$$E(\beta) = \sum_j \beta_j^2 \sigma_j^2 + \lambda \left(1 - \sum_j \beta_j\right)$$

Find β_j and λ that satisfy:

$$\frac{\partial E}{\partial \beta_j} = 2\beta_j \sigma_j^2 - \lambda = 0 \text{ and } \sum_j \beta_j = 1$$

We find:

$$\beta_j = \frac{1/\sigma_j^2}{\sum_l 1/\sigma_l^2} \tag{8}$$

References

Aha, D. W., Kibler, D. &, Albert, M. K. (1991). Instance-Based Learning Algorithms. *Machine Learning* 6: 37–66.

Alpaydın, E. (1990). *Neural Models of Incremental Supervised and Unsupervised Learning*, PhD dissertation, No 869, Department d'Informatique, Ecole Polytechnique Fédérale de Lausanne, Switzerland, 1990.

Alpaydın, E. (1991). *GAL: Networks that Grow When They Learn and Shrink When They Forget*, Berkeley CA, TR-91-032: International Computer Science Institute.

Alpaydın, E. (1993). Multiple Networks for Function Learning. *IEEE International Conference on Neural Networks*, March, San Francisco CA 1: 9–14.

Alpaydın, E. & Gürgen, F. (1995). Comparison of Kernel Estimators, Perceptrons and Radial-Basis Functions for OCR and Speech Classification. *Neural Computing and Applications* 3: 38–49.

Benediktsson, J. A. & Swain, P. H. (1992). Consensus Theoretic Classification Methods. *IEEE Transactions on Systems, Man, and Cybernetics* 22: 688–704.

Breiman, L. (1992). *Stacked Regressions*, TR-367. Department of Statistics, University of California, Berkeley.

Drucker, H., Schapire, R. & Simard, P. (1993). Improving Performance in Neural Networks Using a Boosting Algorithm. In Hanson S. J. Cowan J. & Giles L. (eds.) *Advances in Neural Information Processing Systems 5*, 42–49. Morgan Kaufmann.

Duda, R. O. & Hart, P. E. (1973). *Pattern Classification and Scene Analysis*. Wiley and Sons.

Gates, G. W. (1972). The Reduced Nearest Neighbor Rule. *IEEE Transactions on Information Theory* 18: 431–433.

Guyon, I., Poujoud, I., Personnaz, L., Dreyfus, G., Denker, J. & le Cun, Y. (1989). Comparing Different Neural Architectures for Classifying Handwritten Digits. *International Joint Conference on Neural Networks*. Washington, USA.

Hansen, L. K. & Salamon, P. (1990). Neural Network Ensembles. *IEEE Transactions on Pattern Analysis and Machine Intelligence* 12: 993–1001.

Härdle, W. (1990). *Applied Nonparametric Regression*. Econometric Society Monographs, Cambridge University Press.

Hart, P. E. (1968). The Condensed Nearest Neighbor Rule. *IEEE Transactions on Information Theory* 14: 515–516.

Hastie, T. & Tibshirani, R. (1990). *Generalized Additive Models*. Chapman Hall.

Hines, E. L., Gianna, C. C. & Gardner, J. W. (1993). Neural Network Based Electronic Nose Using Constructive Algorithms. In Taylor, M. and Lisboa P. (eds.) *Techniques and Application of Neural Networks*, 135–154. Ellis Horwood.

Jacobs, R. A., Jordan, M. I., Nowlan, S. J. & Hinton, G. E. (1991). Adaptive Mixtures of Local Experts. *Neural Computation* 3: 79–87.

Krogh, A. & Vedelsby, J. (1995). Neural Network Ensembles, Cross Validation, and Active Learning. In Tesauro, G., Touretzky, D. S. & Leen T. K. (eds.) *Advances in Neural Information Processing Systems 7*. MIT Press.

LeBlanc, M. & Tibshirani, R. (1994). *Combining Estimates in Regression and Classification*. Department of Statistics, University of Toronto.

Lincoln, W. P. & Skrzypek, J. (1990). Synergy of Clustering Multiple Back Propagation Networks. In Touretzky D (ed.) *Advances in Neural Information Processing Systems 2*, 650–657. Morgan Kaufmann.

Mani, G. (1991). Lowering Variance of Decisions by using Artificial Neural Network Ensembles. *Neural Computation* 3: 484–486.

Meir, R. (1994). *Bias, Variance and the Combination of Estimators: The Case of Linear Least Squares*. Department of Electrical Engineering, Technion.

Murphy, P. M. (1994). *UCI Repository of Machine Learning Databases* [http://www.ics.uci.edu/~mlearn/MLRepository.html]. Irvine, CA: University of California, Department of Information and Computer Science.

Omohundro, S. M. (1987). Efficient Algorithms with Neural Network Behaviour. *Complex Systems* **1**: 273–347.

Perrone, M. P. (1993). *Improving Regression Estimation: Averaging Methods for Variance Reduction with Extensions to General Convex Measure Optimization*. PhD Thesis, Department of Physics, Brown University.

Preparata, F. P. & Shamos, M. I. (1985). *Computational Geometry*. Springer.

Reignier, P., Hansen, V. & Crowley, J. (1995). Incremental Supervised Learning for Mobile Robot Reactive Control. In Rembold, U. et al. (eds.) *Intelligent Autonomous Systems*, 287–294. IOS Press.

Rogova, G. (1994). Combining the Results of Several Neural Network Classifiers. *Neural Networks* **7**: 777–781.

Schaffer, C. (1994). A conservation law for generalization performance. In *Proceedings of the Eleventh International Conference on Machine Learning*, 259–265. New Brunswick, NJ: Morgan Kaufmann.

Silverman, B. W. (1986). *Density Estimation for Statistics and Data Analysis*. Chapman & Hall.

Stanfill, C. & Waltz, D. (1986). Toward Memory-Based Reasoning. *Communications of the ACM* **29**: 1213–1228.

Tresp, V. & Taniguchi, M. (1995). Combining Estimators Using Non-Constant Weighting Functions. In Tesauro, G., Touretzky, D. S. & Leen T. K. (eds.) *Advances in Neural Information Processing Systems 7*. MIT Press.

Vapnik, V. (1995). *The Nature of Statistical Learning Theory*. Springer.

Wolpert, D. H. (1992). Stacked Generalization. *Neural Networks* **5**: 241–259.

Xu, L., Krzyzak, A. & Suen, C. Y. (1992). Methods of Combining Multiple Classifiers and Their Applications to Handwriting Recognition. *IEEE Transactions on Systems, Man, and Cybernetics* **22**: 418–435.

Zhang, X., Mesirov, J. P. & Waltz, D. L. (1992). Hybrid System for Protein Secondary Structure Prediction. *Journal of Molecular Biology* **225**: 1049–1063.

Artificial Intelligence Review **11**: 133–155, 1997.

Tolerating Concept and Sampling Shift in Lazy Learning Using Prediction Error Context Switching

MARCOS SALGANICOFF

Applied Science and Engineering Laboratories (ASEL), University of Delaware/Alfred I. duPont Institute, 1600 Rockland Road, Wilmington, Delaware, USA
E-mail: salganic@asel.udel.edu fax: 302-651-6875

Abstract. In their unmodified form, lazy-learning algorithms may have difficulty learning and tracking time-varying input/output function maps such as those that occur in concept shift. Extensions of these algorithms, such as Time-Windowed forgetting (TWF), can permit learning of time-varying mappings by deleting older exemplars, but have decreased classification accuracy when the input-space sampling distribution of the learning set is time-varying. Additionally, TWF suffers from lower asymptotic classification accuracy than equivalent non-forgetting algorithms when the input sampling distributions are stationary. Other shift-sensitive algorithms, such as Locally-Weighted forgetting (LWF), avoid the negative effects of time-varying sampling distributions, but still have lower asymptotic classification in non-varying cases. We introduce Prediction Error Context Switching (PECS), which allows lazy-learning algorithms to have good classification accuracy in conditions having a time-varying function mapping and input sampling distributions, while still maintaining their asymptotic classification accuracy in static tasks. PECS works by selecting and re-activating previously stored instances based on their most recent consistency record. The classification accuracy and active learning set sizes for the above algorithms are compared in a set of learning tasks that illustrate the differing time-varying conditions described above. The results show that the PECS algorithm has the best overall classification accuracy over these differing time-varying conditions, while still having asymptotic classification accuracy competitive with unmodified lazy-learners intended for static environments.

Key words: lazy learning, non-stationary function, concept drift, nearest neighbor learning, time-varying functions

1. Introduction

Many real-world environments in which learning systems have to operate are time-varying. Several aspects of the learning problem can vary, including the mapping to be learned (also known as *concept shift*), and the sampling distribution that governs the input-space location of exemplars that make up the learning set. For example, in robotics applications, the dynamics of a manipulator can change depending on its payload. In communications network routing, the traffic patterns along communication links may change, necessitating the updating of routing decision rules. Therefore, any learning

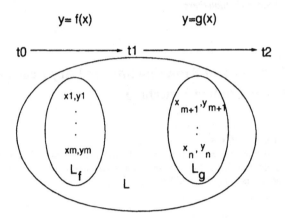

Figure 1. Learning non stationary functions.

system which is to succeed in those environments must not just be able to adapt, but to *re*-adapt as well.

Lazy learning algorithms such as instance-based learning (e.g., IB3) (Aha et al. 1991), k-nearest neighbor (Duda and Hart 1973), and locally-weighted regression (Atkeson 1991) cannot track time-varying functions in their unmodified form. The cause for this shortcoming is illustrated in Figure 1. In this Figure we see that function mapping and sampling distributions can change as a function of time. Function f generates exemplars from time t_0 up to t_1 yielding learning set L_f and function g from time t_1 up to time t_2 yielding learning set L_g. If we train the learner on learning set $L = L_f \cup L_g$ and $f \neq g$ then it is possible that $f(x) \neq g(x)$ for some $x \in L_f \cup L_g$. This one to many mapping makes it impossible for the learner to minimize error at that point for the new observation since the previous observations generated by f will confound the learner. What is required is a method for keeping those exemplars that are predictive and inactivating those that no longer reflect the current mapping.

For lazy learning algorithms, the ability to re-adapt is most often achieved by adding a sliding time-window which keeps only the last m observations in first-in first-out order, as members of the active learning set L. We can consider this technique a "forgetting" policy, since any observation more than m samples old is no longer in the memory-based learning set. Unfortunately, this naive forgetting policy has drawbacks. The maximum number of observations in the learning set is now limited to m samples, which might not be sufficient for the task, depending on the complexity of the learning task and how rapidly the mappings might change over time (Kuh et al. 1991). Many algorithms that are designed for time-varying environments utilize time-weighted forgetting

(Kuh et al. 1991; Hembold and Long 1991; Moore 1991). Additionally, time-weighted forgetting policies inevitably suffer from the problem of catastrophic interference when the sampling distribution varies. This problem is detailed in the next section.

1.1. *Catastrophic interference*

Catastrophic interference is defined as the *unlearning* of learned mappings caused by the intervening presentation of exemplars which interfere with learning (McCloskey and Cohen 1989; Ratcliff 1990). The intervening exemplars lead to a degradation of classification rates on mappings which had previously been learned. This interference phenomenon can occur even when the function to be learned is non-varying. For example, consider a lazy learning algorithm that has a sliding time-window which keeps only the last m observations in the learning set to track changing tasks. A worst case scenario for catastrophic interference occurs when the system is exposed to a sequence of two learning sets, each having m members, with the sets being drawn from disjoint regions of the instance-space. With test queries from the first set, the learner should classify well, assuming that m exemplars are sufficient to predict accurately. If we now sample so that exemplars are chosen from the second disjoint region, the misclassification rate will degrade but will gradually improve as the next m exemplars are provided. If we now switch back to drawing exemplars from the first set, we will see that classification error dramatically increases once again. At the end of the second learning set a total of $2m$ observations will have been presented, but only the last m observations are retained because of the sliding window, and they are all from the second region. Therefore, any new queries from the first region will not have any nearest-neighbors in their proximity, leading to poor classification accuracy immediately after the switch in sampling distribution occurs.

This type of recurring transient error upon sampling distribution switching is extremely wasteful, since m exemplars were already presented from the first region at the start of the task, so we should expect the system to still be able to benefit from these presentations. Secondly this transient increase in misclassification will recur each time the sampling distribution switches because of the finite length of the sliding time-window.

A lazy learner can prevent catastrophic interference by storing all exemplars, which dissociates temporal information from the training sample. Unfortunately, this desirable property comes at the expense of intolerance to time-varying labeling functions since now all of the exemplars for the different mapping function values are intermixed within the learning set.

1.2. *Paper overview*

In this article, three algorithms for handling time-varying learning tasks are described and compared:
1. Time-Weighted Forgetting (TWF)
2. Locally-Weighted Forgetting (LWF)
3. Prediction Error Context Switching (PECS).

TWF is a well-known algorithm for keeping a window of the most recent exemplars and using those as the learning set. LWF is a recently introduced algorithm (Salganicoff 1993) that enhances TWF, and PECS is a novel instance selection algorithm that enhances some aspects of LWF with other mechanisms used in IB3 (Aha et al. 1991) and some novel features (e.g., windowing the resulting prediction accuracy of exemplars). PECS is able to track concept shift, avoid catastrophic interference and has superior asymptotic performance to TWF and LWF on a set of demonstration learning tasks.

These algorithms are detailed in Section 2 and are experimentally compared in Section 3. The relation of this work to previous efforts and areas that warrant further investigation are described in Section 4. A summary of the results and conclusion are given in Section 5.

2. Description of the algorithms

In this section we further describe the three algorithms summarized in Section 1.2.

2.1. *Time-Weighted Forgetting*

TWF is a technique for windowing exemplars that consists of a sliding window which keeps only the most recent experiences presented to the learner in the active learning set. The *active learning set* is the set of exemplars which are used to form predictions. Similar techniques are used in time-series prediction and tracking techniques such as moving average filters and extended Kalman filters (Kalman 1960). However, rather than tracking and predicting the next points of output using a known dynamical model, the learner attempts to approximate a real-valued or categorical function given a learning set L, which consists of the last n experiences presented. In TWF, exemplars are weighted using a function that assigns a weight w_e, initialized to $w_e = 1$, to each observation e. The weights for each observation e are recursively updated to yield an exponential weighting function using the simple rule $w_e \leftarrow \gamma w_e$, with $0 < \gamma \leq 1$, where w_e is the weight associated with an exemplar. An exemplar consists of the input vector X, output value y, and

```
TWF(L,e,γ,θ)                    LWF(L,e,k,θ,τ)
 {                               {
    we ← 1.0                        N ← Nearest_Neighbors(L,e,k)
    L ← L ∪ {e}                     we ← 1.0
    for each e ∈ L                  L ← L ∪ {e}
    {                               for each ei ∈ N
        we ← γ we                   {
        if we < θ                       γ ← Γ(Xe, Xi, Xk, τ)
            L ← L - e                   wei ← γwei
    }                                   if wei < θ
 }                                          L ← L - {ei}
                                    }
                                 }
```

           (a)   (b)

Figure 2. Time-Weighted Forgetting (TWF) and Locally-Weighted Forgetting (LWF). In (a)
L is the learning set, e is the exemplar, γ is the forgetting rate, and θ is the deletion threshold.
For LWF in (b), k is the number of nearest-neighbors, and τ is the maximum decay rate.

a weight w: $e = < X_e, y_e, w_e >$. When w_e decreases below the threshold
value θ, its corresponding exemplar is deleted from L. This is equivalent to
a first-in first-out buffer of length $n = \frac{\log \theta}{\log \gamma}$. A pseudo-code description of
TWF is given in Figure 2(a).

2.2. Locally-Weighted Forgetting

An alternative to TWF is LWF (Salganicoff 1993), which keeps an observation
in L depending on whether data with similar attribute values is subsequently
presented to the learner. When this occurs, the new exemplar eventually super-
sedes the previous one. This effect is realized by decrementing an exemplar's
weight w by a multiplication with the result of $\Gamma()$. Each time a new exemplar is input, the weightings $w_{\{k\}}$ of the k nearest observations, $X_{\{i\}}$ ($i \leq k$),
within a neighborhood of the k nearest-neighbors of the new exemplar X_e
are decreased by multiplication with $\Gamma(X_e, X_{\{i\}}, X_{\{k\}}, \tau)$:

$$w_{\{i\}} \leftarrow \Gamma\left(X_e, X_{\{i\}}, X_{\{k\}}, \tau\right) w_{\{i\}} \tag{1}$$

When an exemplar's weight falls below a threshold value θ, it is deleted
from the learning set. Thus participation is all or none, determined by the
threshold value θ. The variable τ is the minimum value that $\Gamma()$ may take on,
which specifies the maximum forgetting rate. LWF is detailed in Figure 2(b).
    The quantity $\Gamma(X_e, X_{\{i\}}, X_{\{k\}}, \tau)$ is bounded between τ and 1 and is a
truncated quadratic function of the distance between X_e and $X_{\{i\}}$:

$$\Gamma\left(X_e, X_{\{i\}}, X_{\{k\}}, \tau\right) = \begin{cases} \tau + (1 - \tau)\frac{d_{\{i\}}^2}{d_{\{k\}}^2} & \text{if } d_{\{i\}}^2 \leq d_{\{k\}}^2 \\ 1 & \text{otherwise} \end{cases} \quad (2)$$

where $d_{\{i\}}^2 = d^2(X_e, X_{\{i\}})$ is the squared Euclidean distance from the ith nearest-neighbor of exemplar e. Since the radius $d_{\{k\}}$ is that of the sphere containing the k nearest-neighbors of exemplar e, this adapts the decay radius of influence to the local density of exemplars around the new exemplar. This equation is chosen based on a square law analogy to physical systems, such as particle decay. The salient property is that the function be non-decreasing in d, and that it have a maximum value of unity at $d_{\{k\}}$ so that exemplars further than the kth nearest-neighbor are not decayed.

A simple way to implement a bound on the number of exemplars stored in L is to set k, the number of nearest-neighbors, as $k = \lceil \beta \mid L \mid \rceil$ with $0 < \beta \leq 1$. The total number of observations that are kept in L then reaches an asymptotic value when the number of exemplar "births" equals the number of exemplar "deaths" per unit time (an analysis is given in (Salganicoff 1992)). The parameters τ, k and θ determine how many nearby subsequent observations are needed in the neighborhood of a previous observation before it is deleted from the learning set. The decay rate is a function of τ; with smaller values, fewer subsequent observations are necessary in e's neighborhood before it is deleted. The value k controls the volume of input-space subject to decay by a new exemplar.

2.3. Prediction Error Context Switching

PECS is an algorithm that uses the locality principle of LWF, while also taking into account the windowed predictiveness of the nearest-neighbors to subsequent exemplars. Additionally, PECS does not permanently delete (or "forget") exemplars, but instead de-activates and stores them for possible future re-evaluation. When a stored exemplar e_i is one of query e's k-nearest neighbors, then its output value y_{e_i} is checked for agreement with y_e. If an exemplar begins to disagree often with the true outcomes close to it in the input space, it is moved from the active learning set and placed in an inactive set for re-evaluation over future instances. Trends in the reliability of an exemplar are detected by keeping statistics on its most recent agreements and disagreements in its sliding window (a shift register of length l). The probability of agreement for a given exemplar provides a form of context sensing, where an observation can be evaluated in terms of its accuracy in the current task context (i.e., the current mapping). Higher probabilities indicate that the given observation is appropriate for the current mapping context and should be in the active learning set. Lower probabilities indicate that the exemplar should be switched to the dormant set of exemplars.

The approach taken by PECS is similar to that of the lazy learning algorithm IB3 (Aha et al. 1991), although it was developed from the point of view of improving performance in time-varying tasks as a modification of LWF, rather than as a method for improving the robustness of instance-based learners to noisy data, as was the intent with IB3. IB3 removes noisy observations from a learning set by deferring inclusion of an observation in L until it is proven reliable by means of a confidence interval test, which is the same test employed by PECS. In IB3, the agreement confidence interval is computed taking into account the number of agreements and disagreements that have occurred over the *entire lifetime* of the particular exemplar. PECS differs significantly from IB3 in that the agreements statistics used for confidence intervals are windowed over the last l predictions. This permits classification accuracy confidence intervals for an exemplar to track changes in its prediction accuracy such as might occur in time-varying learning situations, without being biased by a large number of previous observation derived from another mapping. Since IB3 keeps cumulative statistics, the amount of time it requires to re-adapt to a new task mapping is proportional to the number of exemplars that it has been exposed to previously. Also, rather than permanently deleting an observation whose classification accuracy is lower than deletion threshold, as is done in IB3, PECS moves this observation to an inactive set. An observation in the inactive set may be re-activated at a future point if the classification accuracy of that observation improves.

PECS is also more aggressive than IB3 in immediately including exemplars in L, whereas IB3 requires a good prediction history before including the exemplar. IB3 also normalizes its lower bound confidence interval with respect to the overall class incidence probabilities to better handle skewed concepts which have a highly dominant class, whereas PECS does not take this into account (see Section 4 for a further discussion of why this design decision was taken).

The PECS algorithm is outlined in Figure 3. Some aspects of the algorithm bear further elaboration. In PECS each new observation e is put into L by default. The unacceptable exemplar set U is initialized as empty. The set N consists of all exemplars in $L \cup U$ that are in the k-nearest-neighbor hyper-sphere centered at e of radius r. The number of nearest-neighbors is set using $k = \lceil \beta \mid L \mid \rceil$, with $0 \leq \beta \leq 1$. Each exemplar e_i is checked for consistency using the agree function, which returns 1 if y_{e_i} agrees with y_e and 0 otherwise. These agreement values are shifted into e_i's shift register SR_{e_i} of length l which stores e_i's recent performance. Note that SR_{e_i} is not

```
PECS(L, e, k, p_min, p_max)
  {
      r ← Nearest_Neighbor_Radius(L,e,k)
      N ← Observations_Within_Radius(L∪U,e,r)
      L ← L∪{e}
      for each e_i ∈ N
        {
            SR_{e_i} ← agree(outcome(e),predict(e_i))
            x ← successes(SR_{e_i})
            n ← attempts(SR_{e_i})
            if lb(x,n) > p_min and e_i ∉ L
              {
                  L ← L∪{e_i}
                  U ← U-{e_i}
              }
            if ub(x,n) < p_max and e_i ∉ U
              {
                  U ← U∪{e_i}
                  L ← L-{e_i}
              }
        }
  }
```

Figure 3. Prediction Error Context Switching (PECS). Here L is the learning set, e is a new exemplar, k represents the number of nearest-neighbors, p_{min} is the agreement acceptance probability, and p_{max} is the inactivation threshold.

a window that slides in time, but only over a given exemplar's most recent predictions.

The upper bound ub and lower bound lb confidence intervals for the probability of agreement are computed using each observation's (x, n) statistics derived from the data in SR_{e_i}. The confidence intervals assume a binomial process, where x is the number of agreements and n is the number of prediction records in SR_{e_i}. The upper bound ub and lower bound lb probability of agreement are calculated according to the binomial confidence interval formula (Larson and Marx 1986; Salganicoff 1993). If the ub on the predictiveness of e_i falls below p_{max} then it is deleted from L and moved to U. However, this same exemplar may eventually be moved back to L if its lower-bound lb predictiveness goes above p_{min}, as may the case when concepts drift cyclicly. If the observation e_i supports the current input/output mapping, its prediction accuracy over its last n participations will be high and it will be kept in L. If it is not consistent with the current context, it will be low and it will be moved to U.

3. Evaluation

In order to better compare the properties of TWF, LWF and PECS, they were run on a set of three different tasks: a task with time-varying function, a task with time-varying input sampling distribution, and a static task. While the chosen learning tasks are not complex, they capture the major types of time-varying phenomenon that can occur and illustrate the strengths and weaknesses of the differing approaches.

Additionally, the three algorithms were compared with a variant of the IB3 algorithm, IB3A. IB3A is essentially the PECS algorithm with an unlimited length shift-register. IB3A can be considered an aggressive version of IB3, where rather than deferring acceptance of an exemplar based on its performance, as is done in IB3, all exemplars are immediately accepted into the set L. If the observation has poor performance then it is moved into the inactive set U (see Section 2.3). IB3A also differs from IB3 in that it does not normalize for concept skew. However the example task were chosen so that concept skew would not be major factor, since properties relating to time-variation of tasks were of most interest for this work.

The parameters for TWF were determined by systematically searching for the γ parameter for LWF for best misclassification performance in the time-varying function task (see Section 3.1). The parameters for LWF were then chosen to yield approximately the same asymptotic sample size as TWF for best performance. The parameters for PECS and IB3A were chosen to give approximately the same misclassification performance as the LWF and TWF algorithms on the time varying function task. By normalizing all algorithms to have similar misclassification performance on the time-varying function task, their differing properties in terms of resistance to catastrophic interference and asymptotic learning rates could be compared fairly. In summary, the parameters for the algorithms over all tasks were as follows: for TWF, $\beta = 0.996$, for LWF, $\tau = 0.8$ and $\beta = 0.04$, for PECS and IB3A, $p_{min} = 0.6$, $p_{max} = 0.4$, $\beta = 0.04$, and a confidence value of 85% for the confidence intervals, with a shift register length of 20 for PECS.

For all of the simulations the misclassification error was estimated using an independent set of 5000 randomly generated exemplars over the current input sampling distribution to get an unbiased estimate of the classification rate.

3.1. *Time-varying function/static sampling distribution*

For a task with time-varying function maps, a simple task with two function maps f and g was chosen. The function f maps all instances inside of a circle of $r = 0.5$ centered at (0,0) to the label $+$ and outside to $-$. The function

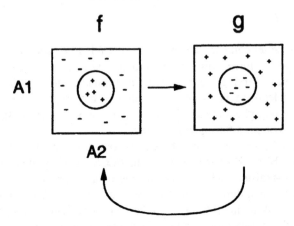

Figure 4(a). The Time-Varying Function Map Task

g is the complement of f. The task switches between f and g every 1000th exemplar presentation. The sampling distribution for both f and g is static and uniform over $-1 \leq a1 \leq 1$ and $-1 \leq a2 \leq 1$. The task is illustrated in Figure 4(a). All of the algorithms are used in conjunction with a nearest-neighbor (1-NN) predictor as the classifier. When IB3A is run on this task, it performs quite poorly in terms of misclassification error (see Figure 4(b)). This occurs because IB3A's consistency statistics for a given exemplar come from the combination of predictions for both the f and g maps, leading to a contaminated active learning set containing a mixture of exemplars derived from both maps. The results for TWF, LWF and PECS are much better in this task, as shown in Figure 4(c). The misclassification error increases whenever the mapping switches between f and g as would be expected, and gradually decreases as newer observations come in until the function switches again. TWF and LWF succeed in this task because they have an asymptotic sample size of approximately 400 with the parameters chosen, which allows them to turn over their active learning set within the 1000 exemplar task switching interval (see Figure 5), while PECS succeeds by switching out exemplars from the incorrect task context within the necessary interval.

3.2. *Time-varying input sampling distribution*

In order to show how the different algorithms would be affected by time-varying input sampling distributions the task in the previous section was modified as follows. Initially, the sampling distribution is uniform over $-1 \leq a1 \leq 1$ and $-1 \leq a2 \leq 1$ and the mapping function is f. After the first epoch of 1000 observations, the sampling distribution is restricted to $0 \leq a1 \leq 1$

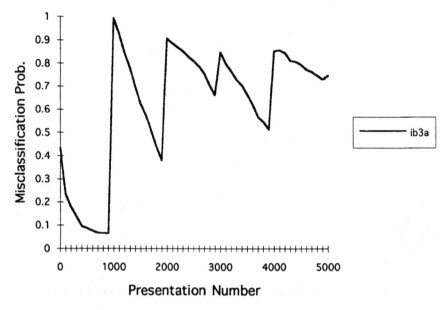

Figure 4(b). Associated Misclassification Error for IB3A.

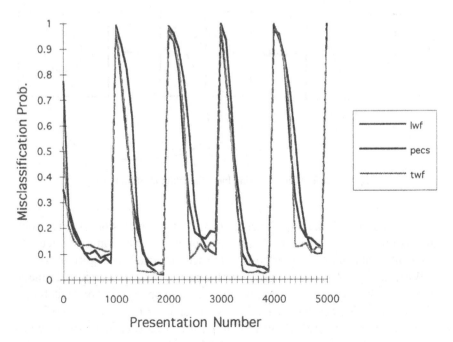

Figure 4(c). Errors for TWF, LWF and PECS.

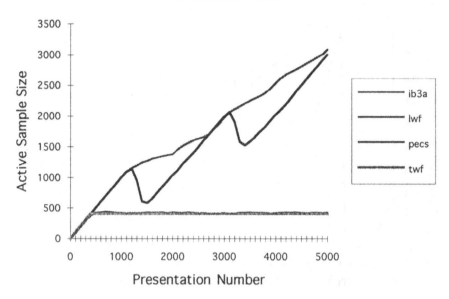

Figure 5. Active Learning Set Sizes for the Time-Varying Function Map Task

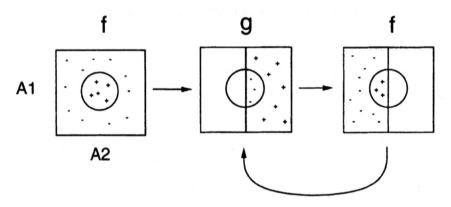

Figure 6(a). The Time-Varying Input Sampling Distribution Task.

and the mapping functions switches to g. At the conclusion of this epoch the mapping switches back to f and the sampling distribution is restricted to $-1 \leq a1 \leq 0$ and the cycle restarts in the second state (see Figure 6(a)).

When using TWF, catastrophic interference occurs, as seen in a dramatic increase in its misclassification rate after each mapping function switch (see Figure 6(b)). The performance on the same task for IB3A, LWF and PECS is shown in Figure 6(c). From this graph it can be seen that IB3A avoids catastrophic interference almost completely, as little transient error increase occurs for the latter concept switches, although it is slowest to recover during

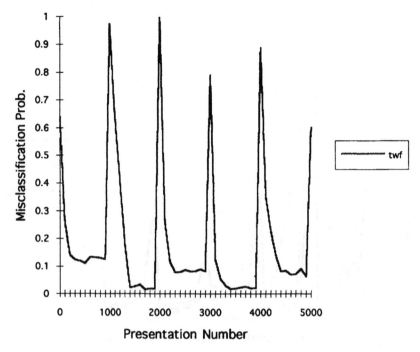

Figure 6(b). Associated Misclassification Error for TWF.

the first switch because of inconsistent exemplars from the first 1000 instances of the f mapping. After the first transient, the sampling distribution switches from the left half to the right half of the domain to yield what are effectively static function values, and switching sampling distributions. This is a condition that is ideal for an algorithm such as IB3A, which will keep almost all of its presented exemplars, and thus avoid catastrophic interference.

LWF and PECS in Figure 6(c) are shown to have decreased interference effects when compared to the TWF algorithm in Figure 6(b), although the effect is still noticeable. These less than perfect performances occur because some "erosion" of the currently inactive half of the task domain may occur as inconsistent exemplars near the border of the two subregions are inactivated. Observations near concept boundaries are more likely to have inconsistencies (Aha et al. 1991), and to be inactivated by PECS. In the case of LWF, exemplars in the inactive sampling regions near the border of the two disjoint sampling regions will be decayed by observations that occur nearby. When the sampling regions switch back, the area near the concept boundary will lack exemplars, which will lead to misclassification error transients. IB3A, on the other hand, uses a cumulative statistic to determine whether to keep

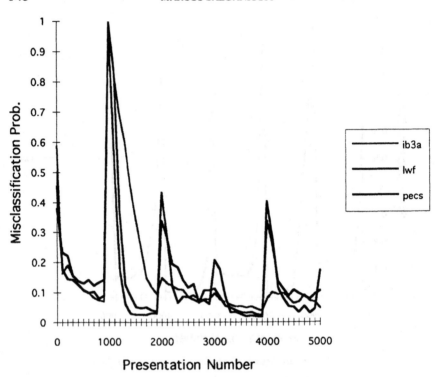

Figure 6(c). IB3A, LWF and PECS.

an exemplar active, which leads to less "erosion" of exemplars by inactivation from the inactive half of the domain. Therefore, when the sampling
distribution switches back, there is less of the domain missing support.

3.3. *Static function and input sampling distribution*

To test the asymptotic classification of the algorithms in a stationary domain,
the task consisted of learning the function f (see Figure 7(a)). The sampling
distribution for f is static and uniform over $-1 \leq a1 \leq 1$ and $-1 \leq a2 \leq 1$.

In Figure 7(b), the asymptotic misclassification rates for IB3A and PECS
are seen to be much lower than that of TWF and LWF. This is because LWF
and TWF both reach an asymptotic size for the learning set $| L |$, which limits
the best classification performance achievable by the 1-NN learner (see Figure
8). PECS and IB3A, on the other hand, have an ever increasing number of
exemplars in L, since the consistency measure of exemplars is good as is
demonstrated by the few exemplars being deleted from L as time goes on.
As L increases, the classification performance of the learner improves to the

f

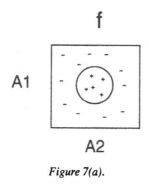

Figure 7(a).

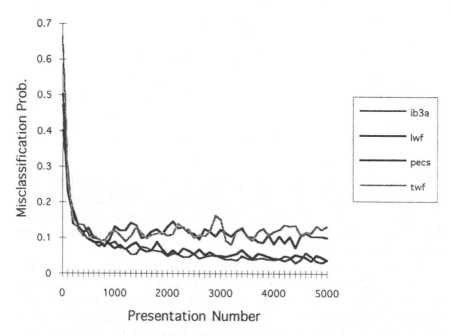

Figure 7(b). The Static Task and Misclassification Errors.

same level it would have if it had no forgetting policy and stored all incoming exemplars.

However, if the mapping function changes, the predictivity of obsolete exemplars will rapidly decrease and those exemplars will be moved to the unacceptable set U. Also, since PECS has the locality property of LWF, it will also avoid catastrophic interference in the same way that LWF does. In contrast, IB3A has a re-adaptation time proportional to the amount of exemplars in the previous mapping. In certain cases the learner may have been acquiring exemplars from a given mapping for a long period of time

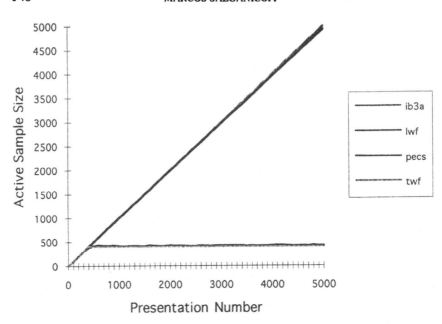

Figure 8. Active Learning Set Sizes for the Static Task.

leading to unacceptably long re-adaptation time for IB3-like algorithms that do not window classification accuracy. An example of this effect may be seen after the first concept shift for the time-varying sampling distribution task in Figure 6(c), where IB3A is slower to recover from the initial concept shift than the other approaches.

The price that we pay for using PECS is that the storage necessary for each exemplar increases because classification accuracy statistics must be kept for each exemplar. However, this may not be a major problem. In many tasks, the amount of real-time that elapses before the storage demands of the instance-based learning algorithm exceed those available in modern computing systems is quite large. Secondly, associative retrieval times can be quite rapid, even for huge data-sets, by the use of efficient indexing schemes such as k-D trees (Friedman et al. 1977; Moore 1991), which can retrieve nearest-neighbors in $\log n$ time where n is the size of the database, and the dimensionality of the attribute space is moderate.

4. Discussion

The average misclassification errors and their standard deviations on all tasks are summarized in Table 1. The results are the mean misclassification error over the task lifetime of 10000 exemplars (measured every 100 presenta-

Table 1. Classification error statistics per task

Task	IB3A	LWF	PECS	TWF
Time varying function	0.672±0.008	0.370±0.004	0.365±0.006	0.324±0.002
Time varying distribution	0.101±0.002	0.117±0.003	0.114±0.004	0.164±0.003
Static task	0.047±0.002	0.112±0.002	0.054±0.003	0.119±0.001

tions), and then averaged over 10 full runs per each condition. As mentioned previously, the misclassification rate is estimated with 5000 independently generated test cases. IB3A has the best asymptotic performance on the static function and sampling task, with PECS close behind, while LWF and TWF converge at approximately twice the error rate. For the time-varying function task, IB3A performs very poorly, while the other algorithms have lower misclassification rates. For the time-varying sampling distribution task the TWF algorithm, in particular, shows the effects of the catastrophic interference, while the other algorithms classify well.

These results, over the three tasks illustrating extremes in time-variation of functions and sampling distributions, show that using PECS for instance selection is a lower risk strategy than the other approaches. PECS will perform better in a variety of different conditions, requiring fewer assumptions about types of non-stationarity present in the environment in order to classify as well. This improved robustness does come at the cost of increased storage requirements when compared to IB3A, which only stores lifetime consistency counts, requiring two counters per exemplar, rather than a shift register. A possible solution for decreasing the necessary storage is briefly discussed in Section 4.2.

4.1. *Relation to previous work*

As mentioned in Section 2.3, PECS has much in common with the IB3 algorithm described by (Aha et al. 1991). However, there are substantive differences between these approaches. IB3 was developed with the intent of increasing the robustness of instance-based learners to noise, which it did very effectively. PECS, on the other hand, was developed from the perspective of being a variation of LWF (Salganicoff 1992; Salganicoff 1993), with the specific intent of improving lazy learning classification performance on time-varying functions and input distributions, while still retaining good classification accuracy in static domains. While the fundamental exemplar classification accuracy mechanism employed by PECS is the same statistical test as that of IB3, a major difference is that the statistics used by PECS are windowed over the last n classification attempts for a particular exemplar, yielding its much improved performance in time-varying domains.

Another important distinction between PECS and IB3 is that PECS does not currently normalize for class incidence as is done in IB3 (Aha et al. 1991) to better handle skewed concepts. This normalization would be problematic for PECS, since for time-varying domains, the class incidence might vary tremendously between contexts, causing misleading incidence statistics, which can cause exemplars being erroneously dropped or added to the active learning set. An important improvement for PECS will be to include some mechanism for accurately tracking class incidence probability so as to better handle concept skew, as could be done by a windowing mechanism for class incidence probabilities.

Other lazy learning approaches, such as those described by Moore (1990, 1991) have employed approaches that combine time-weighting with exemplar classification accuracy in real-valued domains. For example, Moore (1990) extends a kernel regression scheme for weighting nearest-neighbors to time-varying domains by deleting an exemplar if it is both old and inconsistent with the current local estimate at its location, where the local estimate is a function of the output values of the exemplars within a radius r of the query.

In Moore (1991) a very similar approach is taken, but robust regression is used, with the consistency measure for an exemplar defined as the difference between the leave-one-out estimate at the exemplar and the exemplar's output value. Here the weighting relation for the ith exemplar is

$$w_i = \exp\left(-\left((x_i - x_{\text{query}})^2/r^2 + n_i/\tau_{\text{recall}}\right)\right) \tag{3}$$

where r is the kernel radius, x_i and x_{query} are the locations of the ith exemplar and query, respectively, n_i is the number of intervening exemplars that have arrived since exemplar i, and τ_{recall} is a task dependent forgetting rate constant determined by cross-validation. There are two drawbacks for both of these approaches. First as Equation 3 shows, an exemplar will be decayed and become less influential as it becomes older, independent of whether it is still accurate, which implies a good exemplar may be unnecessarily deleted. Secondly, both techniques use a measure for predictive accuracy from the local estimate that is derived from all previous exemplars that are still active. Consider a scenario where a function f has been presented to such a learner using 10000 exemplars and then the mapping switches to a different map g. Using robust regression techniques such as proposed in Moore (1991) the learner may have at best a breakdown point of 50%, meaning that the particular technique is robust to at most 50% of their cases being corrupted. This would imply that for the learner to throw out exemplars from the previous function f would require at least 10000 further exemplars to reach the 50% point, assuming a fixed sampling distribution.

Concept drift, or the changing of mappings over time, was first identified in the context of machine learning by Schlimmer and Granger (1986), who described the STAGGER learning algorithm that is capable of tracking and adapting to time varying mappings and noisy concepts. However, STAGGER is a non-windowed algorithm, which means that it is always biased by previous exemplars. Although it can recover from concept drifts (i.e., drifting functions), its recovery time is also proportional to how many exemplars it has been exposed to from the obsolete concept. Therefore, it may become unacceptably slow to re-adapt in the limit.

More recently, Widmer and Kubat (1992, 1993), introduced the FLORA series of learners that can handle time-varying concepts using a variable length window of exemplars and share some of the principles of the PECS policy. One difference between FLORA and PECS is that in FLORA the size of the most recent consistency record is varied dynamically, based on the overall classification accuracy of the system. Boolean formulae, which form the concept description, have consistency statistics associated with the most recent classification accuracy of each active formula. The least accurate formulae are dropped from the concept description. A similar approach is taken by Blum (1995) for rule-based prediction in a calendar scheduling domain. This performance-based pruning of rules is analogous to what occurs in PECS at the exemplar level. FLORA also attempts to cluster sets of formulae (concept descriptions) and re-invoke them to speed up learning in the event that concepts are cyclic and reappear periodically, and a similar approach could be adopted for PECS to improve performance even further.

Tracking of time-varying concepts has been investigated formally by Kuh et al. (1991) who derive bounds on mistake rates based on two measures of drift: λ, the probability of concept change between the presentation of two examples; and γ, the maximum concept change between exemplars. Hembold and Long (1991) extended the PAC learning model (Valiant, 1984) to time varying environments and proved bounds for the maximum amount of drift that can be sustained as a function of the VC-Dimension. Both Kuh et al. (1991) and Hembold and Long (1991) describe algorithms with sliding time-based sample windows, whereas the PECS approach avoids the problems associated with bounded sample set sizes altogether.

4.2. General issues and future extensions

Extending lazy learning to time-varying domains is crucial for its application to new and important problem domains where its use is currently limited. Many important problems have time-varying characteristics. As an example, consider cyclic phenomenon, such as financial markets. The rules for classifying winning stocks can vary tremendously from year to year (e.g., a time-varying mapping function), and trading activities for different market sectors can vary tremendously (i.e., differing sampling distributions). If lazy learning techniques are to be used in such domains, a means for tracking these changes must be ensured.

Similarly, in robotic tasks, such as learning dynamic control of manipulator arms, the properties of the arm can vary due to differing payloads, wearing out of mechanical components and changing lubrication, all of which must be compensated. In robotic tasks, catastrophic interference can be particularly troubling (Atkeson 1991). In a manufacturing plant, a robotic arm may be run in between some limited repeating set of motions depending on which batch of parts is being produced. Each given motion may be executed and optimized over a long period of time, and then a previously learned motion may be revisited when the production batch changes. If the learning algorithm being used is susceptible to catastrophic interference, the robot will experience undesirably high transient classification errors each time it switches back to a previous motion, if that motion has not been executed for a long period of time. Techniques such as PECS and LWF will permit adaptation while minimizing these transient effects. Traditional adaptive control techniques require persistent excitation, meaning all relevant parts of the manipulator's state-space must be periodically revisited in order to prevent interference. This implies that some percentage of the manipulator time must be spent refreshing parts of the state-space that may be needed again during the future, although the current task may not require it.

An important issue is the selection of appropriate forgetting parameters which are optimal for a given environment. In some situations the concepts may change rapidly, whereas in others the drift might be very slow. If the forgetting parameters are set inappropriately, this can lead to poor performance, due either to slow re-adaptation or an unnecessarily small learning set in the case of TWF. One approach is to apply m-fold cross validation through the attribute space and time, as been successfully done in (Atkeson 1991; Moore 1991) to determine forgetting parameters and feature relevance weightings.

One problem with using absolute thresholds on the predictivity of exemplars is that the appropriate p_{min} and p_{max} rejection and acceptance thresholds may depend on the noise level in a particular domain. Acceptance and rejection threshold criteria that are more robust to different noise levels are an important area to explore in improving PECS, and using cross-validation to select these parameters may also be a viable solution (Atkeson 1991).

The shift register which stores the prediction agreements for each given exemplar uses n bits per exemplar. An alternative, more storage-efficient approach could be to use a decayed count updating rule (Maes and Brooks 1990) of the form

$$t' = \begin{cases} 1 + \tau t & \text{if the prediction is consistent} \\ \tau t & \text{otherwise} \end{cases} \quad (4)$$

and

$$f' = \begin{cases} \tau f & \text{if the prediction is consistent} \\ 1 + \tau f & \text{otherwise} \end{cases} \quad (5)$$

where t' and f' are the approximate number of agreements and disagreements, respectively, where $\tau = \frac{n}{n+1}$ and n is the length of the shift-register that we are approximating. We can then estimate the ub and lb confidence intervals using the decayed statistics for each exemplar, at the expense of some precision when compared to keeping the exact recent consistency history in the shift register.

5. Conclusion

This paper presented three alternative instance selection approaches for improved lazy learning in time-varying domains: Time-Weighted Forgetting (TWF), Locally-Weighted Forgetting (LWF) and a novel Prediction Error Context Switching (PECS) algorithm. These instance selection techniques were evaluated in a set of tasks with differing time-varying conditions: time-varying function mapping and static sampling distribution; static function mapping and time-varying sampling distribution; and static function mapping and sampling distribution. In the first condition, PECS performed as well as TWF and LWF, while an unmodified lazy learning algorithm (IB3A), was not able to classify well. In the second condition, LWF, PECS and IB3A all classified well, while TWF experienced catastrophic interference. Finally, in the static condition, TWF and LWF demonstrated lower asymptotic classification accuracy when compared to PECS and IB3A. The major implication is that we can enjoy the benefits of lazy learning algorithms in more domains by using PECS, which increases robustness to time-variation of functions and distributions, yet avoids undesirable side-effects such as catastrophic interference and poorer asymptotic error rates that are characteristic of the other instance selection algorithms.

Acknowledgments

This work was supported by Navy Grant N00014-92-J-1647, AFOSR Grants 88-0244, AFOSR 88-0296; Army/DAAL 03-89-C-0031PRI; NSF Grants CISE/CDA 88-22719, IRI 89-06770, and ASC 91 0813 and an NSF HPPC Postdoctoral Associateship for MS (CDA-9211136) and a National Institute of Disability and Rehabilitation Research Traineeship Grant.

References

Aha, D. W., Kibler, D. & Albert, M. K. (1991). Instance-Based Learning Algorithms. *Machine Learning* **6**: 37–66.

Atkeson, C. G. (1991). Using Locally Weighted Regression for Robot Learning. In *IEEE Conference on Robotics and Automation*, 958–963. IEEE Press.

Blum, A. (1995). Empirical Support for Winnow and Weighted Majority Based Algorithms: Results on a Calendar Scheduling Domain. *Proceedings of the Twelfth International Conference on Machine Learning*, 64–72. Morgan Kaufmann.

Duda P. O. & Hart P. E. (1973). *Pattern Classification and Scence Analysis*. Wiley and Sons: New York.

Friedman, J. H., Bentley, J. L. & Finkel, R. A. (1977). An Algorithm for Finding Best Matches in Logarithmic Expected Time. *ACM Transactions on Mathematical Software* **3**: 209–226.

Hembold, D. & Long, P. (1991). Tracking Drifting Concepts Using Random Samples. In *Fourth Workship on Computational Learning Theory*, 12–23.

Kalman, R. E. (1960). A New Approach to Linear Filtering and Prediction Problems. *Transactions ASME, Journal of Basic Engineering*: 35–45.

Kuh, A., Petsche, T. & Rivest, R. L. (1991). Learning Time-Varying Concepts. In *Advances in Neural Information Processing Systems 3*, 183–189. Morgan Kaufmann.

Larson, R. & Marx, M. (1986). *An Introduction to Mathematical Statistics*. Prentice Hall: Englewood Cliffs, NJ.

Maes, P. & Brooks, R. A. (1990). Learning to Coordinate Behaviors. In *AAAI-90*, 796–802.

McCloskey, M. & Cohen, N. J. (1989). *The Psychology of Learning and Motivation*, chapter Catastrophic Interference in Connectionist Networks: The Sequential Learning Problem. Academic Press: New York.

Moore, A. W. (1990). Acquisition of Dynamic Control Knowledge for a Robotic Manipulator. In *Proceedings of the Seventh International Conference on Machine Learning*, 244–252. Morgan Kaufmann.

Moore, A. W. (1991). Fast, Robust Adaptive Control by Learning Only Forward Models. In *Advances in Neural Information Processing Systems*. Morgan Kaufmann.

Ratcliff, R. (1990). Connectionist Models of Recognition Memory: Constraints Imposed by Learning and Forgetting Functions. *Psychological Reviews* **97**: 285–308.

Salganicoff, M. (1992). *Learning and Forgetting for Perception-Action: A Projection-Pursuit and Density-Adaptive Approach*. PhD thesis, University of Pennsylvania, Philadelphia, PA, Dept. of Computer and Information Science.

Salganicoff, M. (1993). Density-Adaptive Learning and Forgetting. In *Proceedings of the Tenth International Conference on Machine Learning*. San Francisco, CA: Morgan Kaufmann.

Schlimmer, J. C. & Granger, R. H. (1986). Incremental Learning from Noisy Data. *Machine Learning* **1**: 317–354.

Valiant, L. G. (1984). A Theory of the Learnable. *Communications of the ACM* **27**(11): 1134–1142.

Widmer, G. & Kubat, M. (1992). Learning Flexible Concepts from Streams of Examples: FLORA2. *Proceedings of the Tenth European Conference on Artificial Intelligence*, 463–467. John Wiley & Sons.

Widmer, G. & Kubat, M. (1992). *Effective Learning in Dynamic Environments by Explicit Context Tracking* (Technical Report 93-35). Vienna, Austria: Austrian Institute for Artificial Intelligence.

Artificial Intelligence Review **11**: 157–174, 1997.
© 1997 *Kluwer Academic Publishers.*

Discretisation in Lazy Learning Algorithms

KAI MING TING*
Basser Department of Computer Science, University of Sydney, NSW 2006, Australia

Abstract. This paper adopts the idea of discretising continuous attributes (Fayyad and Irani 1993) and applies it to lazy learning algorithms (Aha 1990; Aha, Kibler and Albert 1991). This approach converts continuous attributes into nominal attributes at the outset. We investigate the effects of this approach on the performance of lazy learning algorithms and examine it empirically using both real-world and artificial data to characterise the benefits of discretisation in lazy learning algorithms. Specifically, we have showed that discretisation achieves an effect of noise reduction and increases lazy learning algorithms' tolerance for irrelevant continuous attributes.

The proposed approach constrains the representation space in lazy learning algorithms to hyper-rectangular regions that are orthogonal to the attribute axes. Our generally better results obtained using a more restricted representation language indicate that employing a powerful representation language in a learning algorithm is not always the best choice as it can lead to a loss of accuracy.

Key words: lazy learning, discretisation, bias, axis-orthogonal representation, empirical evaluation

1. Introduction

Research in lazy learning (Dasarathy 1990; Aha 1990; Cost and Salzberg 1993; Wettschereck 1994) has used different metrics for continuous attributes and nominal attributes. By *metric*, we strictly refer here to a measure used to obtain the value-difference of an attribute. The current naive approach in lazy learning that simply combines different metrics for continuous and nominal attributes in tasks which have both types of attributes can lead to poor performance. In the hypothyroid dataset, for example, the decision tree algorithm, C4.5, has an error rate of 0.8% and the lazy learning algorithm used in this paper has an error rate of 72.4%. When a uniform metric is used (through discretising continuous attributes), the same algorithm achieves an error rate of 1.7%. This huge difference in performance exemplifies the problem. We will provide evidence for this claim in Section 3.1.

---

* Now at the Department of Computer Science, The University of Waikato, Private Bag 3105, Hamilton, New Zealand. E-mail: kaiming@cs.waikato.ac.nz

Here, we investigate an approach of transforming continuous attributes to nominal attributes through discretisation at the outset for lazy learning. One recent discretisation method (Fayyad and Irani 1993) used under the framework of decision trees provides a useful starting point for the work reported here. However, our motivation for using a discretisation method differs. In the framework of decision trees, the emphases are in computational efficiency that results in speeding up the evaluation process for discretising continuous attributes, and producing better decision trees (Catlett 1991; Fayyad and Irani 1993; Van de Merckt 1993). Others have used discretisation in rules (Kerber 1992) and in Naive Bayesian classifiers (Kononenko 1993) because these systems accept only nominal attributes. The ability to treat continuous values directly without discretisation gives lazy learning a seeming advantage over these other systems mentioned above. In fact, research in lazy learning (e.g., nearest neighbour algorithms) began in treating continuous values only. In contrary to the conventional method, we advocate the use of discretisation in lazy learning algorithms. Our experimental results show that discretisation for lazy learning algorithms can improve their performance both in datasets with mixed attribute types and datasets with only continuous attributes. These results are counter-intuitive because discretisation discards information (i.e., order of values and difference between values) in the data. We provide explanation for this outcome in Section 3.2.

Previous experiments (Mooney, Shavlik, Towell and Gove 1989; Weiss and Kapouleas 1989; Quinlan 1994) have shown that using a powerful representation language in a learning system is not always the best choice. Systems using a limited representation language can sometimes outperform those using more complex representation languages which subsume the former language. We show in this paper that this phenomenon occurs in the framework of lazy learning.

The objective of this paper is to investigate the effects on the performance of lazy learning algorithms using discretisation during preprocessing. We intend to characterise the conditions under which the approach can be beneficial to lazy learning.

We begin the next section with a brief description of lazy learning. Section 3 presents the empirical results and is followed by discussion and conclusion.

2. Lazy Learning Algorithms

Lazy learning distinguishes itself from other types of learning that induce theories in the form of decision trees, rules and neural networks. The basic lazy learning algorithm simply stores the training instances and classifies a new instance by predicting that it has the same class as its nearest stored instance

(Stanfill and Waltz 1986; Aha, Kibler and Albert 1991; Cost and Salzberg 1993). For a continuous attribute, the value-difference (usually normalised) between two values is simply an arithmetic difference. In tasks with only nominal attributes the "overlap" metric is usually used. This simply returns a zero value-difference if the two symbolic values are the same, and returns 1 otherwise. Formally, the function that returns a value-difference between two values (v and u) of an attribute i for both metrics is defined as:

$$\delta_i(v, u) = \begin{cases} |v - u| & \text{if attribute } i \text{ is continuous} \\ 0 & \text{if attribute } i \text{ is nominal and } v = u \\ 1 & \text{otherwise} \end{cases} \tag{1}$$

To handle tasks that have both types of attributes, the different metrics are simply combined in the similarity function (e.g., Euclidean distance in the IBn series algorithms by Aha, Kibler and Albert 1991).

Cost and Salzberg (1993) observe that some lazy learning algorithms perform relatively poorly in nominal attribute datasets and identify that it is due to the use of the overlap metric. They introduced MVDM, a modified version of the value-difference metric (Stanfill and Waltz 1986), and empirically showed that MVDM is a better metric than the overlap metric in some nominal attribute datasets.

In MVDM, the value-difference distance between two possible values (v and u) of a nominal attribute i is defined as follows (Cost and Salzberg 1993):

$$\delta_i(v, u) = \sum_{j=1}^{c} \left| \frac{N_{v,j}}{N_v} - \frac{N_{u,j}}{N_u} \right| \tag{2}$$

where c is the number of classes. N_q is the number of times that value q occurred in the training set, and $N_{q,j}$ is the number of times that value q occurred in training instances of class j.

The distance between two instances, $V = \langle v_1, v_2, \ldots, v_n \rangle$ and $U = \langle u_1, u_2, \ldots, u_n \rangle$ is computed using the distance function as follows:

$$Distance(V, U) = \sqrt{\sum_{i=1}^{n} \delta_i(v, u)^2} \tag{3}$$

In the experiments reported in Section 3, we use two variants of IB1 (Aha, Kibler and Albert 1991), namely IB1_o and IB1_m for IB1 with the overlap metric and IB1 with MVDM respectively. We use both metrics for nominal attributes to demonstrate the generality of the experimental results. The basic IB1 (which uses the nearest instance for final prediction) is used because it represents the core and simplest lazy learning method. IB1 uses the linear normalisation method (Aha 1990) to normalise all continuous attributes to the interval [0,1] (i.e., to subtract the minimum observed value and divide by the range).

We will employ a recent discretisation method used in decision trees (Fayyad and Irani 1993) to preprocess instances for IB1, which converts all continuous attributes into nominal attributes at the outset. The details of this discretisation method are given in Appendix A. An appeal of this approach is that it avoids any problems arising from combining two different metrics in tasks which have both types of attributes. Intuitively, using a uniform metric is preferred to using differing metrics because combining different metrics is analogous to summing two numbers of different units, which may bring about poor performance in lazy learning algorithms that use them.

In the following experiments, we first use some real-world datasets that have continuous attributes to investigate the effect of this preprocessing on the performance of IB1. In order to gain insight into the factors that affect the performance of IB1, we then examine some artificial datasets which have specific characteristics.

3. Experiments

The aim of these experiments is to test the following hypothesis:

> *Discretisation of continuous attributes at the outset improves the classification accuracy of IB1 in tasks that have high levels of attribute noise or large numbers of irrelevant continuous attributes.*

Recent machine learning research (Schaffer 1994) has shown that there is no such thing as a universally best learning algorithm. Thus, it is important to discern the conditions under which this bias, i.e., discretising continuous attributes during preprocessing, will improve IB1's performance.

In Section 3.1, we describe experiments with ten well-known datasets that have continuous attributes, obtained from the UCI Repository of machine learning databases (Murphy, 1995). They are the Wisconsin breast cancer (**bcw**), pima diabetes, waveform, Cleveland heart disease (heart), glass, hypothyroid, hepatitis, automobile, echocardiogram (echo) and horse colic datasets. The characteristics of these datasets are given in Table 1. The first five datasets contain only continuous attributes and the other five have both continuous and nominal attributes.

Table 1. Details of experimental datasets

Domain	No. instances	No. classes	No. attr & type	No. missing values
bcw	699	2	9C	16
Diabetes	768	2	8C	0
Waveform	300	3	40C	0
Heart	303	2	13C	6
Glass	214	6	9C	0
Hypothyroid	3163	2	18B+7C	5329
Hepatitis	155	2	13B+6C	167
Automobile	205	6	4B+6N+15C	59
Echo	131	2	1B+6C	40
Horse	368	2	3B+12N+7C	1925

B: Binary, N: Nominal, C: Continuous.

In Section 3.2, we will examine two types of artificial data. We will also investigate the behaviour of the approach when these datasets have attribute noise and irrelevant attributes. In all experiments, discretising continuous attributes during preprocessing is conducted using the training data first, and then the testing data is converted according to the cut-points obtained from the training data conversion. Algorithms run with data conversion are postfixed with * to differentiate from those run without.

3.1 UCI datasets

The first set of experiments employ IB1 and are conducted with the ten UCI datasets. For each dataset, we randomly select 90% of the instances for training and use the remaining 10% for testing, and repeat over 50 trials. The performance results for four variants of IB1 are shown in Table 2. The figures given are the means of the classification error rates over 50 trials together with their standard errors. The best result in each dataset is in boldface.

IB1_o* outperforms IB1_o in all datasets, though in the pima diabetes, glass and hepatitis datasets, the differences are marginal. IB1_m* achieves better results than IB1_m in seven datasets and has equal performance in the **bcw** dataset, and performs marginally worse in the hepatitis and horse colic datasets. IB1_o* achieves the best results for four datasets (**bcw**, glass, hypothyroid and echocardiogram) and IB1_m* has the best performance for the pima diabetes, waveform, heart and automobile datasets. In the hepatitis and horse colic datasets, IB1_m has the best results.

To clarify the comparative error rates, columns 'RER' (for relative error rates) in Table 2 show the differences in average error rates between IB1 and

Table 2. Average error rates for four variants of IB1

Domain	IB1_o	IB1_o*	RER	IB1_m	IB1_m*	RER
bcw	4.5 ± 0.3	**3.3 ± 0.2**	⋆ −1.2	4.6 ± 0.3	4.6 ± 0.3	0.0
Diabetes	29.8 ± 0.8	29.5 ± 0.7	−0.3	29.8 ± 0.8	**28.8 ± 0.6**	−1.0
Waveform	36.5 ± 1.3	31.1 ±1.1	⋆ −5.4	36.5 ± 1.3	**21.7 ± 1.1**	⋆ −14.8
Heart	24.7 ± 1.0	21.1 ± 1.0	⋆ −3.6	24.7 ± 1.0	**19.4 ± 0.9**	⋆ −5.3
Glass	30.0 ± 1.2	**27.3 ± 1.1**	−2.7	30.0 ± 1.2	27.7 ± 1.2	−2.3
Hypothyroid	2.7 ± 0.1	**1.4 ± 0.1**	⋆ −1.3	72.4 ± 0.3	1.7 ± 0.1	⋆ −70.7
Hepatitis	19.3 ± 1.3	19.0 ± 1.2	−0.3	**18.8 ± 1.4**	20.6 ± 1.6	+1.8
Automobile	24.2 ± 1.3	18.8 ± 1.1	⋆ −5.4	23.0 ± 1.3	**14.8 ± 1.0**	⋆ −8.2
Echo	43.9 ± 1.6	**35.4 ± 1.6**	⋆ −8.5	44.4 ± 1.6	36.0 ± 1.9	⋆ −8.4
Horse	24.1 ± 1.0	22.1 ± 1.0	⋆ −2.0	**19.9 ± 0.9**	20.0 ± 1.0	+0.1

⋆: two-tailed, paired t-test with IB1; $p < 0.05$.

IB1*, by taking the average error rate for IB1* as the base. Negative figures in columns 'RER' indicate that the algorithm which uses the converted data performs better than that using the original data, and vice versa. The ⋆ symbol in front of a figure indicates that the difference is significant (t-test, $p < 0.05$). The results clearly show that using the converted data is more desirable for IB1. IB1_m* gains substantially in some datasets, and there is a modest improvement for IB1_o*.

The extremely poor performance of IB1_m in the hypothyroid dataset needs special attention. An analysis on the MVDM produced for the eighteen binary attributes indicates that all the value-differences are less than 0.01. When these value-differences are used in conjunction with the continuous attributes in the distance calculation, they have virtually no impact. Thus, the eighteen binary attributes are deemed irrelevant by IB1_m. Omitting the binary attributes confirmed our analysis by showing similar results. Because of discretisation, the value-differences for the (original) continuous attributes have comparable "weight" to that of the binary attributes. As a result, all twenty-five attributes play a part in classification. Further examination of the data reveals that it has a large proportion of missing values and most of the values (91.8%) of the last attribute are missing. We conducted experiments by deleting the last attribute and using a different scheme[1] that ignores the missing attribute values when

---

[1] The two schemes used in treating missing values are provided in IB1 (Aha 1990). *Max Diff* yields value-differences equal to 1 for nominal attributes and for continuous metric, replaces a missing value with 1 or 0, whichever gives the larger value-difference, and yields 1 if the value is missing for both instances. *Ignore* is a scheme that ignores any missing value attributes when computing the distance between examples. We use the default setting (i.e., Max Diff) for all experiments unless otherwise specified. The Ignore scheme has no obvious advantage except in the hypothyroid datasets.

Table 3. Average error rates for the hypothyroid dataset

No. attribute	Missing value scheme	IB1_o	IB1_m	IB1_o*	IB1_m*
All attr	Max Diff	2.7	72.4	1.4	1.7
Delete 18 binary attr	Max Diff	72.6	72.6	1.7	1.6
Delete last attr	Max Diff	2.7	6.9	1.4	1.6
All attr	Ignore	2.3	2.0	1.4	1.7

computing the distance between instances. The results of these experiments are shown in Table 3, which reveals that IB1_m's poor performance in this dataset is due to the use of different metrics, the missing value scheme used and the peculiar missing values situation.

Since the waveform dataset has nineteen irrelevant attributes, these results seem to suggest that discretisation has increased IB1's tolerance for irrelevant continuous attributes. It is also reasonable to assume these UCI datasets have noise (i.e., the waveform dataset contains Gaussian noise). Discretising continuous attributes could have the effect of noise reduction, which leads to a better performance in almost all the selected datasets. The noise in the data could be reduced by having a coarse division of the real line into several intervals. Assuming appropriate cut-points are found, all values within each interval in the real line, including noise, are converted to one value. Thus, most of the noise in the data can be reduced by making the attribute-values' granularity coarse. We use artificial datasets to test these hypotheses on attribute noise and irrelevant attributes in the following section.

3.2 Artificial datasets

Each of the following experiments was conducted over 50 trials with each trial trained on a randomly generated dataset of a fixed size. All trials in each experiment are tested using the same testing dataset of size 1000. We conducted a two-tailed, paired t-test between the error rates of IB1 and IB1*, and the difference is considered significant if $p < 0.05$.

The purpose of using artificial datasets is to investigate under what conditions discretising continuous attributes will improve/degrade the performance of IB1. The first artificial dataset task, designated as X&Y $\geq$ 0.50, involves two dimensions, where each dimension has values within the interval [0.00,1.00]. Its decision boundaries are orthogonal to the axes. Class 1 is assigned to all points in the top right quarter, and anywhere else is class 0. The two classes are equal-probable. The target concept is:

If $(X \geq 0.50)$ and $(Y \geq 0.50)$ then class 1 else class 0.

Table 4. Average error rates for IB1 and IB1* in the X&Y ≥ 0.50 dataset

Data size	IB1	IB1*
100	3.2 ± 0.1	⋆ 1.1 ± 0.2
150	2.6 ± 0.1	⋆ 0.7 ± 0.2
200	2.4 ± 0.1	⋆ 0.4 ± 0.1

⋆: significant in two-tailed, paired t-test with IB1

Table 4 shows the average error rates for IB1 and IB1* in three different training data sizes. IB1_o and IB1_m behave similarly on this dataset, IB1* outperform IB1 in all cases and the discretisation method employed performs better as the training set size increases.

Another task, which has a non-orthogonal class boundary with respect to the axes, is used for further investigation. The concept description has two continuous attributes[2] and the two classes are equal-probable:

If (X+Y > 1) then class 1, else class 0.

We use both the X&Y ≥ 0.50 and X+Y > 1 tasks in the following experiments by introducing attribute noise.

3.2.1 *Attribute noise*

Gaussian noise with mean zero and varying standard deviations (sd) is introduced to the continuous attributes in another experiment and the noisy data is allowed to be out of range. The results for the 150 training data items in the X&Y ≥ 0.50 and X+Y > 1 datasets are shown in Figures 1(a) and 1(b) respectively. Because IB1_o* and IB1_m* behave similarly, only one result is plotted in Figure 1(a). In the X&Y ≥ 0.50 dataset, discretisation *improves* the performance of IB1 in all cases. In the X+Y > 1 dataset, discretisation *degrades* the performance of IB1 in the noise-free or 'low noise' cases; but *improves* performance for the 'high noise' situations.[3] The performance differences are significant at all noise levels in both tasks.[4] Though the X+Y > 1 concept has a non-orthogonal class boundary with respect to the axes, forcing axis-orthogonal splits through discretisation can still improve IB1's performance at high noise levels. This is because noise has blurred the boundary.

---

[2] Two decimal digits are used here. The range of X and Y is also from 0.00 to 1.00.

[3] Note that the graphs for IB1_o* and IB1_m* are almost identical in Figure 1(b).

[4] The error bars are too small to be visible. In the X&Y ≥ 0.50 dataset, the standard errors range from 0.2% to 0.3% for IB1, and from 0.1% to 0.4% for IB1*. In the X+Y > 1 dataset, the standard errors range from 0.1% to 0.3% for IB1, and from 0.1% to 0.4% for IB1*.

Table 5. Average number of predictions made using more than one instance

Dataset		IB1	IB1_o*	IB1_m*
X&Y ≥ 0.50_150	Noise-free	27.0	1000.0	1000.0
	Noise (sd=0.2)	9.8	1000.0	1000.0
X+Y > 1_150	Noise-free	19.0	970.7	967.5
	Noise (sd=0.3)	6.0	980.9	979.8

At high noise levels, these 'blurring' errors are higher than those caused by axis-orthogonal splits.

The average number of cut-points produced for the 150 training data items is 2.0 for the noise-free data and 2.2 for the noisy data (sd=0.2) in the X&Y ≥ 0.50 dataset. For the X+Y > 1 dataset, they are 7.4 and 5.7 (for noisy data, sd=0.3) respectively. The discretisation method employed produces the right number of cut-points for the X&Y ≥ 0.50 dataset. Some example cut-points for the X+Y > 1 noisy dataset are 0.40, 0.62 and 0.81 for X and 0.07, 0.32 and 0.97 for Y. These cut-points for the X+Y > 1 dataset can only approximate the non-orthogonal decision boundary.

One explanation for the effect of discretisation is that it has made the attribute-values' granularity coarse. For some noise-free or low noise datasets, fine attribute-value granularity would be the best choice. However, in the case of high noise datasets, coarse-grain attribute-value granularity can be a better choice as *this achieves an effect of noise reduction.*

Another issue we would like to explore is to examine the number of predictions made using more than one nearest neighbour. IB1 employs a majority vote when two or more stored instances have the same minimum distance. Table 5 shows the average (over 50 trials with 1000 test instances per trial) number of predictions, N, when they are made using more than one nearest instance for the two artificial dataset tasks. Without discretisation, N in the noisy data is less than that of the noise-free data in both tasks. This coincides with the intuition that noise causes instances to be less similar to each other.[5] As noise corrupts the values, two identical instances can become completely different. In both tasks, discretisation increases the similarity between instances within each hypercube of the discretised description space (indicated by N close or equal to 1000). But this does not necessarily translate into a lower error rate, as shown in the case of the X+Y > 1 noise-free cases. Actually, the increased similarity through discretisation only has the effect of

---

[5] We refer here to instances with continuous attributes. For instances with only nominal attributes, noise can make some different instances become identical.

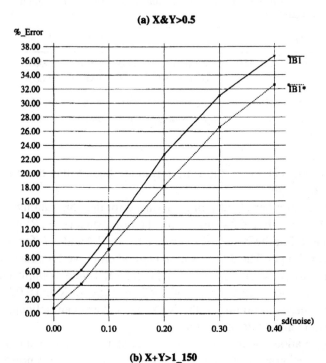

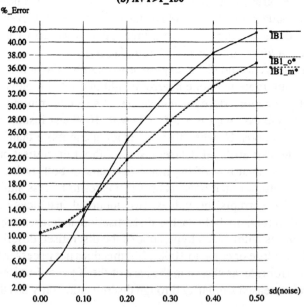

Figure 1. The effect of noise on IB1 and IB1*

Table 6. Relative error rates (IB1 vs IB1*) after
introducing additional noise

Noise level (sd)	IB1_o	IB1_m
(a) The hepatitis dataset		
0.0	−0.3	+1.8
1.0	−1.9	−2.0
2.0	−1.7	⋆ −2.7
(b) The horse colic dataset		
0.0	⋆ −2.0	+0.1
3.0	⋆ −2.4	−0.6
6.0	⋆ −2.1	⋆ −2.8

⋆: significant in two-tailed, paired t-test between
IB1 and IB1*

noise reduction. This effect has brought about the increased performance in
the high noise cases of the X+Y > 1 dataset.

In light of this result, we suspect the only two datasets (i.e., hepatitis and
horse colic) in which IB1_m* performs marginally worse than IB1_m might
be due to low noise levels. An experiment was conducted by adding Gaussian
noise to the continuous attributes in these datasets. Their relative error rates,
shown in Tables 6, indicate that IB1* outperforms IB1 at high noise levels.

3.2.2 Irrelevant attributes

Using noise-free data (150 training data items), the effects of irrelevant
continuous attributes for the X&Y ≥ 0.50 and X+Y > 1 concepts are shown
in Figures 2(a) and 2(b) respectively, where we added a varying number of
irrelevant continuous attributes to the original concepts. Note that the performance of IB1_o is equivalent to that of IB1_m, and their performance
quickly degrades as the number of irrelevant attributes increases (Aha 1990;
Wettschereck 1994). In both cases, the performance of IB1_o* and IB1_m*
degrade more gracefully. The performance differences between IB1 and IB1*
are significant in all cases. These results indicate that *discretisation increases
IB1's tolerance for irrelevant continuous attributes*. In all cases, the irrelevant
continuous attributes are converted into binary attributes. The discretisation
method produces binary attributes with skewed distributions (i.e., one value
occurs more often than the other). This explains why IB1* performs better
than IB1, especially IB1_o*, which uses the overlap metric. The effect of irrelevant binary attributes on the performance of IB1_o decreases as the skewness
of the binary value distribution (of the irrelevant attributes) increases.

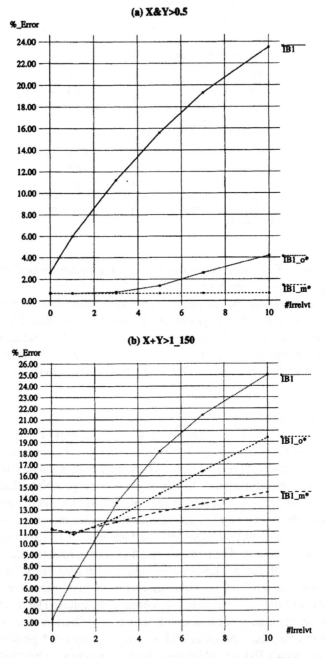

Figure 2. The effect of irrelevant attributes on IB1 and IB1*

Table 7. Average error rates for the waveform dataset

No. irrelevant attr	IB1_o	IB1_o*	IB1_m	IB1_m*
0	26.1 ± 0.8	26.5 ± 1.0	26.1 ± 0.8	**22.1 ± 1.2**
19	36.5 ± 1.3	30.6 ± 1.1	36.5 ± 1.3	**21.7 ± 1.1**

We conducted another experiment by deleting the nineteen irrelevant attributes in the waveform dataset used in Section 3.1. The results, tabulated in Table 7, show that IB1_m* has nullified the impact of irrelevant attributes on IB1_m, and IB1_o* has reduced the impact of irrelevant attributes on IB1_o.

We summarise the experimental results with the two artificial dataset tasks as follows:

i. For the X&Y $\geq$ 0.50 dataset, discretisation improves the performance of IB1 at all noise levels.

ii. For the noise-free or low noise X+Y > 1 datasets, discretisation *degrades* the performance of IB1 because it can only produce cut-points that approximate the non-orthogonal decision boundary in this task.

iii. For the high noise X+Y > 1 datasets, discretisation *improves* the performance of IB1. This is achieved through noise reduction by discretisation.

iv. Discretisation *increases IB1's tolerance for irrelevant continuous attributes* in both tasks by producing binary attributes with skewed distributions.

4. Discussion

Discretisation, at first sight, seems to be antithetical to the idea of lazy learning because it discards information from the data. This is the reason why research on lazy learning algorithms almost never considers using it. On the contrary, lazy learning algorithms are thought to have an advantage over other learning systems that induce decision trees or rules as they can process continuous values directly. Our results here show that, in some situations, discretisation can improve the performance of lazy learning algorithms.

By discretising continuous attributes, we have transferred the source of the errors from those due to using different metrics in tasks that have both types of attributes to discretisation errors (i.e., problems caused by incorrect and spurious cut-points). However, the errors induced by the discretisation mistakes are smaller in most of the datasets studied. The empirical results show that a naive approach in lazy learning which uses two different metrics for continuous and nominal attributes can lead to poor performance in datasets that have both types of attributes. The experiments conducted in the hypothy-roid dataset (shown in Table 3) further reveal that using this naive approach can also increase the sensitivity of the scheme used in treating missing values. When a uniform metric is used instead (i.e., by discretising continu-ous attributes), the sensitivity diminished. Converting continuous attributes to nominal attributes at the outset proves to be a simple yet effective approach. In this way, IB1* uses only one metric rather than two different metrics for continuous and nominal attributes. It provides a coherent approach for the treatment of these two types of attributes.

Experiments with artificial data have provided some insight into the effects of the data character (i.e., attribute noise and irrelevant attributes) on IB1*. Since most real-world cases possibly contain 'high noise' and irrelevant attributes, this explains the better performance of IB1* over IB1 in most of the ten UCI datasets. This finding is also true even if the actual concepts have boundaries not orthogonal to the axes. Although discretisation could only approximate boundaries of this type, it has been shown (e.g., for the X+Y > 1 dataset) that it is better to have coarse axis-orthogonal approximation in 'high noise' situations. This also explains why the nominal attribute treatment is preferable even in datasets with only continuous attributes. Though it is hard to define the level of noise in a dataset, the experimental results seem to suggest that most of the ten UCI datasets contain 'high noise'. Only the hepatitis and horse colic datasets have possibly low noise levels.

Discretisation might also be beneficial for IB1 when using multiple near-est neighbours (i.e., $k > 1$ in k-nearest neighbour algorithms). Using both the k parameter (Wettschereck 1994) and discretisation during preprocessing can produce almost the same effect of noise reduction and improve toler-ance for irrelevant attributes. The k fixes the number of nearest neighbours used in making predictions while discretisation causes the number of nearest neighbours that have the same distance to vary in different regions of the description space.

Since discretisation only provides decision boundaries orthogonal to the axes of the description space, it is anticipated that this approach would degrade the performance of IB1 when the target concept's boundaries are not axis-orthogonal (i.e., in noise-free cases). One weakness of the current discretisation method is that it would fail to find the exact cut-points in the datasets that have correlation between values of different attributes even in noise-free cases (Ting 1995). Because the method determines the cut-points using the whole training set, correlation between values of different attributes in the data 'blurs' the actual cut-points and makes them hard to find using the information gain criterion. We have also attempted five other discreti-sation methods that include variants of the method used in this paper and a discretisation method based on unsupervised learning (Van de Merckt 1993). However, among the six methods, the discretisation method used here seems to work best with IB1 (see Ting 1994). Ting (1994) has also shown that the discretisation method works well with naive Bayesian classifiers (Cestnik 1990). The approach can be applied to other more complex lazy learning algorithms which use other metrics and similarity functions.[6]

Though a few researchers have used discretisation for nearest-neighbour-like algorithms (e.g., Wong and Chiu (1987) use discretisation for their clustering algorithm), no systematic evaluation on when or why discretisation is useful for lazy learning algorithms has been done.

The metric used for nominal attributes does have an effect on the performance of IB1. However, we found no evidence for the claim that MVDM is better than the overlap metric. Our experiments reveal that about half of our experiments favour one metric and the rest favours the other metric (see Table 2).

5. Conclusion

The main contribution of this paper is an analysis of using discretisation during preprocessing in lazy learning algorithms. This approach, though counter-intuitive at first sight, is supported by empirical results. This investigation has also characterised two situations, i.e., datasets that have high level of attribute noise or large numbers of irrelevant attributes, where discretisation can be beneficial to lazy learning. This is because discretisation achieves an effect of noise reduction and increases lazy learning algorithms' tolerance for irrelevant continuous attributes. Although the proposed approach limits the representable concepts to hyper-rectangular regions that are orthogonal to the attribute axes, it has been shown to improve the performance of IB1 in almost all of the ten datasets selected from the UCI Repository that contain continuous attributes.

Acknowledgements

This research was partially supported by an Australia Research Council grant (to J.R. Quinlan) and by a research agreement with Digital Equipment Corporation. This author is partially supported by the Equity and Merit

---

[6] Ting (1995) describes experiments on discretisation during preprocessing for k-nearest neighbour algorithms and a variable-kernel similarity metric algorithm (Wettschereck, 1994; Lowe, 1995).

Scholarship Scheme. Numerous discussions with J.R. Quinlan, N. Indurkhya, M. Cameron-Jones, Z. Zheng, G. Webb, I. Witten and D. Wettschereck have been very helpful. Thanks to D.W. Aha for providing IB1 and many helpful suggestions that improve the presentation of the final version of the paper. Thanks are also due to anonymous referees for their helpful comments.

Appendix A

We use Fayyad and Irani's (1993) discretisation method in this paper to transform all continuous attributes to nominal attributes during preprocessing for the lazy learning algorithm, IB1. Their method considers all possible cut-points (i.e., the values that appear in the training set) and selects the cut-point that gives the highest information gain (see Equation (A.7)). This method is continuously re-applied to the subsets of the previous split until a stopping criterion is satisfied. The stopping criterion based on the minimum description length principle, MDLP (Rissanen 1989), prescribes accepting the partition if and only if the total cost of encoding the binary partition (BP) is less than the total cost of encoding the classes of the examples ($CLASS$).

$$Cost(BP) < Cost(CLASS) \qquad (A.1)$$

Here

$$Cost(CLASS) = N \cdot Ent(S) + c \cdot Ent(S) \qquad (A.2)$$
$$Cost(BP) = log_2(N-1) + |S_1| \cdot Ent(S_1) + |S_2| \cdot Ent(S_2) +$$
$$log_2(3^c - 2) + c_1 \cdot Ent(S_1) + c_2 \cdot Ent(S_2) \quad (A.3)$$
$$Ent(S) = -\sum_{i=1}^{c} P(C_i, S) \cdot log_2(P(C_i, S)) \qquad (A.4)$$

where N is the number of examples in a set S. $Ent(S)$ is the class entropy of set S and c is the number of classes in set S. S_1 and S_2 are two disjoint subsets of S due to the binary partition. $P(C_i, S)$ is the proportion of examples in S that are in class C_i.

Through some mathematical manipulations (see Fayyad and Irani (1993) for details), this criterion can be stated as follows:

MDLP Criterion: the partition induced by a cut-point T of attribute A for a set S of N examples is accepted iff

$$Gain(A, T, S) > \frac{log_2(N - 1)}{N} + \frac{\Delta(A, T, S)}{N} \qquad (A.5)$$

and it is rejected otherwise, where

$$\Delta(A, T, S) = log_2(3^c - 2) - [c \cdot Ent(S) - c_1 \cdot Ent(S_1) - c_2 \cdot Ent(S_2)] \qquad (A.6)$$

$$Gain(A, T, S) = Ent(S) - \frac{|S_1|}{N} \cdot Ent(S_1) - \frac{|S_2|}{N} \cdot Ent(S_2) \qquad (A.7)$$

$Gain(A, T, S)$ is the information gain of a cut-point T of attribute A for a set S.

References

Aha, D. W., Kibler D. & Albert M. K. (1991). Instance-Based Learning Algorithms, *Machine Learning* 6: 37–66.

Aha, D. W. (1990). *A Study of Instance-Based Algorithms for Supervised Learning Tasks: Mathematical, Empirical, and Psychological Evaluations*, PhD Thesis, Department of Information and Computer Science, University of California, Irvine, Technical Report 90-42.

Catlett, J. (1991). On Changing Continuous Attributes into Ordered Discrete Attributes. In Kodratoff (ed.) *Proceedings of the European Working Session on Learning*, pp. 164–178. Springer-Verlag.

Cestnik, B. (1990). Estimating Probabilities: A Crucial Task in Machine Learning. In *Proceedings of the European Conference on Artificial Intelligence*, 147–149.

Cost, S & Salzberg S. (1993). A Weighted Nearest Neighbor Algorithm for Learning with Symbolic Features. *Machine Learning* 10: 57–78.

Dasarathy, B. V. (ed) (1990). *Nearest Neighbor (NN) Norms: NN Pattern Classification Techniques*. IEEE Computer Society Press.

Fayyad, U. M. & Irani K. B. (1993). Multi-Interval Discretization of Continuous-Valued Attributes for Classification Learning. In *Proceedings of the 13th International Joint Conference on Artificial Intelligence*, 1022–1027. Morgan Kaufmann.

Kerber, R. (1992). ChiMerge: Discretization of Numeric Attributes. In *Proceedings of the Tenth National Conference on Artificial Intelligence*, 123–128. AAAI Press/The MIT Press.

Kononenko, I. (1993). Inductive and Bayesian Learning in Medical Diagnosis. *Applied Artificial Intelligence* 7: 317–337.

Lowe, D. G. (1995). Similarity Metric Learning for a Variable-Kernel Classifier. *Neural Computation* 7(1) (January): 72–85.

Mooney, R., Shavlik, J., Towell, G. & Gove, A. (1989). An Empirical Comparison of Symbolic and Connectionist Learning Algorithms. In *Proceedings of the 11th International Joint Conference on Artificial Intelligence*, 775–780. Morgan Kaufmann.

Murphy, P. M. (1995). *UCI Repository of Machine Learning Databases*. Irvine, CA: University of California, Department of Information and Computer Science. [http://www.ics.uci.edu/ mlearn/MLRepository.html].

Quinlan, J. R. (1994). Comparing Connectionist and Symbolic Learning Methods. In Hanson, S. J., Drastal, G. A., & Rivest, R. L. (eds.) *Computational Learning Theory and Natural Learning Systems*, Vol. I, 445–456. The MIT Press.

Rissanen, J. (1989). *Stochastic Complexity in Statistical Inquiry*. World Scientific.

Schaffer, C. (1994), A Conservation Law for Generalization Performance. In *Proceedings of the 11th International Conference on Machine Learning*, 259–265. Morgan Kaufmann.

Stanfill, C. & Waltz, D. (1986). Toward Memory-Based Reasoning. *Communications of the ACM* 29(12): 1213–1228.

Ting, K. M. (1994). *Discretization of Continuous-Valued Attributes and Instance-Based Learning*. Technical Report 491, Basser Dept of Computer Science, University of Sydney.

Ting, K. M. (1995). *Common Issues in Instance-Based and Naive Bayesian Classifiers*, PhD Thesis, Basser Department of Computer Science, University of Sydney.

Van de Merckt, T. (1993). Decision Trees in Numerical Attributes Spaces. In *Proceedings of the 13th International Joint Conference on Artificial Intelligence*, 1016–1021. Morgan Kaufmann.

Weiss, S. M. & Kapouleas, I. (1989). An Empirical Comparison of Pattern Recognition, Neural Nets, and Machine Learning Classification Methods. In *Proceedings of the 11th International Joint Conference on Artificial Intelligence*, 781–787. Morgan Kaufmann.

Wettschereck, D. (1994). *A Study of Distance-Based Machine Learning Algorithms*. PhD Thesis, Department of Computer Science, Oregon State University.

Wong, A. K. C. & Chiu, D. K. Y. (1987). Synthesizing Statistical Knowledge from Incomplete Mixed-mode Data. *IEEE Transactions on Pattern Analysis and Machine Intelligence* **PAMI-9**(6): 796–805.

Artificial Intelligence Review **11**: 175–191, 1997.

Intelligent Selection of Instances for Prediction Functions in Lazy Learning Algorithms

JIANPING ZHANG[1], YEE-SAT YIM[2] and JUNMING YANG[3]

[1]*jianping@zhang.cs.usu.edu;* [2]*Computer Science Department, Utah State University, Logan, UT 84322-4205;* [3]*slw8p@cc.usu.edu*

Abstract. Lazy learning methods for function prediction use different prediction functions. Given a set of stored instances, a similarity measure, and a novel instance, a prediction function determines the value of the novel instance. A prediction function consists of three components: a positive integer k specifying the number of instances to be selected, a method for selecting the k instances, and a method for calculating the value of the novel instance given the k selected instances. This paper introduces a novel method called k *surrounding neighbor* (k-SN) for intelligently selecting instances and describes a simple k-SN algorithm. Unlike k *nearest neighbor* (k-NN), k-SN selects k instances that surround the novel instance. We empirically compared k-SN with k-NN using the linearly weighted average and local weighted regression methods. The experimental results show that k-SN outperforms k-NN with linearly weighted average and performs slightly better than k-NN with local weighted regression for the selected datasets.

Key words: instance-based learning and prediction, function prediction, prediction functions

1. Introduction

The focus of supervised learning has been on generating rules for predicting class categories. However, many real world applications require the prediction of numeric functions. One example of such applications is a highway accident frequency predictor that yields the accident frequency of a given highway section based on its geometric conditions. Accurate predictions of accident frequency may help traffic engineers design and test solutions for the improvement of highway safety.

Prediction of functions has been studied for many years in statistics, but its importance has been recognized by machine learning researchers only recently. Several learning and prediction algorithms have been developed by machine learning researchers in the past few years. Kibler, Aha and Albert (1989), Aha (1990), Moore and Atkeson (1992), and Townsend-Weber and Kibler (1994) applied lazy learning methods for function prediction. Decision tree based learning with numeric functions have been studied by Breiman, Friedman, Olshen and Stone (1984), and Quinlan (1992). Weiss and

Indurkhya (1993) described a rule induction algorithm that generates a list of ordered regression rules for function prediction. Quinlan (1993) developed an algorithm that combines lazy learning and model-based methods to function prediction tasks.

Among these methods, lazy learning methods are popular because of their simplicity and ease in application to function prediction. Lazy learning methods vary in their prediction functions, similarity measures, and ways to select instances to store. Given a set of stored instances along with a similarity measure and a novel instance, a prediction function determines the value of the novel instance. A similarity measure determines the degree of similarity between two instances, and is usually a function of the distance between them. A lazy learning algorithm may save all training instances or only a subset of the training instances.

The focus of this paper is prediction functions. The value of a given novel instance is calculated from the values of a selected subset of stored instances. Thus, a prediction function of a lazy learning method consists of three components: a positive integer k specifying the number of instances to be selected, a method for selecting the k instances, and a method for calculating the value of the novel instance given the k selected instances. This paper introduces a novel method, called k *surrounding neighbor* (k-SN), for selecting instances and a simple k-SN algorithm. Unlike k nearest neighbor (k-NN), k-SN selects k instances that surround the novel instance. Section 2 summarizes the previous work on lazy learning for function prediction with an emphasis on prediction functions. We present the k-SN method in Section 3. Section 4 reports the results of the empirical comparisons of k-SN with k-NN using the linearly weighted average and local weighted regression methods. We conclude in Section 5.

2. Previous Work on Lazy Learning for Function Prediction

In this section we review some lazy learning algorithms for function prediction and the prediction functions used in these algorithms. Throughout the rest of this paper performance will be defined in terms of prediction errors.

2.1 *Lazy learning methods*

Connell and Utgoff (1987) presented a domain-specific lazy learning method for the cart-pole balancing problem. The numeric function to be learned represents the degree of desirability of a cart-pole state. The values of this function range from -1 (undesirable state) to 1 (desirable state). Only small parts of all generated instances are stored, and they are selected by the critic element using domain-specific knowledge. All stored instances are either desirable or undesirable states. The degree of desirability of a new cart-pole state is computed using Shepard's interpolating function with all stored instances.

Kibler et al. (1989) explored a domain independent lazy learning method derived from IB1, a lazy learning algorithm for classification (Aha, Kibler and Albert 1991). The predicted value of a novel instance is the weighted average of N% of all stored instances that are most similar to the novel instance. The weight of an instance depends linearly on its similarity to the novel instance, so that a more similar instance is assigned a larger weight. In (Kibler et al. 1989), it was proven that, given enough instances, IB1 can pac-learn any closed bounded continuous functions. In the same work, IB1 was compared empirically with linear regression using several function prediction tasks. It was concluded that IB1 has some advantages over linear regression: 1) it attained higher prediction accuracy, 2) its training algorithm is simple, 3) it does not require a model of the target function, and 4) it works well with symbolic attributes.

Unfortunately, IB1 has a serious problem. Because IB1 stores all training instances and each prediction of a novel instance involves measuring the distance between the novel instance and each of the stored instances, it becomes very inefficient when the set of training instances grows large. Aha (1990) showed that IB1's storage requirement can be significantly reduced without greatly decreasing its prediction accuracy, and developed a storage reduction lazy learning algorithm called IB2. IB2 saves only those instances for which prediction errors are larger than a given threshold. IB2 is sensitive to noisy training instances, and saves most of these instances because noisy instances often cause large prediction errors. IB3 (Aha 1990) was designed for noise tolerance. IB3 uses only accepted saved instances to predict values for novel instances. Accepted instances are those that display significantly accurate prediction behavior on similar instances.

Quinlan (1993) combined a lazy learning method with model-based methods for function prediction. In his combined method, Quinlan uses the model-based method to adjust the value predicted by the lazy learning method. Three model-based methods: linear regression, neural networks, and model trees, were used in his experiments. Experimental results on several datasets showed that the combined method was significantly better than the individual methods.

Moore and Atkeson (1992) described lazy learning methods for control problems. In their methods, several prediction functions were investigated. Among these prediction functions are *nearest neighbor*, *kernel regression*, and *local weighted regression*. Kernel regression uses the weighted average of all stored instances as the predicted value of the novel instance, and is a nonlinearly weighted average method. The weight of an instance is computed based on its distance to the novel instance, so that the closest instance has the greatest effect. The effect of an instance decreases nonlinearly with its distance to the novel instance, so that a distant instance has little effect. Local weighted regression applies linear regression to find the best local fit to the set of n closest instances. Similar to kernel regression, each instance is nonlinearly weighted based on its distance to the novel instance.

Recently, Townsend-Weber and Kibler (1994) empirically compared the linearly weighted average prediction method with the unweighted average prediction method, proposed two methods to eliminate irrelevant attributes, and developed a method to determine the best k for the k-NN method. Their results showed that the weighted average and unweighted average methods performed equally well, and that choosing the best k with elimination of irrelevant attributes generally reduced the prediction errors.

This paper is concerned with the prediction functions used by lazy learning methods. Therefore, the previous work on prediction functions is discussed in detail in the next section.

2.2 *Prediction functions*

Given a set of instances in memory, a prediction function determines the value of the novel instance. Three issues are involved in a prediction function: 1) how many instances should be selected to predict the value of the novel instance (i.e., determine an integer k), 2) which k instances should be selected, and 3) how to derive the novel instance's value from the k selected instances.

Several researchers (Duda and Hart 1973; Aha 1990) showed that classification/prediction accuracy in k-NN increases with k, peaks at a certain value, and then drops as k continues to grow. The peak value of k varies from one application to another. Thus, it becomes important to determine the best k for each application. In the early k-NN methods, k was a parameter determined by the user. Recently, many algorithms use the leave-one-out cross-validation method to determine the best k. In this method, the value of each instance in the training set is predicted using the instances selected from the rest of the training set with many values of k, and the best k is the one with the lowest average error over all training instances. Although this method for determining the best k works better than the method in which it is a user determined parameter, it can still be improved in the future. The best k determined using the leave-one-out cross-validation method is fixed for an entire application. We believe that the best k actually depends on where the novel instance is located and the number of instances available in this area.

Once k is determined, a prediction function needs to decide which k instances should be selected. Almost all lazy learning algorithms use k-NN, which selects the k instances that are most similar to the novel instance. In this paper, we propose another method called k-SN to select instances. Instead of selecting the k nearest neighbors of the novel instance, k-SN selects k instances that are not only similar to it, but also well distributed around the novel instance.

After the k instances are selected, the value of the novel instance must be derived from them. Several methods were proposed to derive this value. Among these methods *weighted average* (Aha 1990) and *local weighted regression* (Cleveland and Delvin 1988; Moore and Atkeson 1992) are the two most popular ones. In weighted average, the value of the novel instance is the weighted average of the values of the k selected instances. The weight of an instance depends on its similarity to the novel instance, and is generated so that the most similar instances have the largest weights. The weight of a selected instance may be a linear or nonlinear function of the similarity between the selected instance and the novel instance. For nonlinear weighting, the effect of an instance decreases nonlinearly with its similarity to the novel instance, so that a distant instance has little effect.

For each novel instance, local weighted regression performs a linear regression on the k selected instances. Similarly to weighted average, each of the k instances is weighted based on its similarity to the novel instance. The resulting linear equation is then applied to the novel instance.

Although researchers (e.g., Atkeson and Moore 1992) have argued that local weighted regression outperforms weighted average, there are still applications in which weighted average is preferred. Our experiments show that the average best k of local weighted regression is many times larger than that of weighted average. Usually, k should be at least as large as the number of attributes for local weighted regression; otherwise, the solution of the resulting linear equation is not unique. Because it needs a large k, local weighted regression may not perform well when enough local instances are not available. This problem may be overcome by using a different k for different areas of the function to be predicted.

Similar to regression, local weighted regression does not handle multivalued symbolic variables very well. This is because regression methods convert a multivalued symbolic variable to several different binary variables. For example, a symbolic variable with ten values may be converted to ten independent binary variables, and this conversion may cause a dramatic degradation in performance. This problem is severe when the multivalued symbolic variable is irrelevant, because the conversion adds many irrelevant variables. Our experimental results demonstrated this problem. Recently, some researchers have invented methods to treat symbolic attributes and numeric attributes simultaneously (Cost and Salzberg 1993; Mohri and Tanaka 1994). These methods may be used to overcome this problem.

For weighted average, the prediction error of the novel instance x does not exceed $MAX_{i=1,...,k} |f_x - f_i|$, where f_i is the value of the ith selected instance and f_x is the value of x. However, the prediction error of local weighted regression is not bounded (i.e., its prediction error may be infinite). In the experiments conducted, we found that some instances received very large prediction errors when local weighted regression was applied.

In addition, the algorithm of weighted average is simpler and faster than that of local weighted regression.

Experimental results reported in Section 4 show that local weighted regression performs better on some problems, while weighted average performs better on others. Further studies need to be conducted to compare weighted average with local weighted regression. However, this topic is beyond the scope of this paper, and will be the subject of future research.

3. The k-SN Method

This section introduces the idea of the k-SN method and describes a simple k-SN algorithm.

3.1 General idea

The idea of the k-SN method is to select k instances that are not only close to the novel instance, but also well distributed around the novel instance in the instance space. In other words, all selected instances should be close to the novel instance, but they should not be too close to each other. When selected instances are widely distributed around the novel instance, more information is provided to predict the value of the novel instance.

To illustrate this idea, let us consider 2-SN. For a given function $f(x_1, \ldots, x_n)$ and the novel instance $p_x = (x_1 \ldots x_n)$, ideally 2-SN should select two instances $p_y = (y_1 \ldots y_n)$ and $p_z = (z_1 \ldots z_n)$ such that p_y and p_z are close to p_x, and for all $i = 1, \ldots, n$, either $y_i > x_i > z_i$ or $z_i > x_i > y_i$. Figure 1 illustrates this idea using a single variable function. In Figure 1, 2-SN selects p_y and p_z, even though p_w is closer to p_x than p_z. 2-NN would select p_w instead of p_z.

When all selected instances fall in a monotonic subinterval of the target function, k-SN should outperform k-NN when weighted average is used. This is due to the following two facts. First, the predicted value of weighted

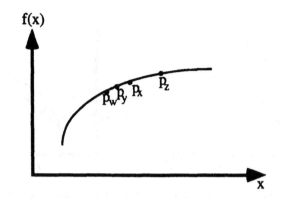

Figure 1. Illustration of the 2-SN method.

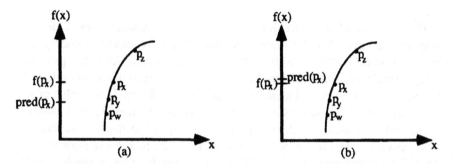

Figure 2. Comparison of 2-NN with 2-SN using the linearly weighted average method. (a) 2-NN selects p_y and p_w to predict the value of p_x. (b) 2-SN selects p_y and p_z to predict the value of p_x.

average is always between the minimum and maximum values of the selected instances. Second, the values of some (ideally half) of the instances selected using k-SN are smaller than the actual value of the novel instance, and the values of the other selected instances are larger than the actual value of the novel instance. This may not be true for instances selected using k-NN. This advantage may become significant when the slope of the monotonic sub-interval is steep. For simplicity, consider 2-NN for a single variable function $f(x)$. The predicted value of the novel instance is always between the values of the two selected instances, but the value of the novel instance could be larger or smaller than both values. In Figure 2(a), p_x is the novel instance and 2-NN chooses instances p_y and p_w, where $f(p_y) > \text{pred}(p_x) > f(p_w)$, and $\text{pred}(p_x)$ is the predicted value of p_x using 2-NN. However, $f(p_x)$ is actually larger than $f(p_y)$. This problem can be overcome by 2-SN. Instead of selecting p_w, 2-SN selects p_z (see Figure 2 (b)).

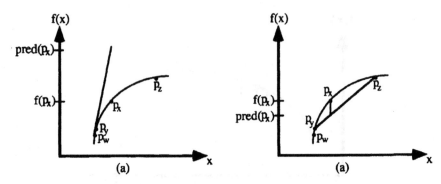

Figure 3. Comparison of 2-NN with 2-SN using the local weighted regression method. (a) How 2-NN works. (b) How 2-SN works.

The problem of local weighted regression with selecting the k nearest neighbors occurs when the slope of the target function changes quickly and instances selected are close to each other. Let us demonstrate the problem using a single variable function $f(x)$ with the two nearest neighbors selected. In Figure 3, p_x is the novel instance and $pred(p_x)$ is the predicted value of p_x. In Figure 3(a), 2-NN selects p_y and p_w, which are the two closest instances to p_x, and then local weighted regression is applied to them to generate a linear equation. From Figure 3(a), one can see the prediction error is very large. This never happens for 2-SN as long as the function is single valued and continuous. Figure 3(b) shows how 2-SN works in this same problem. For k larger than 2, when the majority of the selected instances are close to each other, this problem can also occur.

3.2 *A simple k-SN algorithm*

There are many different algorithms that implement k-SN. Here, we introduce a simple k-SN algorithm. Table 1 gives the algorithm, where p_x is the novel instance. The *repeat* loop is executed $\lceil \frac{k}{2} \rceil$ times. Each repetition selects a pair of instances. The first *for* loop finds p_x's nearest neighbor p_y from the instances in $M - S$. The second *for* loop is executed only if more instances need to be selected and finds the instance p_z that satisfies the following two conditions:

(1) distance$(p_y, p_z) >$ distance(p_x, p_z)
(2) for each instance p_w in memory that satisfies condition (1), distance$(p_w, p_x) \geq$ distance(p_z, p_x).

The first condition implies that the two selected instances are not close to each other and the second condition means that they are close to the novel

Table 1. The simple k-SN algorithm

Input: a novel instance p_x
        a set of instances stored in memory M
        a positive integer $k \leq |M|$

Output: A set of k instances $S \subseteq M$

Let S be empty
Repeat
      Let p_y be the first instance in M − S
      For each $p_w \in$ M − S **do**
        If distance(p_w, p_x) < distance(p_y, p_x)
        Then $p_y = p_w$
      Add p_y to S
      If |S| < k **Then**
        Let p_z be the first instance in M − S
        For each $p_w \in$ M − S **do**
          If distance(p_w, p_x) < distance(p_x, p_z) And
              distance(p_w, p_x) < distance(p_x, p_y)
          Then $p_z = p_w$
        Add p_z to S
    Until k = |S|

---

instance. If there is no such instance p_z in memory such that distance(p_y, p_z) > distance(p_x, p_z), the next nearest neighbor of p_x is selected.

4. Empirical Evaluation

This section describes the experiments conducted to evaluate k-SN. Specifically, we compared k-SN with k-NN using linearly weighted average and local weighted regression. These experiments were performed on the six datasets that are summarized in section 4.1.

4.1 *Datasets and experimental methods*

The six datasets are: *highway-accident, housing, cpu, auto-price, auto-mpg,* and *servo*. The following is a simple description of these datasets. Except the highway-accident dataset, all other datasets were obtained from the UC Irvine Repository (Murphy 1995).

Highway-accident. The highway-accident dataset, provided by the Civil Engineering Department of Utah State University, was compiled by the

Federal Highway Administration. This dataset contains accident data from the main Utah highways for a five year period (1988–1992). It includes a total of 1077 instances, each of which is described by nine attributes. Among these nine attributes, seven are numeric and two are symbolic. The target function is the yearly accident frequency, which ranges from 0 to 665. About 70% of all instances have accident frequencies ranging from 0 to 60.

Housing. The housing dataset contains the housing values in the suburbs of Boston. It contains 506 instances described by 12 numeric and one binary attribute. The target function is the housing value, which ranges from 5 to 50.

CPU. The cpu dataset is the relative CPU performance on different computers. It contains 209 instances described by six numeric and two symbolic attributes. The function values range from 6 to 1150.

Auto-price. The function for this dataset is the 1985 list price of imported cars and trucks and its values range from 5118 to 45400. There is a total of 25 attributes, among which 15 are numeric and ten are symbolic. This dataset contains 201 instances.

Auto-mpg. This dataset concerns the city-cycle fuel consumption in miles per gallon. There are four numeric and four symbolic attributes. It contains a total of 398 instances. The values of this function range from 9.0 to 46.6.

Servo. This dataset concerns the rise time of a servomechanism. It contains 167 instances described by two numeric and two symbolic attributes. The values of this function range from 0.131 to 7.1.

Cross-validation was used in all experiments. All datasets were randomly divided into ten blocks of equal size. Nine of the ten blocks were used as the training sets and the remaining one was used as the test set. This was repeated ten times for each of the different ten partitions. The prediction errors reported are the average of the ten runs on the test sets. In both weighted average and local weighted regression, the best k is determined automatically. To determine the best k, each training set was divided into two subsets, one for training (subtraining set) and one for determining the best k (subtest set). The subtraining set included eight blocks and the subtest set included one block. Instances in the subtest set were classified using the subtraining set with many different values of k (1 to 10 for weighted average and 1 to 100 for local weighted regression). The best k was the one with the lowest error and applied to the test set. We chose different ranges of k for weighted average and local weighted regression because we found that the best k for weighted average was always less than 10 and for local weighted regression was larger than 10 from the results of our early experiments. As we mentioned in Section 2.2, k should be at least as large as the number of attributes for local weighted regression. Otherwise, the solution of the resulting linear equation is not unique. Moreover, regression is a statistical method and needs more data points in order to obtain a reasonable solution. In all experiments, we randomly selected 20%, 40%, 60%, 80%, and 100% of the training instances to store, and then used these stored instances to predict values of all test instances.

4.2 Experiments with weighted average

In this section, we report the experimental result for the comparison of k-SN with k-NN using linearly weighted average. The linearly weighted average method used in these experiments was the one described in (Kibler et al. 1989). In this method, the weight of an instance is its similarity to the novel instance. The similarity is computed by the formula

$$\text{Similarity}(p_x, p_y) = \sum_i (1 - \frac{|x_i - y_i|}{\max_i - \min_i})$$

where x_i (y_i) is the value of the ith attribute of p_x (p_y) and $\max_i$ and $\min_i$ are respectively the largest and smallest value of the ith attribute. The value of the novel instance p_x was calculated using the following formula

$$f_x = \frac{\sum_{i=1,...,k} w_i f_i}{\sum_{i=1,...,k} w_i}, \text{ with}$$
$$w_i = \text{similarity}(p_i, p_x),$$

where f_x is the predicted value of p_x and f_i is the value of a selected instance p_i.

Figure 4 shows the average prediction errors attained by k-SN and k-NN using linearly weighted average with the best k, respectively. The best k was usually smaller than five. k-SN achieved lower prediction errors than k-NN on four of the six datasets: *housing*, *cpu*, *auto-price*, and *servo*. On the *highway-accident* dataset, lower prediction errors were achieved by k-SN when small percentages of training instances were stored. When the sets of stored instances became large, the k-SN and k-NN methods performed about equally well. On the *cpu* dataset, a large improvement of prediction accuracy was attained when the sets of stored instances were small. The results from the *highway-accident* and *cpu* datasets showed that k-SN is superior to k-NN when the number of stored instances is small. On the *auto-mpg* dataset, k-SN gave better prediction accuracy than k-NN when 40% and 60% of training instances were stored, while k-NN attained higher prediction accuracy when 20%, 80%, and 100% of the instances were stored. The prediction errors on *servo* increased with an increase in the number of instances stored. In summary, the experimental results on these six datasets showed that k-SN

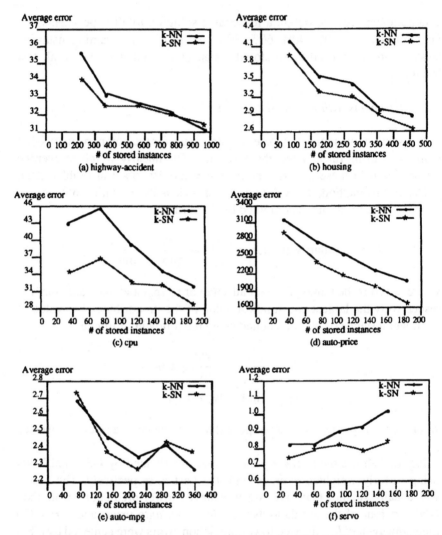

Figure 4. Average prediction errors attained by k-SN and k-NN with the linearly weighted average method.

did perform better than *k*-NN when they were used with linearly weighted average.

4.3 *Experiments with local weighted regression*

The local weighted regression algorithm used in our experiments was the one reported in (Moore and Atkeson 1992). For a problem with D independent variables and k selected instances $(x_{i1}, x_{i2}, \ldots, x_{iD})$ whose values are y_i, this algorithm finds the linear mapping $y = \mathbf{a}^T (x_1, x_2, \ldots, x_D, 1)^T$, where $\mathbf{a}$ is a $D+1$ element column vector, that minimizes the sum of the weighted squares of prediction errors

$$\sum_i w_i^2 (y_i - \mathbf{a}^T (x_{i1}, x_{i2}, \ldots, x_{iD}, 1)^T)^2.$$

The solution to this minimization is the solution to the normal equation

$$\mathbf{X}^T \mathbf{W} \mathbf{X} \mathbf{a} = \mathbf{X}^T \mathbf{W} \mathbf{y},$$

where $\mathbf{X}$ is the k-row, $(D + 1)$-column matrix of k selected instances, $\mathbf{y}$ is the k-element column vector of values of these k selected instances, and $\mathbf{W} = \text{diag}(w_1^2, \ldots, w_k^2)$. The weights w_i are calculated using the formula

$$w_i = \frac{1}{1 + 20(\text{distance}(p_i, p_{\text{novel}})/k_{\text{width}})^2},$$

where p_i is the ith selected instance, p_{novel} is the novel instance, the distance between two instances is computed using the Euclidean measure, and k_{width} is a smoothing kernel width, which was set to 0.05 in all experiments.

Figure 5 gives the average prediction errors attained by k-SN and k-NN with local weighted regression, respectively. We removed one symbolic variable from each of the three datasets: *highway-accident*, *cpu*, and *auto-mpg*. Each of these three symbolic variables had many values and caused great degradation of prediction accuracy. k-SN gave lower prediction errors on three of the six datasets: *highway-accident*, *cpu*, and *servo*, but the improvements were very small on the *highway-accident* and *servo* datasets. On the other three datasets, the results were mixed. k-SN was better on certain numbers of stored instances, but worse on others. The best k in these six datasets ranged from 20 to 80.

As we mentioned above, we removed one symbolic variable from each of the three datasets *highway-accident*, *cpu*, and *auto-mpg*. All of these removed variables had a large number of values, and thus had to be converted to a large number of binary variables in order to apply local weighted regression. After the conversion, both the *cpu* and *auto-mpg* datasets included so many variables that very high average prediction errors occurred. For example, the average prediction errors on *auto-mpg* were around 40, which is about eight times larger than the number obtained with the symbolic variable removed. Figure 6 shows the prediction errors with and without removing the *highway-name* variable using k-NN. Similar results were also obtained using k-SN. These results show that local weighted regression does not work well with multivalued symbolic variables.

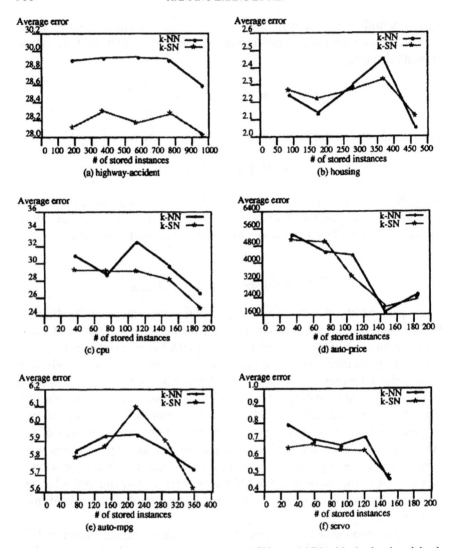

Figure 5. Average prediction errors attained by *k*-SN and *k*-NN with the local weighted regression method.

In comparison with weighted average, local weighted regression performed better on certain datasets and worse on others. Among the three datasets without the symbolic variables removed, local weighted regression performed much better than weighted average on *housing* and *servo*, while weighted average gave much lower prediction errors *on auto-price* which includes ten symbolic variables, particularly when a small percentage of instances were stored. For *the highway-accident* dataset, local weighted regression

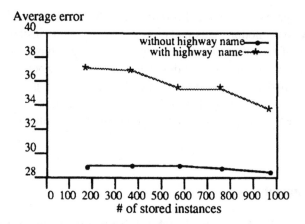

Figure 6. Average prediction errors on the highway-accident dataset attained by the local weighted regression method with and without *highway-name* using *k*-NN.

without *highway-name* attained higher prediction errors than weighted average with *highway-name*. With *highway-name*, local weighted regression performed worse than weighted average. Local weighted regression performed a lot worse than weighted average on *auto-mpg* both with and without the symbolic variable removed. The prediction errors attained by local weighted regression on the *cpu* dataset without the symbolic variable removed were lower than the prediction errors attained by weighted average on the same dataset with the symbolic variable. These results demonstrated that there are still applications in which weighted average is preferred. Determining the preferred algorithm depending on the cases remains the subject of future research.

5. Conclusions

In this paper, we introduced the *k*-SN method for intelligent selection of instances for prediction functions in lazy learning methods for numeric function prediction. A simple *k*-SN algorithm was given, and experiments were conducted to compare *k*-SN with *k*-NN using weighted average and local weighted regression. These experimental results demonstrated that *k*-SN consistently outperformed *k*-NN using weighted average, but performed only slightly better when local weighted regression was used. From these results, we believe that *k*-SN is effective when weighted average is used. It is not clear whether *k*-SN can be effectively used with local weighted regression. Further studies need to be conducted. These experimental results also showed that there are some applications in which weighted average is more appropriate than local weighted regression. Therefore, weighted average is still a worthwhile prediction function. This makes k-SN a worthwhile instance selection method, even if it does not work well with local weighted regression.

To thoroughly evaluate and understand k-SN, more experiments need to be conducted, particularly on some artificial functions to demonstrate clearly when k-SN works well and when it does not. In addition to the simple k-SN algorithm given in this paper, other k-SN algorithms should be investigated in the future.

Acknowledgments

We thank David W. Aha for his insightful comments and suggestions during the preparation of this paper. Thanks also go to Professor Andrew Moore for providing information about the local weighted regression method. Comments from anonymous reviewers have been very useful in improving this paper. Thanks to Mr. Miao Hsi Wang of the Department of Civil Engineering of Utah State University for providing the highway accident database and Patrick Murphy for maintaining the UCI Repository of ML Databases.

References

Aha, D. W. (1990). Efficient instance-based algorithms for learning numeric functions. Unpublished manuscript.

Aha, D. W., Kibler, D. & Albert, M. (1991). Instance-based learning algorithms. *Machine Learning* 6: 37–66.

Breiman, L., Friedman, J., Olshen, R. & Stone, C. (1984). *Classification and Regression Trees*. Monterrey, CA: Wadsworth.

Cleveland W. S. & Delvin S. J. (1988). Locally weighted regression: An approach to regression analysis by local fitting. *Journal of the American Statistical Association* 83(403).

Connell, M. E. & Utgoff, P. E. (1987). Learning to control a dynamic physical system. In *Proceedings of the Sixth National Conference on Artificial Intelligence*, pp. 456–460, Seattle, WA: AAAI Press.

Cost, S. & Salzberg, S. (1993). A weighted nearest neighbor algorithm for learning with symbolic features. *Machine Learning* 10.

Duda, R. & Hart, P. (1973). *Pattern Classification and Scene Analysis*. N.Y.: Wiley.

Kibler, D., Aha, D. W. & Albert, M. K. (1989) Instance-based prediction of real-valued attributes. *Computational Intelligence* 5.

Moore, A. W. & Atkeson, C. G. (1992). An investigation of memory-based function approximators for learning control. Unpublished manuscript.

Mohri, T. & Tanaka, H. (1994). An optimal weighting criterion of case indexing for both numeric and symbolic attributes. In *Working Notes of the AAAI94 Workshop on Case-Based Reasoning*. Seattle, WA: AAAI Press.

Murphy, P. (1995). UCI Repository of machine learning databases [Machine-readable data repository @ics.uci.edu]. Irvine, CA: University of California, Department of Information and Computer Science.

Quinlan, J. R. (1992). Learning with continuous classes. In *Proceedings of the Fifth Australian Joint Conference on Artificial Intelligence*. Singapore: World Scientific.

Quinlan, J. R. (1993). Combining instance-based and model-based learning. In *Proceedings of the Tenth International Machine Learning Conference*, pp. 236–243, Amherst, MA: Morgan Kaufmann.

Salzberg, S. (1991). A nearest hyperrectangle learning method. *Machine Learning* **6**.

Townsend-Weber, T. & Kibler, D. (1994). Instance-based prediction of continuous values. *Technique Report WS-94-01*. Irvine, CA: University of California, Department of Information and Computer Science.

Weiss, S. M. & Indurkhya, N. (1993). Rule-based regression. In *Proceedings of the Thirteenth International Joint Conference on Artificial Intelligence*, pp. 1072–1078, Chambery, France: Morgan Kaufmann.

Artificial Intelligence Review **11**: 193–225, 1997.

The Racing Algorithm: Model Selection for Lazy Learners

ODED MARON[1] and ANDREW W. MOORE[2]

[1] *M.I.T. Artificial Intelligence Lab, NE45-755, 545 Technology Square, Cambridge, MA 02139*
E-mail: oded@ai.mit.edu
[2] *Carnegie Mellon University, 5000 Forbes Ave, Pittsburgh, PA 15213*
E-mail: awm@cs.cmu.edu

Abstract. Given a set of models and some training data, we would like to find the model that best describes the data. Finding the model with the lowest generalization error is a computationally expensive process, especially if the number of testing points is high or if the number of models is large. Optimization techniques such as hill climbing or genetic algorithms are helpful but can end up with a model that is arbitrarily worse than the best one or cannot be used because there is no distance metric on the space of discrete models. In this paper we develop a technique called "racing" that tests the set of models in parallel, quickly discards those models that are clearly inferior and concentrates the computational effort on differentiating among the better models. Racing is especially suitable for selecting among lazy learners since training requires negligible expense, and incremental testing using leave-one-out cross validation is efficient. We use racing to select among various lazy learning algorithms and to find relevant features in applications ranging from robot juggling to lesion detection in MRI scans.

Key words: lazy learning, model selection, cross validation, optimization, attribute selection

1. Introduction

The problem of model selection can be thought of as trying to find the best student in a classroom. The teacher has the task of not only teaching the students some subject, but also of testing them to find out which student has best learned the subject. This problem, in different scaling, turns up repeatedly in the Machine Learning community: which neural net architecture gives the best generalization error? What should the value of k be in a k-nearest-neighbor algorithm? Should I use a decision tree, a neural net, a lazy learner, or a random guesser? Which of the 50 features are relevant for this problem? The answer to these questions changes depending on the training set. We would like to find an answer efficiently, given a training set and a collection of models.

There are a number of popular ways to determine a student's grade, or a model's generalization error (Weiss and Kulikowski 1991). In this paper we will use leave-one-out cross validation. The model is trained on all points but one, and is then queried for the value at that point. This is repeated for every point in the training set and the prediction errors are averaged to give an estimate of the generalization error. Other methods are discussed below.

The idea behind racing (Maron and Moore 1994) is to test the various models in parallel, one test point at a time. This way, a running average can be maintained for each model's error. This is an estimate of the model's true error had it been tested on all of the test points. Using statistical bounds we can also determine how close the estimated error is to the true error of each model. After only a small number of test points, we can usually distinguish the best models (those with lowest error, or highest grade) from the very worst models (those with the highest error). The models that are significantly worse than the best ones are thrown out of the race and are not tested again. The more test points that are seen, the tighter the estimated error is to the true error; therefore, more models can be differentiated from each other and eliminated. This algorithm concentrates the computational effort on the best models, while discarding the inaccurate models and not testing them unnecessarily.

Unlike other machine learning methods, lazy learning algorithms do not force the training points into a decision tree, a neural net, symbolic rules, or any abstract representation. The points act as their own best representation. A direct implication of this fact is that very little work needs to be performed during training – we simply store the points in memory. Most of the computational expense comes when we use the learner for prediction. Racing uses laziness to its advantage, and also attempts to limit the number of predictions.

In this paper, we leverage the laziness in two ways. First, computing leave-one-out cross validation error is cheap because unlike non-lazy methods, there is no need to retrain on all of the points but one. We can simply 'cover up' that point in memory and that is equivalent to retraining. Therefore, we have a quick, reliable estimator for the error of a model by performing leave-one-out cross validation on all the points in the training set. Second, we can examine many different learners without worrying about the initial expense of training all of them. The only significant computation arises when they are tested.

This paper combines the authors' previous work on racing (Maron and Moore 1994; Moore and Lee 1994; Maron 1994), and adds additional experiments, discussion, and connections to lazy learning techniques.

1.1. *Lazy learning algorithms*

The collection of models to which we apply the racing algorithms in this paper are *lazy learning* methods. Lazy learning is an encompassing name for a variety of statistical and machine learning methods such as nearest-neighbor (Dasarathy 1991) and local weighted regression (Cleveland et al. 1988). The underlying principle of lazy learning is to simply remember the training examples. Almost all of the computational work is performed not during training, but only when a query is made. Variants of the nearest-neighbor method are then used for prediction. Further reviews and analysis may be found in, for example (Hastie and Tibshirani 1990; Bottou and Vapnik 1992; Atkeson et al. 1997).

With a lazy learner, data points of the form (<input-vector>, <output-vector>) are kept in memory. The task is for the learner to predict output values when queried with inputs that might not be in memory. When the learner is asked to predict the value at $x = 5$, it looks in memory for a few points whose x-values are closest to 5. The output values at those points are averaged (or regressed (Moore et al. 1992)) and returned as the predicted value. We assume in this paper that both the attributes (inputs) and predictions (outputs) are numeric, though many variations exist (Aha 1990).

Within this general framework, there are still many choices for specifying a model:

- How do we measure *similarity*?
- How many neighbors should we look at?
- What method should be used for averaging the outputs of the neighbors?
- Should we try to perform local regression rather than local averaging?
- How much smoothing, or weighting, should we do over the regression or average?

The following sections describe some possible answers to these questions:

1.1.1. k-nearest-neighbors

The motivation for k-nearest-neighbors is summarized by this quote:

> There seems to be a need for discrimination procedures whose validity does not require the amount of knowledge required by the normality assumption, the homoscedastic assumption, or any assumption of parametric form. ... can reasonable discrimination procedures be found which will work even if no parametric form can be assumed? (Fix and Hodges 1951)

Fix and Hodges answered their own question by introducing nearest-neighbor classification. The principle is simple: when queried for the class of some attributes, return the class of the point with the most similiar attributes. Similarity (or distance) is usually measured by using the Manhattan or Euclidean metric,[1] depending on the type of the attributes. The method generalizes

---

[1] The Manhattan metric assumes that you can travel between two points only along a grid, so the distance between (x_1, y_1) and (x_2, y_2) is $\|x_1 - x_2\| + \|y_1 - y_2\|$. Using a Euclidean metric, the distance is $\sqrt{(x_1 - x_2)^2 + (y_1 - y_2)^2}$.

easily to k-nearest-neighbors, where a majority rule is used to find the correct class, or averaging is used for continuous outputs. A larger value for k makes the rule more stable against outliers and noisy data. However, making k too large destroys the advantage of locality that a nearest-neighbor algorithm inherently owns.

1.1.2. *Weighted distance metric*

Finding an appropriate distance metric is often the toughest hurdle in attempting to use a lazy learning system. The distance metric is responsible for the representation of the memorized data. It decides which attributes are more important than others and aligns all the attributes into the same representation. To give an example, let us say that we are trying to predict hat size from height and weight. The data points are of the form ⟨height, weight, hat-size⟩. Given a query q of the form ⟨6ft,155LB⟩, we look for the point p that minimizes the distance between p and q. However, it is probably not a good idea to use the standard Euclidean distance since differences in pounds are much less significant than differences in feet: someone who is ⟨2ft,155LB⟩ is closer to q than someone who is ⟨6ft,165LB⟩ using the plain Euclidean distance metric. Clearly, we need a weighted metric that forces differences in heights to be comparable to differences in weight. The initial representation (feet and pounds) should be changed to a more suitable one.

However, that is not the end of our problems. What if hat-size is predominantly affected by height, and only marginally by weight? In that case, we need to count the height attribute much more than the weight attribute so that points with similar heights will be close together, even if they have very different weights.

Both problems can be solved with a priori knowledge of the importance and scale of the various attributes, but one of the main reasons for using nearest-neighbor methods is to remove any assumptions about the best representation for the data. The best weighting, like the best value of k, should be searched for. Other, non-symmetric distance measures are possible (Maron 1994), but are not discussed in this paper.

1.1.3. *Kernel regression*

It is intuitive that some neighbors are more important than others. Specifically, neighbors that are closer to the queried point should count more toward its classification than neighbors that are farther away. *Kernel regression* performs weighted averaging (instead of a uniform average) over the space of neighbors. The weighting function which we use is taken from (Moore et al. 1992). The weight of the ith point (x_i) with respect to the query point q is w_i.

$$w_i = \frac{1}{1 + 20 \cdot (distance(x_i, q)/K_{width})^2} \tag{1}$$

The parameter K_{width} determines the width of the weighting (or smoothing) range. The larger it is, the more weight is given to distant points. Again, it is usually not feasible to estimate this parameter before empirically testing various values of it.

1.1.4. *Local regression and local weighted regression*
The computationally intensive part of nearest-neighbor algorithms is usually to find the k neighbors. Once that is done, we can perform more complex operations than averaging to predict the queried value. For example, *local regression* involves finding a least-squares linear fit of the neighbors. *Local weighted regression* (Cleveland et al. 1988) attempts to minimize the weighted error, where the weighting function is Equation 1.

1.2. *Determining the accuracy of a model*

To determine the accuracy of a model, we measure the difference between the predictions of the model and the true answers on a set of points where we have the true answers. However, we need to be careful not to use the training set for testing as well. For example, using a 1-nearest-neighbor method, we can get zero prediction error by testing on the training points. However, the accuracy of 1-nearest-neighbor on new points (the generalization error) can be much lower. What is needed is a way to test not only rote memorization, but also the ability to generalize.

There are a number of popular methods for estimating the learner's ability to generalize. One is partitioning the entire set of the teacher's examples into a training set and a testing set. The learner is trained on the training set, but its performance is determined by its average prediction error for points in the testing set. A prediction query involves giving the learner the attributes, but withholding the correct outputs. The learner's guess at the outputs is then compared to the true outputs.

The second method of estimating generalization is called *leave-one-out cross validation*. Here, we can use the same set of points for both training and testing by performing the following trick: train on all points except one; perform a prediction query on the one point that was held out; repeat this process for all points and return the average prediction error of all the iterations. This method might seem more computationally expensive than the test-set method, but it does have certain advantages, namely in cases where we cannot afford to partition the few training points that we have (i.e., there are not enough points) or when we need a good estimate of the error distribution over the entire space we are trying to learn. Also, for lazy learners, leave-one-out cross validation is efficient.

Another popular method is multi-fold cross validation, where instead leaving just one point out, a different set of points is held out during each iteration and is then used as the test set. The average of the errors gives an estimation of the generalization error.

Cross validation is a special case of a number of statistical reuse techniques such as jackknife and bootstrapping. For a readable overview of these techniques, see (Efron and Tibshirani 1991).

1.3. *Summary*

This paper is organized as follows: we discuss previous approaches to model selection such as brute force, gradient descent and genetic algorithms. We show that they are either slow or inappropriate. We then describe the racing algorithm, and talk about two bounds that can be used to differentiate the various models' errors. We show that using Hoeffing's bound is general and correct, but it is not a very tight bound. We give a Bayesian bound which turns out to be faster in practice. We also discuss various extensions and heuristics that can be made to help the race.

We then describe a set of experiments that show some empirical results of running the various types of races on datasets encountered in the real world. We then discuss a different usage of racing; namely, to find the relevant attributes for prediction. Finally, we conclude with some related work and future directions.

2. Previous approaches to model selection

Traditionally, there have been a number of popular ways to search through a large collection of models. Brute force was always applicable and gave the desired result, but at a high computational price. Descent methods such as hill climbing and conjugate gradient were much faster, yet did not guarantee to return the right result and, even worse, were not applicable in many cases. Other techniques such as genetic algorithms fall into similar traps, since provably convergent versions are too slow to be used in practice. We discuss these approaches in the following subsections. Racing (Maron and Moore 1994) manages to lessen the evils of these techniques, while retaining their benefits.

2.1. *Brute force*

Brute force attacks the problem in the simplest possible way. Given m trained learners and a test set that consists of n points, it performs a prediction query on every point for every single learner. It then computes the mean squared error of the predictions of each learner and selects the learner with the lowest error. This algorithm runs in time $O(n \cdot m)$, which is unacceptably slow, but always returns the best learner.

2.2. *Descent methods*

Gradient descent, or hill climbing (Press et al. 1992), treats the collection of models and their prediction error as a continuous and differentiable surface. It starts at some point on this surface, and proceeds to 'descend' in the direction that has the sharpest decline in error. This approach to optimizing the lazy learner has been used by (Atkeson 1990; Lowe 1995).

The algorithm stops when it reaches a local minimum. In other words, when all of the neighboring models have higher error, the algorithm returns the current model. This algorithm is much faster than brute force since it does not need to find the error of every single model. It only needs to compute the error for the learners that are on the path to the optimal learner. However, there are two major problems: local minima and applicability.

Local minimum is a well documented and analyzed problem with gradient descent. An example of it in the realm of model selection is given in Figure 1. In general, the error at the local minimum can be many times larger than the error at the global minimum. In addition, the chance of starting at a place that will lead to a global minimum can be arbitrarily small.

There is an even more serious problem with gradient descent that was ignored in the last example – namely, there are many instances when it is not even applicable to model selection. At every step of the gradient descent algorithm, we need to find a collection of models that are 'near' the current model. However, the collection of models may not have a distance metric (and therefore no concept of 'near') defined on it. For example, how far is a neural network from a nearest-neighbor model? How far is a decision tree from a local weighted regressor?

It is possible to *impose* a distance metric on any collection of objects, as for example in the k-nearest-neighbor example, or by ordering the models according to simplicity. However, although we can impose a metric, it does not mean that it is correct, or even useful. Just because there is a parameter to tune (e.g., k in k-nearest-neighbor) does not mean that there is a predictable relation between a change in the parameter and the performance of the algorithm. In the cases where there is no clear distance metric among the various models,

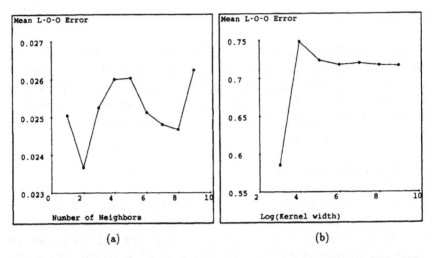

Figure 1. Two examples in which the leave-one-out error varies non-monotonically with a model parameter. (a) shows the error against the number of nearest neighbors for a 300-point two dimensional dataset with output $= x_1 + x_2 + x_1 x_2 + \text{random}(-0.1, 0.1)$, the inputs ranging over $-1 < x_i < 1$. (b) shows the error against the kernel-width smoothing parameter of locally weighted regression (see Atkeson et al. 1997) for a fit to a noisy one-dimensional sinusoid. The left hand of the x-axis denotes almost no smoothing, and the rightmost denotes full smoothing.

all of them must be raced. This is a problem with all minimization methods. Steepest descent, Newton's method (Press et al. 1992) and conjugate gradient are as susceptible to this problem as the plain version of gradient descent.

2.3. *Genetic algorithms*

Genetic algorithms (Goldberg 1989) have been applied with reported success to problems in which the best out of a combinatorial space of bit-strings is selected, but in which each evaluation of a bit-string is relatively cheap. Model selection has different computational economics, because it involves choosing the best from a space which is usually not as large (no more than a few hundred in the subsequent experiments), but the evaluations of each possibility are very expensive.

Worse yet, the problem characteristics that can render hill-climbing meaningless, also apply to genetic algorithms. The usual reason that genetic algorithms are expected to do better than brute force enumeration of all strings is that they exploit assumed underlying structure in the representation. The performance of a substring in one context is assumed non-independent of its performance in another. If the space being searched consists of atomic models without underlying structure, we can no more take advantage of genetic algorithms than we could for identifying the best student using (x, y) coordinates in the classroom.

3. Racing: Hoeffding and Bayes

In this section we formalize the notion of "racing" by defining what it means for one model to be winning the race over another. We use two different statistical bounds to determine with a certain confidence when one model's average error is significantly smaller than another's. Hoeffding's bound is a general bound that only relies on the assumption that the error queries are drawn independently. Using Bayesian bounds gives tighter results, at the expense of assuming that the errors are drawn from a normal distribution.

3.1. *Hoeffding races*

3.1.1. *Hoeffding's bound*
Let us say that we have N points with which to test a given model. If we were to test a model on all of them, then we would have an average error that we will call E_{true}. However, if we only tested the model on ten points, then we only have an estimate of the true average error. We call the average after only n points $(n < N)$ E_{est} since it is an estimate of E_{true}. The more points we test on (the bigger n gets), the closer our estimate gets to the true error. How close is E_{est} to E_{true} after n points? Hoeffding's bound lets us answer that question when the n points are picked with an identical independent distribution from the set of N original test points. In this case, we can say that the probability of E_{est} being more than ϵ away from E_{true} is

$$\Pr(|E_{true} - E_{est}| > \epsilon) < 2e^{-2n\epsilon^2/B^2} \tag{2}$$

where B bounds the greatest possible error that a model can make (Hoeffding 1963). This bound does not make any assumptions other than the independence of the samples.

We would like to say that "we are 99% confident that our estimate of the average error is within ϵ of the true average error", or in other words, $\Pr(|E_{true} - E_{est}| > \epsilon) < 0.01$. We denote the confidence parameter with δ. Equating δ with the right-hand side of Equation 2 gives us an expression for ϵ in terms of n, B, and δ.

$$\epsilon(n) = \sqrt{\frac{B^2 \log(2/\delta)}{2n}} \tag{3}$$

Equation 3 tells us how close the estimated mean is to the true mean after n points with confidence $1 - \delta$. We will discuss how to obtain a value for B

in Section 4.1. We can also determine the number of samples n necessary to obtain a certain accuracy ϵ and confidence δ:

$$n > \frac{B^2 \log(2/\delta)}{2\epsilon^2} \tag{4}$$

The number of samples increases quickly as we attempt to increase the accuracy. This is a problem with using Hoeffding's bound, and we try to resolve it by using Bayesian bounds, which are less general but tighter (see Section 3.2).

3.1.2. *Hoeffding races*

The racing algorithm starts with a collection of learning boxes. We call each model a learning box since we are treating the models as if they were black boxes. We do not consider how complex or time-consuming each prediction is, but only the input and output of the box. Associated with each learning box are two pieces of information: a current estimate of its average error and the number of test points it has processed so far. Assume the dataset has N datapoints.

At each iteration of the algorithm, we randomly select a point from the test set. Then for each learning box:

- compute the leave-one-out error at the point by using that learning box;
- update the learning box's estimate of its own average error rate;
- use Hoeffding's bound and Equation 3 to calculate how close the current estimate is to the true error for each learning box.

Each learning box now has a bound within which its true average error lies. We can eliminate those learning boxes whose best possible error (their lower bound) is still greater than the worst error of the best learning box (its upper bound); see Figure 2. The intervals get smaller as more points are tested (since ϵ gets smaller as n gets larger), thereby "racing" the good learning boxes and eliminating the bad ones.

3.1.3. *Ending the race*

The algorithm iterates, repeatedly picking test points until one of three conditions occurs:

1. All but one of the learning boxes have been eliminated.
2. A sufficient number (e.g., N) of test points have been picked.
3. Alternatively, the algorithm can be stopped once ϵ has reached a certain threshold.

In any case, the algorithm returns a set of learning boxes whose errors are indistinguishable to within $2 \cdot \epsilon(n)$.

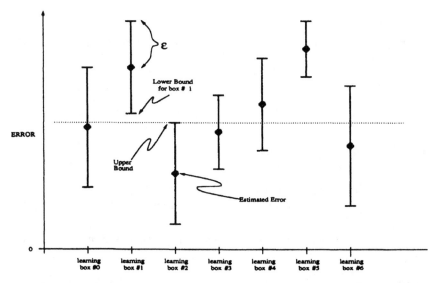

Figure 2. An example where the best upper bound of learning box #2 eliminates learning boxes #1 and #5. The size of ϵ varies since each learning box has its own upper bound on its error range, B.

3.1.4. *Proof of correctness*

Notice that $1 - \delta$ is the confidence in Hoeffding's bound for *one* learning box during *one* iteration of the algorithm. What we need is to prove that the *entire* algorithm has some confidence $1 - \Delta$ of returning the best learning box.

For the sake of a simpler proof, let us make the requirement of a correct algorithm more stringent. We will say that the algorithm is correct if every learning box is within ϵ of its true error at every iteration of the algorithm. This requirement encompasses the weaker requirement that we do not eliminate the best learning box. An algorithm is correct with confidence $1 - \Delta$ if

$$\Pr\{ \text{ all learning boxes are within } \epsilon(n) \text{ on all iterations up to } n\} \geq 1 - \Delta \quad (5)$$

What we would like to do is show the relationship between δ (the chance of being wrong on one learning box in one iteration) and Δ (the chance of being wrong on the whole algorithm), so that when the user wants the algorithm to work with probability 0.999, we can translate that into the confidence that we need for each learning box at each iteration. We will be relying on the *disjunctive probability inequality*, which states that for any events A and B, $Pr\{A \vee B\} \leq Pr\{A\} + Pr\{B\}$.

Assume that there are n iterations, and m learning boxes ($LB_1, \cdots, LB_m$). We start with the fact that:

$$Pr\{\ a\ particular\ LB\ is\ within\ \epsilon(i)\ on\ a\ particular\ iteration\ i\} \geq 1 - \delta \quad (6)$$

Which is equivalent to:

$$Pr\{\ a\ particular\ LB\ is\ wrong\ on\ a\ particular\ iteration\} < \delta \quad\quad (7)$$

Using the disjunctive inequality,

$$Pr\{\quad a\ particular\ LB\ is\ wrong\ on\ iteration\ 1\ \vee$$
$$a\ particular\ LB\ is\ wrong\ on\ iteration\ 2\ \vee$$
$$\cdots$$
$$a\ particular\ LB\ is\ wrong\ on\ iteration\ n\} \leq \delta \cdot n \quad (8)$$

Rewrite this as:

$$Pr\{\ a\ particular\ LB\ is\ wrong\ on\ any\ iteration\ up\ to\ n\} \leq \delta \cdot n \quad (9)$$

And likewise for all learning boxes:

$$Pr\{\quad LB_1\ is\ wrong\ on\ any\ iteration\ \vee$$
$$LB_2\ is\ wrong\ on\ any\ iteration\ \vee$$
$$\cdots$$
$$LB_m\ is\ wrong\ on\ any\ iteration\} \leq \delta \cdot n \cdot m \quad (10)$$

or in other words:

$$Pr\{\ some\ LB\ is\ wrong\ in\ some\ iteration\} \leq \delta \cdot n \cdot m \quad (11)$$

which is equivalent to:

$$Pr\{\ all\ LBs\ are\ within\ \epsilon(n)\ on\ all\ iterations\} \geq 1 - \delta \cdot n \cdot m \quad (12)$$

Clearly, Equation 12 is the same as Equation 5 and we can therefore conclude that $\delta = \frac{\Delta}{n \cdot m}$. When we plug this into Equation 3 (our expression for ϵ from the previous section), we ensure the correctness of this algorithm with confidence Δ. The new ϵ is expressed as:

$$\epsilon(n) = \sqrt{\frac{B^2(\log(2nm) - \log(\Delta))}{2n}} \quad (13)$$

This is an extremely pessimistic bound on Δ and tighter proofs are possible (Omohundro 1993). It is pessimistic in two regards: first, it assumes that all learning boxes are completely independent of each other. Second, it assumes that the error of a learning box after seeing n points is completely independent of its error after seeing $n + 1$ points. This is clearly a worst case assumption, and most PAC bounds are made tighter by leveraging this point (Haussler 1992).

3.2. Bayesian races

Hoeffding's bound is as tight as we can get without making additional assumptions about the distribution of the errors we get from a model. If we assume that the errors are normally distributed, then we can use Bayesian statistics to achieve a tighter bound on the probability that one model is better than another.

The algorithm first randomizes the order of the datapoints. For the jth model the distribution of leave one out errors is Gaussian. Let us say it has unknown mean E_{true}^j and unknown variance V_{true}^j.

As evidence accumulates, the uncertainty of E_{true}^j decreases, since E_{true}^j refers to the leave-one-out errors, not the out of sample errors. Let $\hat{\mu}_{nj}$ and $\hat{\sigma}_{nj}^2$ be the sample mean and variance of model j's errors up to the nth iteration, when all surviving models have been evaluated on n datapoints.

$$\hat{\mu}_{nj} = \frac{1}{n} \sum_{i=1}^{n} e_j(i) \quad \hat{\sigma}_{nj}^2 = \frac{1}{n-1} \sum_{i=1}^{n} \left(e_j(i) - \hat{\mu}_{nj} \right)^2 \qquad (14)$$

defining $e_j(i)$ as the leave-one-out error when the jth model is used to predict the ith datapoint. These statistics can be updated incrementally efficiently: $\hat{\mu}_{(n+1)j}$ and $\hat{\sigma}_{(n+1)j}^2$ can be defined as a closed form of n, $\hat{\mu}_{nj}$, $\hat{\sigma}_{nj}^2$, and $e_j(n+1)$.

For each model we use Bayesian statistics, along with the values $\hat{\mu}_{nj}$, $\hat{\sigma}_{nj}^2$, and n, to put a probability distribution on E_{true}^j. This is a relatively elementary process. Assume that a priori we know nothing about the distribution except that it is normal. The true mean E_{true}^j might be any value between $-\infty$ and $+\infty$. The variance V_{true}^j might be any value between 0 and $+\infty$. This ignorance can be turned into the uninformative priors:

$$p(E_{true}^j) = \text{Constant} \quad p(V_{true}^j) = \text{Constant}/V_{true}^j \qquad (15)$$

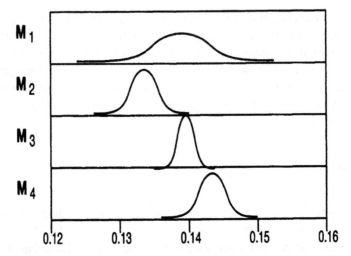

Figure 3. The posterior distributions on the errors of four models involved in a race. The lower the error the better, so it seems very unlikely that model 4 will turn out to be better than model 2 at the end of the race. Thus model 4 is eliminated at this point.

where $p(.)$ denotes a probability density function.[2] The marginal posterior distribution of the mean E_{true}^j is a student distribution with mean $\hat{\mu}_{nj}$, variance $\hat{\sigma}_{nj}^2/n$, and $n-1$ degrees of freedom.

Figure 3 gives an example with four models racing. We eliminate the jth model if there exists some other model j' for which

$$\text{Prob}(E_{true}^j > E_{true}^{j'} \mid e_j(1), \ldots e_j(n), e_{j'}(1), \ldots e_{j'}(n)) > 1 - \delta \qquad (16)$$

$1 - \delta$ again denotes the confidence that is required. Statistics are gathered and models are eliminated until only one model remains, or we run out of datapoints, whereupon we select the model with the lowest $\hat{\mu}_{nj}$. In Figure 3 it would be very probable that E_{true}^2 is lower than E_{true}^4, but only marginally probable that E_{true}^1 is lower than E_{true}^4.

We thus need to compute the probability that the mean μ_1 of one unknown Gaussian distribution is less than the mean μ_2 of another unknown Gaussian distribution, where in each case the posterior distributions of each mean can be computed with Bayesian statistics. This is achieved by the Welch approximation to the Behrens-Fisher problem (Welch 1937).

To use the Welch approximation upon two samples with the same assumptions as before, let the first sample have size n_1, sample mean $\bar{x}_1$ and sample

---

[2] Neither of these priors is a legitimate probability density function. Such an approximation is harmless (see (Schmitt 1969) for more details).

variance s_1^2. The corresponding values for the second sample are n_2, $\bar{x}_2$ and s_2^2. Let

$$u_1 = s_1^2/n_1, \quad u_2 = s_2^2/n_2, \quad b = u_1/(u_1 + u_2). \tag{17}$$

The signed difference between the population means is a random variable, conveniently denoted by $\mu_1 - \mu_2$. Welch's approximation states that $\mu_1 - \mu_2$ has, approximately, a student distribution with mean $\bar{x}_2 - \bar{x}_1$, variance $u_1 + u_2$, and degrees of freedom

$$\left(\frac{b^2}{n_1 - 1} + \frac{(1 - b)^2}{n_2 - 1} \right)^{-1}. \tag{18}$$

By computing the cumulative probability of zero for this student distribution (the probability that a sample drawn from it is negative), we get the probability that $\mu_1 < \mu_2$.

4. Extensions

This section describes several extensions and expansions of the basic racing algorithm. We describe how to determine a bound on B – the maximum error of a model on any test query, to be used in Hoeffding races. We then describe a method for tightening the confidence intervals for each model and for eliminating redundant models in the set (models that are statistically equivalent). We also talk about a statistical method known as *blocking* (Box et al. 1978) that helps with the problems of large variances and dependent models.

4.1. *Bounding errors*

The most obvious obstacle to implementing Hoeffding races is finding a value for B, the maximum error of a learning box. For classification problems, there is no difficulty – B is simply 1. That is because the worst mistake that the algorithm can make is a misclassification which has an error of 1. For regression problems the solution is less straightforward. If we know something about the learner and something about the data, then we can try to put some finite bound on B. If that is not possible, then we can attempt to estimate B by adding a few standard variances to the average error of this learner. Since the average error and variance are updated after every new point, the value of B also gets modified at each iteration. The value of B tends to fluctuate wildly during the first few points until the average and variance

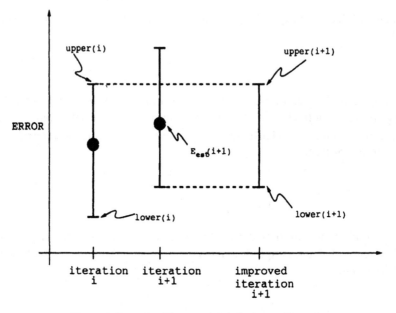

Figure 4. Example of how to shrink the interval bounds.

settle down. To avoid that, we only start racing after collecting errors from about 30 points from each learning box.

4.2. *Shrinking the intervals*

There is a simple heuristic to tighten the bounds around the estimated error for each learning box. First we need to name a few important components of a learning box. Let us call the estimated error for the kth learning box at the ith iteration $E_{est}^k(i)$. We will call the lower bound of that learning box $lower^k(i)$ and likewise the upper bound will be called $upper^k(i)$. These can be calculated by $E_{est}^k(i) - \epsilon(i)$ and $E_{est}^k(i) + \epsilon(i)$ respectively. From now on, we will be dropping the superscript, since we will be talking about one learning box, but applying the ideas to all of them.

During the course of running the race, all three of these components tend to fluctuate. $E_{est}(i)$ moves around with every new point, trying to get closer to the true error. $lower(i)$ and $upper(i)$ move around for two reasons: the first is that ϵ gets smaller at each iteration; the second is that $E_{est}(i)$ changes after almost every new point. However, despite all of this movement, we are guaranteed that with confidence $1 - \Delta$, $E_{est}(i)$ will stay between the lower and upper bounds. What if at iteration $i + 1$ we get a point upon which the learning box performs very badly? In this case, $E_{est}(i + 1)$ is larger than $E_{est}(i)$. The bounds have become tighter because of the decrease in ϵ, but they have been transformed by the increase in E_{est}. However, $E_{est}(i+1)$ is guaranteed to stay not only within the bounds at iteration $i+1$, but also within the bounds at all iterations until now. Therefore, the new upper bound should not be $E_{est}(i+1) + \epsilon(i+1)$, but instead the tighter

$$upper(i+1) = Min(E_{est}(i+1) + \epsilon(i+1), E_{est}(i) + \epsilon(i)). \qquad (19)$$

Likewise, a tighter lower bound at iteration $i+1$ is

$$lower(i+1) = Max(E_{est}(i+1) - \epsilon(i+1), E_{est}(i) - \epsilon(i)) \qquad (20)$$

An example of shrinking the intervals is shown in Figure 4. The bound of iteration $i+1$ can be improved based on previous bounds.

4.3. Eliminating indistinguishable models

So far we have only discussed elimination of models that are considerably worse than the top model. We can also try to speed up the race by eliminating models that seem to be identical in predictive power to other models. In other words, we wish to eliminate any model that we are confident is worse than some other model; we also wish to stop a race between two models that we believe with high confidence to be extremely similar. The latter can be achieved by defining a threshold γ (a small positive number) and eliminating any model that we are confident has an estimated error within γ of another model.

These two rules can be combined into one formulation: given two distinct learning boxes LB_i and LB_j, with an estimated error of E^i_{est} and E^j_{est} respectively, we eliminate LB_j from the race if

$$Pr\{E^i_{true} < E^j_{true} - \gamma \mid e_j(1), \ldots e_j(n), e_{j'}(1), \ldots e_{j'}(n)\} < \delta. \qquad (21)$$

4.4. Blocking

There are two common problems that empirically seem to slow down the races. One problem occurs when learning boxes have a vary large variance in error over the test set. In that case, we cannot eliminate them or use them to eliminate other learning boxes since their confidence are so large. Another problem occurs when two or more learning boxes have some degree of dependence, so that they perform badly on the same points. In that case, we need many test points to distinguish between them.

We deal with both problems by using a statistical method known as *blocking* (Box et al. 1978). Instead of racing to get a tight estimate of a model's error, we race for a tight estimate of the difference in error between two models. Rather than maintaining an average error for each learning box, we maintain an average signed error difference (denoted $ED_{est}^{i,j}$) for every pair of learning boxes (i, j). If we let $e_i(l)$ be the error of the ith learning box on the lth testing point, then our estimate of the error difference after seeing k test points is

$$ED_{est}^{i,j} = \frac{1}{k} \sum_{l=1}^{k} (e_i(l) - e_j(l)) \tag{22}$$

$ED_{est}^{i,j}$ is an estimate of $E_{true}^i - E_{true}^j$. As before, we can use either Hoeffding's Bound or a Bayesian bound to determine whether $E_{true}^i - E_{true}^j < 0$ is significantly unlikely. If so, we know that with high confidence LB_i has a larger mean error than LB_j. This happens when

$$\Pr\{E_{true}^i - E_{true}^j < 0\} < \delta. \tag{23}$$

We check this condition for every pair (i, j) of learning boxes and eliminate LB_i if it is true.

Indistinguishable models can be eliminated if $\Pr\{E_{true}^i - E_{true}^j < -\gamma\} < \delta$, because if the event $E_{true}^i - E_{true}^j < -\gamma$ is found to be highly unlikely, then we know that it is highly unlikely that LB_i is better than LB_j by more than amount γ.

The simplest example of blocking having a beneficial effect is the case where two models in the race are identical – the original racing algorithm would have to race for a long time. The racers would have the same mean at each step of the race, but the race would only end when they both had so many samples that the confidence intervals on its measures of the mean error of each model were both very close to γ (its indifference parameter). In contrast, the blocking race algorithm would maintain, at each step, the difference between the leave-one-out errors on each datapoint. Because the models are the same, this difference would always be zero and it would only require a very small number of statistics (perhaps less than ten, depending on the parameters) before one of the models was eliminated. This example of identical models is extreme, but in the more common case of near-identical models there can also be a large reduction in the time to elimination.

5. Empirical results of Hoeffding and Bayesian racing

We ran races on a wide variety of classification and regression problems that are described below. Some of these results were also presented in (Maron and Moore 1994). The data files are available from the UCI repository (Murphy 1996). The problems were chosen arbitrarily, but turned out to have widely different optimal models: from 3-nearest-neighbor to local weighted regression with a large smoothing kernel.

ROBOT	Given initial and final description of a robot arm, learn the control needed for juggling (Schaal and Atkeson 1993). 10 input attributes, 5 continuous outputs.
PROTEIN	3 inputs, and output is a classification into one of three classes. The famous protein secondary structure database, with some preprocessing (Zhang et al. 1992).
ENERGY	Given solar radiation sensing, predict cooling load for a building. This is taken from the Building Energy Predictor Shootout (Kreider and Haberl 1994). 5 input attributes, 1 output.
POWER	Market data for electricity generation pricing period class for the new United Kingdom Power Market. 11 inputs, 1 output.
POOL	The visually perceived mapping from pool table configurations to shot outcome for two-ball collisions (Moore 1992). 9 input attributes, one output.
DISCONT	An artificial dataset with many discontinuities. Local models should outperform global ones. 2 inputs, 1 output.

We ran the races on a collection of lazy learning algorithms. The learning boxes varied in the number of nearest neighbors that they looked at ($k = 1,3,5,7,9$), in the degree of smoothing performed ($K_{width} = 4, 2, 1, \frac{1}{2}, \frac{1}{4}, \frac{1}{8}, \frac{1}{16}, \frac{1}{32}, \frac{1}{64}$), and whether the function was locally constant or performed local weighted regression (see Section 1.1). These combinations give us either 95 or 189 different models, depending on the permutations used. The distance metric was not varied, and all attributes were held to be equally important. All of the experiments were run using $\delta = 0.01$. We used the techniques mentioned earlier for estimating B and for shrinking the intervals.

In Table 1, we compare the brute force approach to Hoeffding races, Bayesian races, and Bayesian races with blocking. Each of the columns contains the results for one of the datasets described above. The first two rows of the table describe how many points are in each dataset and how many learning boxes (LBs) are in the initial set of models. BRUTE is the number of leave-one-out cross validation (LOOCV) queries made by the brute force algorithm. Likewise, HOEFFDING, BAYES and BLOCK-BAYES show the average number of LOOCV queries made by each of those algorithms over twenty runs. We also show the speedup in terms of the number of queries for each of the algorithms with respect to BRUTE. Hoeffding races usually returns a set of LBs that cannot be distinguished, and for these datasets it always contained the model that BRUTE chose. However, the Bayes-based algorithms returned just one model. We measured its quality by "regret", which is the difference between BRUTE's top model and the model returned, normalized by the standard deviance of the output.

Table 1. Results of various races.

	ROBOT	PROTEIN	ENERGY	POWER	POOL	DISCONT
points	972	4,965	2,444	210	259	500
initial learning boxes	95	95	189	95	95	95
BRUTE	92,340	471,675	461,916	19,950	24,605	47,500
HOEFFDING	15,637	349,405	121,400	13,119	22,095	25,144
LBs left	6	60	40	48	75	29
speedup	**5.91**	**1.35**	**3.80**	**1.52**	**1.11**	**1.89**
BAYES	16,027	207,496	48,016.3	9,318.2	10,824	1,175.55
regret	0.004	0.037	0	0.0001	0	0
speedup	**5.76**	**2.27**	**9.62**	**2.14**	**2.27**	**40.41**
BLOCK-BAYES	2,306.95	4,026.55	14,052.6	5,421.8	1,555.7	913.85
regret	0.003	0.111	0.000006	0.002	0.002	0
speedup	**40.03**	**117.14**	**32.87**	**3.68**	**15.82**	**51.98**

5.1. *Discussion*

There are a few observations to be made from this table:

- Racing never performs more queries than brute force, and its overhead is negligible, except in the case of the blocking race, which has quadratic cost in the number of racers. In addition, the accuracy of the model (or models) selected is very close to the accuracy of the best model in the initial set.
- Bayesian races always improved on Hoeffding races, and Bayes with blocking in turn improved upon Bayesian. The improvement over brute force tends to be greater for larger datasets since a larger dataset means the exhaustive method has to perform proportionally many extra LOOCV evaluations, whereas the racing methods can stop before all datapoints are evaluated.
- The Bayesian methods are faster than Hoeffding, but they do not carry a formal correctness proof. Specifically, they will sometimes throw out good models early in the race, especially if the errors generated by those good models do not fit the priors (i.e., the errors are not Gaussian).
- Hoeffding races (and racing in general) is least effective when a large percentage of the original learning boxes are left at the end. For example, in the POOL problem, where there were 75 learning boxes left at the end of the race, the number of queries is only slightly smaller for Hoeffding races than for brute force. In the ROBOT problem, where only 6 learning

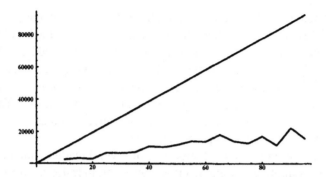

Figure 5. The bottom line shows the number of queries taken by Hoeffding races for the ROBOT problem as the size of the initial set of learning boxes is increased. The top line shows the performance by brute force. At each point, the set of learning boxes was chosen randomly.

boxes were left, a significant reduction in the number of queries can be seen.

- The obvious conclusion from this observation is that *racing is most effective when there exists a small subset of clear winners within the initial set of models.* In fact, the larger the size of the initial set of models, the more effective racing is in comparison to brute force.

To test this conclusion, we created random subsets of increasing sizes from the 95 learning boxes used for the ROBOT experiment. We ran Hoeffding races on each one of the subsets, and tabulated the results in Figure 5. As can be seen, we can search over a large set of models without much concern about the computational expense of a large initial set. In other words, if we have very little knowledge of the problem, we should not preclude any possible solution. Racing lets us do that without much computational expense.

We do not think that there is a general asymptotic relation between races and brute force as the number of models grow. As shown by Table 1, it is problem dependent. However, it is clear that the *Racing algorithms work badly on 'boring' problems,* where any arbitrary model does as well as anything else, and works very well on 'interesting' problems, where only a few models really fit the domain. Using the classroom analogy again, the boring problems can be thought of as picking the best gym student (everybody gets A's in gym), and the interesting problems can be thought of as picking the best history student (where the grade distribution is such that there are only a few excellent students).

5.2. *Segmenting Magnetic Resonance Images*

In addition to the small datasets described above, we used the combination of Hoeffding races and lazy learning in a larger application (i.e., one with a large number of models and training points). The input is a 3-D image of the brain, generated in slices from a Magnetic Resonance machine. Each point in the image becomes a point in the training set. A point is described by its (x, y, z) coordinates in the image and by two descriptive attributes: the proton density and the viscosity of the tissue. This quintuple is mapped into a classification (segmentation) of either gray matter, white matter, fluid, or lesion. The entire data set is quite large: 10 patients, two to four images across time for each patient, and about 0.5 million points per image.

The segmentation problem is important in several medical imaging applications. For example, Multiple Sclerosis causes brain lesions, whose volume needs to be tracked over time to determine if the treatment is working, or the rate of deterioration. If this were to be done by hand, a specialist would need to look through over 50 slices of the brain, determine the location and size of the lesions in each slice, and sum them to get a piece of information for one person during one time point. This becomes horribly time consuming when there are many patients getting scanned on a weekly basis.

We would like to automate the process by training on images from a single patient, taken at different times, and then segmenting future images. An even more ambitious goal is to train on multiple patients and predict on unseen patients' images.

A detailed description of the various experiments and results can be found in (Maron 1994). In summary, using Hoeffding races allowed us to make only 69% of the queries and saved hundreds of hours of CPU time. The best learning box incorrectly classified 18% of points from new patients, and more importantly, produced results that looked reasonable to medical experts.

6. Racing for relevant attributes

A particularly promising use of cross validation is to automatically choose relevant inputs from a wider set of possible inputs. An obvious benefit is in accelerating the learning rate of algorithms that suffer in the face of irrelevant inputs. Other benefits include helping select relevant visual features for visually controlled robot tasks (Moore et al. 1992), and selecting sets of time windows in time series predictions. This problem, known as "subset selection" or "feature selection" is a well-known problem in statistics, surveyed thoroughly in (Miller 1990) and is rapidly gaining attention in the Machine Learning community (Caruana and Freitag 1994; John et al. 1994; Skalak, 1994).

Given D inputs there are 2^D possible input sets, and so performing an exhaustive cross validation search over all of them soon becomes impractical as D rises, even assuming adequate data support to justify searching so many models. Hill climbing is a sensible alternative since the space we are climbing over has a reasonable "neighbor" concept. In this section we provide several hill climbing versions of the racing algorithm; these aim to both speed up the computation and also to reduce the danger of becoming trapped at local maxima.

Sets of inputs can be represented as binary strings. Given four possible inputs, 0101 would denote "ignore inputs 1 and 3, use inputs 2 and 4." The standard non-racing hill climbing algorithm, *forward sequential selection*, begins with a start string (e.g., 0000) then makes all possible 1-feature changes to it (1000, 0100, 0010, 0001) and exhaustively finds which minimizes the leave-one-out cross validation (**LOOCV**) error. It then uses this best string (say 0100) as a new base point, generates all its 1-feature successors (1100, 0000, 0110, 0101), and determines the best. It continues in this way until no single-feature change improves it. The special case of starting with all zeroes is termed forward sequential selection (FOR-SEL), and that of starting with all ones is termed backward elimination (BACK-SEL). Forward sequential selection is better if only a few features are expected to be relevant and backward elimination is better if only a few features are expected to be irrelevant. Unfortunately, such prior knowledge may not be available at the start of the search, meaning that it would be necessary to run both. Running both gives the best of both worlds in finding a good feature set, but the worst of both worlds computationally.

The racing counterparts to these algorithms are straightforward: from the base string generate all 1-feature changes and race them. Proceed until the winner of a race does not improve on its base. In the experiments described later two versions are tested, FOR-RACE and BACK-RACE, that start at all zeroes and all ones respectively.

However, there is an objection to this simple application of racing. Imagine that inputs 4, 5, and 6 are all relevant and independently provide a reduction in the LOOCV error. If we start at string 0000000 and successors 0000100, 0000010, and 0000001 are all good, it will be a shame to run through three separate hill climbing iterations to switch them all on. This motivates the next algorithm, a Gauss-Seidel,[3] version of hill climbing:

- Begin with a predefined start string (e.g., 00000)
- Race between the current string and the current string with the first bit flipped (00000 versus 10000)
- Select the winner of that race as the new current string (e.g., 10000)

---

[3] We give it this name because of the order of the updates. This kind of ordering, in which improved estimates are incorporated immediately instead of at the end of an iteration, are known as Gauss-Seidel methods in the Numerical Analysis literature (Conte and De Boor 1980).

- Now race between the current string and the current string with the second bit flipped (10000 versus 11000)

$$\vdots$$

... until all bits have been raced. Then return to the first bit and proceed until an entire pass through the current string fails to produce an improvement.

Versions of this algorithm, FOR-GS-RACE and BACK-GS-RACE, are tested below. On some occasions they do indeed help, but on others their performance is poor. A further new algorithm, *schemata search* does Gauss-Seidel's job better, and also solves another problem.

6.1. *Schemata search*

Schemata search is a new algorithm described in (Moore and Lee 1994) which aims to solve the same problem that the Gauss-Seidel method addresses – the problem of forward sequential selection taking a long time if many features are relevant, or similarly backward elimination taking a long time if many features are irrelevant. It will also help with a second problem. Suppose there is a family of three features which must all be on simultaneously for any reduction in the LOOCV error. If any family member is ignored then the LOOCV error is as bad as if all family members were ignored. This can happen quite easily, for example if the features are distributed between −1 and 1 and the function being learned is their product. Forward sequential selection would be very likely to miss this family and to converge on something suboptimal. Backward elimination would not have this problem, but if many features are irrelevant then it can become stuck as well (because in the early stages of hill climbing the removal of one irrelevant attribute among many does not improve the LOOCV error).

Schemata search searches over the space of schemata strings, which have 0's, 1's and $\star$'s in them. A $\star$ denotes a fifty percent chance of the attribute being ignored, and a fifty percent chance of it being used. The LOOCV error of such a string is the expected LOOCV error of a binary string generated from the schemata string according to these random rules, for example

$$\text{LOOCVE}(101\star\star) = \tfrac{1}{4}(\text{LOOCVE}(10100) + \text{LOOCVE}(10101) + \text{LOOCVE}(10110) + \text{LOOCVE}(10111))$$

Now a simple algorithm is to begin with all stars (e.g., $\star\star\star\star\star$), and then to find out (by racing) whether it is better to have the first field as a 1 or a 0 (i.e., we would race $1\star\star\star\star$ and $0\star\star\star\star$). Having finished the first race, we could determine the second field by another race, and so on until the entire string is filled with 1's and 0's.

In practice, we can do better than this. Instead of beginning by racing the first field, we can race all fields against each other in parallel:

1⋆⋆⋆⋆	races against	0⋆⋆⋆⋆
⋆1⋆⋆⋆	races against	⋆0⋆⋆⋆
⋆⋆1⋆⋆	races against	⋆⋆0⋆⋆
⋆⋆⋆1⋆	races against	⋆⋆⋆0⋆
⋆⋆⋆⋆1	races against	⋆⋆⋆⋆0

Thus, given D inputs, we have D races occurring in parallel, and we stop all races when any one race produces a winner (to confidence level δ). On each step of the race a random binary string is generated, and then the LOOCV error of one randomly chosen datapoint is computed using that binary string. This statistic is added to the statistics of all the strings in the above sets of races which match the binary string. This continues until one of the pairs of racers becomes significant (i.e., when we believe with probability $1 - \delta$ that one member of the significant pair beats its competitor). Then the next iteration of the race begins with a new set of racers that all have the winning field of the previous race switched on. If, in the above race, ⋆1⋆⋆⋆ became significantly better than ⋆0⋆⋆⋆, then the next iteration would have

11⋆⋆⋆	races against	01⋆⋆⋆
⋆11⋆⋆	races against	⋆10⋆⋆
⋆1⋆1⋆	races against	⋆1⋆0⋆
⋆1⋆⋆1	races against	⋆1⋆⋆0

Astute readers might notice that we could reuse about half the data from the previous iteration: all those samples that match members of the new tournament. Empirically this leads to an algorithmic speed-up, but statistically it is dangerous because the sample that selected the winning field of the previous iteration is biased, *because* it selected that winning field. In the experiments below, the algorithm conservatively begins each iteration with an empty set of samples.

The key idea is that, for example, to identify whether 1⋆⋆⋆⋆ is better than 0⋆⋆⋆⋆ does not require all 2^4 instantiations of the stars to be evaluated, but merely a sufficient random sample for one to show statistically significant superiority. And better yet, we need not commit to choosing which field to instantiate. The trick described above allows us to simultaneously try to identify the best of ⋆0⋆⋆⋆ versus ⋆1⋆⋆⋆, ⋆⋆0⋆⋆ versus ⋆⋆1⋆⋆ etc., using the same random samples. The first field to show significance is the one chosen and fixed for the next iteration.

This may be preferable to our other hill climbing racers for three reasons:
- If any feature is outstandingly good, it will be detected quickly without having to wait for an entire iteration of hill climbing to take place.

Table 2. Syntax of the multivariate functions In experiments.

expr : : =	X_i	the ith input
	expr × **expr**	the product of the subexpressions
	mean(**expr**, **expr**)	the mean of the subexpressions
	max(**expr**, **expr**)	the maximum of the subexpressions
	corrupt(**expr**)	Gaussian random noise of ±0.1 is added to the value of the subexpression
	g(**expr**)	where g is a non-differentiable function $g(x) = -x^2$ if $x > 0$ and $g(x) = -x^2 - 2x$ if $x \leq 0$.

- If several features are independently good then one of them will be quickly selected, without having to wait to determine which precisely is the best, which is a weakness of FOR-RACE and BACK-RACE.
- Small, mutually dependent, families of features that would be missed by the other hill climbers may be found. If features 1, 2 and 3 must all be on to gain any benefit, then schemata string 1***** will eventually win a race against 0***** because 25% of the strings generated from the former have features 1, 2, and 3 all on, whereas 0% of the latter do.

6.2. *Experiments*

We have run all these algorithms on fifty-six randomly generated synthetic datasets. The task was to find the set of features that minimized the leave-one-out cross-validation error of a 1-nearest-neighbor function approximator. The datasets all had between 4 and 12 inputs and one real-valued output that was a noisy multivariate function of a random subset of the inputs. All inputs were randomly generated uniformly in the range $-1 \leq x_i \leq 1$. Each multivariate function was generated from the syntax in Table 2.

The number of terms in the dataset was also randomly decided, and varied between 5 and 30. Thus some datasets were trivial, such as output = $\frac{1}{2}(x_2 + x_7)$, and others complex, such as

output = max(corrupt(product(mean(g(x4) , g(corrupt(x2))), product(x5 , corrupt(x5)))) , g(corrupt(g(g(g(g(corrupt(max(x5 , corrupt(x3))))))))))

It is interesting to note that all the searchers managed to identify the precise set of relevant inputs for this complex dataset, which had 950 datapoints[4]. In all the experiments, $\delta = \gamma = 0.001$.

---

[4] The slowest method was FOR-SEL, needing 19000 evaluations, and the fastest was SCHEMATA+, described shortly, which needed 2215 evaluations

Method	Mean # Evals	P_{IP}	P_{FW}	P_{VW}	Mean relative evals	Median relative evals	Distribution of relative evals (relative to FOR-SEL)
FOR-SEL	17378	17.9	16.1	7.1	1	1	
FOR-RACE	6658	19.6	17.9	5.4	0.51	0.43	
FOR-GS-RACE	7960	17.9	14.3	5.4	0.67	0.53	2 ratios greater than 2
SCHEMATA	7779	16.1	8.9	0	1.7	0.22	12 ratios greater than 2
SCHEMATA+	4159	19.6	14.3	5.4	0.9	0.13	8 ratios greater than 2

Figure 6. Comparing the conventional forward sequential selection algorithm against its racing counterparts, and against schemata search (which has no forwards-backwards bias).

Method	Mean # Evals	P_{IP}	P_{FW}	P_{VW}	Mean relative evals	Median relative evals	Distribution of relative evals (relative to BACK-EL)
BACK-SEL	26358	16.1	14.3	7.1	1	1	
BACK-RACE	13943	16.1	12.5	7.1	0.62	0.57	
BACK-GS-RACE	5611	17.9	16.1	5.4	0.46	0.23	
SCHEMATA	7779	16.1	8.9	0	2.1	0.18	10 ratios greater than 2
SCHEMATA+	4159	19.6	14.3	5.4	1.0	0.11	8 ratios greater than 2

Figure 7. Comparing the conventional backward elimination algorithm against its racing counterparts, and against schemata search (which has no forwards-backwards bias).

Figure 6 shows the performance of the forward searchers and schemata on the 56 random datasets. Each algorithms was run on each dataset. There are two measures of performance.

- **Accuracy.** How often do the searchers end at suboptimal solutions? This is shown by the columns
  - P_{IP} = the percentage of datasets for which the searcher produced an "imperfect" result. A result is imperfect if any other search produced a feature-set with a lower **LOOCV** error.
  - P_{FW} = the percentage of datasets for which the result was fairly wrong, i.e. had a **LOOCV** error more than 0.001 greater than the minimum found by any other search. To give this number some meaning, the minimum **LOOCV** errors found were typically in the range $0.01 - 0.2$ depending on the dataset, with a similar magnitude of variation.
  - P_{VW} = the percentage of datasets for which the result was very wrong, i.e. had a **LOOCV** error more than 0.01 greater than the minimum found by any other search.

- **Search time.** This is given by the number of individual evaluations of LOOCV errors. The mean figure is shown, but this is dominated by the few hard datasets that required tens of thousands of evaluations for all methods. Many other datasets required only thousands, or in some cases, hundreds of evaluations. For this reason, also shown (by scatterplots) are the distributions of the ratio of number of samples needed compared with the number of samples needed by the conventional forward sequential selection method. As can be seen, this distribution is highly skewed, especially for the schemata searches. 50% of the schemata searches took less than a quarter of the time of the conventional search. 12 of the 56 schemata searches took over twice as long, an issue that we discuss below.

Figure 7 is a similar table comparing the various backward methods and the same schemata searches (which have no forward or backward biases).

The forward and backward racing methods were usually faster than the conventional methods with little loss of accuracy. The Gauss-Seidel races were similar in performance. The schemata search was also roughly equal in accuracy, except that in this set of experiments it achieved the distinction of no "very wrong" errors.

Of the twelve schemata searches that were twice as long as the conventional forward method, seven were due to the conventional method quickly becoming stuck with an inferior solution – after considerably more computation schemata search found a better result. Of the other five, four eventually found equally good solutions and one found a slightly inferior solution. Interestingly the schemata searches frequently found all the relevant features very fast, often in a tenth of the total time of their search. This produced strings with only 1's and $\star$'s in them. Unfortunately, they would then spend a very long time convincing themselves that they were justified in putting 0's elsewhere.

As an initial and ugly attempt to address this, we tried an additional algorithm, SCHEMATA+, which would eagerly replace $\star$'s with 0's. If 2000 iterations of one of its races produced no significant winners, it forced one of the stars to zero (using the race statistics to choose the input least likely to be relevant). SCHEMATA+ was the fastest algorithm at converging but was less reliable than SCHEMATA.

6.3. *Feature selection experiments on real world data*

Some of the above algorithms were run on the same datasets that were used in Section 5. To make feature selection more important, three randomly generated (and thus irrelevant) input variables were added to each dataset. The results are given in Table 3. SCHEMATA again outperforms the forward and backwards algorithms, using fewer queries to find a comparable model.

FOR-RACE finds a model quickly for the ENERGY dataset, but it has high error compared to the model found by SCHEMATA.

Table 3. Results of feature selection algorithms on real datasets.

	POOL		ENERGY		ROBOT		POWER	
	Queries	Min error found	Queries	Min error found	Queries	Min error found	Queries	Min error found
FOR-SEL	4,554	0.801	4,888	0.20	47,628	0.177	9,240	0.992
BACK-SEL	4,554	0.801	7,332	0.18	60,264	0.173	9,240	0.888
FOR-RACE	1,668	0.801	171	1.51	10,741	0.186	1,706	0.810
BACK-RACE	3,205	0.801	2,843	0.18	9,792	0.175	2,338	0.796
SCHEMATA	621	0.801	337	0.21	3,909	0.179	773	0.843

7. Conclusion

In this paper, we presented the racing algorithm and some extensions to it, specifically in the framework of model selection. However, racing can be thought of as another searching technique such as A* or hill climbing. It can therefore be used in the many of the applications of search in Machine Learning and Artificial Intelligence. It seems to be especially useful for search in spaces that are riddled with local minima, or spaces in which the collection of models is discretized. The speedup over exhaustive search and the algorithm's ability to quantify the confidence in its result make it a viable alternative to existing heuristic search techniques.

7.1. Related Work

We were motivated to find efficient techniques for model selection by working on Moore's GMBL system (Moore et al. 1992). Haussler's work on generalizations of the PAC model (Haussler 1992) provided a treasure of ideas that, combined with Kaelbling's confidence bounds (Kaelbling 1990), generated the Hoeffding races algorithm. The idea of parallel decision making has been used repeatedly in AI, but the combination of racing with lazy learners gives us the ability to make decisions efficiently, soundly, and incrementally. The notion of racing shows up in related forms in multi-armed bandit problems. To give one example, Rivest and Yin (Rivest and Yin 1993) give a heuristic for picking which arm to pull next according to the probability distributions of the payment of each arm.

An extremely thorough survey and investigation of how the k-armed bandit problem and its solution can be used to minimize wasted computation can be found in (Gratch 1994). In earlier work, (Gratch et al. 1993) uses a related method for choosing appropriate search rules in very large scheduling domains.

Similar questions can be found in the earlier statistics literature. This work is chiefly concerned with detecting an effect in a new drug or industrial process with as few experiments as possible. (Box et al. 1978) is an excellent introduction to this field.

Greiner has independently developed a PALO (Probably Approximately Locally Optimal) algorithm (Greiner and Jurisica 1992) that also uses Hoeffding's bound to decide when one point is better than another. The main differences between our work is that he uses his method for gradient descent, and that he is not trying to select among models, but among Horn clauses and default rules. It is possible to use a descent method in a discretized space by picking among a finite number of discrete gradients. At each iteration, the PALO algorithm compares the estimated error of stopping against the estimated error of each one of the neighboring possibilities. The algorithm then goes in the direction of the least error. The comparison is made faster by using a racing technique.

7.2. *Future Work*

There are many ways to extend this research. In this section, we describe a few of them.

Hoeffding's bound was chosen since it is a tight, distribution-free statistical bound. However, it might not be the best bound to use for classification problems. Other tests, such as the Bayesian methods or other tests such as the f-test (see any elementary statistics text, or Chapter 14 of (Press et al. 1992)), can be used in its place. For a given value of δ (defining the confidence level at which we are prepared to cut off a competitor from the race) the Bayesian approach cuts off far earlier than the Hoeffding approach. The Bayesian approach achieves its superiority by making stronger assumptions about the distribution of the errors, and so might be expected to be less robust than the almost assumptionless Hoeffding approach. In the experiments we have performed to date the Bayesian method does not seem to converge to the wrong model more easily than the Hoeffding approach, but this is an empirical observation that may not be true for all datasets.

Another issue concerns our choice to assume a normal distribution for the errors. In future work it might be more sensible to use a different distribution, such as an exponential or chi-squared. The normal distribution does not take into account the possibility of occasional highly aberrant datapoints (i.e., outliers) in the dataset that might have errors many times greater than the root-mean-square error.

An exciting offshoot of this research is a search for an 'ideal' collection of models. There is not a single model that is a solution to every problem in the world, but it is possible that there is a group of models that will cover a large portion of problems, and only a small number of which are suitable for each problem. This set of models needs to stretch across the space of possible problems without much overlap. This can be thought of as a basis set of vectors that are orthogonal and span the space. Once we have a basis set of models, then racing is the perfect tool for finding the best model out of this idealized collection since, for any given problem, only a few of the models will perform well on it. That is the ideal condition for racing.

Finally, there is the danger of overfitting by searching too many models. If one looks at data long enough, one will begin to see patterns even if it is completely random. If racing is used, it would be statistically wise to use yet another test set at the end of the race to make sure that the chosen model really has its purported error. In addition, users of Hoeffding or Bayesian races should keep in mind Bonferroni's advice that the more models you throw at the data, the better you should expect to perform.

Acknowledgements

The authors thank Mary Soon Lee for help in the development of the Blocking Races algorithm. Thanks also to the reviewers for useful comments. This work is partially supported by an NSF research initiation award. Support for the laboratory's artificial intelligence research is provided in part by the Advanced Research Projects Agency of the Department of Defense under Office of Naval Research contract N00014-91-J-4038.

References

Aha, D. W. (1990). A Study of Instance-Based Algorithms for Supervised Learning Tasks: Mathematical, Empirical and Psychological Evaluations. PhD. Thesis; Technical Report No. 90-42, University of California, Irvine.

Atkeson. C. G., Moore, A. W. & Schaal, S. A. (1997). Locally Weighted Learning. *AI Review*, this issue.

Atkeson, C. G. (1990). Memory-Based Approaches to Approximating Continuous Functions. In *1990 Workshop on Nonlinear Modeling and Forecasting*. Adison-Wesley.

Bottou, L. & Vapnik, V. (1992). Local Learning Algorithms. *Neural Computation* 4: 888–900.

Box, G. E. P., Hunter, W. G. & and Hunter, J. S. (1978). *Statistics for Experimenters*. Wiley.

Caruana, R. A. & and Freitag, D. (1994). Greedy Attribute Selection. In *Machine Learning: Proceedings of the Eleventh International Conference*, pp. 28–36. Morgan Kaufmann.

Cleveland, W. S., Devlin, S. J. & Grosse, E. (1988). Regression by local fitting: Methods, properties, and computational algorithms. *Journal of Econometrics* 37: 87–114.

Conte, S. D. & De Boor, C. (1980). *Elementary Numerical Analysis*. McGraw Hill.

Dasarathy, B. V. (1991). *Nearest Neighbor Norms: NN Patern Classifaction Techniques*. IEEE Computer Society Press.

Efron, B. & Tibshirani, R. (1991). Statistical Data Analysis in the Computer Age. *Science* **253**: 390–395.

Fix, E. & Hodges, J. L. (1951). Discriminatory Analysis: Nonparametric Discrimination: Consistency Properties. Project 21-49-004, Report Number 4, USAF School of Aviation Medicine.

Goldberg, D. (1989). *Genetic Algorithms in Search, Optimization and Machine Learning*. Reading, MA: Addison-Wesley.

Gratch, J., Chien, S. & DeJong, G. (1993). Learning Search Control Knowledge for Deep Space Network Scheduling. In *Proceedings of the 10th International Conference on Machine Learning*, pp. 135–142. Morgan Kaufmann.

Gratch, J. (1994). An effective method for correlated selection problems. Department of Computer Science Technical Report Num. 1893, University of Illinois at Urbana-Champaign.

Greiner, R. & Jurisica, I. (1992). A statistical approach to solving the EBL utility problem. In *Proceedings of the Tenth International conference on Artificial Intelligence*, pp. 241–248. MIT Press.

Hastie, T. J. & Tibshirani, R. J. (1990). *Generalized additive models*. Chapman and Hall.

Haussler, D. (1992). Decision theoretic generalizations of the pac model for neural net and other learning applications. *Information and Computation* **100**: 78–150.

Hoeffding, W. (1963). Probability inequalities for sums of bounded random variables. *Journal of the American Statistical Association* **58**: 13–30.

John, G. H., Kohavi, R. & Pfleger, K. (1994). Irrelevant features and the Subset Selection Problem. In *Machine Learning: Proceedings of the Eleventh International Conference*, pp. 121–129. Morgan Kaufmann.

Kaelbling, L. P. (1990). Learning in Embedded Systems. PhD. Thesis; Technical Report No. TR-90-04, Stanford University, Department of Computer Science.

Kreider, J. F. & Haberl, J. S. (1994). Predicting hourly building energy usage: The great energy predictor shootout – Overview and discussion of results. Transactions of the American Society of Heating, Refrigerating and Air-Conditioning Engineers, 100, Part 2.

Lowe, D. G. (1995). Similarity metric learning for a variable-kernel classifier. *Neural Computation* **7**: 72–85.

Maron, O. & Moore, A. W. (1994). Hoeffding Races: Accelerating model selection search for classification and function approximation. In Cowan, J. D., Tesauro, G. & Alspector, J. (eds.), *Advances in Neural Information Processing Systems 6*. Morgan Kaufmann.

Maron, O. (1994). Hoeffding Races: Model Selection for MRI Classification. Masters Thesis, Dept. of Electrical Engeineering and Computer Science, M.I.T.

Miller, A. J. (1990). *Subset Selection in Regression*. Chapman and Hall.

Moore, A. W. & Lee, M. S. (1994). Efficient Algorithms for Minimizing Cross Validation Error. In *Machine Learning: Proceedings of the Eleventh International Conference*, pp. 190–198. Morgan Kaufmann.

Moore, A. W., Hill, D. J. & Johnson, M. P. (1992). An empirical investigation of brute force to choose features, smoothers and function approximators. In Hanson, S., Judd, S. & Petsche, T. (eds.), *Computational Learning Theory and Natural Learning Systems, Volume 3*. MIT Press.

Moore, A. W. (1992). Fast, robust adaptive control by learning only forward models. In Moody, J. E., Hanson, S. J. & Lippman, R. P. (eds.), *Advances in Neural Information Processing Systems 4*. Morgan Kaufmann.

Murphy, P. M. (1996). UCI repository of machine learning databases. For more information contact ml-repository@ics.uci.edu.

Omohundro, S. (1993). Private communication.

Press, W. H., Teukolsky, S. A., Vetterling, W. T. & Flannery, B. P. (1992). *Numerical Recipes in C: the art of scientific computing*. New York: Cambridge University Press, second edition.

Rivest, R. L. & Yin, Y. (1993). Simulation Results for a new two-armed bandit heuristic. Technical report, Laboratory for Computer Science, M.I.T.

Schaal, S. & Atkeson, C. G. (1993). Open loop stable control strategies for robot juggling. In *Proceedings of IEEE conference on Robotics and Automation.*

Schmitt, S. A. (1969). *Measuring Uncertainty: An elementary introduction to Bayesian Statistics.* Addison-Wesley.

Skalak, D. B. (1994). Prototype and Feature Selection by Sampling and Random Mutation Hill Climbing Algorithms. In *Machine Learning: Proceedings of the Eleventh International Conference*, pp. 293–301. Morgan Kaufmann.

Weiss, S. M. & Kulikowski, C. A. (1991). *Computer systems that learn: Classification and prediction methods from statistics, neural nets, machine learning, and expert systems.* San Mateo, CA: Morgan-Kaufmann.

Welch, B. L. (1937). The significance of the difference between two means when the population variances are unequal. *Biometrika* **29**.

Zhang, X, Mesirov, J. P. & Waltz, D. L. (1992). Hybrid system for protein secondary structure prediction. *Journal of Molecular Biology* **225**: 1049–1063.

Artificial Intelligence Review **11**: 227–253, 1997.
© 1997 *Kluwer Academic Publishers.*

Context-Sensitive Feature Selection for Lazy Learners

PEDRO DOMINGOS
*Department of Information and Computer Science, University of California, Irvine, Irvine,
California 92697, U.S.A.*
E-mail: pedrod@ics.uci.edu

Abstract. High sensitivity to irrelevant features is arguably the main shortcoming of simple lazy learners. In response to it, many feature selection methods have been proposed, including forward sequential selection (FSS) and backward sequential selection (BSS). Although they often produce substantial improvements in accuracy, these methods select the same set of relevant features everywhere in the instance space, and thus represent only a partial solution to the problem. In general, some features will be relevant only in some parts of the space; deleting them may hurt accuracy in those parts, but selecting them will have the same effect in parts where they are irrelevant. This article introduces RC, a new feature selection algorithm that uses a clustering-like approach to select sets of locally relevant features (i.e., the features it selects may vary from one instance to another). Experiments in a large number of domains from the UCI repository show that RC almost always improves accuracy with respect to FSS and BSS, often with high significance. A study using artificial domains confirms the hypothesis that this difference in performance is due to RC's context sensitivity, and also suggests conditions where this sensitivity will and will not be an advantage. Another feature of RC is that it is faster than FSS and BSS, often by an order of magnitude or more.

Key words: lazy learning, feature selection, nearest neighbor, induction, machine learning

1. Introduction and Motivation

Induction is the art and science of generalizing from the known to the unknown, so that appropriate responses to the unknown can be formulated when it appears. Classification is an example of an induction task relevant in a wide variety of domains. Given a set of preclassified examples, each typically represented by a vector of features, inductive learning algorithms attempt to produce class descriptions that will be accurate for new examples. The class assigned to a new example can then be used to decide how to process it (e.g., if the classification task is to diagnose an illness, the diagnosis is used to decide on the treatment). *Eager* approaches to induction explicitly produce generalizations representing the classes under study, often in a language different from that used to represent the examples. *Lazy* approaches, in contrast, delay this generalization until classification time; it is performed implicitly when a new example is compared to the stored instances and the class of the nearest one(s) is assigned to it. Lazy learners, also known as instance-based (Aha 1991), memory-based (Stanfill and Waltz 1986), exemplar-based (Salzberg 1991), case-based (Kolodner 1993) and others, have several advantages when compared to eager methods like decision-tree (Quinlan 1993) and rule induction (Clark and Niblett 1989). They are conceptually simple, and yet able to form complex decision boundaries in the instance space even when relatively little information is available. They combine naturally with analogical reasoning, apply easily to numeric domains, and with appropriate distance measures can also outperform other approaches in symbolic ones (Cost and Salzberg 1993). Special cases that may be missed by abstraction-forming approaches can be retained and recognized. Learning is often simple to perform, because it involves mainly storing the examples, possibly with some selection and indexing.

Lazy learners have some shortcomings, however. The memory cost of the class descriptions they produce is typically greater, and they can be harder for a human to understand. Classification can also take longer, even with suitable indexing schemes. However, the most significant problem for lazy learning is arguably that posed by irrelevant features. If many such features are present in the example descriptions, lazy learners will be confused by them when they compare examples, resulting in a possibly severe degradation of accuracy. A natural solution to this problem is identifying the irrelevant features, and discarding them before storing the examples for future use. Several algorithms have been proposed for this purpose (see (Kittler 1986) for a survey), of which two of the most widely known are forward sequential search (FSS) and backward sequential search (BSS) (Devijver and Kittler, 1982). Many variations of these exist (e.g., (Aha and Bankert 1994)). Their use can have a large positive impact on accuracy.

However, all of these algorithms have the common characteristic that they ignore the fact that some features may be relevant only in context (i.e., given the values of other features). They may discard features that are highly relevant in a restricted sector of the instance space because this relevance is swamped by their irrelevance everywhere else. They may retain features that are relevant in most of the space, but unnecessarily confuse the classifier in some regions.

Consider, for example, an instance space defined by a set of numeric features $\mathbf{F}$, and a class composed of two hyperrectangles, one of which is defined by intervals $f_i \in [a_i, b_i]$ in a subset $\mathbf{F_1}$ of the features, and the other by intervals in a subset $\mathbf{F_2}$ disjoint from the first. Current feature selection algorithms would retain all features in $\mathbf{F_1}$ and $\mathbf{F_2}$, because each of those features is relevant to identifying examples in one of the hyperrectangles. However, the features in $\mathbf{F_2}$ act as noise when identifying examples defined

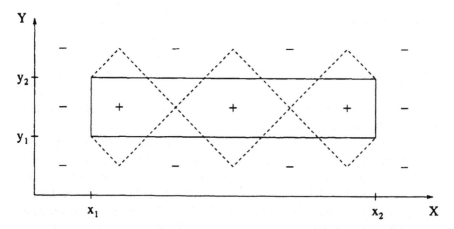

Figure 1. A concept for context-sensitive feature selection.

by F_1, and vice-versa. Instead of storing the same set of features for all instances, a better algorithm would discard the features in F_2 from the stored instances of the first hyperrectangle, and the features in F_1 from those of the second one. This article describes an algorithm that does this.

As another example, consider Figure 1, where the concept to be learned is the rectangle delimited by the solid line, and + and − indicate the positive and negative examples in the training set, respectively. The basic one-nearest-neighbor algorithm would produce the boundary shown as a dashed line, resulting in a large error. A context-free feature selection algorithm would retain both features, producing the same boundary, or delete one of them, collapsing the plane to a line and resulting in an even greater error. A context-sensitive algorithm, on the other hand, would ignore feature X when $Y > y_2$ or $Y < y_1$, because in those areas all examples are negative irrespective of the X coordinate, and it would take X into consideration when $y_1 \leq Y \leq y_2$, because here examples are positive if $x_1 \leq X \leq x_2$, and negative otherwise. X is thus relevant or not depending on the context (i.e., on the value of Y), and recognizing this leads to the correct boundary being induced.

The next section describes the lazy learner used in the studies reported here. Next, the FSS and BSS algorithms are summarized. RC, a context-sensitive feature selection algorithm, is then introduced. The worst-case time complexities of FSS, BSS and RC are compared. An empirical study follows, using datasets from the UCI repository and purposely-constructed ones. Finally RC's relationship to other learning algorithms is discussed, directions for future research are suggested, and some conclusions are drawn.

2. A Lazy Learner

The study described in this article was carried out in the context of RISE, a multistrategy learning system with a lazy-learning component (Domingos 1995; Domingos 1996). In this section we describe the lazy component (LazyRISE), providing the groundwork for the descriptions of the feature selection algorithms to follow.

LazyRISE inputs a *training set* of preclassified *examples*. An example is represented by a vector of *features* and a corresponding *class*. Features can be *symbolic* (nominal, categorical, non-ordinal discrete) or *numeric* (linear, real-valued). In LazyRISE the class is always symbolic. *Test examples* are examples not in the training set and submitted for classification. A distinction is made between examples and *instances*. The former are the input data, and the latter comprise the class description (i.e., instances are the stored examples used to classify new ones). The two may be syntactically identical, but differ semantically: an example represents one point in the instance space, whereas an instance represents the entire region of the space that is closer to it than to any other instance, and therefore inherits its class. Additionally, an instance will differ syntactically from the corresponding example if some features were deemed irrelevant and dropped from it. An instance is said to *win* an example when the example is closer to it than to any other stored instances, according to the distance measure used.

Choosing the distance measure is one of the major design decisions when building a lazy learner. LazyRISE employs normalized Euclidean distance for numeric features, and a simplified version of Stanfill and Waltz's (1986) value difference metric for symbolic ones. Let $E = (e_1, e_2, \ldots, e_F, c_E)$ be an example with value e_i for the ith feature and class c_E, and let $I = (i_1, i_2, \ldots, i_F, c_I)$ be an instance, with similar notation. In instances only, a feature can have the special value '$*$', which means that the feature was found to be irrelevant and discarded. The distance $\Delta(I, E)$ between I and E is then defined as:

$$\Delta(I, E) = \sum_{j=1}^{F} \delta^2(i_j, e_j) \tag{1}$$

where the component distance $\delta(i_j, e_j)$ for the jth feature is:

$$\delta(i_j, e_j) = \begin{cases} 0 & \text{if } i_j = * \\ \delta_{num}(i_j, e_j) & \text{if } i \text{ is numeric and } i_j \neq * \\ SVDM(i_j, e_j) & \text{if } i \text{ is symbolic and } i_j \neq * \end{cases} \tag{2}$$

The component distance for numeric features is defined as:

$$\delta_{num}(i_j, e_j) = \left| \frac{i_j - e_j}{max_j - min_j} \right| \qquad (3)$$

max_j and min_j being respectively the maximum and minimum values of the feature found in the training set. $SVDM(i_j, e_j)$ is the simplified value difference metric, defined as:

$$SVDM(x_i, x_j) = \sum_{h=1}^{C} |P(c_h|x_i) - P(c_h|x_j)| \qquad (4)$$

where x_i and x_j are any legal values of the feature, C is the number of classes, c_h is the hth class, and $P(c_h|x_i)$ denotes the probability of c_h conditioned on x_i. SVDM is a more sophisticated alternative to the commonly-used *overlap* metric (i.e., 0 if $i = j$, and 1 otherwise). $SVDM(x_i, x_j)$ is still always 0 if $i = j$, but it can be less than 1 for two different feature values if they correlate similarly with the class variable. Thus SVDM incorporates into lazy learning some of the information used by eager and Bayesian classifiers. Versions of this measure have been found to produce large improvements in accuracy compared to overlap in some symbolic domains (Cost and Salzberg 1993). SVDM differs from Cost and Salzberg's MVDM in that the latter also includes weights for the instances being compared. Of particular interest is the fact that VDM-type metrics have some ability to mute globally irrelevant features, because they will tend to always be close to zero for them. Thus SVDM eases the task of the feature selection algorithms described in the next two sections, when selecting symbolic features.

The distance from a missing numeric value to any other value is defined as 0. This is equivalent to ignoring a feature when its value is unknown. If a symbolic feature's value is missing, it is assigned the special value "?". This is treated as a legitimate symbolic value, and its SVDM to all other values of the feature is computed and used. In the context of VDM-style metrics, this is a sensible policy: a missing value is taken to be roughly equivalent to a given possible value if it behaves similarly to it, and inversely if it does not.

In its simplest form, LazyRISE simply stores all the training examples as instances, and estimates their accuracy as classifiers using a leave-one-out methodology: each example is removed in turn from the training set, and given to the other instances to classify; the nearest instance is found, and its class assigned to the example. The *accuracy* of an instance is the fraction of the examples it won that were indeed of its class. Because this tends to over-estimate the accuracy of instances that win very few examples, the *Laplace-corrected* accuracy (Niblett 1987) is used instead:

$$LAcc(I) = \frac{N_{corr}(I) + 1}{N_{won}(I) + C} \tag{5}$$

where I is any instance, C is the number of classes, $N_{won}(I)$ is the total number or examples won by I, and $N_{corr}(I)$ is the number of examples that I wins and correctly classifies.

At classification time, LazyRISE compares the new example with each of the stored instances using the distance measure defined in Equation 1, and assigns the example to the nearest instance's class. The previously-computed accuracies are used to choose between instances that are equally close to the test example. The effect of the Laplace correction is to make the estimate of an instance's accuracy converge to the "random guess" value of $1/C$ as the number of examples won by the instance decreases. Thus instances with high apparent accuracy are favored only if they also have high statistical support (i.e., if that apparent accuracy is not simply the result of a small sample). When the closest instances to the test example have the same Laplace accuracy, the most frequent class is chosen, and if the classes are equally frequent, a winner is selected at random.

3. Context-Free Feature Selection

The forward sequential selection algorithm (FSS) starts with an empty feature set and repeatedly adds the "best" feature to it until no further improvement is possible, or all features have been included. The backward sequential selection algorithm (BSS) operates similarly, but starts with the full feature set and repeatedly removes the "worst" feature from it. The implementation of the two algorithms used here is described in pseudo-code in Figures 2 and 3. In both cases, the final feature set can be empty and all examples assigned to the default class, if this leads to the highest accuracy.

The evaluation function $Eval(\ )$ can be a heuristic measure, typically of the quality of the class separation produced by the feature set, or it can be the actual accuracy obtained by applying the classifier using those features. If $Eval(\ )$ is a heuristic measure, the feature selection algorithm acts as a filter, extracting features to be used later by the main algorithm; if it is the actual accuracy, it acts as a wrapper around that algorithm (John, Kohavi and Pfleger 1994). The wrapper strategy has been found to often yield the best results (Aha and Bankert 1994), and this is attributable to the fact that its learning bias is that of the classifier itself, avoiding a possible mismatch between the feature selection and classification biases. Therefore the evaluation function used here is the classifier's accuracy on the training set; it is measured using a

Input: FS is the set of features used to describe examples.

Procedure FSS (FS)

Let $SS = \emptyset$.
Let $BestEval = 0$.
Repeat
  Let $BestF = None$.
  For each feature F in FS and not in SS
    Let $SS' = SS \cup \{F\}$.
    If $Eval(SS') > BestEval$
      Then Let $BestF = F$,
          Let $BestEval = Eval(SS')$.
  If $BestF \neq None$
    Then Let $SS = SS \cup \{BestF\}$.
Until $BestF = None$ or $SS = FS$.
Return SS.

Figure 2. The forward sequential selection (FSS) algorithm.

leave-one-out methodology (i.e., by removing each example from the training set in turn and using the remaining instances to classify it).

4. Context-Sensitive Feature Selection

This section describes RC (Relevance in Context), a context-sensitive feature selection algorithm. RC is in many ways similar to BSS, but with the crucial difference that it makes local, instance-specific decisions on feature relevance, as opposed to global ones. This is done in a clustering-like fashion: each instance looks for the nearest example of the same class, and hypothesizes that the features along which they differ are irrelevant. This is tested by checking whether deleting those features from the instance has a positive or negative effect on the accuracy of the classifier (i.e., a wrapper strategy is used as before). If the effect is positive or null, the features are effectively deleted, and on the following cycle the newly-simplified instance will look for the nearest example of its class that it does not yet cover, and repeat the process. If the effect is negative, the features are retained, and no more feature selection is attempted for this instance. This process is carried out in parallel for all instances, and terminates when feature selection has been attempted

Input: FS is the set of features used to describe examples.

Procedure BSS (FS)

Let $SS = FS$.
Let $BestEval = Eval(SS)$.
Repeat
  Let $WorstF = None$.
  For each feature F in SS
    Let $SS' = SS - \{F\}$.
    If $Eval(SS') \geq BestEval$
      Then Let $WorstF = F$,
            Let $BestEval = Eval(SS')$.
  If $WorstF \neq None$
    Then Let $SS = SS - \{WorstF\}$.
Until $WorstF = None$ or $SS = \emptyset$.
Return SS.

Figure 3. The backward sequential selection (BSS) algorithm.

with negative results for all instances. Notice that duplicate instances may be produced, but are not removed, in keeping with the idea that only feature selection is being performed. The algorithm is summarized in pseudo-code in Figure 4.

A question that arises in this framework is: when should two numeric values be considered different? If two real feature values are similar but not identical, the fact that they differ should obviously not be construed as evidence that the feature is irrelevant. Thus it is necessary to decide where the critical point should be. The policy adopted was to compute the mean and standard deviation of each numeric feature from the sample in the training set, and attempt dropping the feature only when the values for the instance and the example differ by more than one standard deviation.

To understand this choice, suppose that the observed values of a feature fall into two or three clusters. Given any two values, if they differ by less than one standard deviation they are most likely to be in the same cluster, and if they differ by more they are probably in different ones. Thus values in different clusters are judged to be significantly different, and only those. If there is a large number of clusters, the critical value should be less than one standard deviation. The choice made thus reflects a bias towards a low number of

Input: TS is the training set.

Procedure RC (TS)

Let IS be TS.
Compute $Acc(IS)$.
Activate all instances in IS.
Repeat
    For each active instance I in IS,
        Find the nearest example E to I at nonzero distance, and of I's class.
        Let $I' = I$ with all features that differ in I and E removed.
        Let $IS' = IS$ with I replaced by I'.
        If $Acc(IS') \geq Acc(IS)$
            Then replace IS by IS',
            Else deactivate I.
Until all instances are inactive.
Return IS.

Figure 4. The RC feature selection algorithm.

clusters; essentially, it assumes that the goal is either to distinguish between values above and below a certain threshold (the two-cluster case), or between a central range and values outside it (the three-cluster case). This is typically the case in many practical domains, like medical diagnosis (with variables like body temperature, blood pressure, levels of blood chemicals) and fault detection (voltage, stress, design dimensions with tolerances). In practice, an optimum value for this parameter can be determined by cross-validation, although this was not done in the studies described below.

The accuracy of an instance set $Acc(IS)$ is the fraction of the training examples that it correctly classifies using a leave-one-out methodology, as before. Since the accuracy is being measured on the whole training set, not just the examples won by an instance, the sample size is the same for all accuracies being compared, and no Laplace correction is necessary. If N is the training set size and F is the number of features, applying the leave-one-out methodology directly would result in a time cost of $O(N^2F)$ at each step of the algorithm. Fortunately, after the initial computation of $Acc(IS)$, only *differences* in accuracy due to dropping features from one instance need be computed. If each example's current closest instance and assigned class are stored with it, the change in accuracy can then be computed by matching the changed instance with all examples, and finding the ones it wins that it did not before. Previously misclassified examples that are now correctly classified add to the accuracy, and previously correctly classified examples that are now misclassified subtract from it. If the former are more numerous than the latter, the change in accuracy is positive, and the features are dropped. This reduces each step's cost to $O(NF)$.

5. Time Complexity

In this section we show that the worst-case time complexity of RC is similar to that of an efficient implementation of FSS and BSS.

Let N be the training set size, as before. The basic step of FSS/BSS consists of adding/deleting a single feature and checking the results. Since this involves comparing all instances with all examples along $O(F)$ features, the cost of each such step is $O(N^2F)$. This step is repeated for all currently excluded/included features and the best one selected, which means that an $O(N^2F)$ step is repeated $O(F)$ times, resulting in a cost of $O(N^2F^2)$. Since in the worst case all features will be added/dropped, this cycle can be performed $O(F)$ times, resulting in a total cost of $O(N^2F^3)$.

However, this direct implementation of FSS and BSS is inefficient, because it unnecessarily repeats the computation of all distances along all features every time a feature is tentatively added or removed. A more efficient version will cache, for each example, the distances $\Delta(I, E)$ (Equation 1) of all instances to the example, and then, when considering adding or dropping a feature, add or subtract to each $\Delta(I, E)$ the distance component $\delta^2(i_j, e_j)$ along that feature. Once the example's predicted class is found and compared with the correct one, the original distance vector is reinstated, and the process repeats with the next feature. This implementation reduces the worst-case time complexity of FSS and BSS to $O(N^2F^2)$, and is the one used in the studies that follow. Note that it does not require $O(N^2)$ memory instead of $O(N)$, because only the distances for one example at a time are cached. This implies bringing the cycle that classifies each example outside the cycle that tries each feature (i.e., "for each example, add/delete each feature and classify the example," instead of "for each feature, add/delete the feature and classify each example"). Such a process, opening the "black box" of the classification algorithm and bringing the feature selection algorithm inside it, may not be possible for all lazy learning algorithms.

For RC, the basic step consists of finding an instance's nearest example, dropping the features in which they differ, and testing to see if this has a positive effect on global accuracy. Finding the nearest example to a given instance involves comparing the instance with all examples, and takes $O(NF)$

time. Finding and deleting the common features takes $O(F)$ time. Computing the resulting change in accuracy takes $O(NF)$ time, as seen in the previous section. The total cost of finding features to delete in one instance is therefore $O(NF) + O(F) + O(NF) = O(NF)$. In each "repeat" cycle (see Figure 4) this is performed for all instances, leading to a cost of $O(N^2F)$ per cycle. The "repeat" cycle is performed at worst $O(F)$ times, since for each instance in each cycle at least one feature is dropped, and there are at most $O(F)$ features to drop, or the instance is deactivated and the cycle stops early for that instance. Therefore RC's total time cost is $O(N^2F^2)$, similar to that of the efficient implementation FSS and BSS.

An optimization that is possible in RC, as well as in the $O(N^2F^3)$ implementations of FSS and BSS, is the following. When classifying each example using a leave-one-out methodology, the closest instance to it has to be found. This involves computing the distance of each instance to the example, but that computation needs to be carried out only up to the point where the instance's distance is found to be larger than the previous shortest distance found. Similarly, when RC drops features from an instance and searches for the examples it now wins, its distance to each example needs to be computed only until it becomes larger than the current winning rule's one.

This optimization does not change the quadratic (or cubic) exponents in the time complexity, but can significantly reduce the average running time of the algorithm. It was therefore implemented in RC. Unfortunately, it is not possible in the $O(N^2F^2)$ versions of FSS and BSS, due to the inversion of the order of cycles previously mentioned.

6. Empirical Study: UCI Datasets

The central hypothesis of this article is that *RC will produce higher accuracies than FSS and BSS when feature relevance is significantly context-dependent, since it has the ability to select different features for different instances (i.e., to select different features given different values of other features)*. On the other hand, when features are either globally relevant or globally irrelevant, RC should have no advantage. Furthermore, if few examples are available or the data is noisy, BSS and FSS should be able to detect the globally irrelevant features more easily than RC. This is due to the fact that they consider dropping a feature in all instances at once, instead of in one at a time, and so produce larger swings in accuracy, that can be detected over statistical fluctuations even when the examples are noisy and/or few.

To investigate empirically the hypothesis that RC's advantage increases with the context dependency of feature relevance, a measure of the latter is required. Unfortunately, in real-world domains the "true" degree of context dependency for a target concept is necessarily unknown. One way to circumvent this problem is to carry out studies in artificial domains, where the context dependency can be predetermined by the experimenter, and this is done in the next section. Another approach is to find an empirical measure that is thought to correlate positively with context dependency. One possibility is to find out how far RC strays from selecting the same features for all instances (i.e, from doing the same as FSS and BSS). More concretely, a possible measure is the average D for all pairs of instances of the number of features selected by RC for one but not the other:

$$D = \frac{2}{N(N-1)} \sum_{i=1}^{N} \sum_{j=1}^{i-1} \sum_{k=1}^{F} d_{ijk} \tag{6}$$

where N is the number of training examples, F is the number of features, and d_{ijk} is 1 if feature k was selected for instance i but not instance j or vice-versa, and 0 otherwise. This *feature difference* measure is necessarily imperfect, since the context dependency effects exhibited by RC may or may not be really present, but it is a legitimate one, in the sense that observing it can falsify the hypothesis that RC is more accurate relative to FSS and BSS when it detects greater context dependency. The core of the study that follows will thus be to correlate the feature difference D with the differential accuracy of RC and the context-free algorithms.

An empirical study was conducted using 24 datasets from the UCI repository (Murphy 1995). These datasets were chosen so as to provide a wide variety of application areas, sizes, combinations of feature types, and difficulty as measured by the accuracy achieved on them by current algorithms. In this way, any conclusions that are reached can be regarded as having some degree of generality. More precisely, they can be expected to be valid for the population of domains of which the UCI repository is a sample. This population is certainly not the set of all possible induction problems, but it is certainly a set that includes many relevant real-world ones. The choice was also made to use a large number of domains, with the goal of having enough data points to allow statistically sound conclusions. Table 1 summarizes the characteristics of the datasets used.

Twenty runs were carried out for each domain. In each, the training set was composed of two-thirds of the examples, chosen at random, and the remainder were used as test examples. For each of the three algorithms (RC, FSS and BSS), the accuracy obtained, running time and average number of features selected were recorded, and their averages for the 20 runs computed. Table 2 shows, for each domain, the feature difference D (Equation 6), the average accuracy and standard deviation for each algorithm, and the significance of the difference between RC and each of the context-free algorithms using a

Table 1. Datasets used in the empirical study.

Domain[a][b]	Code	Exs.	Feats.	Num.	Classes	Missing	Incons.
Audiology	AD	200	69	0	24	291	No
Breast cancer	BC	286	9	4	2	9	Yes
Credit screening	CE	690	15	6	2	67	No
Pima diabetes	DI	768	8	8	2	0	No
Echocardiogram	EC	131	7	6	2	40	Yes
Glass	GL	214	9	9	6	0	No
Heart disease	HD	303	13	6	2	7	No
Hepatitis	HE	155	19	6	2	167	No
Horse colic	HO	300	22	7	2	1605	Yes
Iris	IR	150	4	4	3	0	No
Labor negotiations	LA	57	16	8	2	326	No
Lung cancer	LC	32	56	0	3	5	No
Liver disease	LD	345	6	6	2	0	No
LED	LI	100	7	0	10	0	Yes
Lymphography	LY	148	18	3	4	0	No
Post-operative	PO	90	8	8	3	3	Yes
DNA promoters	PR	106	57	0	2	0	No
Primary tumor	PT	339	17	0	21	225	Yes
Solar flare	SF	323	12	3	6	0	Yes
Sonar	SN	208	60	60	2	0	No
Soybean	SO	47	35	0	4	0	No
Voting records	VO	435	16	0	2	392	No
Wine	WI	178	13	13	3	0	No
Zoology	ZO	101	16	1	7	0	No

[a] BC: Ljubljana dataset; EC: class is 2nd feature, features 1 and 10-13 deleted, example with unknown class deleted; HD: Cleveland dataset, last feature deleted to yield a two-class problem; HO: class is 24th feature, features 3 and 25-28 deleted; LI: 100 examples, seed = 1, 10% noise; PO: pseudo-discretized values converted to numeric; SF: 1st feature used as class; SO: small dataset.

[b] The columns are, in order: name of the domain; 2-letter code used to refer to it in subsequent tables; number of examples; number of features; number of numeric features; number of classes; number of missing values in the entire dataset; and whether or not the dataset includes inconsistent examples (i.e., identical examples with different classes).

one-tailed paired t test. The t test is appropriate because the accuracies being compared, being means of random samples, are normally distributed by the central limit theorem (DeGroot 1986), and the variances are unknown and also being estimated; the one-tailed test is preferred over the two-tailed one because the goal is to determine in each case whether RC is better than the context-free algorithm, not whether the two are simply different. The more sensitive paired test is made possible by, in each run, testing all the algorithms

Table 2. Percentage accuracies of RC, FSS and BSS, and significances of the difference between RC and FSS/BSS.

Domain	Feature diff.	RC	FSS	Signif.	BSS	Signif.
LC	14.2±11.1	47.7±11.0	42.3±10.3	5.0	44.5±17.2	10.0
PR	**8.6±14.3**	**89.1±6.0**	**84.4±8.9**	**5.0**	**84.9±5.6**	**1.0**
HO	8.1± 2.8	80.6±4.0	75.3±6.1	0.5	78.2±3.4	1.0
AD	6.8± 4.1	77.0±4.9	71.2±5.7	0.5	75.4±4.4	2.5
VO	5.6± 3.5	95.7±1.7	89.5±13.1	2.5	94.7±1.6	2.5
LA	5.0± 2.0	91.1±6.9	87.4±6.7	5.0	85.8±9.2	1.0
PT	**4.9± 2.5**	**40.2±5.9**	**30.0±6.0**	**0.5**	**33.3±5.0**	**0.5**
SO	4.4± 2.9	100.0±0.0	94.4±8.8	1.0	95.0±6.3	0.5
HE	4.1± 2.2	77.1±4.8	80.5±5.2	95.0	75.7±3.8	10.0
LY	3.8± 1.8	81.2±5.6	76.5±5.2	0.5	79.1±6.0	5.0
ZO	3.1± 1.9	93.2±3.8	91.0±5.1	5.0	90.3±5.6	0.5
SF	2.4± 1.8	70.6±3.6	68.2±3.0	1.0	68.9±3.6	5.0
LI	**2.1± 1.3**	**61.4±6.2**	**47.1±13.3**	**0.5**	**54.7±7.8**	**0.5**
CE	2.0± 1.2	83.7±1.9	80.9±2.3	0.5	81.2±2.5	0.5
BC	1.6± 1.1	66.2±5.2	66.7±6.7	60.0	66.9±6.1	65.0
HD	1.5± 1.1	76.8±3.5	74.8±5.0	10.0	76.2±2.8	30.0
EC	0.8± 1.0	60.2±6.1	59.4±5.2	40.0	60.3±5.6	50.0
PO	**0.5± 0.5**	**60.8±6.1**	**68.5±5.0**	**99.5**	**68.0±6.9**	**99.5**
SN	0.5± 0.3	81.4±9.1	73.5±11.2	0.5	80.5±8.7	15.0
LD	0.3± 0.6	60.2±3.9	58.4±5.1	15.0	60.0±4.8	45.0
DI	0.2± 0.5	70.5±2.5	69.6±2.9	20.0	69.2±3.3	2.5
GL	0.0± 0.2	69.2±5.0	70.8±8.1	75.0	71.3±7.4	85.0
IR	0.0± 0.0	94.4±2.4	92.6±2.3	0.5	92.9±2.9	2.5
WI	0.0± 0.1	95.1±2.6	94.1±2.8	10.0	94.5±2.1	25.0

on the same sample. Since 48 individual significance tests are reported, it is possible that some of the differences reported as significant are in fact not so (for example, with 40 tests we can expect 2 non-significant differences to be reported as significant at the 5% level by chance). However, most of the significances are very low, making this effect unlikely. The domains are ordered by decreasing feature difference. Some of the more interesting results are highlighted in boldface.

These results are presented in a more easily comprehended form in Figure 5, which shows the difference in accuracy between each of the algorithms and RC as a function of feature difference. The difference in accuracy between RC and BSS has a significant positive correlation with the feature difference (0.44), and similarly for FSS (0.36). We conclude that RC is indeed able to detect context dependency effects, and from the t test results in Table 2,

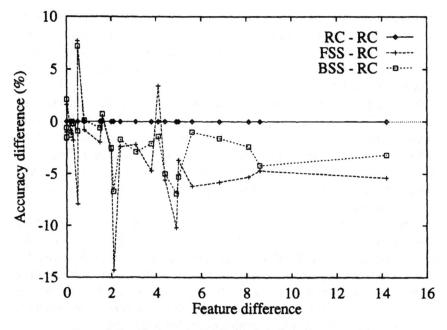

Figure 5. Empirical accuracy as a function of context dependency.

Table 3. Summary of accuracy results.

Measure	FSS	BSS
No. wins	20-4	20-4
No. signif. wins	15-2	14-1
Sign test	0.1	0.1
Wilcoxon test	0.1	0.1

that taking them into account in feature selection can produce significant improvements in accuracy.

Further analysis of the global results is shown in Table 3, and confirms the conclusion that RC is more accurate than FSS and BSS on this set of domains. The first line shows the number of domains in which RC achieved higher accuracy than the corresponding algorithm vs. the number in which the reverse occurred (e.g., RC was more accurate than BSS in 20 domains and less in 4). The second line shows the number of domains in which RC was more accurate than the other algorithm with a significance level of 5% or less, vs. the number in which the opposite occurred (i.e., in which the significance is 95% or more). The results are very favorable to RC. The third line shows the results of applying a sign test to the values in line one (i.e., considering the number of times RC won as a binomial variable and asking how likely the results are under the null hypothesis that the two algorithms are equally accurate). This is expressed as a percentage in the table. For example, RC's 20 wins vs. BSS have only a probability of occurrence of 1/1000. This results in very high confidence that RC is a more accurate algorithm than FSS and BSS on the population of domains from which the 24 used are drawn. Line four shows the result of a Wilcoxon signed-ranks test (DeGroot 1986), a more sensitive procedure that also takes into account the relative magnitudes of the differences observed, though not their absolute values; a large difference in accuracy is considered more significant than a small one. The very small values obtained lend further support to the conclusion that RC is the most accurate algorithm.

It should be remarked that, unlike what is common practice in the machine learning literature, these tests are being performed at the meta level: the question being asked is "Is RC better than the other algorithm on this ensemble of datasets?", as opposed to asking 24 times "Is RC better than the other algorithm on an ensemble of test sets from the same dataset?" Thus the use of a large number of datasets does not undermine the conclusions reached, but instead makes the very high confidences obtained possible.

The gains obtained by using the context-sensitive algorithm, although consistent, are typically moderate (around 2% on average vs. BSS, and 3% vs. FSS). This is consistent with Holte's observation that, for some datasets in the UCI repository, accuracies within a small range of the best recorded values can be obtained using only the single most relevant feature (Holte 1993). If RC, BSS and FSS all incorporate the "best" features, then their accuracies should not be expected to differ by more than this amount.

The number of features that each algorithm selects on average is also an indication of how the algorithms' behavior differs. It is reported in Table 4. Since RC does not select the same set of features for all instances, its feature usage in each trial is defined as the average for all instances of the number of features used in each instance; for example, if a feature is used in only one of the N instances, it counts as only $1/N$ features. This is then averaged across all 20 trials. The average for all trials of the standard deviation *within each trial* of the number of features selected is also reported. As might be expected, it correlates positively with the feature difference, since a high value implies large variation in the features selected, even though the reverse is not true because two instances may have different features but the same number of features.

BSS always selects more features than FSS; this is not surprising, given their respective search strategies. RC almost always selects the most features, but this observation can be misleading: direct inspection of the simplified

Table 4. Average number of features selected by the algorithms, and average feature difference of RC's instances.

Domain	No. feats.	RC	FSS	BSS	Feature diff.
AD	69	64.1± 4.4	11.4	22.0	6.8± 4.1
BC	9	7.7± 1.1	2.3	4.8	1.6± 1.1
CE	15	13.5± 1.2	5.7	9.6	2.0± 1.2
DI	8	7.9± 0.3	1.9	6.6	0.2± 0.5
EC	7	6.6± 0.8	1.5	4.4	0.8± 1.0
GL	9	9.0± 0.1	4.7	5.6	0.0± 0.2
HD	13	12.1± 0.9	4.6	9.3	1.5± 1.1
HE	19	16.4± 2.0	3.5	11.0	4.1± 2.2
HO	22	14.8± 3.4	5.7	15.6	8.1± 2.8
IR	4	4.0± 0.0	2.2	2.6	0.0± 0.0
LA	16	11.3± 2.0	3.0	6.8	5.0± 2.0
LC	56	45.9±11.2	3.2	9.9	14.2±11.1
LD	6	5.9± 0.5	2.1	4.2	0.3± 0.6
LI	7	5.5± 1.2	5.5	6.3	2.1± 1.3
LY	18	15.2± 1.9	5.2	11.3	3.8± 1.8
PO	8	7.7± 0.5	2.0	3.5	0.5± 0.5
PR	57	52.1±11.7	5.4	16.1	8.6±14.3
PT	17	13.5± 2.7	7.5	12.0	4.9± 2.5
SF	12	10.1± 1.9	4.4	5.7	2.4± 1.8
SN	60	59.7± 0.3	5.8	37.2	0.5± 0.3
SO	35	25.2± 1.5	2.0	3.9	4.4± 2.9
VO	16	5.9± 3.5	7.1	9.4	5.6± 3.5
WI	13	13.0± 0.1	4.3	8.4	0.0± 0.1
ZO	16	13.2± 1.8	5.8	6.4	3.1± 1.9

instances output by RC shows that it typically drops most features from just a few of the instances, and it is these highly simplified ones that win most of the test examples; the majority of the instances retain most of the features, but have little impact on classification. Inspection also reveals that the most highly simplified instances differ in the features they retain. This, together with RC's higher accuracies, is further evidence that it is indeed detecting context sensitivity effects. However, it is still true that if the goal is to reduce the feature set size as much as possible, even at some cost in accuracy, RC is clearly not the algorithm of choice: not only does it retain a higher number of features on average, but it only allows the removal of features that do not appear in any final instance.

The post-operative patient data domain (PO) is an example of a situation where FSS's and BSS's bias is more appropriate than RC's. In this domain,

Table 5. Average running time of algorithms, in minutes, seconds, and hundredths of a second; and ratio of running times of FSS and BSS to running time of RC.

Domain	RC	FSS	BSS	FSS/RC	BSS/RC
AD	0:10.68	4:14.60	11:15.61	23.8	63.3
BC	0:06.03	0:25.78	1:31.95	4.3	15.2
CE	1:42.25	7:58.87	7:44.39	4.7	4.5
DI	1:33.12	3:48.80	3:59.52	2.5	2.6
EC	0:01.21	0:03.40	0:05.53	2.8	4.6
GL	0:03.38	0:25.39	0:24.63	7.5	7.3
HD	0:08.10	1:02.13	1:06.16	7.7	8.2
HE	0:02.81	0:10.97	1:32.94	3.9	33.1
HO	0:10.06	2:54.30	2:26.87	17.3	14.6
IR	0:01.12	0:03.50	0:03.52	3.1	3.1
LA	0:00.56	0:01.76	0:04.26	3.1	7.6
LC	0:00.41	0:01.88	0:12.64	4.6	30.8
LD	0:06.47	0:25.89	1:32.14	4.0	14.2
LI	0:00.52	0:02.63	0:00.93	5.1	1.8
LY	0:02.29	0:18.56	0:21.17	8.1	9.2
PO	0:00.76	0:02.00	0:03.27	2.6	4.3
PR	0:03.40	1:34.18	2:29.97	27.7	44.1
PT	0:09.68	2:54.47	1:14.92	18.0	7.7
SF	0:06.81	1:51.47	1:45.35	16.4	15.5
SN	0:24.32	4:47.99	14:49.84	11.8	36.6
SO	0:00.74	0:01.85	0:11.16	2.5	15.1
VO	1:44.70	3:56.94	3:31.63	2.3	2.0
WI	0:03.86	0:26.00	1:33.19	6.7	24.1
ZO	0:01.10	0:07.77	0:10.17	7.1	9.2

most features appear to be globally irrelevant; simply assigning all test examples to the most frequent class, ignoring all feature information, produces higher accuracy than all three algorithms (and also than decision-tree and rule learners, as was found in a separate study (Domingos 1995)). FSS and BSS correctly discard most of the features. However, because the dataset is small (90 examples) and noisy (as evinced by the fact that it contains inconsistent examples) RC has difficulty detecting the global irrelevance of features, and retains most of them for most instances.

Another variable of interest is the running time of the algorithms. These are shown in Table 5. A Sun 670 workstation was used for all runs. Figure 6 shows these values plotted on a log-log scale against $N^2 F^2$, the worst-case asymptotic growth rate for all algorithms (derived in the previous section). RC is always faster than FSS and BSS, sometimes by large factors (see,

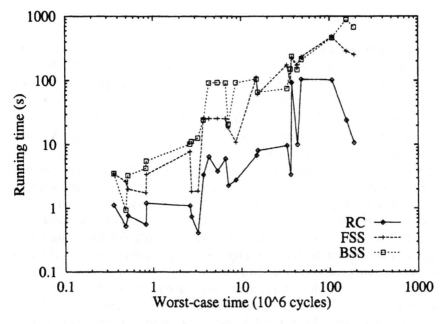

Figure 6. Running time in relation to N^2F^2.

for example, the audiology domain, AD). This can be partly attributed to variations in the number of features that each algorithm actually adds/drops: since RC typically drops fewer features than BSS, and fewer than FSS adds, it finishes in fewer cycles. Another reason for the observed difference in times is that the context-free algorithms have a higher multiplicative coefficient for N^2F^2, and the presence of additional lower-order terms in these. However, the most important factor is the optimization in the distance computation that was used in RC, but is not possible in the efficient versions of FSS and BSS (see previous section).

Considering these effects, and extrapolating from the average slopes of the log-log plots of the algorithms' running times, we are led to hypothesize that RC will still be a viable feature selection algorithm in domains where FSS's and BSS's time cost would exclude them from consideration. In the form used here, none of the algorithms are suitable for very large databases, since they are all necessarily quadratic in N, even in the average case; however, more efficient versions of FSS/BSS-style algorithms exist (Kittler 1986; Aha and Bankert 1994), and similar modifications of RC can be envisioned.

7. Empirical Study: Artificial Domains

The question arises of whether the conclusions formulated in the previous section are generally valid, or the favorable results obtained for RC are specific to the domains used in the study reported in the previous section. In other words, RC's observed benefits might apply only when the biases represented in the UCI repository are verified, independently of the more general hypothesis that they are due to RC's context sensitivity. Another question is whether the feature difference estimate used effectively corresponds to the context dependency we seek to measure, and thus whether the results obtained are meaningful. These two problems were investigated by carrying out experiments in artificial domains. As argued in (Aha 1992) and (Schaffer 1989), more robust and general conclusions will be reached if whole classes of domains are considered, instead of the few individual cases typically used in the machine learning literature. Our hypotheses are that RC is more accurate than FSS and BSS over a broad range of domains ("broad" in the sense that they have no common bias save their context dependency), and that the difference in accuracy increases with the context dependency of feature relevance. In artificial domains, the target concept description is known *a priori*, and, if it is composed of a set of prototypes, the measure of feature difference defined in the previous section applied to that set of prototypes constitutes a suitable measure of context dependency. The empirical study thus proceeded by repeatedly selecting a value of D (Equation 6), generating a large number of domains at random characterized by that value, and observing the resulting accuracies of the three algorithms for that sample of domains.

Two-class problems were considered, with 100 examples in each dataset, described by 32 features. In each domain, each feature was chosen to be numeric or Boolean with equal probability (i.e., the number of numeric features is a binomial variable with expected value $F/2$ and variance $F/4$). Class 1 is defined by ten clusters, and class 0 is the complement of class 1. Each prototype or cluster is defined by a conjunction of conditions on the relevant features. The required value for a Boolean feature is chosen at random, with 0 and 1 being equally probable. Each numeric feature i must fall within a given range $[a_i, b_i]$, with a_i being the smaller of two values chosen from the interval $[-1, 1]$ according to a uniform distribution, and b_i the larger one. A cluster is thus a hyperrectangle in the relevant numeric subspace, and a conjunction of literals in the Boolean one.

The choice of relevant features for each prototype is made at random, but in a way that guarantees that the desired value of D for the set of prototypes is maintained on average. The details of the procedure that does this are described in Appendix A. The feature difference D was varied from 0 to 8,

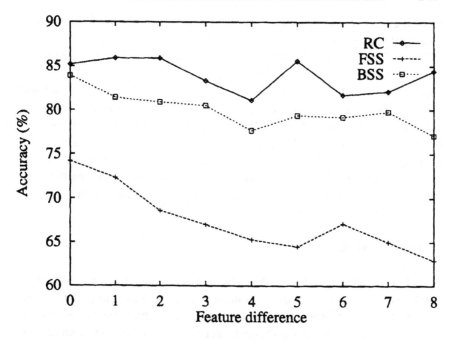

Figure 7. Accuracy as a function of context dependency.

the latter being the maximum value that can be produced given the number of features and prototypes used. Twenty domains were generated for each value of D, and two-thirds of the examples used as the training set. The average accuracy of RC, FSS and BSS on the remaining examples is shown graphically as a function of D in Figure 7.

All differences in accuracy between RC and FSS are significant at the 5% level, as are those between RC and BSS for $D = 1, 2, 4, 5,$ and 8. This confirms our hypothesis that RC is more accurate than FSS and BSS over a broad range of domains. We also note that BSS's performance is sometimes quite close to RC's. The smallest difference occurs when $D = 0$, as might be expected, since this situation exactly fits BSS's bias. More generally, due to the small number of training examples used (100), BSS may benefit from its ability to produce larger, more easily detected swings in accuracy when attempting to delete features, as previously hypothesized. Increasing the training set size should increase the distance between RC and BSS, since RC will then have enough data to detect the finer local dependencies that BSS by definition cannot. FSS's and BSS's time limitations have precluded repeating the experiments with a significantly larger number of examples to investigate this point.[1]

The variation of the algorithms' accuracy with D is also of interest. All accuracies are negatively correlated with D, but the absolute value of the correlation is much smaller for RC (0.49) than for FSS and BSS (0.89 and 0.82, respectively). The downward slope of the regression line for RC's accuracy as a function of D (-0.35) is also much smaller than that for FSS (-1.21) and BSS (-0.61). We thus conclude that RC's higher performance is indeed at least partly due do its context sensitivity, and, pending further evidence, that RC is the feature selection algorithm of choice among the three studied, when feature relevance is significantly context-dependent.

8. Related Work

Variations of FSS and BSS are described and evaluated in (Aha and Bankert 1994). Beyond the pattern recognition approaches surveyed in (Devijver and Kittler 1982) and (Kittler 1986), many methods for feature selection have been proposed in the artificial intelligence literature in recent years (Almuallim and Dieterich 1991; Kira and Rendell 1992; Schlimmer 1993; Vafaie and DeJong 1993; Caruana and Freitag 1994; John et al. 1994; Skalak 1994). Cardie (1993) and Kibler and Aha (1987) use decision trees to select features for use in a lazy learner. Although each path through the tree represents a context-dependent set of relevant features, this information is discarded, and only the unstructured set of all the features used in the tree is passed to the lazy component. Another lazy-learner feature selection method, also based on decision trees, is described in (Langley and Sage 1994). In this case all paths through the tree contain the same set of features, and so the level of context sensitivity is similar to that of BSS.

Decision-tree (Quinlan 1993) and rule induction algorithms (Clark and Niblett 1989) *per se* can be regarded as performing context-sensitive feature selection, and deriving most of their power from it. Because they search in a general-to-specific direction, adding one feature at a time, when seen as feature selectors they are most similar to FSS, and indeed have similar short-comings with regard to detecting feature interactions (Pagallo and Haussler 1990). It makes sense then to also view RC as a prototype specific-to-general rule induction algorithm, and expect it to have the same advantages relative

---

[1] With 100 examples, 20 runs with 9 values of D take approximately 10 hours of CPU time, of which less than 10 minutes is due to RC; 1000 examples would take on the order of $(1000/100)^2 \times 10$ hours, or 40 days. On the other hand, reducing F to allow more examples without increasing time would further reduce the observable range of D.

to algorithms like ID3 and CN2 that BSS has with respect to FSS. This idea was taken further in the RISE system, described in (Domingos 1995; Domingos 1996). RISE is a full-fledged rule learner; starting with one rule per example, it searches for an optimal rule set, taking rule interactions during the induction process into account, allowing deletion of rules, and allowing generalization of numeric values to intervals. In (Domingos 1996) it is compared with ID3 and CN2 on a large number of domains, and found to achieve significantly higher accuracy than either in most datasets, at the cost of increased memory usage, and with comparable running times. Lesion studies and monitoring of the algorithm's internals show that the lazy-learning component is essential to RISE's performance, as are the rule induction aspects and the conflict-resolution strategy used.

A related field is that of feature weighting (Aha 1989; Kelly and Davis 1991; Salzberg 1991; Creecy, Masand, Smith and Waltz 1992; Mohri and Tanaka 1994). Feature selection can be seen as a special case of feature weighting where each weight is either 0 or 1, and thus weighting methods are potentially more powerful. However, because they have more degrees of freedom, they can also be harder to apply successfully, especially when there are few training examples.

Feature weights can be supplied by the designer, as in Skalak's (1992) Broadway system, or learned (see references above). Cain, Pazzani and Silverstein (1991) have an intermediate approach which combines lazy and explanation-based learning, assigning higher weights to features that appear in the derivation of the example's class using a pre-existing domain theory.

Feature weighting methods also vary in what the weights can depend on, and thus in their degree of context sensitivity. In the representationally simplest schemes, there is one weight per feature, and they are therefore completely context-free (Kelly and Davis 1991; Salzberg 1991; Lee 1994; Mohri and Tanaka 1994). More flexible approaches employ one weight per feature value (Nosofsky, Clark and Shin 1989; Stanfill and Waltz 1986), one weight per feature per class (Aha 1989), or a combination of the two (Creecy et al. 1992), and thus exhibit a moderate degree of context sensitivity. In the case of continuous features, it is also possible to take into account the relative values of the feature in the instance and the example being classified, resulting in directional weights (Ricci and Avesani 1995). The most elaborate algorithms have in effect one weight per feature per instance, and are consequently fully context-sensitive; these weights can be assigned at classification time (Atkeson, Moore and Schaal 1997) or at learning time (Aha and Goldstone 1992). Seen as a 0-1 feature weighting algorithm, RC falls into this last category.

9. Concluding Remarks

This article introduced a new feature selection algorithm for lazy learners. It differs from previous approaches in that it accounts for context dependency effects by selecting a possibly different set of relevant features for each instance. Empirical studies show that this often produces significant gains in accuracy, and that these gains increase with the the degree of context dependency of feature relevance.

Directions for future research include:

- Repeating the experiments described using other lazy learners, other context-free feature selection algorithms, and a wider variety of artificial domains, to check if the same qualitative results are obtained.
- Applying the approach described here to algorithms that use the k nearest instances to classify a test example, instead of only the nearest one.
- Combining RC with a context-free algorithm to optimize the selection of both context-free and context-sensitive relevant features, and to reduce the size of the feature set extracted.
- Developing versions of RC suitable for very large datasets and very large feature sets.

Acknowledgments

This work was partly supported by JNICT/Programa Ciência and Fulbright scholarships. The author is grateful to Dennis Kibler and Mike Pazzani for many helpful comments and suggestions, and to all the people who provided the datasets used in the empirical study, in particular M. Zwitter and M. Soklic of the University Medical Centre, Ljubljana, for supplying the lymphography, breast cancer and primary tumor datasets, and Robert Detrano, of the V.A. Medical Center, Long Beach and Cleveland Clinic Foundation, for supplying the heart disease dataset. Please see the documentation in the UCI Repository for detailed information on all datasets.

Appendix A

This appendix describes how, for each one of P prototypes, the relevant features are chosen at random in a way that guarantees that the feature difference between the prototypes (Equation 6) is on average a pre-specified value D.

If P_k is the number of prototypes in which feature k is relevant, Equation 6 can also be written as:

$$D = \frac{2}{P(P-1)} \sum_{k=1}^{F} P_k(P - P_k) \tag{7}$$

where P corresponds to N in (6), and F is the number of features. Let:

$$\rho_k = P_k(P - P_k) \tag{8}$$

and let $\bar{\rho}$ be the average value of ρ for the F features. $\bar{\rho}$ is determined by the desired value of D:

$$\bar{\rho} = \frac{P(P-1)}{2F} D \tag{9}$$

Next, k values of ρ_k such that their average is the value $\bar{\rho}$ above can be obtained from a uniform distribution in the interval $[0, 2\bar{\rho}]$. The corresponding P_ks are found by solving (8) for P_k, which is possible in general iff:

$$D \leq \frac{F}{4(1 - \frac{1}{P})} \tag{10}$$

This constrains the observable range of D given F and P. Finally, feature k is included in each prototype with probability P_k/P.

References

Aha, D. W. (1989). Incremental, Instance-Based Learning of Independent and Graded Concept Descriptions. In Proceedings of *The Sixth International Workshop on Machine Learning*, pp. 387–391. Ithaca, NY: Morgan Kaufmann.

Aha, D. W. (1992). Generalizing from Case Studies: A Case Study. In Proceedings of *The Ninth International Workshop on Machine Learning*, pp. 1–10. Aberdeen, Scotland: Morgan Kaufmann.

Aha, D. W. & Bankert, R. L. (1994). Feature Selection for Case-Based Classification of Cloud Types: An Empirical Comparison. In Proceedings of *The 1994 AAAI Workshop on Case-Based Reasoning*, pp. 106–112. Seattle, WA: AAAI Press.

Aha, D. W. & Goldstone, R. L. (1992). Concept Learning and Flexible Weighting. In Proceedings of *The Fourteenth Annual Conference of the Cognitive Science Society*, pp. 534–539. Evanston, IL: Lawrence Erlbaum.

Aha, D. W., Kibler, D. & Albert, M. K. (1991). Instance-Based Learning Algorithms. *Machine Learning* 6: 37–66.

Almuallim, H. & Dietterich, T. G. (1991). Learning with Many Irrelevant Features. In Proceedings of *The Ninth National Conference on Artificial Intelligence*, pp. 547–552. Menlo Park, CA: AAAI Press.

Atkeson, C. G., Moore, A. W. & Schaal, S. (1997). Locally Weighted Learning. *Artificial Intelligence Review*, this issue.

Cain, T., Pazzani, M. J. & Silverstein, G. (1991). Using Domain Knowledge to Influence Similarity Judgments. In Proceedings of *The Case-Based Reasoning Workshop*, pp. 191–199. Washington, DC: Morgan Kaufmann.

Cardie, C. (1993). Using Decision Trees to Improve Case-Based Learning. In Proceedings of *The Tenth International Conference on Machine Learning*, pp. 25–32. Amherst, MA: Morgan Kaufmann.

Caruana, R. & Freitag, D. (1994). Greedy Attribute Selection. In Proceedings of *The Eleventh International Conference on Machine Learning*, pp. 28–36. New Brunswick, NJ: Morgan Kaufmann.

Clark, P. & Niblett, T. (1989). The CN2 Induction Algorithm. *Machine Learning* 3: 261–283.

Cost, S. & Salzberg, S. (1993). A Weighted Nearest Neighbor Algorithm for Learning with Symbolic Features. *Machine Learning* 10: 57–78.

Creecy, R. H., Masand, B. M., Smith, S. J. & Waltz, D. L. (1992). Trading MIPS and Memory for Knowledge Engineering. *Communications of the ACM* 35(8): 48–63.

DeGroot, M. H. (1986). *Probability and Statistics*, Second Edition. Addison-Wesley: Reading, MA.

Devijver, P. A. & Kittler, J. (1982). *Pattern Recognition: A Statistical Approach*. Prentice/Hall: Englewood Cliffs, NJ.

Domingos, P. (1995). The RISE 2.0 System: A Case Study in Multistrategy Learning. TR-95-2, Department of Information and Computer Science, University of California at Irvine, Irvine, CA.

Domingos, P. (1996). Unifying Instance-Based and Rule-Based Induction. *Machine Learning* 24: 141–168.

Holte, R. C. (1993). Very Simple Classification Rules Perform Well on Most Commonly Used Datasets. *Machine Learning* 11: 63–91.

John, G. H., Kohavi, R. & Pfleger, K. (1994). Irrelevant Features and the Subset Selection Problem. In Proceedings of *The Eleventh International Conference on Machine Learning*, pp. 121–129. New Brunswick, NJ: Morgan Kaufmann.

Kelly, J. D. & Davis, L. (1991). A Hybrid Genetic Algorithm for Classification. In Proceedings of *The Twelfth International Joint Conference on Artificial Intelligence*, pp. 645–650. Sydney: Morgan Kaufmann.

Kibler, D. & Aha, D. W. (1987). Learning Representative Exemplars of Concepts: An Initial Case Study. In Proceedings of *The Fourth International Workshop on Machine Learning*, pp. 24–30, Irvine, CA: Morgan Kaufmann.

Kira, A. & Rendell, L. A. (1992). A Practical Approach to Feature Selection. In Proceedings of *The Ninth International Workshop on Machine Learning*, pp. 249–256. Aberdeen, Scotland: Morgan Kaufmann.

Kittler, J. (1986). Feature Selection and Extraction. In Young, T. Y. & Fu, K. S. (eds.) *Handbook of Pattern Recognition and Image Processing*. Academic Press: New York.

Kolodner, J. (1993). *Case-Based Reasoning*. Morgan Kaufmann: San Mateo, CA.

Langley, P. & Sage, S. (1994). Oblivious Decision Trees and Abstract Cases. In Proceedings of *The 1994 AAAI Workshop on Case-Based Reasoning*, pp. 113–117. Seattle, CA: AAAI Press.

Lee, C. (1994). An Instance-Based Learning Method for Databases: An Information Theoretic Approach. In Proceedings of *The Ninth European Conference on Machine Learning*, pp. 387–390. Catania, Italy: Springer-Verlag.

Mohri, T. & Tanaka, H. (1994). An Optimal Weighting Criterion of Case Indexing for Both Numeric and Symbolic Attributes. In Proceedings of *The 1994 AAAI Workshop on Case-Based Reasoning*, pp. 123–127. Seattle, WA: AAAI Press.

Murphy, P. M. (1995). UCI Repository of Machine Learning Databases. Machine-Readable Data Repository, Department of Information and Computer Science, University of California at Irvine, Irvine, CA.

Niblett, T. (1987). Constructing Decision Trees in Noisy Domains. In Proceedings of *The Second European Working Session on Learning*, pp. 67–78. Bled, Yugoslavia: Sigma.

Nosofsky, R. M., Clark, S. E. & Shin, H. J. (1989). Rules and Exemplars in Categorization, Identification, and Recognition. *Journal of Experimental Psychology: Learning, Memory, and Cognition* 15: 282–304.

Pagallo, G. & Haussler, D. (1990). Boolean Feature Discovery in Empirical Learning. *Machine Learning* **3**: 71–99.

Ricci, F. & Avesani, P. (1995). Learning a Local Similarity Metric for Case-Based Reasoning. In Proceedings of *The First International Conference on Case-Based Reasoning*, pp. 301–312. Sesimbra, Portugal: Springer-Verlag.

Salzberg, S. (1991). A Nearest Hyperrectangle Learning Method. *Machine Learning* **6**: 251–276.

Schaffer, C. (1989). Analysis of Artificial Data Sets. In Proceedings of *The Second International Symposium on Artificial Intelligence*, pp. 607–617. Monterrey, Mexico: McGraw-Hill.

Schlimmer, J. C. (1993). Efficiently Inducing Determinations: A Complete and Systematic Search Algorithm that Uses Optimal Pruning. In Proceedings of *The Tenth International Conference on Machine Learning*, pp. 284–290. Amherst, MA: Morgan Kaufmann.

Skalak, D. B. (1992). Representing Cases as Knowledge Sources that Apply Local Similarity Metrics. In Proceedings of *The Fourteenth Annual Conference of the Cognitive Science Society*, pp. 325–330. Evanston, IL: Lawrence Erlbaum.

Skalak, D. B. (1994). Prototype and Feature Selection by Sampling and Random Mutation Hill Climbing Algorithms. In Proceedings of *The Eleventh International Conference on Machine Learning*, pp. 293–301. New Brunswick, NJ: Morgan Kaufmann.

Stanfill, C. & Waltz, D. (1986). Toward Memory-Based Reasoning. *Communications of the ACM* **29**: 1213–1228.

Vafaie, H. & DeJong, K. (1993). Robust Feature Selection Algorithms. In Proceedings of *The Fifth IEEE International Conference on Tools for Artificial Intelligence*, pp. 356–363. Boston, MA: Computer Society Press.

Artificial Intelligence Review **11**: 255–272, 1997.

Computing Optimal Attribute Weight Settings for Nearest Neighbor Algorithms

CHARLES X. LING and HANDONG WANG
Department of Computer Science, M.C., The University of Western Ontario, London, Ontario, Canada N6A 5B7
E-mail: {ling, hwang}@csd.uwo.ca

Abstract. Nearest neighbor (NN) learning algorithms, examples of the lazy learning paradigm, rely on a distance function to measure the similarity of testing examples with the stored training examples. Since certain attributes are more discriminative, while others can be less or totally irrelevant, attributes should be weighed differently in the distance function. Most previous studies on weight setting for NN learning algorithms are empirical. In this paper we describe our attempt on deciding theoretically optimal weights that minimize the predictive error for NN algorithms. Assuming a uniform distribution of examples in a 2-d continuous space, we first derive the average predictive error introduced by a linear classification boundary, and then determine the optimal weight setting for any polygonal classification region. Our theoretical results of optimal attribute weights can serve as a baseline or lower bound for comparing other empirical weight setting methods.

Key words: nearest neighbor learning algorithms, lazy learning, attribute weight setting, theoretical analyses

1. Introduction

Nearest neighbor learning algorithms, which are examples of the lazy learning paradigm, are some of the most popular and studied learning algorithms. They originated in the field of pattern recognition (Cover and Hart 1967; Dasarathy 1991), and have been well studied and applied in classification tasks in machine learning (e.g., (Stanfill and Waltz 1986; Aha, Kibler, and Albert, 1991; Cost and Salzberg 1993)). Although many variants exist, these algorithms, generally speaking, store all (or selected) training examples, and utilize a similarity (or distance) function to measure the similarity (or distance) of a testing example with the stored training examples when predicting the class of the testing example. That is, they do not induce concept description during the training process; instead, they delay the prediction to the testing period by relying on the training examples. A popular example is the *k-nearest neighbor* (k-NN) algorithm (Dasarathy 1991). It determines the classification of a testing example by selecting a set of *k* closest training examples –

normally the majority class of the k selected training examples. When $k=1$, this algorithm is called the 1-nearest neighbor (1-NN) algorithm. Aha et al. (1991) describe a paradigm of lazy learning algorithms that they refer to as instance-based learning (IBL) algorithms, and their IB1 algorithm is an implementation of 1-NN.

The distance function of k-NN algorithms takes the form:

$$dist(x, y) = \sqrt{\sum (x_i - y_i)^2} \tag{1}$$

where x is the testing example, y is the stored training example, and x_i and y_i are the (normalized) values of the ith attribute.[1] However, this distance function (Equation 1) treats every attribute with equal contribution, which for many cases is not ideal. Sometimes an attribute can be completely irrelevant to the classification, so it should not be included in the distance function. Therefore, a more realistic distance function is[2]

$$dist(x, y) = \sqrt{\sum w_i^2 \times (x_i - y_i)^2} \tag{2}$$

where w_i is a constant (to be determined) that weighs the role of the ith attribute in the similarity function.

Setting the weights in the similarity function appropriately can dramatically improve the generalization of the k-NN algorithms, especially in domains with many irrelevant attributes (e.g., (Aha 1989; Kelly and Davis 1991; Cardie, 1993; Mohri and Tanaka 1994; Ling, Parry, and Wang 1994)). Intuitively, more important attributes should be assigned larger weights than less important attributes, while totally irrelevant attributes should be assigned 0 weight. Many researchers (see Section 2) have proposed algorithms for assigning w_i in Equation 2. However, most of them are empirical; little theoretical work on optimal weight setting is known. Even for a very simple case, where the classification region is an axis-parallel rectangle in a two-dimensional continuous space, it is unknown what the optimal weights w_1 and w_2 are that minimize predictive error.

This paper reports our effort in deciding theoretically optimal weights that minimize the predictive error for 1-NN algorithms. Our results are still quite limited in scope since they apply only to domains of 2-d continuous space. That is, instances are described by two numeric-valued attributes. Also, it is

---

[1] If the attribute is symbolic, then $x_i - y_i = 0$ if $x_i = y_i$; 1 otherwise.

[2] We put a square on the w_i so the transformation along the axes is proportional to w_i instead of to $\sqrt{w_i}$. In addition, we assume that in this paper the attribute weight vector is the same in the whole instance space.

assumed that the examples are uniformly distributed. We first review previous empirical and theoretical work on weight setting algorithms for k-NN in Section 2. In Section 3 we derive formulas for the average predictive error introduced by linear classification boundaries in 2-d continuous space when examples are uniformly distributed. We then use these results to design a method of deciding theoretically optimal weights for 1-NN in Section 4. Our theoretical results in Sections 3 and 4 have also been empirically verified, indicating that several assumptions and approximations in our derivation are reasonable. We discuss how to extend our work to k-NN ($k > 1$) and higher dimensions in Section 5.

Note that in our theoretical analyses of optimal attribute weights, we assume that the classification boundary (i.e., the underlying target concept) is known. Thus, our optimal results can serve as a useful baseline or lower bound for evaluating empirical attribute weight assigning methods on known concepts. We give some specific examples in Section 5. To apply our method in a more realistic setting where only training examples are given, we need to estimate the classification boundary using piecewise linear classifiers before applying our method. See Section 5 for more details.

2. Review of Previous Weight Setting Methods

Quite a few researchers have investigated empirical work on the weight setting of k-NN algorithms. Several studies showed that one can set attribute weights using another popular learning algorithm – the decision tree learning algorithms ID3 (Quinlan 1986) or C4.5 (Quinlan 1993), which use information gain (ratio) to select nodes in decision trees. Kibler and Aha (1987) first presented a simple approach of combining C4.5 and k-NN. Their method uses the presence and absence of attributes in the decision tree built by C4.5 on the same set of training examples to determine the weights (1 and 0 respectively) in the similarity function (Equation 2). The underlying assumption of their method is that if the attributes are not used in the decision tree, they are regarded as irrelevant. Cardie (1993) independently rediscovered the same method. Daelemans, Gillis, Durieux, and van den Bosch (1993) and Wettschereck and Dietterich (1995) presented an approach of assigning continuous weights to all attributes in k-NN algorithms simply by their information gain values. Ling et al. (1994) presented several weight-setting strategies that consider positions of attributes in the decision tree, and showed empirically that these methods improve predictive accuracy dramatically on artificially generated data sets and some real-world data sets.

Other empirical methods on attribute weight setting have been published. Stanfill and Waltz (1986) used statistical information from the stored data to compute weights and applied the method to several tasks including English spelling-to-speech conversion. Aha (1989) changed weights in accordance with success or failure of classification of the training examples. A few methods on assigning binary weights (which is also called feature selection, a special case of numerical weight setting) have also been recently proposed (Aha and Bankert 1994; Caruana and Freitag 1994; Skalak 1994; Moore and Lee 1994). Wettschereck and Aha (1995) reviewed several empirical weight setting methods and explored their comparative empirical behavior.

A few theoretical investigations have focussed on the calculation of predictive error rate of k-NN algorithms with equal attribute weights in the distance function (thus the work does not deal with weight setting). Cover and Hart (1967) and Cover (1968) gave analyses on the asymptotic behaviour of k-NN algorithms and compared the predictive error rate of 1-NN algorithms with the Bayes decision rule. More recently, Albert and Aha (1991) presented PAC-learning analyses for 1-NN algorithms for both symbolic and numeric-prediction tasks. Langley and Iba (1993) and Okamoto and Satoh (1995) presented an average-case analysis on 1-NN predictive accuracy.

The only theoretical work that we are aware of on optimal weight setting for k-NN algorithms is by Mohri and Tanaka (1994) and Satoh and Okamoto (1994). Mohri and Tanaka (1994) proposed a statistical technique on calculating attribute weights, and showed that such weights are optimal in the sense that they maximize the ratio of variance between classes to variance of all cases. However, it is not obvious that this criterion is the same as the optimality of predictive accuracy in 1-NN algorithms. Satoh and Okamoto (1994)'s work assumes that there is *target* weight vector (known to a teacher but unknown to the learner) that classifies pairs of training examples to a qualitative distance, *FAR* and *NEAR*. They showed that if this qualitative distance information is available to the learner, there is a polynomial PAC algorithm that learns (or reconstructs) the target weight vector. However, their work does not aim at choosing weight vectors that minimize the predictive error in classification. Further, the basic assumption of Satoh and Okamoto's work is different from ours; since we presume that the optimal weights for the minimal predictive error is unknown (to the teacher or learner), the teacher cannot provide the qualitative distance information.

3. 1-NN's Predictive Error with a Dividing Line

In this section, we study a very simple problem: what is the predictive error of 1-NN with various attribute weights[3] introduced by an axis-parallel linear classification boundary in a 2-d continuous space? Figure 1 demonstrates such a case (i.e., a vertical line $x = 2$ divides a 10×10 space into two; left side is negative, right side is positive). Clearly, one attribute (x_2) is irrelevant; therefore, w_2 should be set to zero, or the ratio $\theta = w_1/w_2$ infinitely large. What exactly are the theoretical values of the predictive error for different θ values?

Before we derive formulas of the predictive accuracy with various θ, we can first see such an effect graphically. Figure 1 shows the regions of errors of 1-NN with various θ values. The error region of each figure is plotted with the misclassified testing examples out of a total of 40,000 testing examples after training with 500 examples, both uniformly distributed in the space. The predictive error is simply the ratio of the misclassified area over the total area. We can see clearly that the smaller the ratio $\theta = w_1/w_2$, the more the irrelevant attribute x_2 is taken into consideration, and the larger the predictive error. In the extreme case when $\theta = 0$, x_1 (the deciding attribute) is completely ignored, and the classification of testing examples is determined solely by the irrelevant attribute, x_2.

We can in fact calculate the predictive error in this case: for any testing example, it has an 80% of chance of falling into the positive region, a 20% of chance of falling into the negative region. However, its class is determined only by the vertical distance from the closest training example. Since the training examples are uniformly distributed in the space, there is an 80% of chance that the vertically closest training example is a positive example, and a 20% of chance that it is a negative one. Therefore, for any positive example, there is a 20% of chance of being misclassified as negative; and for any negative example, there is an 80% of chance of being misclassified as positive. The overall predicative error is thus $80\% \times 20\% + 20\% \times 80\% = 32\%$. Our experiment with $\theta = 10^{-5}$ yields a similar error (30.6%) (see Figure 1).

This graphical demonstration also gives us an intuitive understanding of the optimal weight ratio for an axis-parallel rectangular classification region. For the two vertical edges, as in Figure 1, the weight ratio θ should be set as large as possible to reduce predictive errors introduced along those edges. However, the two horizontal edges can be regarded just as the vertical edges with the weight ratio $1/\theta$ and, therefore, they require θ to be as small as possible to reduce the predictive errors introduced there. There should be an

---

[3] Since what really matters are the weight ratios, rather than the weights themselves, we will use "weight ratio" and "weight" interchangeably in the rest of the paper.

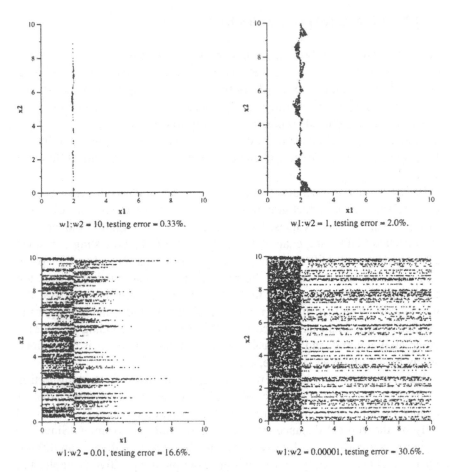

Figure 1. Misclassified testing examples with various weight ratios for the classification boundary $x = 2$ (left side negative, right side positive).

optimal weight ratio that compromises the two sides so that the predictive error is minimal.

3.1. *1-NN with Equal Weights*

We first derive the predictive error rate of 1-NN with an equal weight ratio (i.e., $\theta = 1$) in a 2-d continuous space. Assume that a vertical line divides the instance space into two equal halves with S as the area for both the left half and the right half. See Figure 2(a). For a (positive) testing example O falling into the right half, we can calculate the probability of O being classified as a negative example (i.e., predictive error). For this to happen, there will be a constant-distance boundary centered at O (a circle here since

$w_1 = w_2$) that goes over the vertical line, such that the shaded area (A_1) includes at least one (negative) training example while the area A_2 does not include any (positive) training examples. In this case, the positive example O is misclassified as negative. Assume λ is the density of the uniformly distributed training examples (per unit area), p_1 is the probability of area A_1 having at least one training example, and p_2 is the probability of area A_2 having no training example, then we have (assuming S is very large):

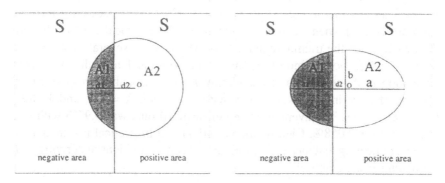

Figure 2. Situations where a positive example (at O) is classified as a negative example. (a): $w_1 = w_2$; (b): $w_1 \neq w_2$.

$$p_1 = 1 - (1 - \frac{A_1}{S})^{S\lambda} \simeq 1 - e^{-\lambda A_1} \tag{3}$$

$$p_2 = (1 - \frac{A_2}{S})^{S\lambda} \simeq e^{-\lambda A_2} \tag{4}$$

Therefore, the error rate at the point O is an integration of $p_1 p_2$ over d_1 (see Figure 2(a)):

$$E_O = \int_0^\infty p_1 p_2 \, dd_1$$

and the error introduced by a unit-length boundary is an integration of E_O over d_2:[4]

$$E = 2 \times \int_0^\infty E_O \, dd_2. \tag{5}$$

Equations 3, 4 and 5 are suitable for calculating error rates in other situations with corresponding A_1 and A_2. In the case of a straight line boundary and $w_1 = w_2$, the areas of A_1 and A_2 are:

---

[4] We multiply the result by 2 to include the misclassified negative testing examples.

$$A_1 = \cos^{-1}(\frac{d_2}{d_1 + d_2})(d_1 + d_2)^2 - d_2\sqrt{(d_1 + d_2)^2 - d_2^2}$$

$$A_2 = \pi(d_1 + d_2)^2 - A_1$$

Unfortunately, there seems to be no closed formula[5] for the double integrations of the predictive error E, so we have to calculate E numerically. As an example, the numerical estimation of E is 1.03% (see Appendix A for more details) when we assume the height of the vertical line[6] is 10, and the density λ of the training examples is 10. To see if several assumptions (such as in Equations 3 and 4) and approximations (such as in the numerical estimation in Appendix A) in calculating E are reasonable, we performed 10 runs of experiments using 1-NN with $w_1 = w_2$, $\lambda = 10$, and 10,000 testing examples. The average testing error of 10 runs was 0.95% with the standard error 0.058%. Clearly, the empirical and theoretical results match closely, indicating that these assumptions and approximations in deriving and estimating E are reasonable.

3.2. 1-NN with Unequal Weights

Assume $\theta = w_1/w_2 \neq 1$, then the constant-distance line formed by the distance equation becomes an ellipse. The vertical radius b of the ellipse is therefore simply equal to $\theta(d_1 + d_2)$. See Figure 2(b). We can use the same method to calculate E, except that E contains a variable θ, and that the areas A_1 and A_2 are defined for ellipses in general. They can be calculated quite easily with Maple V (Char et al. 1992):

$$A_1 = \frac{2b}{a} \int_{d_2}^{d_1+d_2} \sqrt{a^2 - x^2}dx$$

$$A_2 = \pi ab - A_1 = \pi(d_1 + d_2)^2\theta$$

Thus, by using the above formulas for A_1 and A_2, and that $a = d_1 + d_2$, $b = \theta(d_1+d_2)$, we obtain the error rate E (Equation 5) when $\theta = w_1/w_2 \neq 1$. Clearly, it is a function of θ, and we call it $E(\theta)$.

To test our theoretical result $E(\theta)$ (which again is derived with several approximations and assumptions), we conducted an experiment with 1-NN

---

[5] We have tried Maple V (Char, Geddes, Gonnet, Leong, Monagan, and S.M. Watt 1992), and it could not find a closed formula.

[6] When the circle is too close to the top or bottom boundaries, it goes over these boundaries, so the calculation of A_1 and A_2 would be different. To reduce error in E in the top and bottom boundaries, the height is chosen to be large.

with $\theta = 2$ for 10 runs. The average error rate of the 10 runs is 0.511%, while the theoretical error rate $E(\theta)$ is 0.514%. Again, the empirical and theoretical results match closely.

4. Optimal Weight Setting for 1-NN

We have obtained the error rate $E(\theta)$ for a unit length of a dividing line parallel to an axis. We can now calculate the optimal θ for 1-NN algorithms if the classification region is an axis-parallel rectangle. We then extend our method to any polygonal classification region.

4.1. Axis-parallel Rectangular Classification Regions

Clearly, if the width and length of the rectangle are w and l respectively, then the total predictive error introduced by the four sides of the rectangle is[7]

$$E_{rec}(\theta) = 2lE(\theta) + 2wE(1/\theta). \tag{6}$$

One would choose θ such that $E_{rec}(\theta)$ can be minimized for a particular w and l. This could be done by solving the equation $E'_{rec}(\theta) = 0$; i.e., the first derivative with respect to θ is 0.

However, since $E(\theta)$ is a complicated double integration, we could attain only a numeric solution for θ from $E'_{rec}(\theta) = 0$ at best. Alternatively, we use a "short-cut" table look-up method: we compute values of $E(\theta)$ for $\theta = 0.05$, 0.1, 0.15, 0.2, ..., 1.0, and then the corresponding values of $E(1/\theta)$ (i.e., $E(20)$, $E(10)$ and so on). Table 1 lists the values for $E(\theta)$ at multiples of 0.1, and Figure 3 shows such a curve.[8] For a particular w and l, we can just check the table to see which value of θ minimizes $lE(\theta) + wE(1/\theta)$.

As an example, we tried two rectangles with sizes 8×2 and 8×6 respectively (centered in a 10×10 two-dimensional space). The results of $lE(\theta) + wE(1/\theta)$ using Table 1 are plotted in Figures 4(a) and (b). The minimal testing error rates are obtained when θ is equal to 0.5 and 0.9 respectively. An experiment was carried out to determine empirically the actual θ value that minimizes the predictive error. For each rectangle, the 1-NN algorithm was run with randomly generated training and testing examples using different θ (with

---

[7] As discussed in Section 3, a weight ratio of θ for a vertical boundary becomes a weight ratio of $1/\theta$ for the horizontal boundary. Also, there is an overlap in error regions at the corners introduced by the vertical and horizontal edges. Therefore, Equation 6 is an approximation.

[8] Note that values in Table 1 are all *relative* for the purpose of finding the optimal θ that minimizes the total predictive error. Therefore, they can be scaled without affecting the results on the optimal weight selection.

Table 1. The predictive error $E(\theta)$ for various θ values.

θ	0.1	0.2	0.3	0.4	0.5	0.6	0.7	0.8	0.9	1.0
$E(\theta)$	64.2	32.1	21.4	16.1	12.8	10.7	9.17	8.03	7.13	6.42

θ	1/0.1	1/0.2	1/0.3	1/0.4	1/0.5	1/0.6	1/0.7	1/0.8	1/0.9	1.0
$E(\theta)$	0.642	1.28	1.93	2.57	2.89	3.85	4.49	5.14	5.78	6.42

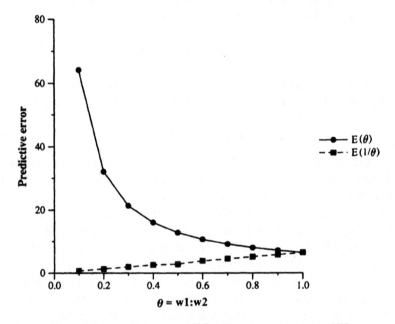

Figure 3. The predictive error $E(\theta)$ with various weights in 1-NN.

an interval of 0.05). The optimal θ values obtained empirically are 0.4 and 0.9 respectively, matching with the theoretical values closely. The predictive errors of the experiment are also plotted in Figure 4.

It is clear that the predictive error curves from the experiments and the theoretical derivation are similar, and the actual optimal θ values are close to the theoretically optimal θ values as well. We can also see that when one side of the rectangle is much larger (or smaller) than the other side, the curve has a more distinctive minimal point; that is, the choice of θ affects the predictive error more dramatically. When the rectangle is close to a square, the optimal

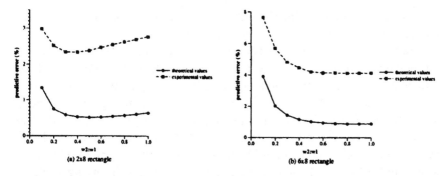

Figure 4. The predictive error with various θ values. The theoretical and experimental curves do not overlap since the theoretically optimal weights are relative, and irrelevant to the actual number of training examples.

Table 2. The optimal θ values predicted by theory and from experiments.

$l : w$	8:1	8:2	8:3	8:4	8:5	8:6	8:7	8:8
$1/\theta$, theory	0.35	0.50	0.60	0.70	0.80	0.85	0.95	1.00
$1/\theta$, exp.	0.25	0.45	0.60	0.65	0.65	0.90	0.95	1.00

θ is close to 1, and the predictive errors are not as sensitive to the θ values close to the optimal value.[9]

Using the same method, we can calculate the optimal θ for rectangles with a length of 8 and various widths from 1 to 8. Again, we can first obtain the theoretically optimal values θ for each width using Table 1. We then ran experiments to see empirically what the optimal values of θ are with each width. The optimal values of θ by our theoretical derivation and from experiments with various $l : w$ ratios are listed in Table 2 for comparison. From Table 2, we can see clearly that they are quite close for most $l : w$ ratios. In addition, the optimal θ values are not proportional to $l : w$.

4.2. *Arbitrary Polygonal Classification Regions*

If the classification boundaries are not parallel to any axis, then we first need to calculate the predictive error rate (a function of θ) along such boundaries. We can then obtain the total predictive error of the whole region by integrating predictive errors along the circumference of the region. The total predictive

---

[9] In either case, however, the absolute difference in predictive errors when θ is near the optimal value is small. As indicated in (Ling et al. 1994), the advantage of weight setting methods for 1-NN is more evident in domains with a large number of irrelevant attributes.

error is again a function of θ. We could find the optimal θ value that minimizes the total error by function minimization techniques.

However, the method described above, though theoretically correct, is not practical. We have again designed a similar table look-up method for finding the optimal θ for polygonal classification regions. The predictive error introduced by a side (of a polygon) of a certain degree with the x axis can be calculated using the same equations (Equations 3, 4 and 5) in Section 3, except that now the areas A_1 and A_2 are more complicated. We constructed a table[10] containing (theoretical) predictive errors introduced by a unit length of a linear boundary at a certain degree (α) with varying θ values. The total predictive errors of the region is the sum of errors introduced by each boundary of the polygon. We can then vary θ to find the optimal value for the minimal predictive error of the polygonal region.

For example, if a classification region can be approximated by a polygon of n sides $l_{\alpha_1}, l_{\alpha_2}, \ldots, l_{\alpha_n}$, and each side intersects with the x axis with angles $\alpha_1, \alpha_2, \ldots, \alpha_n$ respectively, then for a particular θ value, we can obtain the total predictive error introduced by the four edges as

$$l_{\alpha_1} E_{\alpha_1}(\theta) + l_{\alpha_2} E_{\alpha_2}(\theta) + \ldots + l_{\alpha_n} E_{\alpha_n}(\theta)$$

where $E_{\alpha_i}(\theta)$ is the table entry for the angle α_i and the weight ratio θ. By varying θ, we can then obtain the optimal weight ratio θ that minimizes the total predictive error rate above.

We ran an experiment with two simple rectangular shaped regions that are not parallel to any axis (Figure 5). Our experimental results show that the θ value that minimizes the predictive errors is between 0.7 to 0.9[11] for a 8×4 rectangle, and is between 0.7 to 0.8 for a 8×2 rectangle (again, this is obtained by averaging 10 runs). Our theoretical results of the optimal θ value using the table are 0.8 and 0.7, respectively; both fall in the ranges of the experimental results. This suggests that our method, based on theoretical analyses, works well.

5. Discussion

As we indicated in Section 1, our theoretical analyses assume that the classification boundary (i.e., the underlying target concept) is known. Thus, our optimal results can thus serve as a useful baseline or lower bound for evaluating empirical attribute weight assigning methods on known concepts.

---

[10] The table (20×10 in size) is too big to present here. It can be obtained on request.

[11] The predictive error within the range is within 1% of the minimal value.

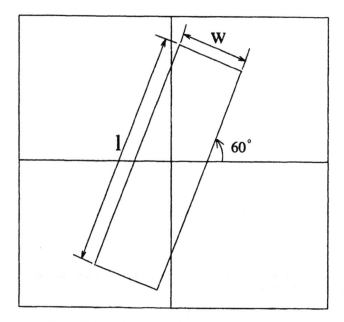

Figure 5. An arbitrary rectangular classification region.

We choose two empirical weight setting methods to compare with our theoretical results on a simple target concept – three 2×8 axis-parallel rectangles centered in a 10×10 2-d continuous space as shown in Figure 6. As we discussed in Section 4.1 (also see Figure 4(a)), the theoretically optimal θ value (w_1/w_2) for the minimal predictive error is 0.5.[12]

The first empirical method, as studied in (Daelemans et al. 1993; Wettschereck and Dietterich 1995; Ling et al. 1994), is to set the attribute weights according to the information gain values of attributes. The second empirical method simply sets the weight (ratio) according to the ratio of the two lengths of a rectangle that is just large enough to enclose all positive examples. This simple heuristic uses one axis-parallel rectangle to approximate the classification boundary. In this case, the weight ratio θ is 1 (i.e., $w_1/w_2 = 1$). Note that when applying empirical methods in (Kibler and Aha 1987) and (Cardie 1993), the weight ratio θ would also be set to 1. We perform 20 runs for the comparison. For each run, 200 training examples and 40,000 testing examples are randomly drawn, and the same training and testing examples are used to evaluate the performance of the 1-NN algorithm with three weight settings: theoretical weight (always 0.5), information-gain

---

[12] Since the three rectangles are relatively far apart, the overlap of errors introduced from edges of adjacent rectangles can be ignored, and the optimal θ value is the same as the one for one rectangle.

Figure 6. A simple concept (shaded areas represent positive examples) for comparing theoretical and empirical weight setting methods.

Table 3. Comparison of the theoretical weight setting method with two empirical methods.

	$\theta = w_1/w_2$	Predictive error
Theoretical	0.5	10.4 ± 0.26
Information-based	0.94 ± 0.06	13.01 ± 0.49
Rectangle ratio	1.0 ± 0.01	13.50 ± 0.30

based weight (determined by the training examples), and the rectangle ratio (around $8/8 = 1$). The results of the comparison are presented in Table 3. From the table, we can see clearly that theoretically optimal weights from our derivation have lower (about 30% lower) predictive error than either of the two empirical methods. The difference is significant in a t-test (at the 0.001 level).

Our theoretical analyses of optimal weight setting can be extended easily to k-NN algorithms. The only difference is at the derivation of p_1 and p_2 (Equations 3 and 4) in Section 3.1. p_1 is now the probability of area A_1 having at least k' (an integer) training examples where $k' > k/2$, and p_2 is the probability of area A_2 having $k - k'$ (0 if negative) training examples. The formulas would be more complex but the rest of the analyses and calculations remain the same.

It should be possible, at least in theory, to extend our method to domains with higher dimensions. In a space with n dimensions, the boundary becomes an n-d hyperplane, and the predictive error introduced by the hyperplane can be calculated by the volumes (similar to areas A_1 and A_2 in Section 3) formed by the intersection of the hyperplane and the hyper-ellipse. The volumes can be obtained by n-dimensional integration, though only numeric approximations are easily attainable. Then an n-dimensional table (similar to Table 1) can be constructed. The $n-1$ dimensions are used to specify the slope of the hyperplane, and the other dimension is for the various θ values. After such a table is constructed, by looking-up the table (i.e., the same method as in Section 4.2) we can determine the optimal θ value that minimizes the predictive error for any polygonal classification region in the n-dimensional space. Clearly, such a method is not practically feasible. We plan to study how optimal weights can be obtained more directly and effectively in higher dimensional spaces.

Another interesting area for future research is optimal weight setting for discrete or Boolean functions. One might think that this problem can be solved by our method in continuous space if we determine a set of boundaries in the continuous space that separate positive and negative examples of the Boolean function. However, the choice of such boundaries critically affects predictive accuracy. Further, the testing error in discrete domains may be quite different from the error introduced along the boundary in the continuous space. The work by Langley and Iba (1993) might be extended to solve this problem.

Finally, we plan to apply our theoretical method to a more realistic learning setting where no concept boundary is known (i.e., the only available information is the set of training examples). With an unknown concept boundary, the techniques described in Section 4.2 cannot be used directly. One feasible approach to this problem is to first estimate a set of linear classifiers that separate positive and negative examples. Several standard techniques for finding piecewise linear classifiers (Fukunaga 1990, pp. 169–173) can be employed. Once the linear classifiers are found, our method (Section 4.2) can be applied to find the optimal weights for the k-NN algorithm. The actual classification boundary formed by the k-NN algorithm with optimal weights is different from the one formed by the piecewise linear classifiers and, therefore, it may be worthwhile to use such a k-NN learning algorithm with optimal attribute weights.

6. Conclusion

Our theoretical work is a first attempt towards computing optimal attribute weight settings that minimize the predictive errors for 1-NN algorithms.

Under the assumption of uniform distribution of training and testing examples in a 2-d continuous space, we first derived the average predictive error introduced by the linear classification boundaries, and used these results to determine the optimal weights in the 1-NN distance function. We verified our theoretical findings with experiments, and found that they match closely, indicating that several assumptions and approximations in our theoretical derivation and numeric estimation are reasonable. Our theoretical results can serve as a baseline or lower bound when evaluating other empirical weight setting methods on known concepts. However, our method is still quite limited in its scope since it only applies to any polygonal classification region in a 2-d continuous space. Several extensions for future work are outlined.

Appendix A

Since we have to calculate E numerically, we need to give finite bounds in the integration. We restrict O within $MaxR$ (some constant) from the boundary. This is because when O is too far away from the boundary, $p_1 p_2$ would be too small to be significant to E. Hence, the integration on d_2 ranges from 0 (when O is on the boundary) to $MaxR$ (when O is $MaxR$ from the boundary). The integration on d_1 could still go from 0 to infinity. We restrict the edge of the circle to expand to at most $2MaxR$ from the boundary. This is because we found that when the circle expands more, it does not contribute much to E_O in integration. Therefore, the maximum diameter of the circle is $2MaxR - d_2$, and the maximum value of d_1 is $2MaxR - d_2 - d_2 = 2MaxR - 2d_2$. Thus, the bound on d_1 ranges from 0 (when the circle just touches the boundary) to $2MaxR - 2d_2$ (when the circle expands to 2 $MaxR$ from the boundary). We found that when $MaxR \geq 2$, E is very close to E with $MaxR = 2$. Thus, we set $MaxR = 2$ (unit length) in the calculation.

Acknowledgements

The authors thank reviewers for many helpful comments. Comments from David Aha were particularly useful in improving the paper.

References

Aha, D. W. (1989). Incremental, instance-based learning of independent and graded concept descriptions. In *Proceedings of the 1989 International Workshop on Machine Learning*, pp. 387–391. Irvine, CA: Morgan Kaufmann.

Aha, D. W. & Bankert, R. L. (1994). Feature selection for case-based classification of cloud types: An empirical comparison. In Aha, D. W. (ed.), *Proceedings of the AAAI-94 Workshop on Case-Based Reasoning* (Technical Report WS-94-01), Menlo Park, CA: AAAI Press.

Aha, D. W., Kibler, D. & Albert, M. K. (1991). Instance-based learning algorithms. *Machine Learning*, 6: 37–66.

Albert, M. K. & Aha, D. W. (1991). Analyses of instance-based learning algorithms. In *Proceedings of the Ninth National Conference on Artificial Intelligence*, pp. 553–558. Menlo Park, CA: AAAI Press.

Cardie, C. (1993). Using decision trees to improve case-based learning. In *Proceedings of the Tenth International Conference on Machine Learning*, pp. 25–32. Morgan Kaufmann, San Mateo, CA.

Caruana, R. & Freitag, D. (1994). Greedy attribute selection. In *Proceedings of the 1994 International Conference on Machine Learning*, pp. 28–36. Morgan Kaufmann, CA.

Char, B., Geddes, K., Gonnet, G., Leong, B., Monagan, M. & Watt S. M. (1992). *First Leaves: A Tutorial Introduction to Maple V*. Springer-Verlag and Waterloo Maple Publishing.

Cost, S. & Salzberg, S. (1993). A weighted nearest neighbor algorithm for learning with symbolic features. *Machine Learning* 10: 57–78.

Cover, T. (1968). Estimation by the nearest neighbor rule. *IEEE Transactions on Information Theory* 14: 50–55.

Cover, T. & Hart, P. (1967). Nearest neighbor pattern classification. *IEEE Transactions on Information Theory* 13: 21–27.

Daelemans, W., Gillis, S., Durieux, G. & van den Bosch, A. (1993). Learnability and markedness in data-driven acquisition of stress. Tech. rep. ITK Research Report No. 43, Institute for Language Technology and AI (ITK), Tilburg University.

Dasarathy, B. (1991). *Nearest neighbor (NN) norms: NN pattern classification techniques*. Los Alamitos, CA: IEEE Computer Society Press.

Fukunaga, K. (1990). *Introduction to Statistical Pattern Recognition* (Second edition). Academic Press.

Kelly, J. D. & Davis, L. (1991). A hybrid algorithm for classification. In Mylopoulos, J. & Reite, R. (eds.), *Proceedings of the Thirteenth International Conference on Artificial Intelligence*, pp. 645–650. Morgan Kaufmann, San Mateo, CA.

Kibler, D. & Aha, D. W. (1987). Learning representative exemplars of concepts: An initial case study. In *Proceedings of the 1987 International Workshop on Machine Learning*, pp. 24–30. Irvine, CA: Morgan Kaufmann.

Langley, P. & Iba, W. (1993). Average-case analysis of a nearest neighbor algorithm. In *Proceedings of the Thirteenth International Joint Conference on Artificial Intelligence*, pp. 889–894. Morgan Kaufmann: San Mateo, CA.

Ling, C. X., Parry, J. J. & Wang, H. (1994). Deciding weights for IBL using C4.5. Submitted.

Mohri, M. & Tanaka, H. (1994). An optimal weighting criterion of case indexing for both numeric and symbolic attributes. Tech. rep. WS-94-01, Case-Based Reasoning: Papers from the 1994 Workshop. Menlo Park, CA: AAAI Press.

Moore, A. W. & Lee, M. S. (1994). Efficient algorithms for minimizing cross validation error. In *Proceedings of the 1994 International Conference on Machine Learning*, pp. 190–198. Morgan Kaufmann, CA.

Okamoto, S. & Satoh, K. (1995). An average-case analysis of k-nearest neighbor classifier. In *Proceedings of the First International Conference on Case-Based Reasoning*, pp. 253–264. Sesimbra, Portugal: Springer-Verlag.

Quinlan, J. (1986). Induction of decision trees. *Machine Learning* 1(1), 81–106.

Quinlan, J. (1993). *C4.5: Programs for Machine Learning*. Morgan Kaufmann: San Mateo, CA.

Satoh, K. & Okamoto, S. (1994). Toward PAC-learning of weights from qualitative distance information. Tech. rep. WS-94-01, Case-Based Reasoning: Papers from the 1994 Workshop. Menlo Park, CA: AAAI Press.

Skalak, D. (1994). Prototype and feature selection by sampling and random mutation hill climbing algorithms. In *Proceedings of the 1994 International Conference on Machine Learning*, pp. 293–301. Morgan Kaufmann, CA.

Stanfill, C. & Waltz, D. (1986). Toward memory-based reasoning. *Communications of the ACM* **29**: 1213–1228.

Wettschereck, D. & Aha, D. (1995). Weighting features. In *Proceedings of the First International Conference on Case-Based Reasoning*, pp. 347–358. Sesimbra, Portugal: Springer-Verlag.

Wettschereck, D. & Dietterich, T. (1995). An experimental comparison of the nearest neighbor and nearest hyperrectangle algorithms. *Machine Learning* **19**: 5–28.

Artificial Intelligence Review **11**: 273–314, 1997.
© 1997 *Kluwer Academic Publishers.*

A Review and Empirical Evaluation of Feature Weighting Methods for a Class of Lazy Learning Algorithms

DIETRICH WETTSCHERECK[1], DAVID W. AHA[2] and TAKAO MOHRI[3]
[1] *GMD (German National Research Center for Information Technology), Schloß Birlinghoven, 53754 Sankt Augustin, Germany*
E-mail: dietrich.wettschereck@gmd.de
[2] *Navy Center for Applied Research in Artificial Intelligence, Naval Research Laboratory, Washington, DC USA*
E-mail: aha@aic.nrl.navy.mil
[3] *Hidehiko Tanaka Lab. Department of Electric Engineering, The University of Tokyo, 7-3-1 Hongo Bunkyo-ku, Tokyo 113 JAPAN*
E-mail: mohri@mtl.t.u-tokyo.ac.jp

Abstract. Many lazy learning algorithms are derivatives of the k-nearest neighbor (k-NN) classifier, which uses a distance function to generate predictions from stored instances. Several studies have shown that k-NN's performance is highly sensitive to the definition of its distance function. Many k-NN variants have been proposed to reduce this sensitivity by parameterizing the distance function with feature weights. However, these variants have not been categorized nor empirically compared. This paper reviews a class of weight-setting methods for lazy learning algorithms. We introduce a framework for distinguishing these methods and empirically compare them. We observed four trends from our experiments and conducted further studies to highlight them. Our results suggest that methods which use performance feedback to assign weight settings demonstrated three advantages over other methods: they require less pre-processing, perform better in the presence of interacting features, and generally require less training data to learn good settings. We also found that continuous weighting methods tend to outperform feature selection algorithms for tasks where some features are useful but less important than others.

Key words: lazy learning, k-nearest neighbor, feature weights, comparison

1. Introduction

The k-nearest neighbor (k-NN) classifier (Dasarathy 1991) is the basis of many *lazy learning* algorithms. k-NN is purely lazy; it simply stores the entire training set and postpones all effort towards inductive generalization until classification time. k-NN generalizes by retrieving the k least distant (i.e., most similar) instances of a given query and predicting their weighted-majority class as the query's class. The quality of k-NN's generalization therefore depends on which instances are deemed least distant, which is determined by its distance function.

In Section 2, we argue that k-NN's distance function is biased: it allows redundant, irrelevant, interacting, or noisy features to have as much effect on distance computations as other features. k-NN can perform poorly when such features are present. This observation motivated the creation of many k-NN variants that compute feature weights, which we review in Section 3. Several of these variants improve its accuracy on some learning tasks (e.g., Kelly and Davis 1991; Aha 1992; Wettschereck 1994). However, many empirical evaluations frequently compare sophisticated algorithms with standard k-NN (e.g., Gorman and Sejnowski 1988; Kohonen et al. 1988; Weiss and Kapouleas 1989; Bounds et al. 1990; Yau and Manry 1991; Bottou and Vapnik 1992; Wettschereck and Dietterich 1992; Michie et al. 1994). While k-NN is frequently shown to have lower classification performance, its own more sophisticated variants are typically ignored.

This paper defines and relates k-NN to the large family of lazy learning algorithms in Section 2, and then introduces a framework and reviews a subclass of k-NN weight learning methods in Section 3. Our objective is to bring attention to these weight learning variants, and their relative merits. No weight learning method can learn optimal weight settings for all learning tasks since each task requires a different learning bias for optimal performance (Mitchell 1990). Therefore, we empirically evaluate a subclass of weight learning methods, present general trends that contrast their capabilities, and investigate these trends in Section 4. We found that weight learning methods which incorporate performance feedback from the classifier showed several advantages, although some weighting methods can locate good weight settings without such feedback. Section 5 discusses the implications of our results in the context of the framework described in Section 3, while Section 6 addresses related work.

2. Context

The focus of our paper is necessarily constrained to a small class of lazy learning algorithms due to lack of space. We examine this constraint by defining the lazy learning paradigm (Section 2.1), by defining a subclass of k-NN classifiers (Section 2.2), and by explaining how this subclass relates to this paradigm. Our subsequent review and empirical study in Sections 3 and 4 examine variants of lazy learners in only this small subclass.

2.1. *Lazy Learning Algorithms*

Purely lazy learning algorithms are characterized by three behaviors:

1. *Defer*: They store all training data and defer processing until queries are given that require replies.

2. *Reply*: Queries are answered by combining the training data, typically by using a *local learning* approach (Bottou and Vapnik 1992) in which (1) instances are defined as points in a space, (2) a similarity function is defined on all pairs of these instances, and (3) a prediction function defines an answer to be a monotonic function of query similarity.

3. *Flush*: After replying to a query, the answer and any intermediate results are discarded.

This definition is purposely vague; it does not define how training instances are stored or represented, nor how they are combined during querying, nor even how similarity is defined. Nonetheless, the k-NN classifier is obviously a "pure" lazy algorithm.

Purity can be compromised in many ways. For example, some training data can be discarded or permanently combined, such as by averaging into prototypes. Many forms of pre-processing can be performed, often to enhance efficiency for incremental learning tasks (e.g., normalizing continuous data, caching similarity or prediction function parameter settings, discretizing continuous data, feature construction). Performance feedback might be recorded and used to guide decision making during query-answering, and intermediate results can be profitably cached for some tasks.

We focus on impure lazy learners in which settings for feature weights are cached (i.e., rather than dynamically computed at query time) and, in some cases, updated via performance feedback information. We also constrain our study in two respects. First, we assume that instances are represented by a set of feature-value pairs rather than, for example, directed acyclic graphs, which are sometimes used in the case-based reasoning literature (Kolodner 1993). Second, we focus on classification as the performance task and ignore issues concerning function learning (Atkeson et al. 1996a), class density estimation (e.g., using parzen windows (Duda and Hart 1973)), or problem solving (Kolodner 1993). Furthermore, we assume classes are disjoint.

2.2. *The k-NN Classifier*

A *classifier* inputs a query instance $\mathbf{q}$ and outputs a prediction for its class. Each *instance* $\mathbf{x} = \{x_1, x_2, \ldots, x_{|\mathbf{F}|}\}$ is a point in a multidimensional space defined by a feature set $\mathbf{F}$ whose class, x_c, is a member of a set of classes $\mathbf{J}$. Each feature is either continuous or ranges over a fixed set of discrete values.

A classifier's performance objective is to minimize *expected loss*, or *misclassification risk*, for each class $c_j \in \mathbf{J}$:

$$R_j = \sum_{c_j' \in J} L_{c_j c_{j'}} p(c_{j'}|\mathbf{q}) \tag{1}$$

where $L_{c_j c_{j'}}$ is the loss (cost) associated with mistakenly classifying an instance of class c_j as in class $c_{j'}$ ($j \neq j'$), and $p(c_{j'}|\mathbf{q})$ is the probability of classifying $\mathbf{q}$ in class $c_{j'}$. k-NN generally assumes that all misclassifications have equal cost:

$$L_{c_j c_{j'}} = \begin{cases} 0 & j = j' \\ 1 & j \neq j' \end{cases} \tag{2}$$

Since k-NN is not given $\mathbf{q}$'s class, it instead outputs the most probable class:

$$k\text{-NN}(\mathbf{q}) = \max_{c_j \in J} p(c_j|\mathbf{q}) \tag{3}$$

k-NN differs from other classifiers in how it defines these posterior class probabilities:

$$p(c_j|\mathbf{q}) = \frac{\sum_{\mathbf{x} \in \mathbf{K_q}} 1(x_c = c_j) \cdot K(d(\mathbf{x},\mathbf{q}))}{\sum_{\mathbf{x} \in \mathbf{K_q}} K(d(\mathbf{x},\mathbf{q}))} \tag{4}$$

where $1(\ )$ yields 1 iff its argument is true, $K(\ )$ is a *kernel* function, here defined as

$$K(d(\mathbf{x},\mathbf{q})) = \frac{1}{d(\mathbf{x},\mathbf{q})}, \tag{5}$$

and where $\mathbf{K_q}$ is the set of $\mathbf{q}$'s k-nearest neighbors among a set $\mathbf{X}$ of (previously supplied) *training* instances as determined by the distance function $d(\ )$. That is, k-NN computes the distance $d(\mathbf{x},\mathbf{q})$ of $\mathbf{q}$ to each $\mathbf{x} \in \mathbf{X}$ using:

$$d(\mathbf{x},\mathbf{q}) = \left(\sum_{f \in F} w(f) \cdot \delta(x_f, q_f)^r\right)^{\frac{1}{r}} \tag{6}$$

where k-NN defines $r = 2$ (i.e., Euclidean distance), function $\delta(\ )$ defines how values of a given feature differ:

$$\delta(x_f, q_f) = \begin{cases} |x_f - q_f| & f \text{ is continuous} \\ 0 & f \text{ is discrete and } x_f = q_f \\ 1 & f \text{ is discrete and } x_f \neq q_f \end{cases} \tag{7}$$

and $w(f)$ defines the *feature weighting* function. k-NN defines this as a constant function:

$$w(f) = w_f \tag{8}$$

Finally, k-NN defines

$$\forall_{f \in \mathbf{F}} \ w_f = s \tag{9}$$

for some scalar constant s. Equation 9's strong constraint provides the motivation for our survey and empirical study.

Some implementation details need mentioning. If there is a tie among the maximal $p(c_j | \mathbf{q})$, then one of the most probable classes is randomly selected. k is set using leave-one-out cross-validation on $\mathbf{X}$ (Weiss and Kulikowski 1991), where ties are broken in favor of smaller values for k. We used a standard function (i.e., subtract the minimum and divide by the observed range) to normalize all continuous values. This ensures that the range of $\delta(\ )$ is [0, 1] for all features. Thus, they have equal maximum and minimum potential effects on distance computations. Unfortunately, this also means that each redundant, irrelevant, and noisy feature has as much potential impact on k-NN's distance function as does any other feature.

2.3. *Scope of our Review*

Arguably, k-NN's description in Section 2.2 is needlessly complex. We had two reasons for showing this detail for what appears, at first, to be a simple classifier. First, this description demonstrates that k-NN is, in fact, but one algorithm in the paradigm of lazy learners. Second, we want to clarify that k-NN's typical description as a *non*-parametric (except for k) classifier is misleading; it simply eliminates many parameters by incorporating them as design decisions.

For example, k-NN's constant loss function is not *class sensitive*; its value for $L_{c_j c_{j'}}$ is invariant for different pairs of classes. Cost-sensitive learning (Turney 1995) variants of k-NN exist (e.g., Tan 1993) that minimize a locally weighted error criterion (Vapnik 1992). The loss function can be arbitrarily complex (e.g., it could vary per class or instance).

Second, k-NN's equation for computing posteriors (Equation 4) is a form of *kernel regression* in statistics (Nadaraya 1964), or the *probability choice model* in cognitive psychology (Luce 1963). It could take on many other forms, such as by replacing $1(\ )$ with a function that relates classes or varies on each instance. Also, many different kernel functions ($K(\ )$) have been investigated (Atkeson et al. 1996a).

Third, while we examine various distance functions, we only examine the effects of replacing Equation 9 with weighting functions that assign unequal weights to features. Many other types of distance functions and weighting methods have been studied. For example, rather than Euclidean or even Minkowskian, distance could be defined using a set-theoretic definition (Tversky 1977; Biberman 1994) or by a function other than one which sums independent contributions of the features. A different distance function could be applied at each query (*query-based*) (Atkeson et al. 1996a) or each instance (*point-based*) (Aha and Goldstone 1992). Similarly, the definition of feature difference (Equation 7) is one of many; functions other than absolute difference for continuous values and more elaborate functions for defining similarity on discrete features have been proposed (Stanfill and Waltz 1986).

Finally, many other classes of weight-learning methods have been examined, frequently in the context of statistical regression, where distance functions on continuous functions have been carefully examined. For example, we restrict our survey to algorithms that use a diagonal weight matrix where there is one weight per feature and no interaction between features. This assumes that the target concept can be best modelled by stretching and shrinking the instance space along its axes. Upper triangular weight matrices, which permit oblique warpings of the instance space, are more appropriate for many tasks. The weighting function (Equation 8) need not be constant, but could be a polynomial or any arbitrarily complex function (e.q., a connectionist network). Furthermore, instead of employing a single set of weights for the entire instance space, separate sets of weights could be associated with specific queries, feature values, instances, classes, or some function of them. For example, a query-specific weighting method would modify Equation 6 by defining the weighting function based on the given query:

$$d(\mathbf{x},\mathbf{q}) = (\sum_{f \in \mathbf{F}} w(f,\mathbf{q}) \cdot \delta(x_f, q_f)^r)^{\frac{1}{r}} \qquad (10)$$

In summary, many of k-NN's "fixed" design decisions are, in fact, optimizable parameters. However, we will focus on only one such decision: the definition of (constant) weighting functions. This is cause for concern. Ideally, these design decisions, and others such as the definition for normalizing continuous values (Turney 1993), should be optimized when comparing the efficacy of alternative constant weighting methods. We leave this as a goal for future research, and fix these other design decisions in our experiments (Section 4). Further information related to lazy classification algorithms can be found elsewhere (e.g., Vapnik 1992; Bottou and Vapnik 1992; Friedman 1994; Atkeson et al. 1996a).

Table 1. Dimensions For Distinguishing Feature
Weighting Methods

Dimension	Possible Values
Bias	{Performance, Preset}
Weight Space	{Continuous, Binary}
Representation	{Given, Transformed}
Generality	{Global, Local}
Knowledge	{Poor, Intensive}

3. A Framework for Feature Weighting Methods

The feature weighting methods reviewed in this section are embedded in lazy algorithms that employ variants of the distance function shown in Equation 6. In particular, they differ in that they do not enforce the constraint shown in Equation 9 (i.e., they allow weight settings to differ among the features). These types of algorithms have been frequently examined in the machine learning literature, but it is not obvious how they all relate nor on what tasks their biases are particularly appropriate.

Feature weighting methods can be organized and dichotomized along several dimensions. We focus on the dimensions shown in Table 1.

By *bias*, we refer to whether the weight learning bias is guided by feedback from the *performance* algorithm (i.e., here, the classifier) or whether it is instead a *preset* bias (e.g., maximize intra-class similarity and minimize inter-class similarity) that does not incorporate performance feedback. By *weight space*, we distinguish *feature weighting* from *feature selection* algorithms. The latter are a proper subset of feature weighting algorithms that employ binary weights (i.e., 0 or 1), meaning that the feature is either retained or deleted. By *representation*, we distinguish algorithms that use the *given* representation from those that *transform* the given representation into one that might yield better performance. Feature weighting algorithms can also be distinguished by their *generality*; while most algorithms learn settings for a single set of weights that are employed *globally* (i.e., over the entire instance space), other algorithms assume weights differ among *local* regions of the instance space. Finally, the *knowledge* dimension distinguishes knowledge-poor algorithms from others that employ domain specific knowledge to set feature weights.

We use these dimensions to frame our discussion of feature weighting methods in this section. Further decompositions of algorithms are described as needed. Some alternatives to feature weighting are mentioned briefly to provide additional intuition. We elaborate on related work in Section 6. We include more detail for algorithms distinguished by the first dimension than the others because our empirical study in Section 4 focuses primarily on this dimension. Space constraints prevent a more detailed discussion for the other dimensions.

3.1. *Bias: Performance vs. Preset*

The distinction between *performance* and *preset* biases is described as *open loop* and *closed loop* in statistics, and as *wrapper* and *filter* models in machine learning (e.g., John et al. 1994). We view this as an issue of learning bias. Weighting methods that use feedback from the performance function during training attempt to incorporate the classifier's bias during weighting. Those that do not incorporate some alternative, preset bias. We further distinguish these two biases into several sub-categories, which are described in Sections 3.1.1 and 3.1.2, respectively. We selected one algorithm from each of the following subsections for our experiments.

3.1.1. *Performance Bias*
Performance bias methods presumably have an advantage; their search for feature weight settings is guided by how well those settings perform. Thus, there should be no mismatch between the biases of the weighting and performance algorithms. We distinguish weighting methods that incorporate performance feedback into two groups: those that perform *online* search in the space of weights (i.e., sequentially processing each training instance once) and those that perform *batch* optimization (i.e., repeatedly pass through the training set).

Online Optimizers

Several lazy algorithms optimize feature weight settings using one pass through the training set. Given a query q to classify, these algorithms iteratively modify feature weights to (a) decrease its distance to nearby[1] instances with the same class and (b) increase its distance with similar instances in other classes. These algorithms are sensitive to the presentation ordering of the training data.

An early example of this approach was used by Salzberg (1991) in EACH, a k-NN variant that updates feature weights by a fixed amount after classifying

---

[1] As defined by the current distance function.

each training instance. The objective of feature weighting was to improve EACH's tolerance of noise. For correct classifications, the weights of all matching features are incremented, using

$$w(f) = w(f) + \Delta, \tag{11}$$

and all mismatching features' weights are decremented by this same amount. Incorrect classifications cause the weights of *mismatching* feature to be incremented, while the weights of matching features are decremented. This procedure was expected to assign high weights to relevant features and lower weights to others. Salzberg found that, by selecting good values for Δ, this algorithm consistently improved classification performance vs. Equation 9.

Salzberg's algorithm influenced the design of IB4 (Aha 1992), which updates weight settings using[2]

$$w(f) = \max \left(\frac{\text{CumulativeWeight}_f}{\text{WeightNormalizer}_f} - 0.5, 0 \right), \tag{12}$$

where CumulativeWeight$_f$ is assumed to asymptote to half of the Weight-Normalizer$_f$ for seemingly irrelevant features. When classifying an instance $\mathbf{x}$ with another (training) instance $\mathbf{y}$, the degree to which IB4 updates CumulativeWeight$_f$ depends on the concept distribution. Let $\Lambda(\mathbf{x}, \mathbf{y}) = \max(p(x_c), p(y_c))$ (i.e., the probability of the more probable class among $\mathbf{x}$ and $\mathbf{y}$'s classes). Then CumulativeWeight$_f$ is incremented by

$$\text{CumulativeWeight}_f \overset{\pm}{=} \begin{cases} 1 - \delta(x_f, y_f) \cdot (1 - \Lambda(\mathbf{x}, \mathbf{y})) & \text{if } (x_c = y_c) \\ \delta(x_f, y_f) \cdot (1 - \Lambda(\mathbf{x}, \mathbf{y})) & \text{Otherwise} \end{cases} \tag{13}$$

and WeightNormalizer is always incremented by $(1 - \Lambda(\mathbf{x}, \mathbf{y}))$. This procedure sensitizes IB4 to skewed concept distributions and avoids the need for a fixed weight adjustment parameter. Aha (1990) reported good results for IB4 vs. 1-NN on tasks involving irrelevant features.

Kira and Rendell (1992) noted that this algorithm assumes a uniform distribution for irrelevant feature values. They introduced a binary (i.e., feature selection) weighting algorithm named RELIEF that removes this constraint. It iterates through a weight-updating procedure m times that (1) selects a random training instance $\mathbf{x}$, (2) locates $\mathbf{x}$'s most similar positive (**p**) and negative (**n**) training instances, and (3) updates each feature's weight using

---

[2] IB4 learns a separate set of weights per concept, but this is ignored here to simplify the presentation.

$$w(f) = w(f) - \delta(x_f, p_f) + \delta(x_f, n_f) \qquad (14)$$

When classifying, RELIEF maps these weights to binary values; if $w_f \geq \tau$, then f's weight is mapped to 1, and otherwise 0, where τ is a user-specified *relevance* parameter. Kira and Rendell reported good results for RELIEF on parity tasks. Kononenko (1994) reported good results when modifying RELIEF to average the contributions of $\mathbf{x}$'s k nearest positive and negative instances, so long as k was properly tuned. He also extended it for application to noisy, incomplete, and multiclass data.

We selected this modification, RELIEF-F, for inclusion in our experiments in Section 4. However, we did not map w_f to a value in $\{0, 1\}$, and allowed it to process each training instance only once.

Online optimizers generally assign low weights to completely irrelevant features and outperform standard k-NN for some applications with many irrelevant features. However, it is not clear to what extent they can recognize redundant or highly interacting features. For example, IB4 performed poorly on a task with many partially relevant features (Aha and Bankert 1994).

Batch Optimizers

These weighting methods optimize feature weights by repeatedly processing instances. Some of these methods require only knowledge of the function value to be approximated at each problem state (e.g., *simulated annealing* and *genetic algorithms*) while others use knowledge of the function's gradient (e.g., Lowe 1995).

Kelly and Davis (1991) and Skalak (1994) used genetic algorithms (GAs) to learn continuous feature weights for lazy learning algorithms. GAs loosely mimic processes of biological evolution. They repeatedly apply genetically-inspired operators (e.g., crossover, mutation) to a population of current problem solutions in the hope of obtaining higher scores on a given *fitness function*, and terminate after a fixed number of iterations or when a heuristic stopping criterion indicates no recent improvement. Kelly and Davis (1991) designed GA-WKNN to learn continuous feature weights using five genetic operators and a fitness function based on both the number of misclassified training instances and recency. GA-WKNN attained lower error rates than k-NN for three datasets.

Skalak (1994) instead used a degenerate GA to select features (i.e., binary weights) for 1-NN. His algorithm repeatedly mutates a single bit sequence, keeps the string with the higher classification accuracy on the training set, and terminates after a fixed number of iterations since finding a new best string.

This algorithm attained higher accuracies than 1-NN on four datasets while halving the number of features used to compute distances.

Other batch weight learning methods increase learning speed by exploiting knowledge of the function's gradient, which can substantially increase learning rates when the target function is reasonably smooth. Lowe (1995) employed this approach in the *variable kernel similarity metric* (VSM), which computes distances using a function similar to Equation 6. Feature weights are optimized using conjugate gradient (Press et al. 1992) to minimize summed leave-one-out classification error (LOOCE) on the training set.[3] The derivative of this error with respect to each feature weight is used to guide the conjugate gradient procedure. Lowe reported that VSM performed as well as or better than several other algorithms on two datasets yet required far less training time than some of the other algorithms.

While we selected a similar weight-optimization method for our empirical evaluation, we did not chose the VSM because it introduces additional complexity that prevents isolation of its feature-weighting algorithm. That is, the VSM assigns weights to instances as defined by an optimized Gaussian function of their distances, and then uses these weights to bias classification predictions. We instead selected a simplification of the VSM, named k-NN$_{VSM}$ (Wettschereck 1995a), which replaces the Gaussian kernels of Lowe's VSM with a differentiable k-NN function and eliminates the use of pre-assigned instance weights.

k-NN$_{VSM}$ employs a distance-weighted voting scheme (e.g., Dudani 1975, see also Equation 4). This algorithm first computes the distances between all pairs of training instances using Equation 9. It then assigns to k the value that minimizes LOOCE on the training set. Finally, it, like the VSM, uses conjugate gradient to optimize feature weights so as to minimize LOOCE training error. The error function is

$$E = \sum_{x \in X} \sum_{c_j \in J} \left(1(x \in c_j) - p(c_j|x)\right)^2 \qquad (15)$$

where $p(c_j|x)$ is defined as in Equation 4. Wettschereck (1995a, 1994) discusses further details on k-NN$_{VSM}$, including the derivation of the gradient of E with respect to each feature weight. He found that k-NN$_{VSM}$ can learn good feature weights in a variety of domains although a relatively large number of design decisions can heavily influence its performance.

---

[3] Error is a function of the differences between the probabilities computed by the VSM and the target class. A stabilizing term is added to this error to prevent large weight changes for small training sets.

3.1.2. *Preset Bias*

This section summarizes approaches that do *not* use feedback from the classifier to assign weight settings. Instead, they use a pre-existing model's bias. Three groups of these *preset bias* methods are described in this section: those based on (simple) *conditional probabilities, class projection,* and *mutual information,* respectively.

Conditional probabilities

Creecy et al. (1992) introduced two simple feature-weighting methods that use conditional probabilities to assign feature weights. Both algorithms work only with binary features, so they discretize continuous features and *binarize* discrete features (i.e., each discrete feature f defined over a set V_f of values was replaced with $|V_f|$ binary features).

First, their *cross-category feature importance* (CCF) method averages weights across classes using

$$w(f) = \sum_{c_j \in \mathbf{J}} p(c_j|f)^2 \qquad (16)$$

Creecy et al.'s (1992) motivation for designing CCF was to assign higher weights to features that occurred in fewer classes. However, this algorithm is not sensitive to the distribution of a feature's values across classes (i.e., a feature's weight is independent of the class), which seems unrealistic for practical applications. Therefore, they designed a second weighting method, named *per category feature importance* (PCF), which assigns feature weights using

$$w(f, c_j) = p(c_j|f) \qquad (17)$$

That is, the weight value of a feature f for a class c_j is defined as the conditional probability that an instance is a member of c_j given its value for f, averaged across all values for f. This algorithm assigns high weight values to features that have high correlations with the given class. They concluded that their weighted methods outperform non-weighted methods, but did not compare these two weighting methods.

Mohri et al. (1993) found that PCF is sensitive to concept distributions; it tends to classify too many instances according to the majority class. PCF performed poorly in their experiments (Mohri and Tanaka 1994). For example, the simpler CCF attained higher accuracies than PCF on six of eight tasks.

Class projection

Stanfill and Waltz (1986) introduced the *value-difference metric* (VDM), a more sophisticated similarity function defined for discrete features. This was the predecessor of CCF and PCF; it assigns higher weights to features whose distribution of values across classes are highly skewed. Although it also computes conditional probabilities, it does not binarize features. Previously, most similarity functions on discrete values either binarized them or employed the simple *overlap* function, which simply counts the number of mismatching features. In contrast, the VDM allows similarity to vary among individual feature values. Distance is defined as the sum of feature differences for two instances using

$$d(\mathbf{x}, \mathbf{y}) = \sum_{f \in \mathbf{F}} w(f, x_f) \cdot \delta(f, x_f, y_f) \tag{18}$$

$$w(f, v) = \sqrt{\sum_{c_j \in \mathbf{J}} p(\mathbf{x} \in c_j | \mathbf{x} \in \mathbf{X}, x_f = v)^2} \tag{19}$$

$$\delta(f, v_1, v_2) = \sum_{c_j \in \mathbf{J}} (p(\mathbf{x} \in c_j | \mathbf{x} \in \mathbf{X}, x_f = v_1) - p(\mathbf{x} \in c_j | \mathbf{x} \in \mathbf{X}, x_f = v_2))^2 \tag{20}$$

where Equation 19 computes f's weight when its value is v, and $p(\mathbf{x} \in c_j | \mathbf{x} \in \mathbf{X}, x_f = v)$ is the observed relative frequency that instances in the training set with value v for feature f are in class c_j. Equation 20 computes the difference of two values for a given feature. It assigns greater differences to values whose corresponding sets of instances have highly disparate class distributions. Thus, two instances are similar if they have feature values whose respective projections on the training set have similar class distributions.

Stanfill and Waltz (1986) used the VDM on a vowel pronunciation task, but did not compare it with other weighting methods. A few non-weighting variants of the VDM (e.g., Cost and Salzberg's (1993) MVDM and its extension to continuous features by Ting (1994)) have performed well on some tasks. However, surprisingly little evidence exists that feature-weighting variants of the VDM improve classification performance compared to unweighted variants. Furthermore, Daelemans and van den Bosch (1992) report that a method that assigns weights using information gain (see Section 3.1.2) outperforms the VDM on a grapheme to phoneme conversion task, and Aha (1990) reported that even the overlap function outperforms the VDM on some classification tasks. We also found little performance difference for the MVDM with and without weights in our experiments in Section 4.3. Thus, additional research is required to determine the conditions under which feature weighting can improve the classification performance of VDM variants.

Mutual information

This section describes a third approach for assigning feature weights using conditional probabilities. Like class projection, discrete features are not binarized. This approach also easily admits extensions for use with continuous features, which we discuss after describing the basic algorithm.

A feature weighting algorithm should assign low weights to (less relevant) features that provide little information for classification and higher weights to features that provide more reliable information. Towards this goal, the *mutual information* (MI) (Shannon 1948; McGill 1955) between the values of a feature and the class of the training examples can be used to assign feature weights. The MI of two variables is the reduction in uncertainty of one variable's value given knowledge of the other's value (Cover and Thomas 1991). This can be computed using

$$w(f) = \sum_{v \in V_f} \sum_{c_j \in \mathbf{J}} p(c_j, x_f = v) \cdot \log \frac{p(c_j, x_f = v)}{p(c_j) \cdot p(x_f = v)} \tag{21}$$

where $p(c_j)$ is the frequency of class c_j among the training set $\mathbf{X}$ and $p(x_f = v)$ is the frequency of value v for f among instances in $\mathbf{X}$. This equation assigns zero to features that provide no information about the class, and a value proportional to $\log(|J|)$ to features that completely determine the class (i.e., assuming a uniform distribution on classes).

Daelemans and van den Bosch (1992) introduced an extension of this approach that assigns a feature's (normalized) *information gain* (Quinlan 1986) as its weight rather than Equation 21:

$$w(f) = - \sum_{c_j \in \mathbf{J}} p(c_j) \log(p(c_j))$$

$$- \sum_{v \in V_f} \sum_{c_j \in \mathbf{J}} -p(c_j | x_f = v) \log p(c_j | x_f = v) p(x_f = v) \tag{22}$$

This equation subtracts the average information entropy of a feature from the information entropy of the training set $\mathbf{X}$. They reported that this weighting method substantially improved k-NN's accuracy on a word hyphenation task. Subsequently, van den Bosch and Daelemans (1993) found similarly good results for this weighting method on a grapheme-to-phoneme conversion task, and Daelemans et al. (1993) reported that it obtained the best performance, among three algorithms, for a stress assignment task.

These two equations do not define how to compute the MI for *continuous* features. Wettschereck and Dietterich (1995) used a simple approach to do this; it divides continuous features into a pre-determined number I of intervals, treating all values within a given interval as equal. They found that this batch weighting method improved the performance of EACH (Salzberg 1991) compared to its online algorithm for setting weights (Equation 11). We use a similar approach in Section 4 that avoids the need to predetermine I. Features are instead discretized using Fayyad and Irani's (1993) algorithm[4] and then treated in the same manner as discrete features. Both Mohri and Tanaka (1994) and Ting (1994) have shown the utility of this discretization method for lazy learning algorithms.

3.2. *Weight Space: Weighting vs. Selection*

In Section 3.1, we discussed the first dimension for distinguishing feature weighting algorithms (i.e., whether they tune weights using feedback from the classifier). This section addresses the second dimension, which concerns the space of values explored for assigning feature weights.

Feature selection algorithms assign binary weights to features. Thus they are restricted to a subset of the weight assignments learnable using continuous feature weights. Feature selection has been studied for several decades (e.g., Fu 1968; Mucciardi and Gose 1971; Cover and van Campenhout 1977). Several researchers have recently used various feature selection methods for lazy learning algorithms. These methods select features using

- an induced decision tree (Cardie 1993; Kibler and Aha 1987),
- random mutation hill-climbing (Skalak 1994),
- parallel search (Moore and Lee 1994),
- beam search with stepwise selection (Aha and Bankert 1994), and
- stepwise feature removal in oblivious decision trees (Langley and Sage 1994).

The first of these methods employs a preset weighting bias while the others exploit performance feedback. All report accuracy and/or speed improvements over 1-NN or k-NN. Feature selection algorithms can often reduce the dimensionality of a learning task. If the de-selected features are completely irrelevant, then this could significantly increase an algorithm's learning rate.

---

[4]This discretization algorithm computes the entropy of a set of possible discretization points and recursively accepts binary splits that yield maximal entropy reduction as long as the minimum description length principle is satisfied.

Aha and Bankert (1994) reported that their feature selection algorithm had benefits over IB4, the online feature weighting algorithm, for a task with a large number (204) of features. They hypothesized that IB4 fares poorly under such conditions because it trades off learning rate for a much larger space of continuous weights. Thus, its learning rate is slow.

More recently, Kohavi et al. (1995) empirically compared a weighting and selection method. Their DIET algorithms, performance biased methods that respectively use best first and hill climbing searches through a constrained space of feature weights, outperformed a similar feature selection algorithm in tasks where features vary in their relevance for classification. They also anticipate the tradeoff between learning rate and weight space size.

In summary, these studies and similar ones using other learning algorithms suggest that feature selection algorithms perform best when the features used to describe instances are either highly correlated with the class label or completely irrelevant. Feature weighting is more appropriate for tasks where features vary in their relevance, but such methods search larger spaces of weight assignments. Additional research is required to further investigate this tradeoff.

3.3. Representation: Given vs. Transformed

A third dimension for distinguishing feature weighting algorithms concerns whether the set of features used to represent the instances is transformed (i.e., replaced with a different set) before weighting. A substantial shortcoming of all methods that simply assign weights to individual features is their insensitivity to interacting or correlated features. This can be addressed either by using distance functions that combine weights (e.g., using upper triangular weight matrices) or by transforming the given representation before weighting features.

QM2m (Mohri and Tanaka 1994) is an example of this latter approach. It assigns the absolute values computed by *Quantification Method II* (QM2) (Hayashi 1952) to set its feature weights in the following variant of Equation 6:[5]

$$d(\mathbf{x}, \mathbf{q}) = \sqrt{\sum_{f \in \mathbf{F}} \left(\sum_{f' \in \mathbf{F'}} |w(f', f)| \cdot \delta(x_f, q_f) \right)^2} \tag{23}$$

where $\mathbf{F'}$ is the set of transformed (i.e., new) features and $w(f', f)$ is the weight of the given feature f for the transformed feature f'. This representation

---

[5] Symbolic features with V_f values are replaced with $|V_f|$ binary features before this transformation.

transformation is performed using QM2, which is a supervised version of *principal components analysis* (PCA).[6] QM2 locates a new set of features such that the sums of the squared distances of each instance to its projections on the successive feature dimensions are minimized. The value of transformed feature f' for transformation of $\mathbf{x}$ is computed using

$$\sum_{f \in F} w(f', f) x_f \tag{24}$$

where these weights are calculated to maximize, for each new feature f', the ratio of the variance between each class' instances to the variance of all instances. Kawaguchi (1978) describes this algorithm in more detail.

Mohri and Tanaka (1994) reported good performance for QM2m. QM2 can be used to reduce the dimensionality of the data by removing the transformed features with the lowest variation (Mohri and Tanaka 1995; Wettschereck 1994). Mohri and Tanaka (1995) investigate how to determine the number of transformed features that can be removed.

Mohri and Tanaka (1994, 1995) also introduced QM2y, which uses a different distance function:

$$d(\mathbf{x}, \mathbf{q}) = \sum_{f' \in F'} \left(\sum_{f \in F} w(f', f) x_f \cdot \sum_{f \in F} w(f', f) q_f \right)^2 \tag{25}$$

This algorithm performed best among their selected set of lazy algorithms, but hypotheses explaining why have not yet been investigated.

Another lazy learning algorithm that supports feature transformation is IB3-CI (Aha 1991). This is a knowledge-intensive extension of the noise-tolerant IB3 algorithm (Aha et al. 1991). It uses a Bayesian approach, adapted from (Schlimmer 1987), to direct its search through a space of logical feature combinations, and uses a competitive feature selection approach to assign binary weights. Aha (1991) reported good results for IB3-CI in comparison with lazy algorithms that do not perform representation change. However, it requires domain-specific knowledge to constrain and intelligently prune the space of feature combinations.

A significant disadvantage of feature transformation methods is that the transformed features are often not meaningful. This can constitute a significant shortfall of these methods if inspection of the (transformed) classifier

---

[6]QM2 is preferable to PCA, which can lose information since (1) PCA orders principal components by decreasing functions of their input data variations and (2) the variable with the lowest variation might actually be the one with the highest predictive relevance (Kshirsager 1972). QM2 also is sensitive to concept skew when ordering the new variables.

is necessary (i.e., additional constraints on the transformation process are required to guarantee comprehensibility).

3.4. *Generality: Global vs. Local*

A fourth dimension for distinguishing feature weighting algorithms concerns whether the weights apply *globally* (i.e., over the entire instance space) or *locally* (i.e., differ in different parts of the instance space). Although many feature-weighting algorithms use a global scheme, their assumption that feature relevance is invariant over the instance space is constraining and sometimes inappropriate.

Two types of local weighting schemes are popular. The first assigns a different weight to each value of a feature (e.g., the VDM (Section 3.1.2)). Although this allows feature relevance to vary over the values of a feature, it still constrain weights to be identical for all instances with the same feature value. The second local weighting scheme removes this constraint by allowing feature weights to vary as a function of the instance. We discuss several examples of this approach below.

The asymptotic error rate of first nearest neighbor is no more than twice that of the Bayes optimal classifier (Cover and Hart, 1967). Short and Fukunaga (1980, 1981) and Fukunaga and Flick (1982, 1984) utilized this fact to compute feature weights for a weighted distance function. They estimated the finite sample risk from the local neighborhood of a given instance. They then minimized the difference between the finite sample risk and the asymptotic risk to obtain a local distance function for each instance. Hence, to classify a query the authors first find its k nearest neighbors, as defined by k-NN, and then compute each neighbor's local distance function to find the nearest neighbor. Myles and Hand (1990) extended this approach for multiclass problems.

Fukunaga and Flick (1984) noted two disadvantages of this local weighting approach. First, it lacks regularization; one noisy sample can cause an improper distance computation. Second, the large number of distinct local distance functions can obscure useful feature information. Therefore, they propose a global distance function that combines the information from all local functions into one global set of weights for a weighted Euclidean distance function.

In this vein, Aha and Goldstone (1992) combined local with global distance functions to compute instance-specific weights for their GCM-ISW algorithm. Distance for continuous features was defined as

$$d(\mathbf{x}, \mathbf{q}) = \sqrt{\sum_{f \in \mathbf{F}} w(f, \mathbf{x}, \mathbf{q}) \cdot \delta(x_f, q_f)^2} \qquad (26)$$

where instance specific weights are dynamically assigned using

$$w(f, \mathbf{x}, \mathbf{q}) = w(f, \mathbf{x}) \cdot \sqrt{1 - |x_f - q_f|}$$
$$+ w(f) \cdot \left(1 - \sqrt{1 - |x_f - q_f|}\right) \quad (27)$$

Equation 27 adds the contributions of stored instance $\mathbf{x}$'s instance-specific weight $w(f, \mathbf{x})$ and the global weight $w(f)$. As the difference between the values of f for these instances decreases, $\mathbf{x}$'s instance-specific weight contributes more to the dynamically assigned weight $w(f, \mathbf{x}, \mathbf{q})$. Likewise, the global weight $w(f)$ is used more as this difference increases. Thus, this distance function depends more on instance-specific weights when the new instance is similar to the stored instance, and depends more on the global weights when they are not similar. Similarly, the updating algorithm for instance-specific weights has more influence when these instances are similar.

GCM-ISW was shown to correlate significantly better with subject data than did its non-weighting and global weighting variants (Aha and Goldstone 1992). The subjects' target concept was designed such that feature relevance varied in different parts of the instance space.

GCM-ISW's definition of similarity is not symmetric; frequently, it yields $d(\mathbf{x}, \mathbf{y}) \neq d(\mathbf{y}, \mathbf{x})$. Ricci and Avesani (1995) noted that asymmetric local similarity functions defined on continuous features have another degree of freedom: a feature's weight can differ depending on whether a query's value for that feature is greater or less than the value of the stored instance. Assuming that a feature f is continuous, they defined an anisotropic and asymmetric distance measure with *directed* weight settings using

$$w(f, \mathbf{x}, \mathbf{q}) = \begin{cases} w_{x_{f>}} & \text{if } x_f \geq q_f \\ w_{x_{f<}} & \text{if } x_f < q_f \end{cases} \quad (28)$$

where $w_{x_{f<}}$ and $w_{x_{f<}}$ are the weights of instance $\mathbf{x}$ at feature f on the respective "sides" of x_f. They obtained favorable results with their local weighting scheme as compared to standard 1-NN and Salzberg's (1991) EACH on four data sets from the UCI repository (Murphy 1995).

Other purely local (and lazy) approaches were recently introduced by Hastie and Tibshirani (1994) and by Friedman (1994). Hastie and Tibshirani (1994) compute a separate distance metric for each query through an iterative process. The main idea is to employ discriminant analysis to shrink the neighborhood around each query in directions orthogonal to the decision boundary (i.e., thus giving greater weight to features whose axes are closer to perpendicular with this boundary). Their weighting algorithm works as follows:

1. Initialize a weight matrix $\mathbf{D}$ with the identity matrix.
2. Find $\mathbf{K_q}$, the k nearest neighbors to a query $\mathbf{q}$ using $\mathbf{D}$.
3. Use $\mathbf{K_q}$ to compute the weighted within and between sum of squares matrices $\mathbf{W}$ and $\mathbf{B}$.
4. Update the weight matrix using $\mathbf{D} = \mathbf{W}^{-1/2}[\mathbf{W}^{-1/2}\mathbf{B}\mathbf{W}^{-1/2} + \epsilon\mathbf{I}]\mathbf{W}^{-1/2}$, where ϵ is a user-chosen parameter. (Steps 2-4 can be repeated indefinitely.)
5. Use $\mathbf{D}$ to classify $\mathbf{q}$ using k-NN.

The local statistics $\mathbf{W}$ and $\mathbf{B}$ used to compute the new local metric about $\mathbf{q}$ are the deviation of each pattern from its class-mean ($\mathbf{W}$) and the deviation of each of the class-means from the mean of all k nearest neighbors ($\mathbf{B}$).

A computationally more efficient approach is taken by Friedman (1994). He employs recursive partitioning to find the k nearest neighbors to a query. His *scythe* algorithm recursively zooms in on the query along the most relevant feature. That is, the most relevant feature is scaled at each step such that a fixed fraction of the given training examples fall outside of a predetermined range around the query. The training examples outside of that range are then discarded, the new "most relevant" feature is determined, and the process is repeated until only k training examples remain. The (local) relevance of each variable is estimated from the estimated reduction in prediction error that the knowledge of the value of that variable would yield.

Both Hastie and Tibshirani (1994) and Friedman (1994) report favorable results for their local approaches, in comparison to unweighted k-NN, on synthetic and "real" data sets. Atkeson, Moore, and Schaal (1996a, 1996b) survey the literature on locally weighted learning algorithms and report similar results for several robotic control tasks using locally weighted regression (LWR) algorithms for learning numeric functions. They distinguish *point-based* and *query-based* weighting methods, based on whether distances are computed for each stored instance or dynamically, for a specific query, as is done in LWR algorithms (Cleveland and Loader 1994). Finally, several case-based reasoning researchers have advocated using local distance functions with pre-determined weight assignments (e.g., Ashley and Rissland 1988; Skalak 1992). We expect that local weighting methods will continue to be a fruitful area for future research.

3.5. *Knowledge: None vs. Domain-Specific*

The fifth, final, and most important dimension for distinguishing feature weighting algorithms concerns their use of domain-specific knowledge. Such valuable information is frequently used to constrain the representation of instances and selection of features (e.g., Stanfill and Waltz 1986). Several researchers have also demonstrated the utility of using knowledge to assign feature weights (e.g., Ashley and Rissland 1988; Skalak 1992). Approaches more closely related to the focus of this paper are algorithms that combine automated weight-learning components with domain intensive knowledge or heuristics (e.g., the set of possible transformations assumed when defining tangent distance functions (Simard et al. 1993)). We described some knowledge-intensive algorithms earlier (e.g., IB3-CI), and briefly detail two more below.

Cain et al. (1991) use a domain theory of rules to assign instance-specific weights. Like other algorithms that define local distance functions, their CBR+EBL algorithm combines instance-specific with global feature weights. They assign instance-specific weights to discrete features using an explanation-based learning (EBL) approach (Mitchell et al. 1986). Any feature appearing in an EBL tree that was generated to explain the instance's class is assigned a weight of 1. All other features for that instance are assigned an instance-specific weight of 0. Their distance function is

$$d(\mathbf{x}, \mathbf{q}) = -\text{similarity}(\mathbf{x}, \mathbf{q}) \tag{29}$$

where

$$\text{similarity}(\mathbf{x}, \mathbf{q}) = \frac{\sum_{f \in \mathbf{F}} \alpha \cdot (1 - \delta(x_f, q_f)) + \sum_{f \in \mathbf{F}} \beta \cdot w(f, \mathbf{x}) \cdot (1 - \delta(x_f, q_f))}{\alpha |\mathbf{F}| + \sum_{f \in \mathbf{F}} \beta \cdot w(f, \mathbf{x})} \tag{30}$$

where α determines the degree to which the nearest neighbor algorithm is used to classify instances and β determines the degree to which EBL-determined feature weights are used to influence its similarity function. That is, previous instances are ignored when $\alpha = 0$ while the domain theory is ignored when $\beta = 0$. In an experiment with a sparse dataset (i.e., 50 instances, 76 features), they reported substantial leave-one-out accuracy improvement when using both previous instances and the domain theory in comparison with using only one of these. Thus, they demonstrated the utility of using knowledge to set instance-specific weights for a lazy learning algorithm.

PROTOS (Porter et al. 1990) is a sophisticated *case-based reasoning* system designed initially for a clinical audiology classification task. It builds a semantic network whose links relate features, instances, and classes. It uses feedback from the user to refine its knowledge. The initial settings for PROTOS' instance-specific feature weights are determined from the certainty with which the feature's presence can be inferred from category membership when PROTOS builds explanations of a given instance's classification.

Knowledge-based pattern matching is used to generate these explanations; it determines whether two values of a feature match by searching for chains of relations in the semantic network linking the two instances' features. Domain-specific heuristics help determine the degree to which two features match. Feature weights can be subsequently modified by the domain expert whenever PROTOS fails to retrieve the correct case to a query. PROTOS' distance function uses a variant of the *context model* (Medin and Schaffer 1978): it subtracts, from 1.0, the contributions of non-matching features according to their relevance weights. Bareiss (1989) reported that PROTOS recorded higher accuracies than did knowledge-poor k-NN on the audiology task.

In summary, knowledge can be used to assign feature weights for use in a k-NN variant, as in CBR+EBL, or through an expert's critique of the algorithm's predictions for feature relevance, as is done in PROTOS. In both cases *instance-specific* weights are used, and we expect this trend to continue in knowledge-intensive approaches.

4. Comparative Evaluation

It is difficult to predict the comparative behavior of feature weighting methods for lazy learning algorithms. Although large scale empirical comparisons exist for other classes of algorithms (e.g., Michie et al. 1994), they do not exist for this class. Instead, most previous comparisons among feature weighting algorithms tend to focus on a specific pair of algorithms (e.g., Wettschereck and Dietterich 1995; Kohavi et al. 1995).

In this section we investigate the comparative capabilities of some of the algorithms described in Section 3. The purpose of this empirical study is to formulate and evaluate a set of trends[7] regarding the relative strengths and weaknesses of groups of feature weight learning algorithms. We focus on the first two dimensions described in Section 3 (i.e., bias and weight space), ignoring the others due to space constraints. The following subsections describe the selected algorithms, the selected datasets, our empirical methodology, and the results. We then summarize these results with explanatory hypotheses and evaluate them. Section 5 includes a discussion on our findings with respect to our framework in Section 3.

---

[7] We prefer the term "trend" over "hypothesis" to indicate that the design and execution of this as well as many other empirical studies does not allow the formulation of hypotheses that withstand statistical scrutiny.

Table 2. Algorithms Selected for Experimentation

Name	Category	Sub-category
k-NN	Control	–
RELIEF-F	Performance	Online Optimizer
k-NN$_{VSM}$	Performance	Batch Optimizer
CCF	Preset	Conditional probabilities
VDM	Preset	Class projection
MVDM	Preset	Class projection
MI	Preset	Mutual information

4.1. *Selected Algorithms*

No weight learning algorithm will perform best for all applications since each implements a different bias; they will have substantially different performance on some problems (Mitchell 1990; Schaffer 1994). We selected one weight-learning method from each sub-category of the bias dimension (Section 3.1) to compare their capabilities. These algorithms, including the baseline k-NN algorithm, are shown in Table 2.

The MVDM (i.e., VDM without feature weights) is also included so we can evaluate the influence of the modified feature difference function (Equation 20) independent of the feature weighting method (Equation 19) on VDM's behavior.[8]

To allow for controlled experimentation along the second dimension (i.e., continuous vs. binary weight space), selected experiments were conducted with one preset bias method (MI) and one performance bias method (RELIEF-F).[9] In these experiments, we set a varying number of the lowest-valued weights to 0 and all other weights to 1.

4.2. *Selected Data Sets*

We selected fourteen datasets for our study. Ten of these were chosen to evaluate the selected algorithms' capabilities under controlled conditions for specific data characteristics. These were designed to evaluate the selected algorithms in the context of tasks with irrelevant features, interacting features, redundant features, and/or features with varying relevance. Four of these datasets were created for this study, three of which are shown in Figure 1:

---

[8] This is necessary since the VDM is the only method that differs from k-NN in more than the definition of Equation 9.

[9] These two were selected because they are the most computationally efficient methods in their respective categories.

- The *banded* task has axis-parallel decision boundaries. The horizontal dimension of this task is completely irrelevant.
- The decision boundary in the *sinusoidal* task is a sine curve. The vertical dimension in this task is nearly completely irrelevant.
- The *gauss-band* task was constructed by combining the input features of the *banded* task and four Gaussian distributions (variance 0.025). A fifth boolean feature indicates whether the inputs from the *banded* task or the Gaussian distribution determine the output. Therefore, this task is an example of a task with interacting features.
- Another task with highly interacting features is the parity problem. We selected a *parity* task with 11 boolean features; seven are irrelevant while the sum of the other four determines the output (i.e., if the sum is an even number, then the class is 1 and otherwise is 0).

Figure 1. The distribution of examples from the different classes in three two-dimensional artificial data sets. The *banded* task has ten classes. *Sinusoidal* is a binary classification task. The rightmost graph depicts two of the five features of the *gauss-band* task with data points drawn from four Gaussian distributions (variance = 0.025), where different symbols indicate different classes. Lines represent the decision boundaries used to label the data.

The remaining datasets were drawn from the UC Irvine Repository (Murphy 1995). Some characteristics of these datasets are shown in Table 3. Additional dataset characteristics that are relevant to the evaluation are:

- The LED Display and Waveform datasets are also constructed from a data generator. The relevant features of the LED task are interacting, which allows us to further compare the abilities of performance and preset bias methods on such tasks. Some features in the Waveform task are more relevant than others; we will use this knowledge to examine the effect of continuous vs. binary feature weights.
- The Waveform-40 (LED-7+17B, LED-7+17C) task is identical to the Waveform-21 (LED-7) task with the addition of 19 (17) irrelevant features (i.e., having random values). These tasks were chosen to compare how

well different feature weighting algorithms tolerate irrelevant features when a relatively large number of features are irrelevant.

- The Cleveland, Hungarian, and Voting databases contain redundant features (i.e., some features can be removed in these datasets without any significant effect on the performance of k-NN (Wettschereck 1994)). In contrast, some datasets have no redundant features (e.g., Waveform, Isolet, and NETtalk).

Table 3. Characteristics of the selected datasets. B = Boolean, C = Continuous, D = Discrete. The relevant features in the datasets located above the horizontal divider are approximately equally relevant.

Domain	Set Size		Number and Type of Features	Number of Irrelevant Features	Classes
	Training	Test			
Banded	350	150	2 C	1	10
Sinusoidal	350	150	2 C	1	2
Gauss-band	350	150	4 C, 1 B	2	14
Parity	350	150	11 B	7	2
LED-7 Display	200	1000	7 B	0	10
LED-7+17B	200	1000	24 B	17	10
LED-7+17C	200	1000	7 B, 17 C	17	10
Waveform-21	300	100	21 C	0	3
Waveform-40	300	100	40 C	19	3
Cleveland	212	91	5 C, 3 B, 5 D	0	2
Hungarian	206	88	5 C, 3 B, 5 D	1	2
Voting	305	130	16 B	0	2
Isolet	1040	1040	617 C	0	26
NETtalk*	5000	2500	7 D	0	54

* Phonemes only

In summary, these datasets were selected to evaluate the selected algorithms' ability to tolerate different types of problematic features. We suspect that performance feedback methods will attain higher accuracies than the preset bias weighting methods discussed in Section 3.1 for datasets with interacting or redundant features because these preset bias methods compute weights independently for each feature.[10] Feature weighting methods should outperform feature selection methods for datasets with no irrelevant or redundant features (e.g., the NETtalk, Isolet, and Waveform-21 datasets).

---

[10] John, Kohavi, and Pfleger (1994) argued that performance feedback (*wrapper*) methods are preferable for feature selection algorithms, and empirical evidence now exists that supports their hypothesis (e.g., Doak 1992; Aha and Bankert 1994).

Finally, irrelevant features are often seen as *the* cause for k-NN's poor performance. Hence, several datasets with different numbers and types of irrelevant features were selected. However, we expect no substantial performance differences among the different feature weight learning algorithms for datasets with completely irrelevant features since such features are easily detected.

4.3. *Methodology and Initial Results*

We used the training/test set methodology to evaluate the generalization performance of the selected learning algorithms. Each dataset was randomly partitioned into a training and a test set. After training, the percentage of correct classifications on the test set was measured. This procedure was repeated 25 times to reduce statistical variation. The same training and test sets were used for each algorithm.

Leave-one-out cross-validation was used to tune the free parameters of the selected algorithms for all but the two largest datasets. Due to computational restrictions, the training sets for the NETtalk and Isolet datasets were split into two subsets: a sub-training and a cross-validation set. The algorithms were then trained on the sub-training set with various parameter settings and tested on the cross-validation set. The best parameter settings were then employed during classification in combination with the entire training set. The optimal value of k was estimated for all preset bias methods after feature weights were computed and for all performance feedback methods before and after learning feature weights. For k-NN$_{VSM}$, the number of training epochs was limited to the number of epochs required for minimization along one conjugate direction (see Press et al. 1992; Wettschereck 1995a). CCF, VDM, and MVDM have no free parameters. Fayyad and Irani's (1993) discretization algorithm was used to discretize continuous features for CCF, VDM, MVDM, MI (i.e., during feature weight computation), and RELIEF-F (i.e., when computing distance in the presence of missing feature values).

Using this methodology, we applied each algorithm to each dataset. Table 4 summarizes the results.

4.4. *Summary: Trends and their Evaluation*

These results, combined with additional insights gained during informal testing, suggest the following trends,[11] which we investigate later in this section:

- **T1:** Preset bias methods can suffer substantially when the data are not carefully pre-processed.

---

[11] Of course, these trends may be limited to the datasets tested.

Table 4. The effect of different feature weight learning algorithms on the generalization accuracy of k-NN. Shown are the average accuracy (and standard deviations) of k-NN with uniform feature weights and the relative percentage point differences in average accuracy attained by several feature weighting variants. We use boldfaced numbers in our tables to indicate that differences between the weighted and unweighted approach are more than three standard errors.

| | Feature Weight Learning Algorithm | | | | | | |
| | Control | Performance Bias Method | | Preset Bias Method | | | |
Dataset	none	Relief-F	k-NN$_{VSM}$	CCF	VDM	MVDM	MI
Banded	83.0±0.4	**11.2**		**12.8**	**12.8**	**12.8**	**12.8**	10.8
Sinusoidal	74.2±0.8	**5.9**		**14.4**	**-9.1**	**-9.1**	**-9.2**	**-4.6**
Gauss-band	78.3±0.5	**8.6**		**16.6**	**14.9**	**15.5**	**17.5**	**12.1**
Parity	67.3±0.1	**32.7**		**32.7**	1.3	1.7	1.9	2.2
LED-7 Display	72.7±0.4	-1.0		0.0	-1.5	-1.4	-1.3	-1.2
LED-7+17B	52.5±0.5	**19.2**		**15.5**	9.2	**19.4**	**18.9**	**19.4**
LED-7+17C	68.8±0.6	**3.3**		**2.0**	**-5.6**	**2.0**	**2.3**	**3.6**
Waveform-21	82.1±0.4	0.3		-0.5	**-6.1**	**-3.7**	**-3.9**	0.5
Waveform-40	81.3±0.9	1.7		1.2	**-3.4**	-0.7	-0.4	1.0
Cleveland	82.4±0.8	-0.5		0.0	-1.3	0.2	0.7	-0.6
Hungarian	82.6±0.7	**-2.5**		-0.4	-0.1	0.1	0.0	0.1
Voting	92.6±0.7	**2.9**		**2.5**	1.0	**2.1**	**2.1**	**2.0**
Isolet	84.2±0.3	0.4		**1.9**	**-1.1**	**-3.9**	**1.6**	**1.6**
NETtalk	69.6±0.2	**9.2**		**6.6**	**7.7**	**10.0**	**12.1**	**9.7**

- T2: Performance bias methods attain higher accuracies than preset bias methods for tasks with interacting features.
- T3: Performance bias methods have faster learning rates than preset bias methods.
- T4: Feature weighting algorithms achieve higher generalization accuracies than feature selection algorithms for tasks where some features are useful but less important than others.

We also found that most feature weight learning algorithms can tolerate completely irrelevant features unless there are many highly interacting features, which agrees with findings from previous studies of weight learning algorithms (e.g., Aha 1992; Kira and Rendell 1992). An exception is the performance of the preset bias methods on the *sinusoidal* task, which we investigate in T1 below. A further interesting result was obtained for the Waveform-40 task; k-NN's average performance dropped by less than one percentage point when the 19 irrelevant continuous features were added. Simultaneously, the *relative* accuracies of all the feature weighting algorithms increased as expected. However, despite the large number of irrelevant features, and that RELIEF-F, k-NN$_{VSM}$, and MI correctly computed low weights for them (e.g., Figure 2), none of the algorithms substantially outperformed k-NN. We surmised that k-NN's surprisingly good performance was because 300 training instances suffice to create a densely populated manifold in the instance space for this task. Therefore, we ran experiments on this task with a smaller training set (i.e., 100 training examples). The results (Table 5) reveal that 300 training examples are indeed too many to illustrate the faster learning rates of feature weighting algorithms for these Waveform tasks.

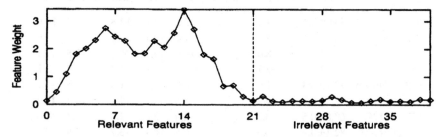

Figure 2. Feature weights computed by MI for the Waveform-40 task.

Table 5. Average accuracies for the Waveform-21 and Waveform-40 tasks for differently sized training sets.

Training Set Size	Feature Weight Learning Algorithm			
	control	Performance bias method		Preset bias method
	none	Relief-F	k-NN$_{VSM}$	MI
Waveform-21				
300	82.1±0.9	82.4	81.6	82.6
100	77.0±1.0	79.1	77.2	78.0
Waveform-40				
300	81.3±0.9	83.0	82.5	82.3
100	73.4±1.0	**78.4**	**76.7**	**78.6**

T1: This trend explores an explanation for the poor performance of the preset bias methods on the *sinusoidal* task. One form of pre-processing involves discretizing continuous features, which is required by the four preset bias algorithms (i.e., CCF, VDM, MVDM, and MI). Inspection of the discretizations computed by Fayyad and Irani's (1993) method revealed that features were improperly discretized for the *sinusoidal* task.[12] The comparatively

---

[12] The vertical, more relevant, dimension was generally split into only three intervals of which one interval covered nearly the entire range.

lower accuracies recorded by these four methods on this task (i.e., in comparison to k-NN$_{VSM}$) indicates their dependence on proper pre-processing methods, in this case discretization.

To test this hypothesis, we repeated our experiments for the *sinusoidal* task but manually provided the correct discretizations (i.e., 16 (4) equally sized intervals for the horizontal (vertical) feature, see Figure 6). The accuracies of all four preset bias methods then improved from at least three standard errors below k-NN's accuracy to at least three standard errors above (Table 6). Discretization had no positive effect on either k-NN$_{VSM}$'s or RELIEF-F's performance.

Table 6. Average accuracies for the *sinusoidal* task with Fayyad and Irani (1993) discretization intervals and manually assigned discretization intervals.

Discretization Method	Feature Weight Learning Algorithm					
	control	Performance bias method	Preset bias method			
	none	k-NN$_{VSM}$	CCF	VDM	MVDM	MI
none	74.2±0.7	**88.6**				
Irani and Fayyad			**65.1**	**65.1**	**65.0**	**69.6**
Manually			**81.6**	**82.8**	**83.3**	**88.5**

T2: The accuracy differences between the performance and preset bias methods for the *parity* task indicate that a main advantage of performance bias methods might be higher accuracy in the presence of interacting features. An additional experiment in a boolean task with ten input features, where the output was computed as the parity of a varying number of input features, supported this trend; k-NN$_{VSM}$ substantially outperformed MI when using two to four parity features. For larger numbers of interacting features, both algorithms had difficulty learning the concept given the small training set employed (i.e., 50 training examples).

T3: The experiment described in Table 5 showed that, for one task, feature weighting methods may have a substantially higher learning rate than k-NN. An issue closely related to this is whether different weighting methods have different learning rates. In particular, we hypothesize that performance bias methods have faster learning rates than preset bias methods. We selected the two most computationally efficient methods from each of these categories (i.e., MI and RELIEF-F) to investigate this hypothesis. We selected three tasks where these two methods achieved approximately equal accuracies as reported in Table 4. Results from these experiments indicate that the generalization accuracy of RELIEF-F is indeed higher than MI's for small training sets (Figure 3).

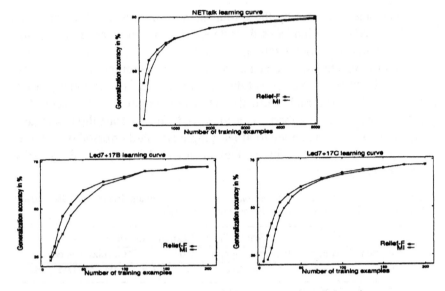

Figure 3. Learning curves for MI and RELIEF-F from three tasks.

T4: The second dimension for distinguishing feature weighting methods as described in Table 1 is the weight space employed by the algorithms. Kohavi et al. (1995) describe evidence that feature weighting methods lead to superior performance as compared to feature selection methods for tasks where some features are useful but less important than others.

We investigated this hypothesis by examining the performance of RELIEF-F and MI with continuous vs. binary weight settings (i.e., feature selection), where we removed an increasing number of lowest-weighted features. They were applied to two learning tasks: Waveform-40 (19 irrelevant, 21 relevant features, where feature relevance varies) and LED-7+17B (17 irrelevant features, seven others with approximately equal relevance). Figure 4 displays the results for RELIEF-F. Similar results were achieved for MI (not shown). For both tasks, the weighted approach is generally superior to the feature selection approach. The only improvement achieved by feature selection methods was for the LED-7+17B task when all 17 irrelevant features were removed. These results provide further support for T4. Our evidence suggests that, despite searching a larger weight space, feature weighting methods may outperform feature selection methods even in domains that are thought to be most suited to feature selection methods, i.e., domains that contain either approximately equally relevant or completely irrelevant features. This claim might hold unless the correct subset of (relevant) features is located by the feature selection methods. Additional research is needed to investigate this claim.

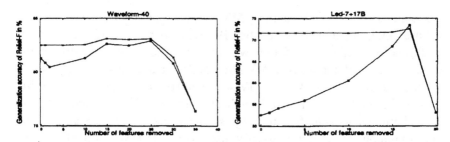

Figure 4. The performance of RELIEF-F when an increasing number of features with the lowest computed weights are removed. The remaining features are either continuously weighted (×) or assigned a weight value of 1 (□).

4.4.1. *Intra-model comparisons*

This section addresses differences in performance within the families of performance feedback and preset bias methods.

Performance bias methods

RELIEF-F and k-NN$_{VSM}$ had substantial performance differences on several datasets. We suspect that one cause is that k-NN$_{VSM}$ appears to be insufficiently biased towards giving zero weight to irrelevant features. We tested this hypothesis by varying the number of irrelevant features in the LED-7 task, and our results supports this claim. When the number of irrelevant features is increased from zero to 17, k-NN$_{VSM}$'s performance is initially superior, but RELIEF-F outperforms k-NN$_{VSM}$ when there are more than two irrelevant features. Furthermore, several experiments showed that RELIEF-F has a faster learning rate than k-NN$_{VSM}$.

Preset bias methods

VDM, MVDM, and CCF performed poorly compared with MI on the Waveform and *sinusoidal* tasks. A possible cause is that these methods retain the discretization of continuous features even after feature weights are learned. We tested this claim using the Waveform tasks. When feature values are left discretized for MI, even after feature weights are computed, its performance drops by 6.0% and 3.8% for the Waveform-21 and Waveform-40 tasks, respectively. This indicates that a substantial amount of information is lost when these datasets are discretized. Ting (1994) reported that discretization in lazy learning algorithms can be useful for noisy tasks. Further research is needed to explain why discretization does not improve performance for these noisy Waveform tasks.

A comparison of VDM and MVDM's accuracies in Table 4 reveals that the feature weights computed by Equation 19 have no beneficial effect on VDM's performance. Furthermore, feature weights computed via mutual information (Equation 21) did not improve MVDM's performance for the *banded*, *sinusoidal*, and Waveform tasks. The MVDM's good performance for the *banded*, Led-7+17B, and Led-7+17C tasks indicates that the class projection method is an alternative to using feature weights when irrelevant features are present and continuous features are properly discretized. MVDM recorded the best result for the NETtalk task, which is not surprising since the VDM was designed for this task.

4.4.2. *Summary*

In summary, these results provide strong but sometimes incomplete evidence for our four trends. For example, our evidence for trend **T1** requires additional investigations with other forms of pre-processing steps that could decrease the performance of the preset bias methods (e.g., normalization).

Our trends were designed to help determine which algorithms should perform well for some given task characteristics. Specifically, these trends predict the behavior of several feature weight learning algorithms – in the presence of irrelevant, redundant or interacting features, or features with varying relevance – according to their categorization in our framework in Section 3.

5. Discussion and Implications

The dimensional framework in Section 3 can be used to relate different methods for weighting features, motivate experiments to distinguish their comparative abilities, and suggest future work (e.g., combining multiple approaches, such as a feature selection followed by a weighting algorithm). For example, new weighting methods could be categorized according to this framework, which could simplify their comprehension and provide a context for understanding their comparative abilities.

We also used this framework to organize our investigation in Section 4, whose purpose was to investigate the comparative abilities of feature weighting methods for a subclass of lazy algorithms with respect to two of this framework's dimensions. However, instead of simply reporting case study results (i.e., from applying each algorithm to each dataset), we also introduced and briefly evaluated trends that attempt to explain these results.

First, we introduced trends **T1**, **T2**, and **T3** to address the first dimension. That is, they concern the distinctive capabilities of performance and preset bias methods. Although we provide some evidence for them, they are limited to the selected algorithms and datasets. For example, trend **T2** suggests performance biases are preferred for tasks with interacting features. This trend could be invalidated by methods that use preset biases designed to account for such features (e.g., a mutual information method that considers all combinations of features). Thus, in situations when a preset bias might otherwise be preferable (e.g., for computational reasons), yet the task is known to involve interacting features with high probability, steps can be taken to either modify the dataset's characteristics through representation change or on designing a preset bias method that tolerates such characteristics. The initial studies described in Section 4.4.1 likewise require further investigation since their implications might also be limited to the algorithms and datasets involved.

Second, trend **T4** addresses the second dimension of our framework defined in Section 3. Like Kohavi et al. (1995), we found some evidence that weighting is preferable to binary selection in some tasks where feature relevance varies. This provides motivation for designing algorithms that explore the tradeoffs of searching larger weight spaces, as done by continuous weighting algorithms, versus the computational efficiency gained by reducing the size of this space.

Finally, our framework can be used to suggest and direct future research efforts. For example, we envision algorithm designs that profitably exploit aspects of multiple framework dimensions. Algorithms could be designed to address the space/time tradeoff mentioned above by locally estimating where continuous weighting could be profitably explored. Larger weight spaces could then be searched for those regions of instance space. Alternatively, this could provide a focus for extracting domain-specific knowledge (i.e., for those local regions) (e.g., Domingos 1996), or for applying local feature transformation methods so as to reduce the size of the weight space (e.g., Hastie and Tibshirani 1994).

As another example, comparative evaluations could be focussed according to the sub-category structure. Our trends did not address differences *within* sub-categories of the framework (i.e., a comparison of two types of preset bias methods), although we briefly addressed these issues in Section 4.4.1. More detailed studies of this nature, which are strongly suggested by our framework, are left for future research.

6. Related Work

6.1. *Similar Studies*

Several studies have introduced feature weighting algorithms. Some compared new algorithms to unweighted k-NN (e.g., Kelly and Davis 1991; Aha 1992). Some studies have also compared weighting algorithms in a specific context. For example, Wettschereck and Dietterich (1995) showed that a mutual information method traded off higher computational complexity for higher accuracies when compared with an online algorithm in the context of learning hyperrectangles (Salzberg 1991). Mohri and Tanaka (1994) reported a more extensive comparison, in which they review several feature weighting algorithms while motivating the introduction of QM2. This algorithm assigns weight values by optimizing specific statistical criteria. They reported that two lazy variants of QM2 attain good results in comparison with four other feature weighting algorithms, although they (also) have higher computational costs.

6.2. *Performance vs. Preset Biases*

Doak (1992), among others, noted the utility of using the classifier to guide feature selection. John et al. (1994) clarified this distinction. Aha and Bankert (1994), among others, subsequently provided additional empirical evidence for preferring performance feedback biases, and Kohavi et al. (1995) advocated using performance biases for continuous weighting methods.

Kohonen's (1990) *learning vector quantization* (LVQ) algorithm employs a hill-climbing performance bias method to cluster instances defined by continuous features. Although no current LVQ variant explicitly computes weights for input features, one could argue that these algorithms implicitly learn the relevance of features. Wettschereck and Dietterich (1992) showed how LVQ-type algorithms can be used to adjust the coordinates of irrelevant input features for all stored exemplars such that they are identical, which effectively eliminates them. They showed this for generalized radial basis networks (Poggio and Girosi 1990), where the centers of basis functions are moved during training. After training, the mean distances between the center locations' features reflected the relevance of the original input features.

6.3. *Information Theory*

In Section 3.1.2 we described feature weighting algorithms that use preset biases based on information theory. Several other learning algorithms have a similar basis. Quinlan (1986) used an information gain measure to select features when inducing decision trees in ID3. Wolpert (1990, 1994) used an information theoretic approach to set feature weights for a four-nearest neighbor algorithm and reported favorable results in comparison with Back-propagation on a word pronunciation task. Bakiri (1991) employed a modification of a MI weighting procedure proposed by Lucassen and Mercer (1984) that ranked features. This ranking was then used to determine which ones were used to induce decision trees.

The MI approach described in Section 3.1.2 assumes that features are independent (i.e., in their correlation with class). This can lead to inferior performance for tasks with interacting or redundant features. Battiti (1994) describes an approach that addresses this problem by first computing the MI between each pair of features and then decreasing the weight of highly interacting features.

Another concern is that the MI computed for many-valued features will frequently be larger than the MI of features with few distinct values, even if both features carry the same amount of information. This can be counteracted by normalizing each feature's MI value by a function of its number of possible values. However, this can still lead to sub-optimal behavior, such as when two continuous features differ greatly in relevance, yet the more relevant feature is discretized into a much larger number of intervals.

6.4. *Instance Weighting*

The topic of this paper concerns methods that set parameter values (i.e., feature weights) in the distance functions in a subclass of lazy learning algorithms. An alternative and frequently used approach for enhancing distance functions involves assigning weights to instances themselves. Weights can be assigned either before computing distances (e.g., Salzberg 1991; Aha et al. 1991) or afterwards (e.g., Connell and Utgoff 1987; Atkeson 1989). Both approaches bias the prediction of lazy algorithms by emphasizing the contributions of some instances over others. Wettschereck (1995b) described evidence that non-equal instance weights are often preferable. Atkeson et al. (1996a) survey alternative kernel functions, which effectively modify instance weightings. We expect that future research will determine which feature weighting methods are also useful for weighting instances.

6.5. *Alternative Architectures for Lazy Algorithms*

Finally, we note that several lazy learning algorithms have been implemented using alternative computational architectures. For example, connectionist network architectures have been used to implement many lazy learning algorithms. Volper and Hampson (1987) were early advocates of using specific instance information in such networks. Radial basis networks (e.g., Poggio and Girosi 1990; Broomhead and Lowe 1988) are closely related to lazy learning algorithms that cache weight settings; they replace a sigmoidal squashing function with a Gaussian whose activation is a function of its distance to the inputs. Kruschke (1992), among others, reported that his modified radial basis network correlates significantly well with a surprising amount of subject data collected over several decades. Carpenter et al. (1992) modified and implemented Salzberg's (1991) EACH algorithm as a connectionist network. Several of these systems use some form of feature weighting that could be more closely compared with the algorithms reviewed here.

Several other algorithms blur the distinction between lazy and eager processing. For example, some incremental decision tree induction algorithms retain specific instances (e.g., Utgoff 1989), and some algorithms combine rules with specific instances to represent concepts (e.g., Zhang 1990). Each architecture highlights a unique perspective on weighting features, which may provide insights not easily obtained when using a traditional k-NN architecture.

7. Conclusions

In this paper we investigated issues on estimating feature weight parameters for the distance functions in a subclass of lazy learning algorithms. We reviewed several such feature weighting methods, outlined a framework composed of five dimensions for distinguishing them, and described example algorithms defined by each dimension. Our empirical evaluation compared several such algorithms, and suggested several trends. We described additional supporting evidence for each trend.

These trends suggest certain directions for future research. For example, since most of the algorithms tested successfully assign low weights to irrelevant features, empirical demonstrations of new feature weighting algorithms in the presence of irrelevant features are not particularly valuable. Instead, they should be compared with existing feature weighting algorithms, where the framework used in our review can be used to both categorize the new algorithm and motivate the selection of algorithms in empirical comparisons. Alternatively, researchers could use some of these trends to motivate the design of algorithms that contradict them (i.e., by avoiding some problems with their predecessors). Finally, we investigated only the first two dimensions of our framework, and did not address function learning tasks. This suggests additional research directions based on this framework.

This article focussed on empirical evaluations. Although several mathematical analyses exist for lazy learning algorithms (e.g., Cover and Hart 1967; Langley and Iba 1993) few address feature weighting (e.g., Satoh and Okamoto 1994; Ling and Wang 1996). Therefore, a theoretical analysis of these algorithms would provide a valuable companion for this article.

Acknowledgements

Thanks to our reviewers, whose comments helped us to greatly improve this article. We thank Igor Kononenko for providing the source code for Relief-F. Thanks also to Gert Durieux and Steven Gillis for testing whether the difference in performance between MVDM and MVDM with MI was statistically significant. Finally, we thank Patrick Murphy for maintaining the UCI Repository of ML Databases and Robert Detrano for making available the datasets on heart disease diagnoses.

References

Aha, D. W. (1991). Incremental constructive induction: An instance-based approach. In *Proceedings of the Eighth International Workshop on Machine Learning*, pp. 117–121. Evanston, IL: Morgan Kaufmann.

Aha, D. W. (1992). Tolerating noisy, irrelevant, and novel attributes in instance-based learning algorithms. *International Journal of Man-Machine Studies* 36: 267–287.

Aha, D. W. & Bankert, R. L. (1994). Feature selection for case-based classification of cloud types: An empirical comparison. In D. W. Aha (ed.) *Case-Based Reasoning: Papers from the 1994 Workshop* (Technical Report WS-94-01). Menlo Park, CA: AAAI Press.

Aha, D. W. & Goldstone, R. L. (1992). Concept learning and flexible weighting. In *Proceedings of the Fourteenth Annual Conference of the Cognitive Science Society*, pp. 534–539. Bloomington, IN: Lawrence Erlbaum.

Aha, D. W., Kibler, D. & Albert, M. K. (1991). Instance-based learning algorithms. *Machine Learning*, 6: 37–66.

Ashley, K. D. & Rissland, E. L. (1988). Waiting on weighting: A symbolic least commitment approach. In *Proceedings of the Seventh National Conference on Artificial Intelligence*, pp. 239-244. St. Paul, MN: Morgan Kaufmann.

Atkeson, C. (1989). Using local models to control movement. In D. S. Touretzky (ed.), *Advances in Neural Information Processing Systems 2*. San Mateo, CA: Morgan Kaufmann.

Atkeson, C., Moore, A. & Schaal, S. (1996a). Locally weighted learning. *Artificial Intelligence Review*, this issue.

Atkeson, C., Moore, A. & Schaal, S. (1996b). Locally weighted learning for control. *Artificial Intelligence Review*, this issue.

Bakiri, G. (1991). *Converting English text to speech: A machine learning approach*. Doctoral dissertation, Department of Computer Science, Oregon State University, Corvallis, OR.

Bareiss, R. (1989). The experimental evaluation of a case-based learning apprentice. In *Proceedings of a Case-Based Reasoning Workshop*, pp. 162–167. Pensacola Beach, FL: Morgan Kaufmann.

Battiti, R. (1994). Using mutual information for selecting features in supervised neural net learning. *IEEE Transactions on Neural Networks* 5: 537–550.

Biberman, Y. (1994). A context similarity measure. In *Proceedings of the European Conference on Machine Learning*, pp. 49–63. Catania, Italy: Springer-Verlag.

Bottou, L. & Vapnik, V. (1992). Local learning algorithms. *Neural Computation* 4: 888–900.

Bounds, D., Lloyd, P. & Mathew, B. (1990). A comparison of neural network and other pattern recognition approaches to the diagnosis of low back disorders. *Neural Networks* 3: 583–591.

Broomhead, D. S. & Lowe, D. (1988). Multivariable functional interpolation and adaptive networks. *Complex Systems* 2: 321–355.

Cain, T., Pazzani, M. J. & Silverstein, G. (1991). Using domain knowledge to influence similarity judgement. In *Proceedings of the Case-Based Reasoning Workshop*, pp. 191–202. Washington, DC: Morgan Kaufmann.

Cardie, C. (1993). Using decision trees to improve case-based learning. In *Proceedings of the Tenth International Conference on Machine Learning*, pp. 25–32. Amherst, MA: Morgan Kaufmann.

Carpenter, G.A., Grossberg, S., Markuzon, N., Reynolds, J.H. & Rosen, D.B. (1992). Fuzzy ARTMAP: A neural network architecture for incremental supervised learning of analog multidimensional maps. *IEEE Transactions on Neural Networks* 3: 693–713.

Cleveland, W. S. & Loader, C. (1994). *Computational methods for local regression* (Technical Report 11). Murray Hill, NJ: AT&T Bell Laboratories, Statistics Department. Available by FTP from netlib.att.com in /netlib/att/stat/doc/94/11.ps.

Connell, M. E. & Utgoff, P. E. (1987). Learning to control a dynamic physical system. In *Proceedings of the Sixth National Conference on Artificial Intelligence*, pp. 456–460. Seattle, WA: Morgan Kaufmann.

Cost, S. & Salzberg, S. (1993). A weighted nearest neighbor algorithm for learning with symbolic features. *Machine Learning* 10: 57–78.

Cover, T. M. & Hart, P. E. (1967). Nearest neighbor pattern classification. *Institute of Electrical and Electronics Engineers Transactions on Information Theory* 13: 21–27.

Cover, T. M. & Thomas, J. (1991). *Elements of Information Theory*. New York: John Wiley and Sons.

Cover, T. M. & van Campenhout, J. M. (1977). On the possible orderings in the measurement selection problem. *IEEE Transactions on Systems, Man, and Cybernetics* 7: 657–661.

Creecy, R. H., Masand, B. M., Smith, S. J. & Waltz, D. L. (1992). Trading MIPS and memory for knowledge engineering. *Communications of the ACM* 35: 48–64.

Daelemans, W., Gills, S. & Durieux, G. (1993). *Learnability and markedness in data-driven acquisition of stress* (Technical Report 43). Tilburg, Netherlands: Tilburg University, Institute for Language Technology and Artificial Intelligence.

Daelemans, W., van den Bosch, A. (1992). Generalization performance of backpropagation learning on a syllabification task. In *Proceedings of TWLT3: Connectionism and Natural Language Processing*, pp. 27–37. Enschede, The Netherlands: Unpublished.

Dasarathy, B. V. (Ed.). (1991). *Nearest neighbor(NN) norms: NN pattern classification techniques*. Los Alamitos, CA: IEEE Computer Society Press.

Doak, J. (1992). *An evaluation of feature selection methods and their application to computer security* (Technical Report CSE-92-18). Davis, CA: University of California, Department of Computer Science.

Domingos, P. (1996). Context-sensitive feature selection for lazy learners. *Artificial Intelligence Review*, this issue.

Duda, R. O. & Hart, P. E. (1973). *Pattern classification and scene analysis*. New York, NY: Wiley.

Dudani, S. (1975). The distance-weighted k-nearest neighbor rule. *IEEE Transactions on Systems, Man, and Cybernetics* 6: 325–327.

Fayyad, U. M., & Irani, K. B. (1993). Multi-interval discretization of continuous-valued attributes for classification learning. In *Proceedings of the Thirteenth International Joint Conference on Artificial Intelligence*, pp. 1022–1029. Chambery, France: Morgan Kaufmann.

Friedman, J. H. (1994). Flexible metric nearest neighbor classification. Unpublished manuscript available by anonymous FTP from playfair.stanford.edu (see pub/friedman/README).

Fu, K. S. (1968). *Sequential methods in pattern recognition and machine learning*. New York: Academic Press.

Fukunaga, K. & Flick, T. (1982). A parametrically-defined nearest neighbor distance measure. *Pattern Recognition Letters* 1: 3–5.

Fukunaga, K. & Flick, T. (1984). An optimal global nearest neighbor metric. *IEEE Transactions on Pattern Analysis and Machine Intelligence* 6: 314–318.

Gorman, R. & Sejnowski, T. (1988). Analysis of hidden units in a layered network trained to classify sonar targets. *Neural Networks* 1: 75–89.

Hastie, T. J. & Tibshirani, R. J. (1994). Discriminant Adaptive Nearest Neighbor Classification. Unpublished manuscript available by anonymous FTP from playfair.stanford.edu as /pub/hastie/dann.ps.Z.

Hayashi, C. (1952). On the prediction of phenomena from qualitative data and the quantification of qualitative data from the mathematical-statistical point of view. *Annals of the Institute of Statistical Mathematics* 3: 69–98.

John, G., Kohavi, R. & Pfleger, K. (1994). Irrelevant features and the subset selection problem. In *Proceedings of the Eleventh International Machine Learning Conference*, pp. 121–129. New Brunswick, NJ: Morgan Kaufmann.

Kawaguchi, M. (1978). *Introduction to Multivariate Analysis II* (in Japanese). Morikita-Shuppan.

Kelly, J. D., Jr. & Davis, L. (1991). A hybrid genetic algorithm for classification. In *Proceedings of the Twelfth International Joint Conference on Artificial Intelligence*, pp. 645–650. Sydney, Australia: Morgan Kaufmann.

Kibler, D. & Aha, D. W. (1987). Learning representative exemplars of concepts: An initial case study. In *Proceedings of the Fourth International Workshop on Machine Learning*, pp. 24–30. Irvine, CA: Morgan Kaufmann.

Kira, K. & Rendell, L. A. (1992). A practical approach to feature selection. In *Proceedings of the Ninth International Conference on Machine Learning*, pp. 249–256. Aberdeen, Scotland: Morgan Kaufmann.

Kohavi, R., Langley, P. & Yun, Y. (1995). Heuristic search for feature weights in instance-based learning. Manuscript submitted for publication.

Kohonen, T., Barna, G. & Chrisley, R. (1988). Statistical pattern recognition with neural networks. In *Proceedings of the International Joint Conference on Neural Networks*, pp. 61–88. IEEE Press.

Kohonen, T. (1990). The self-organizing map. *Proceedings of the IEEE* 78: 1464–1480.

Kolodner, J. (1993). *Case-based reasoning*. San Mateo, CA: Morgan Kaufmann.

Kononenko, I. (1994). Estimating attributes: Analysis and extensions of RELIEF. In *Proceedings of the 1994 European Conference on Machine Learning*, pp. 171–182. Catania, Italy: Springer Verlag.

Kruschke, J. K. (1992). ALCOVE: An exemplar-based connectionist model of category learning. *Psychological Review* 99: 22–44.

Kshirsager, A. (1972). *Multivariate Analysis*. New York: Dekker.

Langley, P. & Iba, W. (1993). Average-case analysis of a nearest neighbor algorithm. *Proceedings of the Thirteenth International Joint Conference on Artificial Intelligence*, pp. 889–894. Chambery, France: Morgan Kaufmann.

Langley, P. & Sage, S. (1994). Oblivious decision trees and abstract cases. In D. W. Aha (ed.), *Case-Based Reasoning: Papers from the 1994 Workshop* (Technical Report WS-94-01). Menlo Park, CA: AAAI Press.

Ling, X. C. & Wang, H. (1996). Towards optimal weights setting for the 1-nearest neighbour learning algorithm. *Artificial Intelligence Review*, this issue.

Lowe, D. (1995). Similarity metric learning for a variable-kernel classifier. *Neural Computation* 7: 72–85.

Lucassen, J. & Mercer, R. (1984). An information theoretic approach to the automatic determination of phonemic base forms. In *Proceedings of the International Conference on Acoustics Speech Signal Processing* (42.5.1-42.5.4).

Luce, R. D. (1963). Detection and recognition. In R. D. Luce, R .R. Bush & E. Galanger (eds.), *Handbook of mathematical psychology*. New York, NY: Wiley.

McGill, W. (1955). Multivariate information transmission. *IEEE Transactions on Information Theory* 1: 93–111.

Medin, D. L. & Schaffer, M. M. (1978). Context theory of classification learning. *Psychological Review* 85: 207–238.

Michie, D., Spiegelhalter, D. J. & Taylor, C. C. (Eds.) (1994). *Machine learning, neural and statistical classification.* London: Prentice Hall.

Mitchell, T. M. (1990). The need for biases in learning generalizations. In J. W. Shavlik & T. G. Dietterich (eds.), *Readings in machine learning.* San Mateo, CA: Morgan Kaufmann.

Mitchell, T., Keller, R. & Kedar-Cabelli, S. (1986). Explanation-based learning: A unifying view. *Machine Learning* 1: 47–80.

Mohri, T., Nakamura, M. & Tanaka, H. (1993). Weather forecasting using memory-based reasoning. In *Second International Workshop on Parallel Processing for Artificial Intelligence*, pp. 40–45.

Mohri, T. & Tanaka, H. (1994). An optimal weighting criterion of case indexing for both numeric and symbolic attributes. In D. W. Aha (ed.), *Case-Based Reasoning: Papers from the 1994 Workshop* (Technical Report WS-94-01). Menlo Park, CA: AAAI Press.

Mohri, T. & Tanaka, H. (1995). Comparison between attribute weighting methods in memory-based reasoning and multivariate analysis. Manuscript submitted for publication.

Moore, A. W. & Lee, M. S. (1994). Efficient algorithms for minimizing cross validation error. In *Proceedings of the Eleventh International Conference on Machine Learning*, pp. 190–198. New Brunswick, NJ: Morgan Kaufmann.

Mucciardi, A. N. & Gose, E. E. (1971). A comparison of seven techniques for choosing subsets of pattern recognition properties. *IEEE Transaction on Computers* 20: 1023–1031.

Murphy, P. (1995). *UCI Repository of machine learning databases* [Machine-readable data repository @ics.uci.edu]. Irvine, CA: University of California, Department of Information and Computer Science.

Myles, J. & Hand, D. (1990). The multi-class metric problem in nearest neighbor discrimination rules. *Pattern Recognition* 23: 1291–1297.

Nadaraya, E. A. (1964), On estimating regression. *Theory of Probability and its Applications* 9: 141–142.

Poggio, T. & Girosi, F. (1990). Regularization algorithms for learning that are equivalent to multilayer networks. *Science* 247: 978–982.

Porter, B. W., Bareiss, R. & Holte, R. C. (1990). Knowledge acquisition and heuristic classification in weak-theory domains. *Artificial Intelligence* 45: 229–263.

Press, W. H., Teukolsky, S. A., Vetterling, W. T. & Flannery, B. P. (1992). *Numerical Recipes in C.* Cambridge, UK: Cambridge University Press.

Quinlan, J. R. (1986). Induction of decision trees. *Machine Learning* 1: 81–106.

Ricci, F. & Avesani, P. (1995). Learning a local similarity metric for case-based reasoning. In *Proceedings of the First International Conference on Case-Based Reasoning*, pp. 301–312. Sesimbra, Portugal: Springer-Verlag.

Salzberg, S. L. (1991). A nearest hyperrectangle learning method. *Machine Learning* 6: 251–276.

Satoh, K. & Okamoto, S. (1994). Toward PAC-learning of weights from qualitative distance information. In D. W. Aha (ed.) *Case-Based Reasoning: Papers from the 1994 Workshop* (Technical Report WS-94-01). Menlo Park, CA: AAAI Press.

Schaffer, C. (1994). A conservation law for generalization performance. In *Proceedings of the Eleventh International Conference on Machine Learning*, pp. 259–265. New Brunswick, NJ: Morgan Kaufmann.

Schlimmer, J. C. (1987). Incremental adjustment of representations for learning. In *Proceedings of the Fourth International Workshop on Machine Learning*, pp. 79–90. Irvine, CA: Morgan Kaufmann.

Shannon, C. E. (1948). A mathematical theory of communication. *Bell Systems Technology Journal* 27: 379–423.

Short, R. & Fukunaga, K. (1980). A new nearest neighbor distance measure. In *Proceedings of the Fifth International Conference on Pattern Recognition*, pp. 81–86. Los Alamitos, CA: IEEE Press.

Short, R. & Fukunaga, K. (1981). The optimal distance measure for nearest neighbor classification. *IEEE Transactions on Information Theory* 27: 622–627.

Simard, P., Le Cun, Y. & Denker, J. (1993). Efficient pattern recognition using a new transformation distance. In Hanson, S. J., et al. (eds.), *Advances in Neural Information Processing Systems 5*. San Mateo, CA: Morgan Kaufmann.

Skalak, D. (1992). Representing cases as knowledge sources that apply local similarity metrics. In *Proceedings of the Fourteenth Annual Conference of the Cognitive Science Society*, pp. 325–330. Bloomington, IN: Lawrence Erlbaum.

Skalak, D. (1994). Prototype and feature selection by sampling and random mutation hill climbing algorithms. In *Proceedings of the Eleventh International Machine Learning Conference*, pp. 293–301. New Brunswick, NJ: Morgan Kaufmann.

Stanfill, C. & Waltz, D. (1986). Toward memory-based reasoning. *Communications of the Association for Computing Machinery* 29: 1213–1228.

Tan, M. (1993). Cost-sensitive learning of classification knowledge and its application in robotics. *Machine Learning* 13: 7–34.

Ting, K. M. (1994). *Discretization of continuous-valued attributes and instance-based learning* (Technical Report). Sydney, Australia, University of Sydney, Basser Department of Computer Science.

Turney, P. D. (1993). Exploiting context when learning to classify. In *Proceedings of the European Conference on Machine Learning*, pp. 402–407. Vienna, Austria: Springer-Verlag.

Turney, P. D. (1995). Cost-sensitive classification: Empirical evaluation of a hybrid genetic decision tree induction algorithm. *Journal of Artificial Intelligence Research* 2: 369–409.

Tversky, A. (1977). Features of similarity. *Psychological Review* 84: 327–352.

Utgoff, P. E. (1989). Incremental induction of decision trees. *Machine Learning* 4: 161–186.

van den Bosch, A. & Daelemans, W. (1993). *Data-oriented methods for grapheme-to-phoneme conversion* (Technical Report 42). Tilburg, Netherlands: Tilburg University, Institute for Language Technology and Artificial Intelligence.

Vapnik, V. (1992). Principles of risk minimization for learning theory. In R. P. Lippmann & J. E. Moody (eds.), *Advances in Neural Information Processing Systems 3*. Denver, CO: Morgan Kaufmann.

Volper, D. J. & Hampson, S. E. (1987). Learning and using specific instances. *Biological Cybernetics* 57: 57–71.

Weiss, S. M. & Kapouleas, I. (1989). An empirical comparison of pattern recognition, neural nets, and machine learning classification methods. In *Proceedings of the Eleventh International Joint Conference on Artificial Intelligence*, pp. 781–787. Detroit, MI: Morgan Kaufmann.

Weiss, S. M. & Kulikowski, C. A. (1991). *Computer systems that learn: Classification and prediction methods from statistics, neural nets, machine learning, and expert systems*. San Mateo, CA: Morgan Kaufmann.

Wettschereck, D. (1994). *A study of distance-based machine learning algorithms*. Doctoral dissertation, Department of Computer Science, Oregon State University, Corvallis, OR. Available via WWW at http://nathan.gmd.de/persons/dietrich.wettschereck.html

Wettschereck, D. (1995a). *A description of the mutual information approach and the variable similiarty metric* (Technical Report 944). Sankt Augustin, Germany, German National Research Center for Computer Science, Artificial Intelligence Research Division.

Wettschereck, D. (1995b). *Weighted kNN versus majority kNN: A recommendation* (Technical Report 943). Sankt Augustin, Germany, German National Research Center for Computer Science, Artificial Intelligence Research Division.

Wettschereck, D. & Dietterich, T. G. (1992). Improving the performance of radial basis function networks by learning center locations. In J. Moody, S. Hanson, & R. Lippmann (eds.), *Neural Information Processing Systems 4*. Denver, CO: Morgan Kaufmann.

Wettschereck, D. & Dietterich, T. G. (1995). An experimental comparison of the nearest neighbor and nearest hyperrectangle algorithms. *Machine Learning* 19: 5–28.

Wolpert, D. H. (1990). Constructing a generalizer superior to NETtalk via a mathematical theory of generalization. *Neural Networks* **3**: 445–452.

Wolpert, D. H. (1994). Personal communication.

Yau, H. C. & Manry, M. T. (1991). Iterative improvement of a nearest neighbor classifier. *Neural Networks* **4**: 517–524.

Zhang, J. (1990). A method that combines inductive learning with exemplar-based learning. In *Proceedings for Tools for Artificial Intelligence*, pp. 31–37. Herndon, VA: IEEE Computer Society Press.

Artificial Intelligence Review **11**: 315–342, 1997.
© 1997 *Kluwer Academic Publishers.*

Lazy Acquisition of Place Knowledge

PAT LANGLEY[1,3], KARL PFLEGER[2] and MEHRAN SAHAMI[3]
[1] *Institute for the Study of Learning and Expertise, 2164 Staunton Court, Palo Alto, CA 94306*
E-mail: Langley@cs.stanford.edu
[2] *Knowledge Systems Laboratory, Computer Science Department, Stanford University, Stanford, CA 94305*
E-mail: KPfleger@hpp.stanford.edu
[3] *Robotics Laboratory, Computer Science Department, Stanford University, Stanford, CA 94305*
E-mail: sahami@cs.stanford.edu

Abstract. In this paper we define the task of place learning and describe one approach to this problem. Our framework represents distinct places as evidence grids, a probabilistic description of occupancy. Place recognition relies on nearest neighbor classification, augmented by a registration process to correct for translational differences between the two grids. The learning mechanism is lazy in that it involves the simple storage of inferred evidence grids. Experimental studies with physical and simulated robots suggest that this approach improves place recognition with experience, that it can handle significant sensor noise, that it benefits from improved quality in stored cases, and that it scales well to environments with many distinct places. Additional studies suggest that using historical information about the robot's path through the environment can actually reduce recognition accuracy. Previous researchers have studied evidence grids and place learning, but they have not combined these two powerful concepts, nor have they used systematic experimentation to evaluate their methods' abilities.

Key words: place acquisition, case-based learning, evidence grids, robot learning

1. Introduction and Basic Concepts

A physical agent exists in an environment, and knowledge about that environment can aid its achievement of goals. One important type of environmental knowledge concerns the spatial arrangement of the agent's surroundings. For this reason, research on the representation, use, and acquisition of spatial knowledge has occupied an important role in the field of robotics. However, work on spatial learning has seldom made contact with the systematic experimental methodology that predominates in other areas of machine learning. In this paper, we consider a novel approach to this area that incorporates ideas from both of these disciplines.

We begin with some definitions of concepts and tasks that appear central to spatial reasoning. Consider a physical agent, say a robot, that is situated in the world. We can say that:

Definition 1. The POSITION of an agent is a coordinate in 2D or 3D space.

Position corresponds to ground truth, giving the actual location of the agent in some established coordinate system. We might also define the related concept of agent *orientation*, but here we will assume the agent has a 360 degree field of view, making this notion unnecessary.

A physical agent does not typically have direct access to knowledge of its position, but it does have indirect information.

Definition 2. A SENSOR READING is a description of the environment around the agent's position that has been filtered through its sensors.

The information in sensor readings may be imperfect in various ways. For example, it may be incomplete in that it describes only certain characteristics of the local environment, and it may be noisy in that sensor readings for the same position may produce different results at different times.

Nevertheless, the agent must find some way to use this information to make useful inferences. This suggests a natural task for a physical agent:

Definition 3. LOCALIZATION involves determining the position of the agent in the environment from a set of sensor readings.

Other tasks, such as navigating from position A to position B, are certainly possible. But an agent cannot begin to carry out such a task without first knowing A and without knowing when it has achieved B. Thus, localization seems more basic than navigation, and we will focus our attention on it here.

However, in many situations humans seem to care less about their exact position in space than about more abstract spatial regions. This suggests another, somewhat different, concept:

Definition 4. A PLACE is a contiguous set of positions in 2D or 3D space.

Robotics researchers have paid relatively little attention to the notion of place, but its central role in human spatial reasoning suggests it deserves a closer look. Naturally, this new concept lets us define an associated performance task by analogy with the localization task:

Definition 5. PLACE RECOGNITION involves determining the place in which the agent currently resides from a set of sensor readings.

At least in principle, the place recognition task seems more tractable (in terms of accuracy) than localization, in that it transforms a problem of numeric prediction into one involving discrete classification. One can also carry out localization within the context of a given place, and this in turn may be easier than global localization. Navigation between two places may also be simpler than navigation between two positions, as the former involves less precision than the latter.

Of course, reliance on places rather than positions also introduces a problem: one must specify some descriptions in memory that let the agent map sensor readings onto place names. One might attempt to enter such descriptions manually, but it seems desirable to automate this process, suggesting a final task:

Definition 6. PLACE LEARNING involves the induction of descriptions, from the sensor readings and place names for a set of training positions, that let the agent accurately recognize the places of novel positions.

Note that this task formulation makes minimal demands on the teacher, who does not have to give the agent information about its actual positions. Rather, the agent collects its own sensor readings, and the teacher must only label each reading as an instance of one place or another. This formulation assumes supervised training data, but unsupervised versions, in which the agent decides on its own place names, are also possible. We will touch briefly on unsupervised place learning in Section 5, but we will focus on the supervised version in this paper.

In the pages that follow, we present one approach to dealing with knowledge about places. First we describe a representational formalism for storing place knowledge – evidence grids – and then examine a method for place recognition that operates on this representation, along with a simple learning process that acquires and refines knowledge of places. This approach to place learning is *lazy* rather than *eager*, in that the storage process involves only the retention of evidence grids, while generalization occurs at retrieval time, during the matching of new grids against those in memory. After describing this approach, we present some hypotheses about its behavior and some experimental tests of those hypotheses, then present some additional studies of the role that historical information plays in place recognition. Finally, we review related work on spatial learning and discuss some directions for future work.

One important difference between our approach and earlier robotics work on spatial knowledge lies in our incorporation of ideas from the experimental study of machine learning.[1] In particular, we view place recognition as a classification task and we view place learning as a supervised concept induction task. This suggests not only certain learning methods, but also the use of experimental methods prevalent in machine learning (Kibler and Langley, 1988) to evaluate our technique. However, the tasks of place recognition and place learning introduce some difficulties not usually present in such learning research, such as the pervasive presence of significant sensor noise, and our approach to the problem is designed with these issues in mind. These tasks also provide some information not available for most classification problems, such as historical context about previous places, which we consider later in the paper.

2. Representation, Use, and Acquisition of Place Knowledge

With the above definitions in hand, we can examine one approach to learning place knowledge. However, before we address the acquisition process, we should first consider the manner in which we represent knowledge about places and the performance element that takes advantage of that spatial knowledge base.

2.1. *The Evidence Grid Representation*

Robotics researchers have explored a variety of formalisms for representing spatial knowledge. One approach relies on geometric primitives to describe the edges or surfaces of obstacles in the environment. For example, one can use a set of lines to approximate the walls of an office and the furniture it contains. Such representations are precise, but Schiele and Crowley (1994) note that they can be difficult to use when sensors are noisy.

Another common scheme involves dividing the environment into a rectangular grid of mutually exclusive cells, each corresponding to a distinct position in space. In this framework, each cell is specified as either occupied (containing an obstacle) or open (containing none). This approach is well suited to navigation tasks in which one already knows the structure of the environment (i.e., which cells are occupied) and the position of the agent within the grid. However, this scheme is not designed to handle the uncertainty that arises when the position is unknown or when the agent has yet to learn the structure of the environment.

---

[1] Other work in robotic learning (e.g., Atkeson 1989; Moore 1990) has fared much better in terms of experimental methodology, especially in the use of well-defined performance tasks.

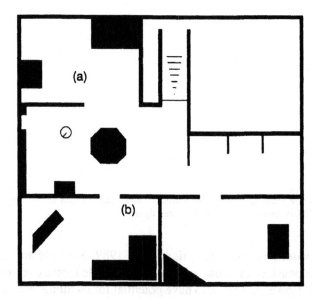

Figure 1. A simulated office environment with a number of distinct places.

An alternative framework uses the *evidence grid* (Elfes 1989; Moravec and Blackwell 1992), a data structure that is specifically designed to tolerate uncertainty. In this approach, each cell C has an associated probability that C is occupied by some tangible object that would block the agent's path if it tried to move through the cell. These probabilities range from near zero (nearly certain a cell is open) to near one (nearly certain a cell is occupied), with the middle corresponding to cells for which little information is available (e.g., behind a wall or inside an object). We will adopt this framework in the current paper.

Figure 1 shows the position of an agent in a room within a larger office environment, similar in structure to an actual area at Stanford University. Figure 2 depicts evidence grids constructed from simulated sensor readings taken from positions (a) in the top left room and (b) in the lower left room from the same orientation. Open regions within the agent's view have low probability of being occupied (lighter shades), whereas edges of obstacles and walls within view have high probability (darker shades). However, areas that are occluded, such as those behind obstacles and walls, have probabilities around $\frac{1}{2}$ (empty regions), since the agent's sensors provide no information about them. Of course, the agent can construct a more complete evidence grid by moving around the environment to collect sensor readings from different viewpoints.

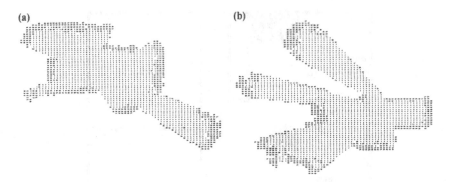

Figure 2. Evidence grids generated from simulated sonar readings for (a) the top left room in Figure 1 and (b) the lower left room in the same figure.

Previous work with evidence grids (Elfes 1989; Moravec and Blackwell 1992) has emphasized their use in representing single rooms over a relatively short period. However, they also have potential for handling large-scale spatial knowledge over longer time spans. An agent could store its knowledge about an entire building or even a city in a single, large evidence grid. But this scheme seems impractical due to the difficulties inherent in integrating information from distant regions into a single map.

A more tractable approach to representing large-scale spatial knowledge, which we take here, involves storage of separate evidence grids for each distinct place. For example, one might use a different grid to encode each room in a building. This knowledge can be augmented by geometric relations among places, which would support navigation planning, but we will not address that aspect here. The retention of place descriptions in memory has much in common with the storage of a *case library* in work on case-based reasoning (Aamodt and Plaza 1994; Kolodner 1993). In both frameworks, the stored items represent alternative situations in which the agent can find itself, and which suggest different inferences.

2.2. *Lazy Recognition of Places*

Now that we have described the nature of evidence grids, we can examine their use in place recognition. Let us assume the agent has a stored place library, with each place described as an $R \times C$ evidence grid with an associated place name. Our approach to place recognition relies on a three-step process that, like other lazy methods, carries out much of the induction at performance time.

First, the agent constructs a temporary or short-term evidence grid for its current position from a set of sensor readings. This involves transforming each sensor reading into a probability of occupancy for each cell. Following Moravec and Blackwell (1992), we assume a sensor model that specifies this mapping. The result is a temporary evidence grid, based on the sensor reading, that characterizes the region in the vicinity of the agent. The agent may repeat this process a number of times, in each case incorporating the result into the temporary grid using a Bayesian updating scheme. We will not describe this updating process in depth, but readers can find details in Elfes (1989) and in Moravec and Blackwell (1992).

Next, the agent matches the short-term evidence grid against each of the grids stored in the place library. The evaluation function used in this comparison process measures the degree of match between two grids. Specifically, if $S_{r,c}$ is the probability associated with the rth of R rows and the cth of C columns for the short-term grid, and if $L_{r,c}$ is the analogous probability for the stored, long-term grid, then

$$M = \sum_r^R \sum_c^C F(S_{r,c}, L_{r,c})$$

computes the similarity between the short-term and stored grids. One can instantiate the function F in many ways, provided they satisfy certain properties: two cells should be treated as similar if they are confident in the same direction, as dissimilar if they are confident in opposite directions, and generally ignored if either is uncertain.

Moravec and Blackwell (1992) implement this cell-to-cell component of grid similarity as the expression

$$F(S_{r,c}, L_{r,c}) = log_2 \left[S_{r,c}L_{r,c} + (1 - S_{r,c})(1 - L_{r,c}) \right] + 1,$$

which varies from one (a perfect match) to negative infinity (the worst possible match). Reflection suggests that this scheme might give very low match scores to reasonably similar grids if even a few cells are confident in opposite directions. For this reason, we decided to use an alternative metric:

$$F(S_{r,c}, L_{r,c}) = \begin{cases} 1 & \text{if } S_{r,c} > \frac{2}{3} \text{ and } L_{r,c} > \frac{2}{3} \\ 1 & \text{if } S_{r,c} < \frac{1}{3} \text{ and } L_{r,c} < \frac{1}{3} \\ -1 & \text{if } S_{r,c} > \frac{2}{3} \text{ and } L_{r,c} < \frac{1}{3} \\ -1 & \text{if } S_{r,c} < \frac{1}{3} \text{ and } L_{r,c} > \frac{2}{3} \\ 0 & \text{otherwise .} \end{cases}$$

We felt this measure would be less sensitive to situations in which disagreements arise between cells having high certainty, thus eliminating the problem predicted for the Moravec/Blackwell measure. There is nothing special about the choice of $\frac{1}{3}$ and $\frac{2}{3}$ as thresholds, as few cells have probabilities near them; the important point is to divide experience into three qualitative states.

The above metrics assume that the stored and temporary grids are described in the same coordinate system. One can plausibly assume the presence of a reasonably accurate compass to determine the relative rotations, but possible differences in translation requires some form of registration that coerces the temporary evidence grid into the same coordinate system as the stored place. To this end, our system carries out an exhaustive search using operators that modify the position by one grid row or column, evaluating each alternative using the metric M defined above.[2] The system selects the translation that gives the highest M score; the resulting registered grid localizes the agent with respect to that grid. If the compass is not accurate, one can extend this approach to correct for small offsets in rotation.

Finally, the agent compares the match scores for the various registered grids and selects the best of these competitors. This strategy provides both the place name associated with the selected evidence grid and the estimated position within that place description. Because adjacent evidence grids may cover overlapping regions, this scheme has some potential for misclassifying a place based on its outlying rather than its central cells. An alternative strategy would let the agent associate distinct place names with different cells in the same stored grid, then predict the name specified for the cell nearest to the estimated position. However, this issue has not been a problem in our studies to date, so our current system relies on the simpler classification strategy.

As we noted earlier, this approach has much in common with other methods for lazy recognition. Here the evidence grids in the place library correspond to stored experiences, whereas the short-term grid maps on to a test case for which one wants to make a prediction. The match function corresponds to the similarity metric that determines the nearness of the test case to each stored case in an $R \times C$ dimensional space, and the final classification step is similar to that used in the nearest neighbor method, perhaps the simplest lazy technique. The fact that each evidence grid is a probabilistic summary, computed from a set of sensor readings, differs from the prototypical lazy approach, but some systems partially generalize from experience at storage time. A more intriguing difference concerns the registration process. Many

---

[2] When translation causes two grids to overlap on only $R' \times C'$ cells, the metric uses only these cells in its summation. This creates a bias toward stored grids that share more cells with the temporary grid, which seems reasonable, but it does not actively punish a stored grid for having only partial overlap. Although the current registration algorithm is exhaustive and thus computationally expensive, Alan Schultz (personal communication, 1995) reports encouraging results with a more efficient registration algorithm that uses genetic search with a similar match function.

lazy systems incorporate some *adaptation* method (Aamodt and Plaza 1994; Leake 1994), but usually this occurs after retrieval, whereas here adaptation (registration) takes place during the evaluation (match) process itself.

2.3. *Lazy Learning of Place Knowledge*

Now let us consider an approach to learning place knowledge that is stored as evidence grids. We would like an incremental process, since the agent encounters its environment sequentially. However, we are not concerned here with the task of effectively exploring an unknown world, so we will assume that the agent is led to a position, given time to observe its surroundings, given a place name, led to another position, and so forth.

Given our commitment to a place library and to a method for place recognition described above, we naturally assume a lazy learning scheme. In particular, at each position to which it is led, the agent constructs a short-term evidence grid S using the method described above. The system then simply adds the new grid to the place library, along with the specified place name. The same place name may be associated with multiple evidence grids, but this seems appropriate if they produce different sensor readings.

At first glance, this approach to place learning sounds guaranteed to work, in that one simply stores a description for each place, after which recognition will be perfect. However, this view ignores the central feature of the task – uncertainty. Even with noise-free sensors, the same place typically looks different from different positions, if only because different regions are occluded. Moreover, standard robotic sensors such as sonar are notoriously noisy, and will produce different sensor readings, and thus different evidence grids, even when repeated from the same position.

In addition, the dimensionality of the resulting space is high, with one attribute for each cell in the $R \times C$ evidence grid. Among others, Aha (1990) and Langley and Sage (in press) have shown that the learning rate of lazy methods like nearest neighbor can be drastically slowed by the presence of irrelevant attributes. Since typical rooms contain large open areas, it seems plausible that the cells that describe such areas will make place learning difficult. Thus, the adequacy of this approach remains an open question that is best answered by experiment.

2.4. *Lazy vs. Eager Approaches to Place Learning*

In addition to the lazy approach to place learning we have described above, we also considered eager methods that incorporated the evidence grid representation. However, the latter proved problematic in that nearly all eager learning methods, including connectionist and decision-tree techniques, assume a fixed set of attributes or features,[3] whereas evidence grids can have different sizes and thus different numbers of cells.

We considered one response to this problem that would coerce the training grids into a single size by padding extra cells with $\frac{1}{2}$ probabilities, thus ensuring a fixed feature set. However, this scheme would not guarantee that still larger grids would not occur in the test set, which would make it difficult to apply the learned knowledge. Moreover, this strategy would increase the number of features in an already high-dimensional space, exacerbating the effect of irrelevant attributes.

The need to register evidence grids also poses difficulties for purely eager methods. Although one can imagine an eager learning scheme inducing higher-order, translation-invariant features, this would seem to require many more training grids than our lazy approach, since it would need to find regularities over many translated grids of the same places. An alternative approach would coerce all training grids for a given place into a single coordinate system, then use an eager method to learn place descriptions in terms of those coordinates. However, the resulting system would still have a strong lazy component, in that test grids would still require registration.

In summary, the evidence grid framework lends itself nicely to a lazy approach to place recognition and learning, but raises significant problems for eager techniques. Of course, this does not imply that eager approaches to place learning are impossible, as we will find in Section 4 when we discuss related work on this task. But for now our focus will remain on the lazy framework outlined above.

3. Experimental Studies of Place Learning

In Section 1 we formulated the place learning task in terms similar to those used to describe other induction problems. Thus, we can use the experimental methods developed for machine learning to evaluate the robustness of our framework. In this section we present a number of hypotheses about the system's behavior, followed by experimental tests of those hypotheses, most of which we have reported previously (Langley and Pfleger 1995). Our primary measure of performance was recognition accuracy for places in a test set of evidence grids that differ from those in the training set.

---

[3] The main exceptions are methods for inductive logic programming (Lavrac and Dzeroski, 1993), but their first-order representations hardly seem suitable for dealing with evidence grids.

3.1. *The Experimental Setting*

The experiments we designed to evaluate the abilities of our approach relied on both a physical robot – a Nomad 200 with a 16-sensor sonar ring – and a high-fidelity simulation of this machine. The physical environment was a suite of offices and common areas at Stanford University, and the simulated environment was an idealized layout of a similar suite, depicted earlier in Figure 1. We used the physical Nomad to ensure realism in our results, while the simulation gave us experimental control over device parameters not possible with the actual robot.

We generated each training or test case by placing the physical or simulated robot in a position, collecting readings from the sonar ring to construct an initial evidence grid (Elfes, 1989), rotating and/or moving the robot (as described below), collecting new sonar readings and updating the evidence grid, and repeating this process many times. For the simulated robot, we generated six different grids for each of six distinct places,[4] giving 36 total evidence grids. For the physical robot, we produced only three grids for each place (because the process took longer), giving 18 total grids.

The Nomad simulator incorporates a number parameters that affect the quality of sonar information. For example, the `error` parameter controls random variation in the distance returned by the sonar sensors, `critical` controls the angle of incidence at which specular reflection occurs (giving distances farther than the actual ones), and `halfcone` controls the angular width of each sonar signal. Unless otherwise specified, we set `error` to 0.15, which was our best estimate of the error encountered by the physical robot, and we left all other parameters at their default values, which produce a 25 degree field of view for each sensor and specular reflection at angles of incidence with the sensed surface of 30 degrees or less.

For each experimental condition with the simulated environment, we ran the learning system 400 times with different random partitions of the evidence grids into 33 training and three test cases, randomly ordering the storage of training cases. For the physical environment, we randomly partitioned the grids into 17 training cases (with randomized orders) and one test case, again averaging over 400 runs for each condition.

3.2. *Improving Place Recognition with Experience*

Following Kibler and Langley (1988), we can divide the factors that affect the learner's behavior into two broad types, those involving characteristics

---

[4]These places corresponded to the lower left, lower right, middle right, and upper left rooms in Figure 1, and to the areas to the left and right of the octagonal table in the figure.

Table 1. Confusion matrices with probabilities of labeling for the six places used in the experiments. Rows indicate the correct place names, whereas columns show the predicted place after training.

PHYSICAL ROBOT						
	(a)	(b)	(c)	(d)	(e)	(f)
(a)	1	0	0	0	0	0
(b)	0	1	0	0	0	0
(c)	0	0	1	0	0	0
(d)	0	0	$\frac{2}{3}$	$\frac{1}{3}$	0	0
(e)	$\frac{2}{3}$	0	$\frac{1}{3}$	0	0	0
(f)	0	0	0	0	0	1

SIMULATED ROBOT						
	(a)	(b)	(c)	(d)	(e)	(f)
(a)	$\frac{5}{6}$	0	$\frac{1}{6}$	0	0	0
(b)	0	1	0	0	0	0
(c)	0	0	1	0	0	0
(d)	0	0	$\frac{1}{6}$	$\frac{5}{6}$	0	0
(e)	0	0	$\frac{1}{6}$	0	$\frac{5}{6}$	0
(f)	0	0	0	0	0	1

of the environment and those involving features of the learner. The most basic environmental characteristic is the number of training cases available. Naturally, we hypothesized that the accuracy of place recognition would improve as the agent encounters more positions. However, the literature sometimes reports actual decreases in performance, so we needed to explicitly test this expectation.

As we report elsewhere (Langley and Pfleger, 1995), our first study used the physical Nomad robot to generate 18 evidence grids based on 45 sonar readings, taken from a single position but with successive rotations incremented by one degree (though still merged into a stored grid with a single orientation). As expected, the system's ability to recognize places gradually increases as it observes and stores more training cases. However, the learning task is not trivial, in that multiple cases for each place are needed to achieve even 70% accuracy.

Inspection of the inferred structures reveals that, from certain views, the registered evidence grids for two different places occasionally appear more similar than the grids for two different positions within the same place. This should not be surprising, given the noise inherent in sonar sensors and given that objects can occlude portions of a place from some positions. Table 1 shows the actual confusions that occur, on average, for the physical robot after 17 training cases; because we included three grids for each place and used leave-one-out to estimate error rates, all entries are divisible by three. The table reveals that most errors involve the misclassification of place (e), which is confused with places (a) and (c), and the mislabeling of (d), which is classified as (c).

We also found that runs with the simulated robot produce a learning curve with a very similar shape to that for the physical device, but that the rate of learning is somewhat higher. Table 1 also shows the averaged confusion matrix for this experimental condition after the learner has seen 35 training

(a)   (b)

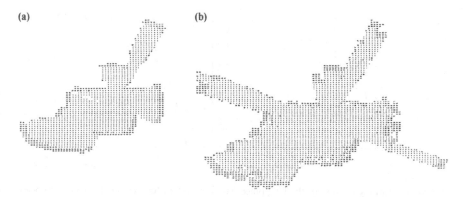

Figure 3. Evidence grids generated from 45 simulated sonar readings for the lower left room in Figure 1 using (a) zero sensor noise and (b) a 0.45 noise setting.

cases; here we used six grids for each place, so each entry is divisible by six. Although a few errors still occur, the performance component generally assigns the correct place name to the test cases. The same experiment revealed that the method's ability to identify the precise position of the robot within a given place, based on the registration process, also improved with training.

3.3. *Sensor Noise and Grid Quality*

The amount of sensor noise constitutes a more interesting environmental factor. We might expect increased noise to reduce the asymptotic accuracy, as it can produce confusions between similar places, but it should have an even greater effect on the rate of place learning, in that it should increase the number of training cases needed to reach a given accuracy level. Nevertheless, we hoped that the probabilistic nature of evidence grids would let our approach degrade gracefully with increasing amounts of sensor noise.

Figure 3 shows two evidence grids constructed from simulated sonar signals collected from the same position and orientation within the lower left room in Figure 1. For grid (a), we set the simulator's error parameter to zero, so that there was no sensor noise. For grid (b), we set this parameter to 0.45, producing significant noise. The resulting evidence grids are similar but contain noticeable differences, suggesting that the basic inference method is robust but that sensor noise also has some effect.[5]

Fortunately, our reliance on evidence grids suggests a natural response to noisy sense data. Because each stored grid can be based on multiple sensor

---

[5] The inferred "arms" in (b) appear to be artifacts of the grid updating scheme; the more generic effect of sensor noise is to create more ragged boundaries along the edges of objects.

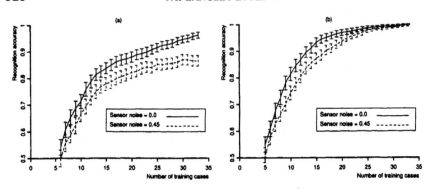

Figure 4. Learning curves for the lazy place learning system for two levels of sensor noise when evidence grids are based on (a) 45 readings from one position and (b) 90 readings from two nearby positions.

signals, we can attempt to improve the *quality* of these grids by increasing the number, or altering the arrangement, of the signals used to generate them. We hypothesized that place descriptions based on more sensor readings would be less affected by increases in sensor noise. Thus, we predicted an interaction between these two independent variables, specifically one that affects both learning rate and asymptotic accuracy.

To test this hypothesis, we used the Nomad simulator to produce four different levels of sensor noise, in which the error parameter was set to 0.0, 0.15, 0.30, and 0.45, respectively. We also attempted to vary the quality of the stored grids by using two different sensing strategies. In one, we based each evidence grid (both training and test cases) on 45 sonar readings collected from a single position but produced at orientations one degree apart, as used to generate the earlier results. In the other, we based each grid on 90 readings, produced by repeating this strategy in two nearby positions within the same room.

Figure 4 (a) shows the learning curves that result for the zero and 0.45 noise levels using the one-position sensing strategy, whereas Figure 4 (b) presents analogous results for the two-position strategy. (The results for the 0.15 and 0.3 settings fell between these extremes; we have omitted them for the sake of clarity.) The two-position scheme clearly fares better than the simpler strategy, and the curves generally agree with our predictions. The rate of learning for the two-position method is much higher than for the one-position method, even when no sensor noise is present. Also, the introduction of sensor noise clearly affects both strategies, but it alters only the learning rate for the more sophisticated scheme, while it actually appears to reduce the asymptotic recognition accuracy for the simpler one.

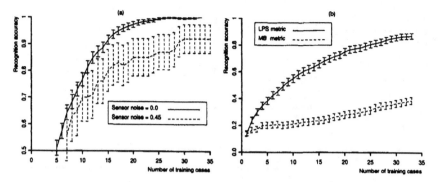

Figure 5. (a) Learning curves for two levels of sensor noise when evidence grids are based on 45 readings taken at equal intervals along a line between two positions. (b) Learning curves using the Langley/Pfleger/Sahami (LPS) similarity metric and the Moravec/Blackwell (MB) metric.

The general superiority of the two-position strategy is hardly surprising, in that its evidence grids are based on twice as many sonar readings. Ideally, we would prefer a sensing scheme that is robust with respect to noise but that requires no more sensing than the initial strategy. To this end, we explored a third method that takes three sonar readings at an initial position, with rotational increments of 7.5 degrees, moves a fixed amount along a straight line and takes another three readings in the same manner, then repeats this process until completing a total of 45 readings. The resulting evidence grid is based on sensing over the entire path, reducing the chance of occlusion and hopefully reducing the effect of sensor noise.

Figure 5 (a) presents learning curves for this sensing strategy on two of the simulated noise levels. For the noise-free situation, the behavior is nearly identical to that for the 90-reading strategy, even though grids are based on half as many sonar signals. However, sensor noise significantly degrades this strategy's behavior, though its accuracies remain well above those for the one-position method. Clearly, basing evidence grids on a number of distinct positions within a given place gives better results than basing them on one position, but increasing the number of readings also has desirable effects. It seems likely that more sophisticated sensing strategies, which sample readings in a more intelligent manner, would produce even better results.

3.4. *Effect of the Similarity Metric*

In Section 2.2 we described the similarity metric used to assign a short-term evidence grid to the stored grid that best matches it. This metric sums over the cells on which the two grids overlap, using a function F to measure the similarity of individual cells. We contrasted our implementation of F,

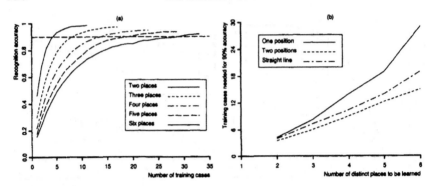

Figure 6. (a) Learning curves for different numbers of distinct places, based on 45 sonar readings from one position. (b) Scaling curves that map, for different sensing strategies, the number of training cases needed to achieve 90% accuracy as a function of the number of places.

which takes on the values 1, 0, and −1, with the implementation used by Moravec and Blackwell (1992), which ranges from one to negative infinity. We presented some intuitive arguments for preferring our formulation, but the question of which measure behaves better in practice is ultimately an empirical one.

Figure 5 (b) presents experimental results for the two similarity metrics, using training and test cases from six places based on 45 simulated sonar readings from one position. The learning curve for our version of the F function is similar to those we have seen earlier in the paper. In contrast, the curve for the Moravec and Blackwell metric reveals learning at a much slower rate, reaching only 39% accuracy after 33 training cases, as compared with 87% for our measure. These results do not imply that our approach is the only viable option, but they do show that the similarity measure can make a substantial difference in place recognition, and that our metric performs much better than one proposed alternative, at least on this task.

3.5. *Number of Distinct Places*

Some real-world environments contain many distinct places, making it desirable for a learning method to scale well as the number of places increases. We obtained preliminary results along these lines by examining our algorithm's behavior with different subsets of the places available in our environment. Figure 6 (a) shows the learning curves that result for two through six places, with each grid based on 45 simulated sonar readings from one position. Each reported accuracy is averaged over 400 runs for each possible subset of k out of six places, using 35 randomly selected training cases and one test case. Thus, when $k = 2$ we carried out $\binom{6}{2} \times 400 = 6000$ runs, and when $k = 3$

we carried out $\left(\begin{smallmatrix} 6 \\ 3 \end{smallmatrix}\right) \times 400 = 8000$ runs. We have not reported confidence intervals here, since the accuracies are averages of averages.

Naturally, increasing the number of places decreases the speed of learning, but we can also examine the rate of this decrease. Note that the figure also shows where each learning curve crosses the level of 90 percent accuracy. These crossover points produce the *scaling* curve in Figure 6 (b), which maps the number of distinct places against the number of training cases needed to reach this accuracy level. This higher-order curve seems to be either linear or quadratic, but the analogous scaling curves for the two-position and straight-line sensing strategies, also shown, definitely appear linear. These results suggest that our approach requires, more or less, a fixed number of training cases per place, independent of the total number of places. This encourages us to believe that the method will scale well to domains that involve many more different places than the six we have examined, though ultimately we should test this prediction using larger environments.

3.6. *Summary of Experimental Results*

In this section, we reported on a number experiments designed to evaluate our lazy approach to the acquisition of place knowledge. We used a method common in research on machine learning, stating explicit hypotheses and running experiments designed to test them. In each case, we varied one or two independent variables and observed their effects on some performance measure.

The experiments revealed a number of encouraging behaviors. Our approach to place learning generally improves its recognition accuracy as it observes more training cases, with similar results occurring for both the physical and simulated robot. The learning rate slows in the presence of sensor noise, but one can mitigate this effect by increasing the quality of the inferred evidence grids. The rate of learning also slows with increasing numbers of places, but no more than expected in any multiclass learning situation. In addition, we found that our similarity metric performs significantly better than another metric proposed in the literature on this domain.

Clearly, there exist many other factors that could influence the behavior of our place-learning method. These include the resolution of the evidence grids and the distinctiveness of the places one must learn to distinguish. However, we will reserve these issues for future studies, as the current experiments have been sufficient to show that our approach is a promising one.

4. The Role of History in Place Learning

The above experiments dealt with place recognition in isolation, but this seems unrealistic for most robotics settings.[6] More often, a physical agent will have strong expectations about its current place based on knowledge about the place it has just left. Such historical information about the connections among places should be particularly useful for distinguishing between places that are otherwise similar.

One can encode knowledge of this sort in a topological map that takes the form of a Markov model. Each node in the map corresponds to a distinct place, while links indicate adjacency relations between pairs of places, along with the probability of moving from one place to a neighbor. Each node also specifies the prior probability that the agent is located there, lacking other information. In this section we provide an analysis of this framework, followed by initial experiments on the effects of previous place knowledge that moves beyond our earlier work.

4.1. Analysis of Historical Information

Suppose a robot has constructed an evidence grid E based on sensor information, and we would like to predict the current place C based not only on E but also on knowledge about the place B in which the robot was previously. Mathematically, we would like to compute $P(C|E, B)$, the probability that the robot is in current place C given previous place B and evidence grid E. As we show in the Appendix, under simple assumptions this term can be rewritten as

$$P(C|E, B) = \frac{P(C|E)P(B|C)}{\sum_C [P(C|E)P(B|C)]} \quad .$$

However, to make this expression operational, we must define $P(B|C)$ and $P(C|E)$. We can expand the former to

$$P(B|C) = \frac{P(B)P(C|B)}{\sum_B P(B)P(C|B)} \quad ,$$

in which the terms $P(B)$ and $P(C|B)$ are known, provided we make Markov assumptions about the environment. We can expand the latter to

[6] Such place recognition might occur when a robot is first turned on or when it reenters a known place during exploration, but these hardly seem typical.

$$P(C|E) = \frac{\sum_g match(C_g, E)}{\sum_D \sum_h match(D_h, E)} \quad,$$

where the summation in the numerator is over all stored grids g for place C, where those in the denominator are over all places D and all grids h for those places, and where $match(K_j, E)$ is the match score between the stored evidence grid j for place K and the sensory grid E. This expansion only approximates $P(C|E)$, but the accuracy of the approximation should increase with the number of grids stored for each place.

The above method takes the "proper" Bayesian approach of using a weighted vote over all candidate grids, but it differs from the best-match scheme we used in our earlier studies. We can obtain an analogous probabilistic version of the best-match method by defining the probability of a place $P(C)$ given a grid E, $P(C|E)$, as

$$P(C|E) = \frac{\max_g match(C_g, E)}{\sum_D \max_h match(D_h, E)} \quad.$$

In the absence of information about previous places, this best-match expression should give the same predictions as the method described in Section 2.

We use a simple algorithm that incorporates these expressions to make predictions about the current place C. First we initialize the distribution over previous places $P(B)$; in the studies reported below, we assumed a uniform distribution. Next, for each possible place C, we define the term

$$R(C) = \sum_B [P(C|E, B)P(B)]$$

using the expressions described above, which includes the match score for the current evidence grid and which marginalizes over all possible previous places. We then predict the place C with the highest $R(C)$ probability. Finally, we use the $R(C)$ value for each place as the prior probability for each previous place in the next round of reasoning, and we update $P(B|C)$ using this new prior. This updating process makes the Markovian assumption that knowledge of previous places on the current time step depends only on knowledge of the previous time step. This seems reasonable, as we are not concerned with how the agent has reached its current location, but only with the location itself.

4.2. Experimental Studies with Historical Information

We designed a simulated environment that would let us evaluate experimentally the influence of historical knowledge on place recognition and learning. Figure 7 shows the layout, which includes two distinctive rooms, A and C,

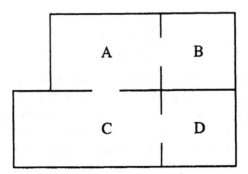

Figure 7. Simulated office environment with four rooms, two of which (B and D) should be difficult to distinguish without historical path information.

and two identical rooms, B and D. We hypothesized that both the averaging and best-match schemes would fare better in this domain when historical information was available than when it was absent. To provide an upper bound on the effect of history, we decided to include a condition in which the programmer told the classifier the correct label for the previous place, thus providing perfect knowledge of the previous path.[7]

We used the Nomad simulator to generate six grids for each place in this environment, giving a total of 24 grids, which we split into six disjoint sets, each containing one grid from each place. From these sets we generated six separate training/test splits by taking the union of five sets for training and reserving the remaining set for testing. For each group of training grids, we ran the learning system on ten distinct paths through the space; these were randomly selected from the possible paths of length seven or nine for the environment in Figure 7 in which each place was visited at least once, and excluding paths in which the robot remained in the same place across a time step. In addition to storing each training grid and its place name in memory, the learner used the training paths to estimate $P(C|B)$ for each combination of places. We measured the classification accuracy on the test set for each path and for each split, then averaged the scores.

The leftmost columns of Table 2 show the results, a number of which are unexpected. First, in the absence of historical information, the best-match scheme is 27% more accurate than the Bayesian averaging method. Even more surprising, the use of probabilistic historical knowledge, inferred from previous grids along the path, actually decreases the accuracy for both the best-match and averaging strategies. The availability of certain knowledge

---

[7] We also included a condition in which we gave the system the correct label for only its starting place. Although we do not report the precise results here, this condition always gave accuracies between those for probabilistic and certain historical knowledge.

Table 2. Place recognition accuracies (with standard errors in parentheses) with and without knowledge of previous places, for both averaging and best-match strategies, in environments with rooms that have open and closed doors.

Type of previous	Open Doors		Closed Doors	
place knowledge	Averaging	Best Match	Averaging	Best Match
None	0.611 (0.003)	0.878 (0.001)	0.908 (0.000)	0.908 (0.000)
Probabilistic	0.550 (0.002)	0.558 (0.007)	0.553 (0.004)	0.608 (0.004)
Certain	0.847 (0.001)	0.969 (0.000)	1.000 (0.000)	0.969 (0.000)

about the previous place, provided by the programmer, helps for both the best-match and the averaging methods.

Inspection of the evidence grids inferred for this environment gives a partial explanation of the behavior. Because the sonar signals reach into adjacent rooms, the grids for B and D can appear quite different, even though the rooms themselves are identical. In other words, sonar information about adjacent rooms provides context that offsets the advantage of historical knowledge about path traversal. Moreover, this situation can lead to high variation in the grids generated for different positions within a given place, as the adjacent room will only be visible from some viewpoints.

These observations explain why knowledge of previous places provides little aid in this environment, but not why the probabilistic version actually hurts accuracy. Our hypothesis for this effect is that even occasional errors in place recognition early in the robot's path propagate to decisions later in the path, causing errors that do not occur when using only sensory information. This explanation is supported by the fact that, when provided by the programmer, historical information increased rather than reduced accuracy.

Because rooms were more distinguishable than we had expected, we decided to repeat the study with a similar environment that had closed doors. This configuration should remove any sensory context and thus make rooms B and D more difficult to discriminate. Table 2 also shows the results of this experimental condition. The main difference from the previous world is that the averaging and best-match methods give identical results in the absence of historical knowledge, which can be explained by the reduction in variability among the stored grids for each place. However, the use of probabilistic knowledge about previous places still reduces accuracy for both strategies over simple use of the current evidence grid.[8] As before,

---

[8] Because places A and C occur more often than B and D in this environment, the expected accuracy is 82% for the closed-door world in the absence of historical knowledge, but this is considerably lower than the 91% observed. Inspection of the confusion matrix shows that, as expected, place D was misclassified half of the time, but that B was always correctly classified.

programmer-provided historical knowledge improves both strategies, again suggesting that classification errors early in the path are responsible for the decrements with the probabilistic scheme.

These results raise serious questions about the usefulness of topological knowledge to constrain the process of place recognition. At least for the techniques and environments explored to date, the simple use of sensory information, transformed into an evidence grid and combined with a lazy classification method, appears to be the method of choice. Historical information can aid place recognition, but only when this knowledge is accurate enough to keep from introducing new errors.

5. Related Work on Learning Spatial Knowledge

Our research on the acquisition of spatial knowledge is certainly not the first in this area. Clearly, our work owes a strong intellectual debt to Elfes (1989), Moravec and Blackwell (1992), and other developers of the evidence grid framework. Our basic representation and our performance system directly employ techniques developed by these researchers. However, most research in this framework has focused on the construction of a single global map, rather than a collection of evidence grids for distinct places. Although such approaches clearly acquire spatial knowledge, they do not involve induction in the sense of using training instances to improve performance on novel test cases, whereas our work on place learning fits easily into this paradigm. Thrun (1993) has used reinforcement learning to improve sensor interpretation for evidence-grid construction, but his goal was to construct a global map. Mahadevan (1992) describes a method that forms generalizations expressed as evidence grids, but his aim was to learn not places but action models.

Nevertheless, some researchers outside the evidence grid formalism have studied place learning. For example, Yamauchi and Beer (1996) describe ELDEN, a system that represents places in terms of means and variances of direct sensor readings, rather than inferred grid occupancies. Their place descriptions also include features for the robot's position as estimated through dead reckoning and connections to recently visited places. Place recognition involves passing each attribute's value through Gaussian functions associated with each place, then selecting the competitor with the highest sum. Learning consists of updating the means and variances for recognized places, creating new places when no existing ones match well enough, and adding predictive

---

This appeared to result from differences in the evidence grids due to specular reflection, which occurred more in B than in D due to chance.

connections between places. Yamauchi and Beer's reliance on a Gaussian distance metric makes their method similar to our approach, though ELDEN differs in the eager nature of its instance-averaging process, its use of raw sensor data, and the unsupervised nature of the learning processes.[9]

Lin, Hanson, and Judd (1994) have taken a similar approach to representing and using spatial knowledge. Their system also describes places[10] as means and variances of sonar readings and uses a Gaussian metric to determine the degree of match against the current sensor signals. However, their learning mechanisms, which are best described as eager rather than lazy, include not only the creation and updating of place descriptions, but also a reinforcement process designed to improve estimates of the robot's location. This latter technique can lead the learner to add a new place or remove an existing one if these actions reduce errors in location estimates.

Kuipers and Byun's (1988) NX system also operates on direct sensory readings, but it stores only places that are distinctive in terms of optimizing certain measures. For example, NX defines the central point in a hallway corner as being symmetrical and being equidistant from the walls, in addition to containing information about the angles and distances to obstacles. The system also describes edges, which connect distinctive places, in terms of length, width, and similar characteristics. Whenever NX encounters a local optimum L on one of its measures, it compares the sensor readings to each known place P stored in memory; if the descriptions for L and P are similar, and if their locations are metrically or topologically close, the system classifies L as the known place P. Otherwise, NX creates a new place based on L's description and stores this in memory, along with its edge connections to other places. This approach to place learning is lazy, like our own, in that little processing takes place at storage time. Mataric (1991) describes a similar scheme, though the details of place creation are different.

In methodological terms, Kortencamp and Weymouth's (1994) work is perhaps the most similar to our own. Their approach emphasizes *gateways* such as doors that connect two regions, but their system represents these locations using a grid structure and they evaluate its behavior in terms of recognition accuracy. However, their scheme uses hand-coded descriptions for a few gateway types to recognize candidate places and create new ones, rather than actual supervised training data, and they compare a number of

---

[9] Yamauchi and Beer's system also incorporates an evidence grid representation, but it constructs a global map and uses this map for correcting errors in dead reckoning rather than for place recognition.

[10] Lin et al. refer to their descriptions as *landmarks*. However, this term usually indicates a feature of the environment used to distinguish among different places, rather than to places themselves.

different recognition strategies, including one that combines evidence from sonar and visual sensors.

On another dimension, our approach is most similar to Yeap's (1988) work on spatial reasoning. His framework also posits the storage of distinct places, the descriptions of which are not direct sensory readings but inferred summaries. However, his "absolute space representation" does not take the form of evidence grids but rather consists of a connected sequence of line segments that, except for occasional openings, enclose an area. Yeap does not describe a performance element that uses these descriptions in place recognition but, as in our own framework, learning involves the simple storage of the inferred place descriptions, which suggests the use of a lazy method.

6. Concluding Remarks

Although our experimental studies of place learning have revealed some insight into our approach, clearly more work remains to be done. The most immediate extension would replace the current supervised learning method with an unsupervised one. Such a system must identify distinctive places on its own, as it cannot rely on a tutor for this information. To this end, we plan to employ a technique similar to that used by Anderson and Matessa (1992) for classification and by Yamauchi and Beer (1996) for place recognition, but adapted to operate on evidence grids rather than direct sensor descriptions. As the agent moves through the environment, it would regularly stop and construct a short-term evidence grid, merging this with the previous place description if the match is high enough and using the short-term grid as the basis for a new place otherwise.[11] Discontinuities caused by passage through doors and past obstacles should be enough to identify distinguishable places.

Most methods for place learning, including those discussed above, also construct topological maps that connect different places. Clearly, this is another important direction in which to extend our approach. We expect that storing rough estimates of the direction of movement between one place and its successor will be sufficient for many navigation tasks. Upon executing a navigation plan, the agent would still need to register its location upon entering each place along the path, but expectations about the next place and its rough translation should greatly simplify the registration process. Although our preliminary results with the use of historical information to reduce confusion among similar places were not entirely positive, it seems likely that including additional information, such as direction of movement,

---

[11] This scheme is somewhat less lazy than the current version, but the reliance on a sophisticated retrieval mechanism would remain.

would improve the situation. Such context should also reduce the computational complexity of place recognition by providing expected positions and orientations from which to hill climb toward a good registration.

In future work, we also hope to develop methods for detecting distinctive features in evidence grids that would simplify the place recognition process. We envision such features as being configurations of grid cells with large differences in their probabilities, such as might occur along a wall or at a door. The recognition mechanism would use the presence of these features as cues during retrieval of candidate places and during registration, and the learning process would use the features to index places in memory. Such learned features could also play the role of landmarks, in the sense used by Levitt, Lawton, Chelberg, and Nelson (1987), that qualitatively distinguish places. One simple approach to detecting useful configurations of grid cells would draw on recent methods for feature selection with nearest neighbor methods (e.g., Langley and Sage, in press), which use estimates of accuracy obtained through cross validation to direct search through the space of feature combinations.

In summary, we have presented a framework for representing, using, and learning knowledge about places in which evidence grids play a central role. Our approach draws on earlier work for updating these probabilistic summaries, but diverges from previous schemes by storing a set of local grids in a place library, then retrieving and matching them for use in place recognition. Experimental studies adapted from the machine learning literature indicate that this lazy approach improves recognition accuracy with experience, that sensor noise degrades the learning process, and that improving the quality of stored cases can offset this effect. The experiments also revealed that our method scales well to increased numbers of places, and that some of its power comes from the particular similarity metric used in the matching process. However, additional experiments suggested that using historical knowledge of the places just visited can reduce rather than increase accuracy. Many other environmental and system factors remain to be examined, but the basic approach to lazy learning of place knowledge appears promising and suggests many natural extensions.

Acknowledgements

We owe thanks to Hans Moravec for making his evidence grid software available for use, to Brian Yamauchi for integrating that code with the Nomad interface, to Cathay Yu for carrying at the experiments on historical information, and to Bill Adams for additional software support. Alan Schultz, Brian Yamauchi, and David Aha made many useful suggestions, as did the anonymous reviewers, and Barbara Hayes-Roth and Nils Nilsson provided access to a Nomadics robot. This research was supported in part by Grant Number N00014-94-1-0505 from the Office of Naval Research to the Institute for the Study of Learning and Expertise.

Appendix: Derivation of Previous Place Influences

Recall that our goal is to compute $P(C|E, B)$, the probability that the robot is in current place C given that previous place B and evidence grid E. By applying Bayes rule, we can rewrite the probability in question as

$$P(C|E, B) = \frac{P(E, B|C)P(C)}{P(E, B)} \quad .$$

Now we can expand the denominator by marginalizing over C, giving

$$P(C|E, B) = \frac{P(E, B|C)P(C)}{\sum_C [P(E, B|C)P(C)]} \quad .$$

If we are willing to assume that E and B are independent given C (as in the naive Bayesian classifier), we obtain

$$P(E, B|C) = P(E|C)P(B|C) \quad .$$

Substituting the above equation for $P(E, B|C)$ in our original expression, we have

$$P(C|E, B) = \frac{P(E|C)P(B|C)P(C)}{\sum_C [P(E|C)P(B|C)P(C)]}$$

and replacing $P(E|C)$ with $\frac{P(C|E)P(E)}{P(C)}$ (by Bayes Rule) gives

$$P(C|E, B) = \frac{\frac{P(C|E)P(E)}{P(C)} P(B|C)P(C)}{\sum_C [\frac{P(C|E)P(E)}{P(C)} P(B|C)P(C)]} \quad .$$

Cancelling the $P(C)$ terms in the numerator gives the simplified expression

$$P(C|E, B) = \frac{P(C|E)P(E)P(B|C)}{\sum_C [\frac{P(C|E)P(E)}{P(C)} P(B|C)P(C)]} \quad ,$$

whereas cancelling the $P(C)$ terms in the denominator gives

$$P(C|E,B) = \frac{P(C|E)P(E)P(B|C)}{\sum_C [P(C|E)P(E)P(B|C)]} \quad.$$

Since $P(E)$ is independent of C, we can move $P(E)$ out of the sum in the denominator, producing

$$P(C|E,B) = \frac{P(C|E)P(E)P(B|C)}{P(E)\sum_C [P(C|E)P(B|C)]} \quad.$$

Finally, we can cancel the $P(E)$ terms in the numerator and denominator to obtain

$$P(C|E,B) = \frac{P(C|E)P(B|C)}{\sum_C [P(C|E)P(B|C)]} \quad,$$

which can be expanded in a number of ways, as described in Section 4.

References

Aamodt, A. & Plaza, E. (1994). Case-based reasoning: Foundational issues, methodological variations, and system approaches. *AI Communications* 7: 39–59.

Aha, D. W. (1990). *A study of instance-based algorithms for supervised learning tasks: Mathematical, empirical, and psychological evaluations.* Doctoral dissertation, Department of Information & Computer Science, University of California, Irvine.

Anderson, J. R. & Matessa, M. (1992). Explorations of an incremental, Bayesian algorithm for categorization. *Machine Learning* 9: 275–308.

Atkeson, C. (1989). Using local models to control movement. In Touretzky, D. S. (ed.), *Advances in Neural Information Processing Systems* (Vol. 2). San Francisco: Morgan Kaufmann.

Elfes, A. (1989). Using occupancy grids for mobile robot perception and navigation. *IEEE Computer Magazine*, June, 46–58.

Kibler, D. & Langley, P. (1988). Machine learning as an experimental science. *Proceedings of the Third European Working Session on Learning* (pp. 81–92). Glasgow: Pittman.

Kolodner, J. L. (1993). *Case-based reasoning.* San Francisco: Morgan Kaufmann.

Kortencamp, D. & Weymouth, T. (1994). Topological mapping for mobile robots using a combination of sonar and vision sensing. *Proceedings of the Twelfth National Conference on Artificial Intelligence* (pp. 979–984). Seattle, WA: AAAI Press.

Kuipers, B. & Byun, Y. T. (1988). A robust, qualitative method for robot spatial learning. *Proceedings of the Eighth National Conference on Artificial Intelligence* (pp. 774–779). St. Paul, MN.

Langley, P. & Pfleger, K. (1995). Case-based acquisition of place knowledge. *Proceedings of the Twelfth International Conference on Machine Learning* (pp. 244–352). Lake Tahoe, CA: Morgan Kaufmann.

Langley, P. & Sage, S. (in press). Scaling to domains with irrelevant features. In Greiner, R., Petsche, T. & Hanson, S. J. (eds.), *Computational learning theory and natural learning systems* (Vol. 4). Cambridge, MA: MIT Press.

Lavrac, N. & Dzeroski, S. (1993). *Inductive logic programming: Techniques and applications.* New York: Ellis Horwood.

Leake, D. B. (1994). Case-based reasoning. *Knowledge Engineering Review* 9: 61–64.

Levitt, T. S, Lawton, D. T., Chelberg, D. M. & Nelson, P. C. (1987). Qualitative landmark-based path planning and following. *Proceedings of the Sixth National Conference on Artificial Intelligence* (pp. 689–694). Seattle, WA: AAAI Press.

Lin, L., Hanson, S. J. & Judd, J. S. (1994). *On-line learning for landmark-based navigation* (Technical Report No. SCR-94-TR-472). Princeton, NJ: Siemens Corporate Research, Learning Systems Department.

Mahadevan, S. (1992). Enhancing transfer in reinforcement learning by building stochastic models of robot actions. *Proceedings of the Ninth International Conference on Machine Learning* (pp. 290–299). Aberdeen: Morgan Kaufmann.

Mataric, M. J. (1991). Behavioral synergy without explicit integration. *Sigart Bulletin* 2: 130–133.

Moore, A. W. (1990). Acquisition of dynamic control knowledge for a robotic manipulator. *Proceedings of the Seventh International Conference on Machine Learning* (pp. 244–252). Austin, TX: Morgan Kaufmann.

Moravec, H. & Blackwell, M. (1992). Learning sensor models for evidence grids. *Robotics Institute Research Review*. Pittsburgh, PA: Carnegie Mellon University.

Schiele, B. & Crowley, J. L. (1994). A comparison of position estimation techniques using occupancy grids. *Robotics and Autonomous Systems* 12: 163–171.

Thrun, S. B. (1993). Exploration and model building in mobile robot domains. *Proceedings of the IEEE International Conference on Neural Networks*. San Francisco: IEEE.

Yamauchi, B. & Beer, R. (1994). Spatial learning for navigation in dynamic environments. *IEEE Transactions on Systems, Man, and Cybernetics – Part B* 26: 496–505.

Yeap, Y. K. (1988). Towards a computational theory of cognitive maps. *Artificial Intelligence* 34: 297–360.

Artificial Intelligence Review **11**: 343–370, 1997.
© 1997 *Kluwer Academic Publishers.*

A Teaching Strategy for Memory-Based Control

JOHN W. SHEPPARD and STEVEN L. SALZBERG
*Department of Computer Science, The Johns Hopkins University, Baltimore,
Maryland 21218*
E-mail: lastname@cs.jhu.edu

Abstract. Combining different machine learning algorithms in the same system can produce benefits above and beyond what either method could achieve alone. This paper demonstrates that genetic algorithms can be used in conjunction with lazy learning to solve examples of a difficult class of delayed reinforcement learning problems better than either method alone. This class, the class of differential games, includes numerous important control problems that arise in robotics, planning, game playing, and other areas, and solutions for differential games suggest solution strategies for the general class of planning and control problems. We conducted a series of experiments applying three learning approaches – lazy Q-learning, k-nearest neighbor (k-NN), and a genetic algorithm – to a particular differential game called a pursuit game. Our experiments demonstrate that k-NN had great difficulty solving the problem, while a lazy version of Q-learning performed moderately well and the genetic algorithm performed even better. These results motivated the next step in the experiments, where we hypothesized k-NN was having difficulty because it did not have good examples – a common source of difficulty for lazy learning. Therefore, we used the genetic algorithm as a bootstrapping method for k-NN to create a system to provide these examples. Our experiments demonstrate that the resulting joint system learned to solve the pursuit games with a high degree of accuracy – outperforming either method alone – and with relatively small memory requirements.

Key words: lazy learning, nearest neighbor, genetic algorithms, differential games, pursuit games, teaching, reinforcement learning

1. Introduction

When two people learn a task together, they can both benefit from the different skills that each brings to the table. The result is that both will learn better than they would have on their own. Likewise, machine learning methods should be able to work together to learn how to solve difficult problems. This paper describes how a lazy learning algorithm and a genetic algorithm can work together to produce better solutions than either method could produce by itself.

To explore our hypothesis that two learning algorithms can work together to outperform either individually, we focused on a particular problem in which an agent must perform a task, and the task requires several steps to accomplish. We limit feedback on how well the agent is performing to the end of the task. Several learning algorithms have been applied to this family of problems, called *delayed reinforcement problems* (Widrow 1987; Atkeson 1990; Watkins 1989; Barto, Sutton and Watkins 1990; Millan and Torras 1992; Moore and Atkeson 1993), but little has been done to evaluate the power of combining different types of learning algorithms to these problems.

One way of characterizing these delayed reinforcement problems is as learning to solve a *Markov decision problem* (van der Wal 1981). Markov decision problems are those in which an agent develops a mapping from a set of states to a set of actions, possibly different ones for each state, and the optimal strategy from a given state depends only on the current state. The actions are directed toward achieving some goal or performing some task, and payoff or penalty for that action is awarded immediately. Delayed reinforcement problems apply zero payoff at intermediate states and apply the actual reward at the end of the sequence.

One class of problems frequently modeled as a Markovian decision problem is the class of differential games. Differential games require the players to make a long sequence of moves where the behaviors and strategies are modeled by differential equations. Finding a solution to the differential game consists of computing the "value" of the game in terms of expected payoff and determining the optimal strategies for the players that yield this value. Differential games are difficult to solve yet are important for solving a wide variety of multi-agent tasks. They have had widespread application in the military and entertainment industries, but more recently, systems for intelligent highways, air traffic control, railroad monitoring, and ship routing are using differential game theory to assist agents in optimizing their often competing goals. More generally, strategies for solving these games can be used for planning and intelligent agents, thus making the approach discussed applicable to the broader domain of control problems.

For this study, we begin by considering a differential game that involved one agent trying to pursue and capture another (i.e., a pursuit game). Earlier research showed that at least one implementation of this task, known as *evasive maneuvers* (Grefenstette, Ramsey and Schultz 1990), can be solved by a genetic algorithm (GA). We developed a lazy learning approach using *k*-nearest neighbor (*k*-NN) for the same task, hoping to demonstrate lazy learning could perform as well or better than the GA. Then we made the task substantially harder to study the limitations of lazy learning methods on this class of problems. The more complicated task, which is described further in Section 3.2, also resembles complicated planning tasks in which an agent has to satisfy several goals simultaneously (Chapman 1987).

As our experiments will show, we were successful at developing a method to solve our difficult reinforcement learning task. The key idea behind our success was the combined use of both lazy learning and GAs. We observed after comparing two lazy methods (k-NN and an adaptation of Q-learning) with genetic algorithms that lazy methods can learn to solve the task, but were dependent on having good examples in the database. Later, we found that the best learning agent first used a GA to generate examples, and then switched to k-NN after reaching a certain performance threshold. Our experiments demonstrate significant improvement in the performance of lazy learning, both in overall accuracy and in memory requirements, as a result of using these techniques. The combined system also performed better than the GA alone, demonstrating how two learning algorithms working together can outperform either method when used alone.

2. Previous Work

Recently, considerable work has been done applying learning algorithms to Markov decision problems. To date, little has been done to apply these algorithms to differential games. One exception to this is Grefenstette's SAMUEL system, which uses a genetic algorithm. In addition to the evasive maneuvers task, Grefenstette (1991) has applied SAMUEL to aerial dogfighting and target tracking. Ramsey and Grefenstette (1994) have used a case-based method of initializing SAMUEL with a population of "solutions" dependent on the current environment. Where we use a GA to "jump start" a lazy learner, Ramsey and Grefenstette use a lazy learner to jump start a GA. This suggests that a combined strategy where the lazy learner and the GA transmit information in both directions could be a powerful combination.

In related research, Gordon and Subramanian (1993a, 1993b) use an approach similar to explanation based learning (EBL) to incorporate advice into a genetic algorithm, using SAMUEL for the GA. In their multistrategy apprach, a *spatial knowledge base* and high-level strategic guidance from a human teacher are encoded using rule compilation that operationalizes the rules, by encoding them in a form suitable for SAMUEL to use. SAMUEL then uses and refines the advice with its genetic algorithm.

The idea of using lazy learning methods for delayed reinforcement tasks has only recently been studied by a small number of researchers. Atkeson (1990) employed a lazy technique to train a robot arm to follow a prespecified trajectory. Moore (1990) took advantage of the improved efficiency provided by storing examples in kd-trees in using a lazy approach to learn several robot control tasks. More recently, Moore and Atkeson (1993) developed their prioritized sweeping algorithm, in which "interesting" examples in a Q table are the focus of updating.

McCallum (1995) developed the "nearest sequence memory" algorithm, which is a lazy algorithm for solving control problems plagued by hidden state. Hidden state is an artifact of *perceptual aliasing* in which the mapping between states and perceptions is not one-to-one (Whitehead 1992). McCallum showed through his algorithm that lazy methods can reduce the effects of perceptual aliasing by appending history information with state information. Since our approach stores complete sequences, we too have minimized the effects of hidden state.

In another study, Aha and Salzberg (1993) used nearest-neighbor techniques to train a simulated robot to catch a ball. In their study, they provided an agent that knew the correct behavior for the robot, and therefore provided corrected actions when the robot made a mistake. This approach is typical in nearest-neighbor applications that rely on determining "good" actions before storing examples. In our case, we had no idea which examples were good and needed an approach to determine these examples.

One of the most popular approaches to reinforcement learning has been using neural network learning algorithms, most often the error back-propagation algorithm. This has been used for simple multi-step control problems (Widrow 1987; Nguyen and Widrow, 1989), using knowledge of the correct control action to train the network. Millan and Torras (1992) used a reinforcement learning algorithm embedded in a neural net in which the control variables were permitted to vary continuously. They addressed the problem of teaching a robot to navigate around obstacles.

Considerable research has been performed using a form of reinforcement learning called *temporal difference* learning (Sutton 1988). Temporal difference methods apply reinforcement throughout a sequence of actions to predict both future reinforcement and appropriate actions in performing the task. Specifically, predictions are refined through a process of identifying differences between the results of temporally successive actions. Two popular temporal difference algorithms are ACE/ASE (Barto, Sutton and Anderson 1983; Barto et al. 1990) and Q-learning (Watkins 1989). The original work by Barto et al. (1983) demonstrated that the cart and pole problem could be solved using this method. Clouse and Utgoff (1992) later used ACE/ASE with a separate teacher for the cart and pole problem, and applied Q-learning to navigating a race track. Lin (1991) used Q-learning to teach a robot to navigate the halls of a classroom building and plug itself into a wall socket to recharge its batteries. Below we describe a lazy variant of Q-learning, and show that it is also capable of learning complex control tasks.

In addition, Dorigo and Colombetti (1994) and Colombetti and Dorigo (1994) describe an approach to using reinforcement learning in classifier systems to teach a robot to approach and pursue a target. Their approach uses a separate reinforcement program to monitor the performance of the robot and provide feedback on performance. Learning occurs through a genetic algorithm applied to the classifiers with fitness determined by the reinforcement program.

More recently, Michael Littman (1994) observed that reinforcement learning can be applied to multi-agent activities in the context of *Markov games*. Littman expanded Watkins' Q-learning algorithm to cover two players in a simplified game of soccer. He embedded linear programming to determine the optimal strategy prior to play, and applied a modified Q backup operator (which accounted for the competitive goals of the players) to update the estimates of the expected discounted reward for each player.

Some other recent work in learning strategies for game playing has begun to deal with issues of co-learning at a superficial level with strategic games such as chess and othello. Pell (1993) developed an environment for deriving strategies in what he calls "symmetric chess-like games." His METAGAMER focused on translating the rules and constraints of a game into a strategy using a declarative formulation of the game's characteristics. METAGAMER has been applied to chess, checkers, noughts and crosses (i.e., Tic-Tac-Toe), and Go, and has yielded performance at an intermediate level for each of these games. Smith and Gray (1993) applied what they call a *co-adaptive* genetic algorithm to learn to play Othello. A co-adaptive GA is a genetic algorithm in which fitness values of members of the population are dependent on the fitness of other members in the population. They found they were able to control the development of niches in the population to handle several different types of opponents. Finally, Tesauro used temporal difference learning (Tesauro 1992) and neural networks (Tesauro and Sejnowski 1989) to train a backgammon program called TD-GAMMON. Backgammon's stochastic component (each move is determined in part by a roll of dice) distinguishes it from deterministic games such as chess, but despite this additional complexity, TD-GAMMON is currently playing at a master level.

3. The Problem

Reinforcement learning (RL) is challenging in part because of the delay between taking an action and receiving a reward or penalty. Typically an agent takes a long series of actions before the reward, so it is hard to decide which of the actions were responsible for the eventual payoff. Both lazy and eager approaches to reinforcement learning can be found in the literature. The

most common eager approach is the use of temporal-difference learning on
neural networks (Barto et al. 1983, 1990; Clouse and Utgoff 1992; Tesauro
1992). The advantages to a lazy approach are three-fold. First, minimal computational time is required during training, since training consists primarily of
storing examples (in the most traditional lazy approach, k-nearest neighbor).
Second, lazy methods have been shown to be good function-approximators in
continuous state and action spaces (Atkeson 1992). As we will see, this will
become important for our task of learning to play differential games. Third,
traditional eager approaches to reinforcement learning assume the tasks are
Markov decision problems. When the tasks are non-Markovian (e.g., when
history is significant), information must be appended to the state to encapsu-
late some of the prior state information, in order to approximate a Markov
decision problem. Since the lazy approach stores complete sequences,
non-Markovian problems can be treated in a similar fashion to Markovian
problems.

The class of RL problems studied here has also been studied in the field
of *differential game theory*. Differential game theory is an extension of traditional game theory in which a game follows a sequence of actions through a
continuous state space to achieve some payoff (Isaacs 1963). This sequence
can be modeled with a set of differential equations which are analyzed to
determine optimal play by the players. We can also interpret differential
games to be a version of optimal control theory in which players' positions
develop continuously in time, and where the goal is to optimize competing
control laws for the players (Friedman 1971).

3.1. *Differential games and pursuit games*

Differential game theory originated in the early 1960s (Isaacs 1963) as a
framework for a more formal analysis of competitive games. In a differential
game, the dynamics of the game (i.e., the behaviors of the players) are modeled
with a system of first order differential equations of the form

$$\frac{dk_j^t}{dt} = h_j^t(k^t, a^t), j = 1, ..., n \tag{1}$$

where $a^t = (a_1^t, ..., a_p^t)$ is the set of actions taken by p players at time t,
$k^t = (k_1^t, ..., k_n^t)$ is a vector in real Euclidean n-space denoting a position in
play (i.e., the state) for the game, and $h_j^t()$ is the history of the game for the
jth dimension of the state space. In other words, the differential equations
model how actions taken by the players in the game change the state of the
game over time. In these games, the initial state of the game k^0 is given. The
object of analyzing a differential game is to determine the optimal strategies

for each player of the game and to determine the value of the game (i.e., the expected payoff to each player) assuming all of the players follow the optimal strategies. For more details, see (Sheppard and Salzberg 1993).

A pursuit game is a special type of differential game that has two players, called the pursuer (P) and the evader (E). The evader attempts to achieve an objective, frequently to escape from a fixed playing arena, while the pursuer attempts to prevent the evader from achieving that objective. Examples include such simple games as the children's game called "tag," the popular video game PacMan, and much more complicated predator-prey interactions in nature. These examples illustrate a common feature of pursuit games – the pursuer and the evader have different abilities: different speeds, different defense mechanisms, and different sensing abilities.

One classic pursuit game studied in differential game theory is the *homicidal chauffeur* game. In this game, we can think of the playing field being an open parking lot with a single pedestrian crossing the parking lot and a single car. The driver of the car (the chauffeur) is trying to run down the pedestrian. Although the car is much faster than the pedestrian, the pedestrian can change direction much more quickly than the car. The typical formulation has both the car and the pedestrian traveling at fixed speeds, with the car having a fixed minimum radius of curvature, and the pedestrian able to make arbitrarily sharp turns (i.e., the radius of curvature is zero) (Basar and Olsder 1982).

In analyzing this game, it turns out that the solution is relatively simple and depends on four parameters – the speed of the car, the speed of the pedestrian, the radius of curvature of the car and the "lethal envelope" of the car (i.e., the distance between the car and the pedestrian that is considered to be "close enough" to hit the pedestrian). Isaacs (1963) shows that, assuming optimal play by both players, the ability of P to capture E (or conversely for E to escape) depends on the ratio of the players' speeds and P's radius of curvature. Intuitively, optimal play for P is to turn randomly if lined up with E and to turn sharply toward E otherwise. The optimal strategy for E is to head directly towards P until inside P's radius of curvature, and then to turn sharply. Since E's strategy is the more interesting, we will focus on learning to evade in a similar game.

3.2. *The evasive maneuvers task*

The evasive maneuvers task as a differential game is a variation on the homicidal chauffeur game. Even though the solution to the homicidal chauffeur game is intuitive, the actual surface characterizing the solution is highly nonlinear. Thus we should reasonably expect the surface for extensions to the problem (such as those discussed in this paper) to be more difficult to characterize. Grefenstette et al. (1990) studied the evasive maneuvers task to demonstrate the ability of genetic algorithms to solve complex sequential decision making problems. In their two-dimensional simulation, a single aircraft attempts to evade a single missile.

We initially implemented the same pursuit game as Grefenstette et al., and later we extended it to make it substantially more difficult. In this game, play occurs in a relative coordinate system centered on the evader, E. Because of the relative frame of reference, the search space is reduced and games are determined by their starting positions. P uses a fixed control law to attempt to capture E, while E must learn to evade P. Even the basic game is more difficult than the homicidal chauffeur game, because the pursuer has variable speed and the evader has a non-zero radius of curvature. Our extended version includes a second pursuer, which makes the problem much harder. Unlike the single-pursuer problems, the two-pursuer problem has no known optimal strategy (Imado and Ishihara 1993), and for some initial states, there is no possibility of escape. Second, we gave the evader additional capabilities: in the one-pursuer game, E only controls its turn angle at each time step. Thus E basically zigzags back and forth or makes a series of sharp turns into the path of P to escape. In the two-pursuer game, we gave E the ability to change its speed, and we also gave E a bag of "smoke bombs," which will for a limited time help to hide E from the pursuers.

In our definition of the two-pursuer task, both pursuers ($P1$ and $P2$) have identical maneuvering and sensing abilities. Further, they use the same control strategy: they anticipate the future location of E and aim for a location where they can capture in the fewest time steps. They begin the game at random locations on a fixed-radius circle centered on the evader, E. The initial speeds of $P1$ and $P2$ are much greater than the speed of E, but they lose speed as they maneuver, in direct proportion to the sharpness of the turns they make. The maximum speed reduction is 70%, scaled linearly from no turn (with no reduction in speed) to the maximum turn angle allowed of 135°. They can regain speed by traveling straight ahead, but they have limited fuel. If the speed of both $P1$ and $P2$ drops below a minimum threshold, then E escapes and wins the game. E also wins by successfully evading the pursuers for 20 times steps (i.e., both $P1$ and $P2$ run out of fuel). If the paths of either $P1$ or $P2$ ever pass within a threshold range of E's path during the game, then E loses (i.e., the pursuer will "grab" E) (Figure 1). We use the term "game" to include a complete simulation run, beginning with the initial placements of all of the players, and ending when E either wins or loses, at most 20 time steps later.

When playing against one pursuer, the capabilities of E are identical to the simulated aircraft used by Grefenstette et al. Against one pursuer, E controls only its turn angle, which is sufficient to play the game well. With

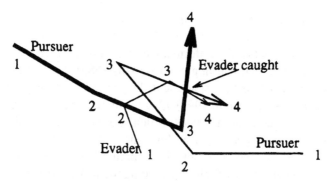

Figure 1. A game where E is caught.

two pursuers $P1$ and $P2$ in the game, E has additional information about its opponents. This information includes 13 features describing the state of the game, including E's own speed, the angle of its previous turn, a game clock, the angle defined by $P1$-E-$P2$, and the range difference between $P1$ and $P2$. It also has eight features that measure $P1$ and $P2$ individually: speed, bearing, heading, and distance. Bearing measures the position of the pursuer relative to the direction that E is facing (e.g., if E is facing north and $P1$ is due east, then the bearing would be 3 o'clock). Heading is the angle between E's direction and the pursuer's direction. When fleeing two pursuers, E can adjust its speed and turn angle at each time step, and it can also periodically release a smoke bomb, which introduces noise into the sensor readings of $P1$ and $P2$. If smoke is released, the turn angle of the pursuer is shifted by a random factor up to 50% of the current turn angle. As the severity of the turn increases, so does the potential effect from smoke.

4. The Learning Algorithms

The following sections discuss the details of the experiments with the three learning algorithms and motivate the need for a learning strategy combining eager learning (as a teacher) and lazy learning (as a performer). We explored several algorithms to determine the applicability of lazy learning to control problems in general, and pursuit games in particular. We began by examining the ability of Q-learning to learn to play the evasive maneuvers game. We had to adapt Q-learning because of the large, continuous state space, which resulted in a lazy variant of standard Q-learning. We then tried a traditional lazy learning approach, k-nearest neighbors. Finally, we experimented with an eager learning method, genetic algorithms, to compare with the two lazy methods.

4.1. *Lazy Q-learning for evasive maneuvers*

Q-learning solves delayed reinformement learning problems by using a temporal difference (TD) learning rule (Watkins 1989). TD methods usually assume that both the feature space and the variables being predicted are discrete (Sutton 1988; Tesauro 1992). Q-learning represents a problem using a lookup table that contains all states, which naturally causes problems with large, continuous state spaces such as those encountered in differential games. We therefore had to develop a method for predicting the rewards for some state-action pairs without explicitly generating them. The resulting algorithm was a lazy version of Q-learning.

Rather than constructing a complete lookup table, our implementation of Q-learning stores examples similar to the set of instances produced for a lazy method such as k-NN. It begins by generating a set of actions at random for a particular game; these actions do not have to result in successful evasion. Instead, the algorithm applies a payoff function (defined below) to determine the reward for that sequence of state-action pairs. Initially, it stores the actual payoff values with these pairs. After generating the first set of pairs, learning proceeds as follows.

First, assuming that neighboring states will require similar actions, we specify two distance parameters: one for the states and one for the actions ($d_1 = 0.01$ and $d_2 = 0.005$ respectively), noting that all distances are normalized. The purpose of these parameters is to guide a search through the instance database. The system begins an evasive maneuvering game by initializing the simulator. The simulator passes the first state to the state matcher which locates all of the states in the database that are within d_1 of the current state. If the state matcher has failed to find any nearby states, the action comparator selects an action at random. Otherwise, the action comparator examines the expected rewards associated with each of these states and selects the action with the highest expected reward. The resulting action is passed to the simulator, and the game continues until termination. It also has a probability (0.3) of generating a random action regardless of what it finds in the table. This permits it to fill in more of the database; i.e., it is exploring the state space as it is learning. It passes the resulting action to the simulator, and the game continues until termination, at which point the simulator determines the payoff. The Q function then updates the database using the complete game.

At the end of a game, the system examines all of the state-action pairs in the game. It stores in the database any state-action pair that is new, along with the reward from the game. If the pair already exists, the predicted reward is updated as follows:

$$Q(x,a) = Q(x,a) + \eta[\rho + \gamma E(y) - Q(x,a)] \tag{2}$$

where $Q(x, a)$ is the predicted reward for state x with corresponding action a, η is a learning rate, ρ is the actual reward, γ is a discount factor, and $E(y)$ is the maximum Q value for all actions associated with state y. State y is the state that follows when action a is applied to state x. Reward is determined using the payoff function in (Grefenstette et al. 1990), namely

$$\rho = \begin{cases} 1000 & \text{if } E \text{ evades the pursuers} \\ 10t & \text{if } E \text{ is captured at time } t. \end{cases} \tag{3}$$

Each of the pairs in the game are then compared with all of the pairs in the database. If the distance between a stored state and action are less than d_1 and d_2 respectively for some state-action pair in the game, then the stored state-action pair's Q value is updated.

4.2.   K-NN for evasive maneuvers

Lazy learning is a classical approach to machine learning and pattern recognition, most commonly in the form of the k-nearest neighbor algorithm. K-NN is rarely used for Markov decision problems, so we had to represent the pursuit game in a format amenable to this algorithm. Further, to be successful, a lazy approach must have a database full of correctly labeled examples, because k-NN expects each example to be labeled with its class name. The difficulty here, then, is how to determine the *correct* action to store with each state.

We formulate Markov decision problems as classification problems by letting the state variables correspond to features of the examples, and the actions correspond to classes. Typically, classification tasks assume a small set of discrete classes to be assigned. We do not require quantization of the state space or the action space, but instead use interpolation so that any action can be produced by the k-NN classifier.

In order to know the *correct* action to store with each state, we must at least wait until we have determined the outcome of a game before deciding how to label each step. (One example can be added at each time step). However, even after a successful game where E evades P, we cannot be sure that the actions at *every* time step were the correct ones; in general, they were not.

To construct an initial database of instances, the simulator generated actions randomly until E evaded P for a complete game. The corresponding state-action pairs for that engagement were then stored. At that point, k-NN was used for future games. States were passed by the simulator to a classifier which searched the database for the k nearest neighbors and selected an action by averaging the associated actions. If k-NN failed to produce a game that ended in successful evasion, the game was replayed with the example generator randomly selecting actions until play ended in evasion. Once evasion occurred, the corresponding sequence of states and actions (i.e., the complete game) was stored in the database.

Evasion usually occurred after 20 time steps since it was rare in the lazy learner that the pursuers' speeds dropped below the threshold. Thus a stored game typically consisted of 20 state-action pairs. Our implementation uses Euclidean distance to find the k nearest neighbors and the arithmetic mean of their control values to determine the appropriate actions. Distance is computed as follows:

$$dist(state, instance) = \sqrt{\sum_{\forall attrib} (state_{attrib} - instance_{attrib})^2} \qquad (4)$$

Then the nearest neighbor is determined simply as

$$nn = \arg \min_{\forall instance} \{dist(state, instance)\} \qquad (5)$$

If E fails to evade when using the stored instances, we reset the game to the starting position and generate actions randomly until E succeeds. We also generate random actions with probability 0.01 regardless of performance. The resulting set of examples is added to the database.

For the initial experiments using k-nearest neighbors, we varied k between 1 and 5 and determined that $k = 1$ yielded the best performance. (This was not completely surprising in that averaging control values with $k > 1$ tended to "cancel out" values that were extreme. For example, if three instances indicated turns of 90 degrees left, 5 degrees right, and 85 degrees right, the selected action would have been no turn. Of course, we are averaging "cyclic" values where, for example, 359 degrees is close to 1 degree. Improving the averaging process might enable $k > 1$ to perform better.) Examples consisted of randomly generated games that resulted in success for E; thus we could assume that at least some of E's actions were correct. (In random games, every action taken by E is random; the database is not checked for nearby neighbors.)

4.3. *GA for evasive maneuvers*

Grefenstette, et al. demonstrated that genetic algorithms perform well in solving the single pursuer game. Typically, GAs use rules called classifiers, which are simple structures in which terms in the antecedent and the consequent are represented as binary attributes (Booker, Goldberg and Holland 1989; Holland 1975). The knowledge for the evasive maneuvers problem requires rules in which the terms have numeric values; we therefore modified the standard GA representation and operators for this problem, using a formulation similar to (Grefenstette et al. 1990).

We call a set of rules a *plan*. For the GA, each plan consists of 20 rules with the general form:

IF $low_1 \leq state_1 \leq high_1 \wedge \ldots \wedge low_n \leq state_n \leq high_n$

THEN $action_1, \ldots, action_m$

Each clause in the antecedant compares a state variable to a lower and upper bound. "Don't care" conditions can be generated by setting the corresponding range to be maximally general. To map this rule form into a chromosome for the GA, we store each of the attribute bounds followed by each action. For example, suppose we have the following rule (for the single pursuer problem):

IF $300 \leq$ speed $\leq 350 \wedge$

$25 \leq$ previous turn $\leq 90 \wedge$

$3 \leq$ clock $\leq 10 \wedge$

$875 \leq$ pursuer speed $\leq 950 \wedge$

$8 \leq$ pursuer bearing $\leq 10 \wedge$

$180 \leq$ pursuer heading $\leq 270 \wedge$

$300 \leq$ pursuer range ≤ 400

THEN   turn $= 45$

The chromosome corresponding to this rule would be:

[300 350 25 90 3 10 875 950 8 10 180 270 300 400 45]

Associated with each rule is a rule strength, and associated with each plan is a plan fitness. A population may contain up to fifty plans, all of which compete against each other in the GA system. Strength and fitness values, described below, determine the winners of the competition.

Initially, all rules are maximally general. As a result, all rules will match all states, and one rule will be selected with uniform probability. Following each training game, the rules that fired are generalized or specialized by the GA, using hill-climbing to modify the upper and lower limits of the tests for each state variable as follows:

$$LB_i = LB_i + \beta(state_i - LB_i) \tag{6}$$

$$UB_i = UB_i - \beta(UB_i - state_i) \tag{7}$$

where LB_i and UB_i are the lower and upper bounds, respectively, of the rule that fired for $state_i$ and β is the learning rate. If the current state is within the bounds of the predicate, the bounds shift closer to the state based on the learning rate ($\beta = 0.1$ for this study). On the other hand, if the state is outside the bounds, only the nearer bound is adjusted by shifting it toward the value $state_i$. Following a game the strengths of the rules that fired are updated based on the payoff received from the game (the same payoff used in Q-learning).

Given the payoff function, the strength for each rule that fired in a game is updated using the profit sharing plan (Grefenstette 1988) as follows:

$$\mu(t) = (1 - c)\mu(t - 1) + c\rho \tag{8}$$
$$\sigma(t) = (1 - c)\sigma(t - 1) + c(\mu(t) - \rho) \tag{9}$$
$$strength(t) = \mu(t) - \sigma(t) \tag{10}$$

where c is the profit sharing rate ($c = 0.01$ for our experiments), ρ is the payoff received, μ is an estimate of the mean strength of a rule, and σ is an estimate of the variance of rule strength. Plan fitness is calculated by running each plan against a set of randomly generated games, and computing the mean payoff for the set of tests. During testing, the plan with the highest fitness is used to control E.

The heart of the learning algorithm lies in the application of two genetic operators: *mutation* and *crossover*. Rules within a plan are selected for mutation using *fitness proportional selection* (Goldberg 1989). Namely, probability of selection is determined as

$$\Pr(r) = \frac{strength_r(t)}{\sum_{\forall s \in rules} strength_s(t)} \tag{11}$$

where *rules* is the set of rules in a plan and r is the rule of interest. Probability of selection for plans is determined similarly using plan fitness rather than rule strength. For more details of the implementation, see (Sheppard and Salzberg 1993).

4.4. Results

For each of the algorithms and for both variations of the evasive maneuvers game, we ran ten experiments. To produce learning curves, we combined the results of the ten experiments by averaging the algorithm's performance at regular intervals. We estimated the accuracy of each algorithm by testing the results of training on 100 randomly generated games.

The results of the Q-learning experiments were encouraging and led to the next phase of our study in which we applied a traditional lazy learning method, k-nearest neighbors (k-NN), to the evasive maneuvers task. When we found that k-NN did not work well, we considered an eager learning

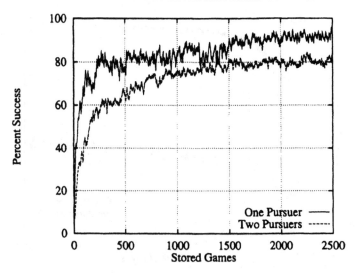

Figure 2. Performance of *Q*-learning on one- and two-player pursuit games.

algorithm, the genetic algorithm. This choice was motivated by the previous work by Grefenstette et al. which indicated the GA was capable of solving this type of task. In fact, we were able to replicate those results for the one-pursuer problem and scale up the GA so that it still worked quite well for the two-pursuer game.

4.4.1. *Performance of lazy Q-learning*

In the one-pursuer task, *Q*-learning did extremely well initially (Figure 2), reaching 80% evasion within the first 250 games, but then performance flattened out. Peak performance (when the experiments were stopped) was about 90%. There was an apparent plateau between 250 games and 1500 games where performance remained in the range 80%–85%. Then performance jumped to another plateau at 90% for the remainder of the experiment.

Q-learning's performance on the two-pursuer task was also encouraging. It reached 60% evasion within 250 games and continued to improve until reaching a plateau at 80%. This plateau was maintained throughout the remainder of the experiment. Since our implementation of *Q*-learning uses a form of lazy-learning, these results led us to believe it might be possible to design a more traditional lazy method (i.e., *k*-NN) to solve the evasion task. At first, however, our hypothesis was not supported, as we see in the next section.

4.4.2. *Performance of k-NN*

Figure 3 shows how well *k*-NN performed on the two versions of the evasive maneuvers game as the number of training examples (and games) increased.

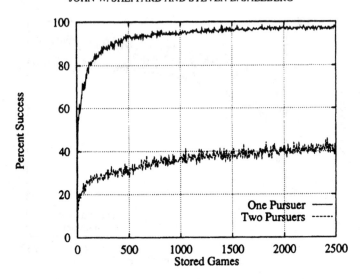

Figure 3. Performance of *k*-NN on one- and two-player pursuit games.

This figure compares the performance on the two problems with respect to the number of games stored, where a game contains up to 20 state-action pairs.

These experiments indicate that the problem of escaping from a single pursuer is relatively easy to solve. K-NN developed a set of examples that was 95% successful after storing approximately 1,500 games, and it eventually reached almost perfect performance. The distance between P and E at the start of the game guarantees that escape is always possible. However, the results were disappointing when E was given the task of learning how to escape from two pursuers. In fact, the lazy learning approach had difficulty achieving a level of performance above 45%. This demonstrates that the two-pursuer problem is significantly more difficult for k-NN.

One possible reason for k-NN's poor performance on the two-pursuer task is presence of irrelevant attributes, which is known to cause problems for nearest neighbor algorithms (Aha 1992; Salzberg 1991). We experimented with a method similar to stepwise forward selection (Devijver and Kittler 1982) to determine the set of relevant attributes. However, determining relevant attributes in a dynamic environment is difficult for the same reason that determining good examples is difficult: we do not know which attributes to use until many successful examples have been generated.

Another possible reason for the poor performance of k-NN on the two pursuer task is the size of the search space. For the one-pursuer problem, the state space contains $\approx 7.5 \times 10^{15}$ points, whereas for two-pursuer evasion, the state space has $\approx 2.9 \times 10^{33}$ points. The one-pursuer game showed good

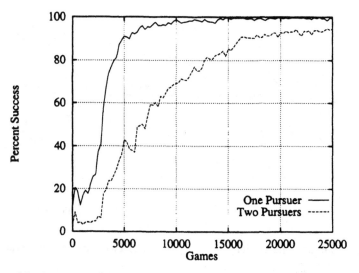

Figure 4. Performance of the genetic algorithm on one- and two-player pursuit games.

performance after 250 games; to achieve similar coverage of the state space in the two-pursuer game would require roughly 2.7×10^{21} games (assuming similar distributions of games in the training data).

But the most likely reason for k-NN's troubles, we concluded, was that we were generating bad examples in the early phases of the game. As stated above, a lazy learner needs to have the "correct" action, or something close to it, stored with almost every state in memory. Our strategy for collecting examples was to play random games at first, and to store games in which E succeeded in escaping. However, many of the actions taken in these random games will be incorrect. E might escape because of one or two particularly good actions, but a game lasts for 20 time steps, and all 20 state-action pairs are stored. Since our lazy learning approach had no way (at first – see section 5.2) to throw away examples, if it collected many bad examples it could get stuck forever at a low level of performance.

4.4.3. *Performance of the GA*

We show the results of the GA experiments in Figure 4. As with k-NN, the GA performs well when faced with one pursuer. In fact, it achieves near perfect performance after 15,000 games and very good performance (above 90%) after only 5,000 games. The number of games is somewhat inflated for the GA because it evaluates 50 plans during each generation, thus we counted one generation as 50 games. In fact, the simulation ran for only 500 generations (i.e., 25,000 games) in these experiments.

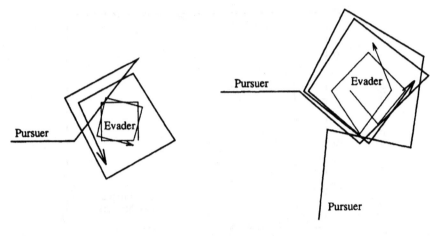

a) One pursuer, one evader   b) Two pursuers, one evader

Figure 5. Sample games where E successfully evades.

The most striking difference in performance between k-NN and the genetic algorithm is that the GA learned excellent strategies for the two-pursuer problem, while nearest neighbor did not. Q-learning's performance, though much better than k-NN, is still inferior to the GA. Indeed, the GA achieved above 90% success after 16,000 games (320 generations) and its success rate continued to improve until it reached approximately 95%.

4.4.4. *Comparing one- and two-pursuer evasion*

Figure 5a shows a sample game in which E evades a single pursuer, which gives some intuition of the strategy that E had to learn. Essentially, E just keeps turning sharply so that P will be unable to match its changes of direction. Although all three algorithms did well on this task, a closer examination of the results reveals some interesting differences.

K-NN eventually reached a successful evasion rate of 97%–98%, and it reached 93% evasion after only 500 games. This was superior to Q-learning's asymptotic performance, and k-NN performed better than the GA through 250 games. Of course, the GA eventually achieved near perfect performance. Q-learning also learned very rapidly in the beginning, exceeding the GA's ability through the first 150 games, but then its learning slowed considerably. In fact, at the point the GA was performing nearly perfectly, Q-learning's performance was only around 85%. After twice as many games as the GA, Q-learning (now achieving 91% evasion) was still performing considerably poorer than both the GA and k-NN.

Table 1. Comparing learning for the evasive maneuvers task at convergence.

Algorithm	One Pursuer	Two Pursuers
k-NN	96.9%	42.3%
Q-learning	93.3%	81.7%
GA	99.6%	94.5%

Table 1 shows the results of comparing the three algorithms on the two evasion tasks at convergence. We considered the algorithms to have converged when they showed no improvement through 500 games (for k-NN and Q-learning) or through 100 generations (for the GA). Recognizing the difficulty of the two-pursuer task (relative to the one-pursuer task), we now see profound differences in the performance of the three approaches. (See Figure 5b for a sample game where E evades two pursuers.) As before, the GA started slowly, being outperformed by both k-NN and Q-learning. After about 3,000 games (60 generations), the GA began to improve rapidly, passing k-NN almost immediately, and catching Q-learning after an additional 5,000 games (100 generations). The end results show the GA surpassing both Q-learning (by a margin of 11%) and k-NN (by a margin of 52%). The more striking result, though, is the poor performance of k-NN for the two-pursuer game. We next set out to improve this figure.

5. Combining the GA with Lazy Learning

Initially, we were surprised with k-NN's performance on the two-pursuer task. In an attempt to improve its performance, we considered how to provide "good" examples to k-NN, based on our hypothesis that the primary cause of its poor performance is the poor quality of its training experiences. For lazy learning to work effectively on control tasks, the stored examples must have a high probability of being good ones; i.e., the action associated with a stored state should be correct or nearly correct. Because of this credit assignment problem, and because of the difficulty of the tasks we designed, initial training is very difficult for a lazy learner. In contrast, a GA initially searches a wide variety of solutions, and for the problems we studied tends to learn rapidly in the early stages. These observations suggested the two-phase approach that we adopted, in which we first trained a GA, and then used it to provide examplars to bootstrap k-NN.

```
algorithm GLL;
init population;
do
      run genetic algorithm;           /* Run the GA for one generation */
      perf = select best plan;         /* Determine performance of GA */
      if perf ≥ θ                      /* Evaluate performance against θ = 0, 50, 90 */
            do i = 1, n                /* For our experiments n = 100 */
                  evade = evaluate best;  /* Determine if best plan from GA evades */
                  if evade
                        store examples;  /* Stores up to 20 examples */
      evaluate lazy;                   /* Test on 100 games */
```

Figure 6. Pseudocode for GLL.

5.1. *Bootstrapping nearest neighbor*

Our bootstrapping idea requires that one algorithm train on its own for a time, and then communicate what it has learned to a second algorithm. At that point, the second algorithm takes over. Later, the first algorithm adds additional examples. This alternation continues until the combined system reaches some asymptotic limit. Because the GA learned much better for the two-pursuer game, we selected it as the first learner, with k-NN second. Details of the communication or "teaching" phase are given in Figure 6. Using this approach, the examples continue to accumulate as the genetic algorithm learns the task.

The results of training k-NN using the GA as the teacher are shown in Figure 7. We call this system GLL because it first uses a GA and then uses a lazy learning algorithm (i.e., k-NN). All points shown in the graph are the averages of 10 trials.

The first threshold was set to 0%, which meant that the GA provided examples to k-NN from the beginning of its own training. The second threshold was set to 50% to permit the GA to achieve a level of success approximately equal to the best performance of k-NN on its own. Thus only plans that achieved at least 50% evasion were allowed to transmit examples to k-NN. Finally, the threshold was set at 90% to limit examples for k-NN to games in which a highly trained GA made the decisions about which examples to store.

When $\theta = 0\%$, GLL almost immediately reaches a level equal to the best performance of k-NN on its own (around 45%). From there, it improves somewhat erratically but steadily until it reaches a performance of approximately 97% success. The figure shows performance plotted against the number of examples stored. The number of examples stored here is higher than the number of examples stored for k-NN alone. If we halt learning after 50,000

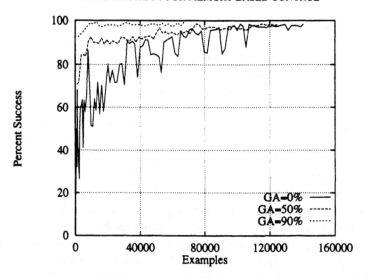

Figure 7. Results of GA teaching *k*-NN.

examples (which is consistent with the earlier *k*-NN experiments), performance would be in the 85% range, still an enormous improvement over *k*-NN's performance, but not better than the GA on its own.

When $\theta = 50\%$, GLL starts performing at a very high level (above 70%) and quickly exceeds 90% success. After 50,000 examples, GLL obtained a success rate above 95%, with some individual trials (on random sets of 100 games) achieving 100% success. In addition, the learning curve is much smoother, indicating that *k*-NN is probably not storing many "bad" examples. This confirms in part our earlier hypothesis that *k*-NN's fundamental problem was the storage of bad examples. If it stores examples with bad actions, it will take bad actions later, and its performance will continue to be poor whenever a new state is similar to one of those bad examples.

Finally, with $\theta = 90\%$, GLL's performance was always superb, exceeding the GA's 90% success rate on its very first set of examples. GLL converged to near-perfect performance with only 10,000 examples. One striking observation was that GLL performed better than the GA throughout its learning. For example, when $\theta = 0\%$, GLL achieved 50–80% success while the GA was still only achieving 2–10% success. Further, GLL remained ahead of the GA throughout training. Even when $\theta = 90\%$, GLL achieved 98–100% evasion while the GA was still only achieving around 95% evasion. Neither the GA nor *k*-NN were able to obtain such a high success rate on their own, after any number of trials.

5.2. *Reducing memory size*

Our bootstrapping algorithm, GLL, performs well even when only a small number of examples are provided by the GA, and it even outperforms its own teacher (the GA) during training. But the amount of knowledge required for the GA to perform well on the task was quite small – only 20 rules are stored as a single plan. The number of examples used by GLL, though small in comparison with k-NN, still requires significantly more space and time than the rules in the GA. Consequently, we decided to take this study one step further, and attempted to reduce the size of the memory store during the lazy learning phase of GLL (Zhang 1992; Skalak 1994).

In the pattern recognition literature, e.g., in (Dasarathy 1991), algorithms for reducing memory size are known as *editing* methods. However, because lazy learning is not usually applied to control tasks, we were not able to find any editing methods specifically tied to our type of problem. We therefore modified a known editing algorithm for our problem, and call the resulting system GLE (GA plus lazy learning plus editing).

GLL performs quite well as described above, and we would like to reduce its memory requirements without significantly affecting performance. Early work by Wilson (1972) showed that examples could be removed from a set used for classification, and suggested that simply editing would frequently improve classification accuracy (in the same way that pruning improves decision trees (Mingers 1989)). Wilson's algorithm classifies each example in a data set with its own k nearest neighbors. Those points that are incorrectly classified are deleted from the example set, the idea being that such points probably represent noise. Tomek (1976) modified this approach by taking a sample (> 1) of the data and classifying the sample with the remaining examples. Editing then proceeds using Wilson's approach. Ritter et al. (1975) described another editing method, which differs from Wilson in that points that are *correctly* classified are discarded. The Ritter method, which is similar to Hart's (1968), basically keeps only points near the boundaries between classes, and eliminates examples that are in the midst of a homogenous region.

The editing approach we took combined the editing procedure of Ritter et al. and the sampling idea of Tomek (Devijver 1986). We began by generating ten example sets with $\theta = 90$ where each set consisted of a single set of examples from the GA. We then selected the set with the best performance on 10,000 test games, which in this case obtained nearly perfect accuracy with 1,700 examples. Next we edited the memory base by classifying each example using all other examples in the set. For this phase, we used the five nearest neighbors. If a point was correctly classified, we deleted it with probability 0.25. (This probability was selected arbitrarily, and was used to

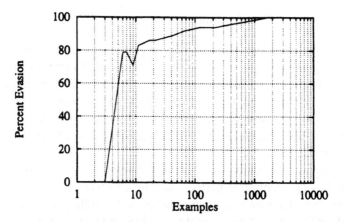

Figure 8. Results of editing examples provided by the genetic algorithm for k-NN.

show how performance changed as editing occurred.) Prior to editing and after each pass through the data, the example set was tested using 1-NN on 10,000 random games.

One complication in "classifying" the points for editing was that the class was actually a three-dimensional vector of three different actions, two of which were real-valued (turn angle and speed) and one of which was binary (emitting smoke). It was clear that an exact match would be too strict a constraint. Therefore we specified a range around each 3-vector within which the system would consider two "classes" to be the same. In addition, the three values were normalized to equalize their effect on this range measurement.

The results of running GLE on the 1,700 examples are summarized in Figure 8.

A logarithmic scale is used on the x-axis to highlight the fact that accuracy decreased very slowly until almost all the examples were edited. When read from right to left, the graph shows how accuracy decreases as the number of examples decreases. With as few as 11 examples, GLE achieved better than 80% evasion, which is substantially better than the best ever achieved by k-NN alone. With 21 examples (comparable in size to a plan in the GA), GLE achieved 86% evasion. Performance remained at a high level (greater than 90% success) with only 66 examples. Thus it is clear that a small, well chosen set of examples can yield excellent performance on this difficult task. Furthermore, such a small memory base guarantees that the on-line performance of k-NN will be quite fast.

6. Discussion and Conclusions

This study considered approaches to developing strategies for learning to play differential games. In particular, we examined several methods for learning evasion strategies in pursuit games. Optimal strategies for differential games are determined by solving a system of differential equations; for even simple games, the resulting strategies are complex. Many games do not have known closed-form solutions. We illustrated the complexity of differential strategies with the pursuit game.

These experiments demonstrated the ability of three algorithms (GA, k-NN, and lazy Q-learning) to perform well on a simple task with one pursuer, and then show how increasing the difficulty by adding a second pursuer adversely affects two of the algorithms (k-NN and lazy Q-learning). K-NN, in particular, had considerable difficulty scaling up to the more complex task. Thus we were left with the question of whether it is even possible for lazy learning techniques such as k-nearest neighbor to perform well on problems of this type. This motivated the second phase of the study, in which we used a GA-based teacher to train k-NN for the two-pursuer task.

The experiments reported here show that it is possible to use genetic algorithms in conjunction with lazy learning to produce agents that perform well on difficult delayed reinforcement learning problems. The experiments also demonstrate clearly the power of having a teacher or other source of good examples for lazy learning methods. For complex control tasks, such a teacher is probably a necessary component of any lazy or memory-based method. Our experiments show how a genetic algorithm can be used to learn plans or control laws in complex domains, and then to train a lazy learner by using its learned rules to generate good examples. The result was a hybrid system that outperformed both of its "parent" systems. This hybrid approach can of course be applied in many ways; for example, standard Q-learning is notoriously slow to converge, and approaches such as ours could be used to accelerate it.

One surprising result was that the performance of GLL outperformed the GA at the same point in training. We hypothesize this was because only the best examples of a given generation were passed to k-NN, rather than all of the experiences of the GA during that generation. The fact that GLL outperformed GA right away indicates that perhaps it could have been used to teach the GA, instead of the other way around.

In addition, we found that editing the example set produced a relatively small set of examples that still play the game extremely well. Again, this makes sense since editing served to identify the strongest examples in the database, given that poor examples were still likely to be included in the early stages of learning. It might be possible with careful editing to reduce the size of memory even further. This question is related to theoretical work by Salzberg et al. (1991) that studies the question of how to find a minimal-size training set through the use of a "helpful teacher," which explicitly provides very good examples. Such a helpful teacher is similar to the oracle used by Clouse and Utgoff (1992) except that it provides the theoretically minimal number of examples required for learning.

7. Next Steps

Our current implementation takes only the first step towards a truly combined learning system in which the two learners would assist each other in learning the task. Our approach uses one algorithm to start the learning process and hands off the results of the first algorithm to a second algorithm to continue learning the task. We envision a more general architecture in which different learning algorithms take turns learning, depending on which one is learning most effectively at any given time. Such an architecture should expand the capabilities of learning algorithms as they tackle increasingly difficult control problems.

One possible future direction is to use genetic operators (or other methods) directly on the examples in a lazy learning approach. That is, rather than producing rules, we can begin with a set of examples and mutate those directly using genetic operators to evolve a database (i.e., example set) to perform the task. One such approach might be to examine the frequency with which the examples are used to successfully evade and then select the n most frequently used examples. These examples can then be converted into a plan for the GA by specifying a range about each attribute in each example. This results in a new set of rules which is sufficient to construct a plan, and the new plan can be seeded into the population for the GA to use.

The general problem of determining optimal strategies in differential games is complex. Solving the games involves solving a system of differential equations. Learning solutions to the games involves simultaneous learning by all of the players. This means that the players must learn in a highly dynamic environment. Rather than a player learning to counter a single, constant strategy, the player must adapt its strategy to the changing strategy of the opponent. In such an environment, one must avoid prematurely converging on a fixed solution.

To study these problems, we are building an environment for analyzing learning algorithms in multi-agent environments. Specifically, we wish to explore the effects on sequential decision making when several agents are learning at the same time. We are exploring the ability of an agent to apply one approach to learn evasion tactics while another agent is using the same or perhaps a different approach to develop pursuit strategies. We will also pit a strategy against itself and study whether a single learning algorithm can develop multiple solutions for the same reactive control task.

Acknowledgments

Thanks to David Aha and the anonymous reviewers of this special issue for their many valuable comments on an earlier draft of this paper. Also thanks to Diana Gordon, John Grefenstette, Simon Kasif, and S.K. Murthy for helpful comments and ideas during the formative stages of this work. This material is based upon work supported in part by the National Science foundation under Grant Nos. IRI-9116843 and IRI-9223591.

References

Aha, D. & Salzberg, S. (1993). Learning to catch: Applying nearest neighbor algorithms to dynamic control tasks. In *Proceedings of the Fourth International Workshop on AI and Statistics*, pp. 363–368. Ft. Lauderdale.

Aha, D. W. (1992). Tolerating noisy, irrelevant, and novel attributes in instance-based learning algorithms. *International Journal of Man-Machine Studies* 16: 267–287.

Atkeson, C. (1990). Using local models to control movement. In Touretzky, D. S. (ed.), *Advances in Neural Information Processing Systems* 2, 316–323. San Mateo, CA: Morgan Kaufman.

Atkeson, C. G. (1992). Memory-based approaches to approximating continuous functions. In Casdagli, M. & Eubanks, S. (eds.), *Nonlinear Modeling and Forecasting*, pp. 503–521. Addison Wesley.

Barto, A., Sutton, R. & Anderson, C. (1983). Neuronlike adaptive elements that can solve difficult learning control problems. *IEEE Transactions on Systems, Man, and Cybernetics* 13: 835–846.

Barto, A., Sutton, R. & & Watkins, C. (1990). Learning and sequential decision making. In Gabriel & Moore (eds.), *Learning and Computational Neuroscience*, pp. 539–602. Cambridge: MIT Press.

Basar, T. & Olsder, G. J. (1982). *Dynamic Noncooperative Game Theory*. Academic Press: London.

Booker, L., Goldberg, D. & Holland, J. (1989). Classifier systems and genetic algorithms. *Artificial Intelligence* 40: 235–282.

Chapman, D. (1987). Planning for conjunctive goals. *Artificial Intelligence* 32: 333–377.

Clouse, J. & Utgoff, P. (1992). A teaching method for reinforcement leraning. In *Proceedings of the Ninth International Conference on Machine Learning*, pp. 92–101. Aberdeen, Scotland: Morgan Kaufman.

Colombetti, M. & Dorigo, M. (1994). Training agents to perform sequential behavior. *Adaptive Behavior* 2(3): 247–275.

Dasarathy, B. V. (ed.) (1991). *Nearest Neighbor (NN) Norms: NN Pattern Classification Techniques*. Los Alamitos, CA: IEEE Computer Society Press.

Devijver, P. A. (1986). On the editing rate of the multiedit algorithm. *Pattern Recognition Letters* 4: 9–12.

Devijver, P. A. & Kittler, J. (1982). *Pattern Recognition: A Statistical Approach*. Englewood Cliffs, New Jersey: Prentice-Hall.

Dorigo, M. & Colombetti, M. (1994). Robot shaping: Developing autonomous agents through learning. *Artificial Intelligence* **71**(2): 321–370.

Friedman, A. (1971). *Differential Games*. New York: Wiley Interscience.

Goldberg, D. (1989). *Genetic Algorithms in Search, Optimization, and Machine Learning*. Reading, Massachusetts: Addison-Wesley.

Gordon, D. & Subramanian, D. (1993a). A multistrategy learning scheme for agent knowledge acquisition. *Informatica* **17**: 331–346.

Gordon, D. & Subramanian, D. (1993b). A multistrategy learning scheme for assimilating advice in embedded agents. In *Proceedings of the Second International Workshop on Multistrategy Learning*, pp. 218–233. George Mason University.

Grefenstette, J. (1988). Credit assignment in rule discovery systems based on genetic algorithms. *Machine Learning* **3**, 225–245.

Grefenstette, J. (1991). Lamarkian learning in multi-agent environments. In *Proceedings of the Fourth International Conference of Genetic Algorithms*, pp. 303–310. Morgan Kaufmann.

Grefenstette, J., Ramsey, C. & Schultz, A. (1990). Learning sequential decision rules using simulation models and competition. *Machine Learning* **5**: 355–381.

Hart, P. (1968). The condensed nearest neighbor rule. *IEEE Transactions on Information Theory* **14**(3): 515–516.

Holland, J. (1975). *Adaptation in Natural and Artificial Systems*. Ann Arbor, Michigan: University of Michigan Press.

Imado, F. & Ishihara, T. (1993). Pursuit-evasion geometry analysis between two missiles and an aircraft. *Computers and Mathematics with Applications* **26**(3): 125–139.

Isaacs, R. (1963). Differential games: A mathematical theory with applications to warfare and other topics. Tech. Rep. Research Contribution No. 1, Center for Naval Analysis, Washington, D.C.

Lin, L. (1991). Programming robots using reinforcement learning and teaching. In *Proceedings of the Eight National Conference on Artificial Intelligence*, pp. 781–786. AAAI Press.

Littman, M. (1994). Markov games as a framework for multi-agent reinforcement learning. In *Proceedings of the Eleventh International Machine Conference*, pp. 157–163. New Brunswick, NJ: Morgan Kaufmann.

McCallum, R. A. (1995). Instance-based state identification for reinforcement learning. In *Advances in Neural Information Processing Systems 7*, pp. 377–384.

Millan, J. & Torras, C. (1992). A reinforcement connectionist approach to robot path finding in non-maze-like environments. *Machine Learning* **8**: 363–395.

Mingers, J. (1989). An empirical comparison of pruning methods for decision tree induction. *Machine Learning* **4**(2): 227–243.

Moore, A. (1990). *Efficient Memory-Based Learning for Robot Control*. Ph.D. thesis, Computer Laboratory, Cambridge University.

Moore, A. & Atkeson, C. (1993). Prioritized sweeping: Reinforcement learning with less data and less time. *Machine Learning* **13**: 103–130.

Nguyen, D. & Widrow, B. (1989). The truck backer-upper: An example of self learning in neural networks. In *Proceedings of the International Joint Conference on Neural Networks*, Vol. 2, pp. 357–363.

Pell, B. D. (1993). *Strategy Generation and Evaluation for Meta-Game Playing*. Ph.D. thesis, University of Cambridge, Cambridge, England.

Ramsey, C. L. & Grefenstette, J. J. (1994). Case-based anytime learning. In Aha, D. W. (ed.), *Case Based Reasoning: Papers from the 1994 Workshop*, pp. 91–95. Menlo Park, California: AAAI Press.

Ritter, G., Woodruff H., Lowry S. & Isenhour, T. (1975). An algorithm for a selective nearest neighbor decision rule. *IEEE Transactions on Information Theory* **21**(6): 665–669.

Salzberg, S. (1991). Distance metrics for instance-based learning. In *Methodologies for Intelligent Systems: 6th International Symposium*, pp. 399–408.

Salzberg, S., Delcher, A., Heath, D. & Kasif, S. (1991). Learning with a helpful teacher. In *Proceedings of the Twelfth International Joint Conference on Artificial Intelligence*, pp. 705–511. Sydney, Australia: Morgan Kaufmann.

Sheppard, J. W. & Salzberg, S. L. (1993). Memory-based learning of pursuit games. Tech. Rep. JHU-93/94-02, Department of Computer Science, Johns Hopkins University, Baltimore, Maryland. Revised May, 1995.

Skalak, D. (1994). Prototype and feature selection by sampling and random mutation hill climbing algorithms. In *Proceedings of the Eleventh International Machine Learning Conference*, pp. 293–301. New Brunswick, NJ: Morgan Kaufman.

Smith, R. E. & Gray, B. (1993). Co-adaptive genetic algorithms: An example in othello strategy. Tech. Rep. TCGA Report No. 94002, University of Alabama, Tuscaloosa, Alabama.

Sutton, R. (1988). Learning to predict my methods of temporal differences. *Machine Learning* 3: 9–44.

Tesauro, G. (1992). Practical issues in temporal difference learning. *Machine Learning* 8: 257–277.

Tesauro, G. & Sejnowski, T. J. (1989). A parallel network that learns to play backgammon. *Artificial Intelligence* 39: 357–390.

Tomek, I. (1976). An experiment with the edited nearest-neighbor rule. *IEEE Transactions on Systems, Man, and Cybernetics* 6: 448–452.

van der Wal, J. (1981). *Stochastic Dynamic Programming*. Amsterdam: Morgan Kaufmann.

Watkins, C. (1989). *Learning with Delayed Rewards*. Ph.D. thesis, Cambridge University, Department of Computer Science, Cambridge, England.

Whitehead, S. (1992). *Reinforcement Learning for the Adaptive Control of Perception and Action*. Ph.D. thesis, Department of Computer Science, University of Rochester.

Widrow, B. (1987). The original adaptive neural net broom-balancer. In *International Symposium on Circuits and Systems*, pp. 351–357.

Wilson, D. (1972). Asymptotic properties of nearest neighbor rules using edited data. *IEEE Transactions on Systems, Man, and Cybernetics* 2(3): 408–421.

Zhang, J. (1992). Selecting typical instances in instance-based learning. In *Proceedings of the Ninth International Machine Learning Conference*, pp. 470–479. Aberdeen, Scotland: Morgan Kaufman.

Artificial Intelligence Review **11**: 371–405, 1997.
© 1997 *Kluwer Academic Publishers.*

371

Lazy Incremental Learning of Control Knowledge for Efficiently Obtaining Quality Plans

DANIEL BORRAJO[1] and MANUELA VELOSO[2]

[1] *Departamento de Informática, Universidad Carlos III de Madrid, 28911 Leganés (Madrid), Spain*
E-mail: dborrajo@grial.uc3m.es
[2] *Computer Science Department, Carnegie Mellon University, Pittsburgh, PA 15213-3891, USA*
E-mail: veloso@cs.cmu.edu

Abstract. General-purpose generative planners use domain-independent search heuristics to generate solutions for problems in a variety of domains. However, in some situations these heuristics force the planner to perform inefficiently or obtain solutions of poor quality. Learning from experience can help to identify the particular situations for which the domain-independent heuristics need to be overridden. Most of the past learning approaches are fully deductive and eagerly acquire correct control knowledge from a necessarily complete domain theory and a few examples to focus their scope. These learning strategies are hard to generalize in the case of nonlinear planning, where it is difficult to capture correct explanations of the interactions among goals, multiple planning operator choices, and situational data. In this article, we present a *lazy* learning method that combines a deductive and an inductive strategy to efficiently learn control knowledge incrementally with experience. We present HAMLET, a system we developed that learns control knowledge to improve both search *efficiency* and the *quality* of the solutions generated by a nonlinear planner, namely PRODIGY4.0. We have identified three lazy aspects of our approach from which we believe HAMLET greatly benefits: lazy explanation of successes, incremental refinement of acquired knowledge, and lazy learning to override only the default behavior of the problem solver. We show empirical results that support the effectiveness of this overall lazy learning approach, in terms of improving the efficiency of the problem solver and the quality of the solutions produced.

Key words: speedup learning, nonlinear planning, lazy learning, multistrategy learning, learning to improve plan quality

1. Introduction

Planning uses generalized operators, describing the available actions in a task domain, to search for a solution to a problem by selecting, instantiating, and chaining appropriate operators. Control knowledge can be added to the planning procedure to guide the search, thus improving the planning performance. It has been the focus of attention of several researchers, present authors included, *to learn* control knowledge, i.e., to automate the acquisition of knowledge that guides the problem solving search process.

One approach to learning control knowledge consists of generating explanations for the local decisions made during the search process (DeJong and Mooney 1986; Laird et al. 1986; Mitchell et al. 1986; Minton 1988; Pérez and Etzioni 1992; Katukam and Kambhampati 1994). These explanations become control rules that are used in future situations to prune the search space. These deductive approaches invest a substantial explanation effort to produce provably correct and complete control rules from a single (or few) problem solving examples and a correct underlying domain theory. They also require a complete domain theory to obtain the explanations,[1] although there has been some work on learning with incomplete, or intractable theories, such as (Tadepalli 1989). Alternatively, inductive approaches incrementally acquire correct knowledge by observing a large set of problem solving examples. These approaches strongly depend on the particular examples seen, but can also acquire simple and useful rules (Cohen 1990; Leckie and Zukerman 1991).

This article presents a method that combines a deductive and an inductive approach, integrating three aspects of lazy learning. The results show that the combination of these three lazy components has several advantages over eager deductive approaches, such as: reduced learning effort; no need for a complete domain theory as specified by domain axioms; and reduced cost of utilizing the learned knowledge. The lazy aspects we have identified are:

- **Bounded explanation.** The learning method explains the successes of the problem solving episodes first by loosely following the dependencies among choices, and by selecting a bounded set of features that will be used in the explanations. No proof of correctness or completeness for the explanations generated is attempted as in eager approaches.

- **Incremental refinement.** Upon experiencing new problem solving episodes, the learning algorithm lazily refines these explanations with examples of its successful or failed applications. It incrementally acquires increasingly correct control knowledge. Since the learned rules are approximately correct, there should be no need to use a large number of examples for refining them, as do many inductive methods. As discussed in the editorial of this special issue, there is a difference between incremental and lazy learning, in that the first one refers to how examples are provided to the learning system, while the second refers to how the system handles those examples. With respect to this difference, HAMLET is

---

[1] In addition to the set of operators and inference rules that describe the primitive problem solving actions, a complete domain theory includes a set of domain axioms that enables the proof of the universal truth of the learned knowledge in the domain.

both a lazy and an incremental system: examples are given incrementally, and each one is handled lazily.

- **Lazy learning to override only the default behavior.** With respect to identifying which are the learning opportunities, our system can operate in two learning modes: *eager* or *lazy*. In *eager* mode, it generates a positive example from every decision that leads to a solution. In *lazy* mode, it generates a positive example only if the decision leads to one of the globally best solutions and it was not the choice selected by the problem solving default heuristics.

We implemented our learning approach in a system called HAMLET, standing for *Heuristics Acquisition Method by Learning from sEarch Trees* (Barrajo and Veloso 1994; Veloso and Barrajo 1994). HAMLET is integrated with PRODIGY4.0, the current nonlinear problem solver of the PRODIGY architecture for planning and learning (Carbonell et al. 1992). HAMLET learns control knowledge incrementally and inductively to improve both the search *efficiency* of the problem solver and to improve the *quality* of the plans generated.

The article is divided into seven sections. Section 2 briefly presents PRODIGY4.0, the substrate nonlinear planner, identifying its choice points and learning opportunities. It also introduces HAMLET's architecture, presenting the generation of the meta-level control rules and their incremental refinement. Section 3 describes the Bounded Explanation component of HAMLET. Section 4 discusses the Refinement module with the generalization and specialization algorithms. Section 5 shows empirical results in the blocksworld domain and in an elaborated logistics transportation domain, where HAMLET learns rules that improve PRODIGY's efficiency and the quality of the solutions of complex planning problems with up to 50 goals and hundreds of literals in the initial state. Section 6 relates our work with other strategy learning approaches. We discuss how HAMLET extends the explanation-based strategy learning method for applications to nonlinear planning. Finally, Section 7 summarizes our conclusions.

2. Overview of PRODIGY4.0 and HAMLET

HAMLET is integrated in the planning and learning architecture PRODIGY (Carbonell et al. 1990). The current nonlinear problem solver in PRODIGY, PRODIGY4.0, follows a means-ends analysis backward chaining search procedure reasoning about multiple goals and multiple alternative operators relevant to the goals (Veloso et al. 1995).[2] The inputs to the problem solver algorithm are:

- Domain theory, $\mathcal{D}$ (or, for short, domain), that includes the set of operators specifying the task knowledge and the object hierarchy;
- Problem, specified in terms of an initial configuration of the world (initial state, $\mathcal{S}$) and a set of goals to be achieved ($\mathcal{G}$); and
- Control knowledge, $\mathcal{C}$, described as a set of control rules, that guides the decision-making process.

PRODIGY's planning algorithm interleaves backward-chaining planning with the simulation of plan execution by applying operators found relevant to the goal to an internal world state. Figure 1 shows an abstract view of PRODIGY's planning algorithm. The function backtrack will return to a prior node, undoing the effects of applied operators. All select- functions return the best alternative according to the control knowledge.[3]

The planning/reasoning cycle, as shown in Figure 1, involves several decision points, namely:

- the *goal* to select from the set of pending goals and subgoals (step 3.1.1);
- the *operator* to choose to achieve a particular goal (step 3.1.2);
- the *bindings* to choose to instantiate the chosen operator (step 3.1.3);
- *apply* an operator whose preconditions are satisfied or continue *subgoaling* on an unsolved goal (step 3): and
- the *operator* to be applied (step 3.2.1).

Default decisions at all these choices can be directed by explicit control knowledge. Figure 2 sketches the general decision search tree considered by PRODIGY. The decision cycle first encounters steps 3.1.x (i.e., selection of goal, operator, and bindings), followed by the same set of steps 3.1.x, or by applying an operator in steps 3.2.x.

Although PRODIGY uses powerful domain-independent heuristics (Stone et al. 1994) that guide the decision making process, it is still difficult and costly to characterize when these heuristics are going to succeed or fail. Therefore, learning is used for automatically acquiring control knowledge to *override the default behavior*, so that it guides the planner more efficiently to solutions of good quality.[4]

---

[2] PRODIGY4.0 is a successor of the previous linear planner, PRODIGY2.0 (Minton et al. 1989), and PRODIGY's first nonlinear planner, NOLIMIT (Veloso 1989). We use the term "nonlinear" for a planner that can fully interleave subplans for different goals.

[3] We will use **boldface** for functions whose definitions appear in the article, and typescript font for functions whose definitions do not appear. We will not study PRODIGY4.0 in detail, and, therefore, we did not use any boldface in its definition.

[4] Independently of the base-level planning algorithm, researchers should find learning opportunities to override the planning default behavior when it leads the planner into failure, inefficient performance, or solutions of poor quality (Veloso and Blythe 1994).

Function **Prodigy4.0** (S, G, D, C)

S is the state of the problem
G is the set of goals to be achieved, *pending goals*
D is the domain description: operators and objects hierarchy
C is the set of control rules (control knowledge)
P is the plan, initially $\emptyset$
O is a variablized operator (from the set of operators in D)
B is a substitution (bindings) of the variables of an operator
O_B is the operator O instantiated with bindings B
$\mathcal{O}$ is the set of chosen instantiated operators not yet in P, initially $\emptyset$
$\mathcal{A}$ is the set of applicable operators (a subset of $\mathcal{O}$)
$G_\mathcal{O}$ is the set of preconditions of all operators in $\mathcal{O}$, $G_\mathcal{O} = \cup_{O_B \in \mathcal{O}}$ preconditions(O_B)

While $G \not\subseteq S$ AND search tree not exhausted
   1. $G = G_\mathcal{O} - S$
   2. $\mathcal{A} \leftarrow \emptyset$
      Forall $O_B \in \mathcal{O}$ | preconditions$(O_B) \subseteq S$ do $\mathcal{A} \leftarrow \mathcal{A} \cup \{O_B\}$
   3. If select-subgoal-or-apply$(G, \mathcal{A}, S, C)$=*subgoal*
     Then **3.1.1.** $G \leftarrow$ select-goal(G, S, C)
         3.1.2. $O \leftarrow$ select-relevant-operator(G, D, S, C)
         3.1.3. $B \leftarrow$ select-bindings(O, S, C)
         3.1.4. $\mathcal{O} \leftarrow \mathcal{O} \cup O_B$
     Else **3.2.1.** $O_B \leftarrow$ select-applicable-operator$(\mathcal{A}, S, C)$
         3.2.2. $S \leftarrow$ apply(O_B, S)
         3.2.3. $\mathcal{O} \leftarrow \mathcal{O} - O_B$
         3.2.4. $P \leftarrow$ enqueue-at-end(P, O_B)
   4. If there is a reason to suspend the current search path
     Then backtrack.
$ST \leftarrow$ the planning search tree.
Return plan P and ST

Figure 1. PRODIGY4.0's planning algorithm.

HAMLET is integrated with the PRODIGY planner. The inputs to HAMLET are a task domain (D), a set of training problems (P), a quality measure (Q), a learning mode (L), and an optimality parameter (O). Q, L, and O will be explained shortly. The output is a set of control rules (C). HAMLET has two main modules: the Bounded Explanation module, and the Refinement module. Figure 3 shows HAMLET's modules and their connection to PRODIGY.

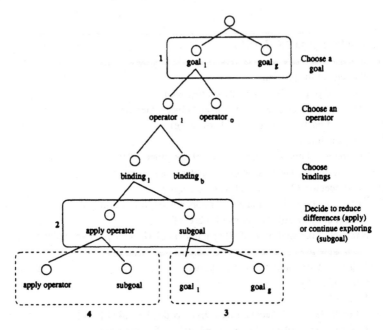

Figure 2. Tree of decisions generated by PRODIGY when searching for a solution to a problem. Decisions 3 and 4 enclosed in dashed rectangles are of the same type as 1 and 2, respectively.

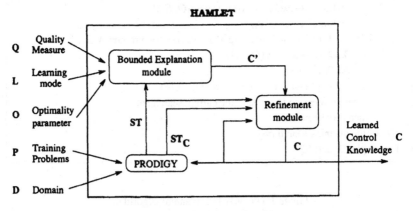

Figure 3. HAMLET's high level architecture.

The Bounded Explanation module generates control rules from a PRODIGY search tree. These rules might be overly specific or overly general. The Refinement module solves the problem of being overly specific by generalizing rules when analyzing positive examples. It also replaces overly general rules with more specific ones when it finds situations in which the learned rules lead to wrong decisions. HAMLET gradually learns and refines control rules, in an attempt to converge to a concise set of correct control rules (i.e., rules that are individually neither overly general, nor overly specific). ST and ST_C are planning search trees generated by two calls to PRODIGY's planning algorithm, C is the set of control rules, and C' is the new set of control rules learned by the Bounded Explanation module.

Figure 4 outlines HAMLET's learning algorithm.

Function **Hamlet** $(\mathcal{P}, \mathcal{D}, Q, L, O)$

$\mathcal{P}$ is the set of training problems
$\mathcal{D}$ is the domain description
Q is a quality measure
L is the learning-mode, which can be either *lazy* or *eager*
O is the boolean *optimality parameter*
C is the set of learned control rules, initially $\emptyset$
P is a problem
ST is the search tree for solving a problem P without control knowledge, $C = \emptyset$
ST_C is the search tree for solving a problem P with control knowledge C
C' is the new set of control rules learned from solving P

Forall $P \in \mathcal{P}$ do
   $ST \leftarrow$ search-tree(**Prodigy4.0**(initial-state(P),goal(P),$\mathcal{D}, \emptyset$))
   $ST_C \leftarrow$ search-tree(**Prodigy4.0**(initial-state(P),goal(P),$\mathcal{D}, C$))
   $C' \leftarrow$ **Bounded-Explanation**(ST, Q, L, O)
   $C \leftarrow$ **Refinement**(ST, ST_C, C, C')
Return C

Figure 4. A high-level description of HAMLET's learning algorithm.

For each problem P in the set of training problems $\mathcal{P}$, HAMLET calls PRODIGY4.0 twice. In the first call, PRODIGY generates a search tree ST to identify the optimal solutions. This is done by solving P without any control rules, exhausting the search space.[5] HAMLET generates new positive examples from ST, as ST was not pruned by any control rules. In the second call, PRODIGY uses the current set of learned control rules C and produces a search tree ST_C. HAMLET identifies possible negative examples by the pruned search tree, ST_C, with the complete search tree ST. Positive and negative examples are used to refine the learned rules to produce the new set of control rules C.

---

[5] PRODIGY also generates a plan that HAMLET does not use.

3. Bounded Explanation

The Bounded Explanation module learns control rules by lazily choosing "key" decisions (as will be characterized later) made during the search for a solution and extracting the information that justifies these decisions from the search space. The explanation procedure consists of three phases: Labeling the search tree; Credit assignment; and Generation of control rules. The Bounded Explanation module behaves lazily in two aspects:

- In contrast with *eager* approaches that learn control knowledge for planning (e.g., (Minton 1988; Etzioni 1993)), HAMLET does not require learning initially correct or complete knowledge. Incremental refinement will be responsible for the correctness of the control knowledge at the end of the learning process. Therefore, there is no need for additional domain axioms.

- It does not require to learn from all search paths, as opposed to an *eager* learner that would learn from all decision nodes. In our experiments with multiple domains, we found that there is no need to learn from all decision nodes. Instead, one could only learn from the ones that: lead to successful solutions; were not the best alternative considered; and belonged to the path of the best solution (according to a quality measure, Q).

Function **Bounded-Explanation** (ST, Q, L, O)

ST is the search tree of solving a problem P without control knowledge, $C = \emptyset$

Q is a quality measure

L is the learning-mode, which can be either *lazy* or *eager*

O is the boolean *optimality parameter*

C' is the set of new learned control rules

$C' \leftarrow$ **Label**($\text{root}(ST), Q, L, O$)

If $O = True$

Then Return $\text{follow-best-path}(\text{root}(ST))$

Else Return C'

Figure 5. Bounded Explanation high level algorithm.

Figure 5 shows a high level description of the Bounded Explanation algorithm. The algorithm takes as input a search tree ST generated without using the learned control knowledge, the *quality measure Q*, the *learning-mode L*, and the *optimality parameter O*. It returns a new set of control rules learned from the search tree decisions. The function Label, explained in subsection 3.1, assigns labels to each node of the search tree and possibly learns control rules. If the *optimality parameter* is true, then it will delay learning until it finishes labeling the whole tree, so that it learns only from the path to the best solution (function follow-best-path). If false, it will learn at the same time that it labels the nodes of the search tree.

Function **Label** (N, Q, L, O)

N is the node HAMLET is going to label
Q is a quality measure
L can be either *eager* or *lazy*
O is the optimality parameter
C is the set of new control rules without refinement, initially $\emptyset$
S is the set of successors of node N

Forall $s \in S$ do $C \leftarrow C \cup$ **Label**(s, Q, L, O)
Case of
 • If $S = \emptyset$
  Then Case of
      If solution-path(N) Then node-label(N)←*success*
      If failed-path(N) Then node-label(N)←*failure*
      If untried(N) Then node-label(N)←*unknown*
 • If $\exists s \in S$ | node-label(s)=*unknown*
  Then If L =*eager* AND $\exists s' \in S$ | node-label(s')=*success*
     Then $C \leftarrow C \cup$ **Store-or-learn-rule**(N, Q, L, O)
     Else node-label(N)←*unknown*
 • If $\exists s \in S$ | node-label(s)=*success* AND $\not\exists s' \in S$ | node-label(s')=*unknown*
  Then $C \leftarrow C \cup$ **Store-or-learn-rule**(N, Q, L, O)
 • If $\forall s \in S$ node-label(s)=*failure*:
  Then node-label(N)←*failure*
Return C

Figure 6. High level description of HAMLET's labeling procedure.

3.1. *Labeling the Search Tree*

HAMLET traverses the search tree bottom-up, starting from the leaf nodes. After labeling the leaf nodes, the algorithm propagates the labels up to the root of the search tree, using the algorithm described in Figures 6 and 7.

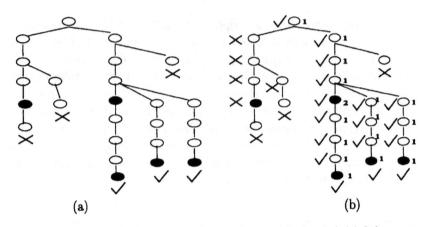

Figure 7. (a) A sketch of a PRODIGY search tree, where each leaf node is labeled as success (√) or failure (X); (b) The same tree after HAMLET labels it and attaches the optimal solution length from each node. The black nodes correspond to the operators applied to the state. A solution is the sequence of applied operators in a path from the root node to a success leaf node.

HAMLET assigns three kinds of labels to each node of the tree:

- *success*, if the node corresponds to a correct solution plan;
- *failure*, if the node is a dead end in the search space; and
- *unknown*, if the planner did not expand the node, and thus we do not know whether this node can lead to a solution.

The parameter *learning-mode* controls the way to label a node, as well as the way in which it assigns credit (discussed in next subsection). If its value is *eager*, HAMLET will eagerly label as *success* every node that has at least one success child, even if it did not explore all its subtrees. If its value is *lazy*, then HAMLET will label as *success* only the nodes that explored all their subtrees, and had at least one *success* child. The function `Store-or-learn-rule` (Figure 9) decides first whether to learn from the node's decision. If it decides learning, it also considers whether directly learning a control rule from the node's decision (function `learn`), or delaying the learning process until the end of the tree labeling: it stores now the decision with function `store` and later learns it with function `learn`. In the second case, HAMLET would only learn from nodes in the optimal path (see subsection 3.2). The function `learn` creates and returns a new control rule according to the target concept corresponding to the decision made in the node, the state at that node, and the meta-level information from the search tree (see Subsection 3.3). Figure 7 shows an illustration of the labelling procedure.[6]

---

[6] In this example, there are no unknown labeled nodes.

Figure 7(a) shows an example of a typical search tree, in which each leaf node is labeled by the PRODIGY planner as success ($\sqrt{}$) or failure (X). Figure 7(b) shows how HAMLET propagates labels to the root of this tree. In general, there might be several solutions to a problem as shown by the different solution paths. The nodes in each solution path are also labeled with the length of the optimal solution that can be reached from this node.

3.2. Credit Assignment

Credit assignment is the process of selecting important branching decisions for which learning will occur. It is done concurrently with labeling. Two parameters, *optimality parameter O* and *learning-mode L*, control the way in which HAMLET assigns credit. If O is *true*, the system learns only from the paths that lead to optimal solutions of the problem. It waits until the whole tree is labeled to generate the control rules, since this is the only way to know when a node is in an optimal solution path. If *optimality parameter* is *false*, HAMLET learns from every path to a solution. In this case, it does not have to wait to finish the credit assignment and labeling to generate the control rules. Instead, it interleaves credit assignment and generation of the control rules.

When we first designed HAMLET, it would learn from every node in a solution path. If all the possible solutions to a given problem are of the same quality (according to a given criteria), or one is only concerned with learning to produce the solutions more efficiently, then this eager approach is correct. However, we wanted to create a learning system capable of also improving the quality of the solutions provided. Therefore, we created a parameter, *learning-mode*, that would control the way in which HAMLET assigns credit. If it is *eager*, HAMLET views a branching decision as a learning opportunity only if the decision leads to any solution. If *lazy*, a decision is a learning opportunity if it leads to an optimal solution and differs from the default decision made by the domain-independent heuristics. As discussed in Section 5, *eager* mode learns many more rules than *lazy* mode. We found that *lazy* mode was almost always more efficient in solving problems, and also the solutions obtained were better according to the quality measure Q.

Figure 8 shows the learning opportunities that HAMLET finds in the example search tree of Figure 7(b). In Figure 8(a), the thick solid lines show the branching decisions that would be learned in *lazy* mode. In Figure 8(b), the dashed lines indicate the additional decisions learned in *eager* mode.

3.3. Generation of Control Rules

At each decision choice to be learned, HAMLET has access to information on the current state S, and on the meta-level planning information, such as the

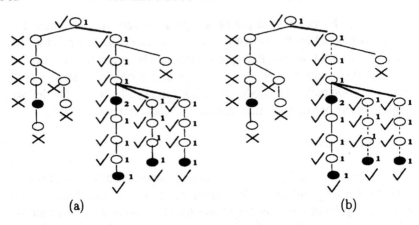

(a)   (b)

Figure 8. The learning opportunities corresponding to the example labeled tree of Figure 7(b). The default decisions are the left-most successors of every node.

goals that have not been achieved, the goal the planner is working on, and the possible applicable operators. This information is used by the generation module (the function learn in Figure 9) to create the applicability conditions (i.e., the antecedents of the control rules). The relevant predicates of the current state are selected using *goal regression* (Waldinger 1981).

Function **Store-or-learn-rule** (N, Q, L, O)

N is the node HAMLET is going to label
Q is a quality measure
L can be either *eager* or *lazy*
O is the optimality parameter
B is the set of best successors of N according to Q

---

node-label$(N) \leftarrow success$
If $L = eager$ OR default-alternative$(N) \notin B$
Then If O=True
       Then store(N, B)
            Return $\emptyset$
       Else Return $\{$learn$(N, B)\}$
Else Return $\emptyset$

Figure 9. Auxiliary function for HAMLET's labeling procedure.

HAMLET learns five kinds of *select* control rules, corresponding to PRODIGY's decisions as discussed in Section 2. These are the generalized target concepts:[7]

- decide to apply an *operator* for achieving a *goal*;
- decide to subgoal on an unachieved *goal*;
- select an unachieved *goal*;
- select an *operator* to achieve some *goal*; and
- select bindings for an *operator* when trying to achieve a *goal*.

They are instantiated on each domain by replacing the above variables (words in italics) by specific names of operators and goals. For instance, there will be one target concept of the type select-operator for each possible <*operator, goal*> pair, where *goal* refers to the goals that can be achieved by *operator*. As an example in the blocksworld, two target concepts will be *select unstack for achieving holding-object* and *select pick-up for achieving holding-object*. HAMLET generates a set of rules for each target concept, where the antecedent of each rule is described as a conjunctive set of tests.[8] As HAMLET can learn several rules for the same target concept, the set of all rules can be viewed as the disjunction of conjunctive rules.

Each of the five kinds of generalized target concepts has a template for describing its antecedents as shown in Figure 10. The templates share a set of common predicates for all kinds of control rules, but each kind has certain local predicates. Below are the predicates used in the antecedents of all five types of control rules (i.e., the common predicates):

- True-in-state *assertion*: tests whether *assertion* is true in the current state of the search.
- Other-goals *list-of-goals*: tests whether any of the goals in *list-of-goals* is an unachieved goal.
- Prior-goals *list-of-goals*: tests whether any goal in *list-of-goals* is the top-level goal that created the subgoal which the planner is currently trying to achieve.
- Type-of-object *object type*: tests whether *object* is of type *type*.

The local predicates that are used in some, but not all, kinds of control rules, are:

- Target-goal *goal*: tests whether *goal* is one of the unachieved goals.
- Current-goal *goal*: tests whether *goal* is the current goal the planner is trying to achieve.

---

[7] HAMLET does not yet learn rules to control the choice of which operator to apply (see step 3.2.1 in Figure 1), as this decision has only been recently added to PRODIGY4.0 as a control choice point.

[8] Some of the tests are, in fact, disjunctive, such as *other-goals* and *prior-goals*.

(control-rule *name*
   (if (and (current-goal *goal-name*)
      [(prior-goals (*literal**))]
      (true-in-state *literal*)*
      (other-goals (*literal**))
      (type-of-object *object type*)*))
   (then select **operators** *operator-name*))

(a)

(control-rule *name*
   (if (and (current-operator *operator-name*)
      (current-goal *goal-name*)
      [(prior-goals (*literal**))]
      (true-in-state *literal*)*
      (other-goals (*literal**))
      (type-of-object *object type*)*))
   (then select **bindings** *bindings*))

(b)

(control-rule *name*
   (if (and (applicable-op *operator*)
      [(prior-goals (*literal**))]
      (true-in-state *literal*)*
      (other-goals (*literal**))
      (type-of-object *object type*)*))
   (then decide {**apply|sub-goal**}))

(c)

(control-rule *name*
   (if (and (target-goal *literal*)
      [(prior-goals (*literal**))]
      (true-in-state *literal*)*
      (other-goals (*literal**))
      (type-of-object *object type*)*))
   (then select **goals** *literal*))

(d)

Figure 10. Templates (regular expressions) of the five kinds of target concepts. They correspond to the decisions: (a) operator decision; (b) bindings decision; (c) decide to apply or subgoal, (both have the same antecedent); and (d) goal decision.

- Current-operator *operator*: tests whether *operator* is the operator PRODIGY is considering to achieve a goal.
- Applicable-op *instantiated operator*: tests whether *instantiated operator* is applicable in the current state.

After a rule is generated, HAMLET replaces specific constants inherited from the considered planning situation with variables of corresponding types. Distinct constants are replaced with differently named variables. When the rule is applied, different variables must always be matched with distinct constants. The latter heuristic can be relaxed when generalizing rules.

3.4. *Example*

We show now a simple example of how control knowledge can be generated. The domain we use is a logistics-transportation domain (Veloso 1994b). In this domain, packages must be delivered to different locations in several cities. Packages are carried within the same city in trucks and across cities in airplanes. At each city, there are several locations, such as post offices and airports. The domain consists of a set of operators to load and unload

packages into and from the carriers at different locations, and to move the
carriers between locations. Consider the problem in Figure 11, where there are
three cities, each with one airport. Initially, there is one package, *package1*,
at *airport1*, and one airplane, *plane1*, at *airport2*. The goal of the problem is
to bring both *package1* and *plane1* to *airport3*.

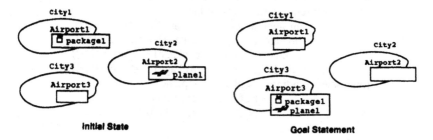

Figure 11. An illustrative example – initial state and goal statement.

```
(control-rule select-bind-fly-airplane-1
  (if (and (current-operator fly-airplane)
        (current-goal
          (at-airplane <plane1> <airport3>))
        (true-in-state
          (at-airplane <plane1> <airport2>))
        (other-goals
          ((at-object <package1> <airport3>)))))
  (then select bindings ((<plane> . <plane1>)
        (<from> . <airport1>)
        (<to> . <airport3>))))
            (a)
```

```
(operator FLY-AIRPLANE
  (preconds
    ((<plane> AIRPLANE)
     (<from> AIRPORT)
     (<to> AIRPORT))
    (at-airplane <plane> <from>))
  (effects
    ((add (at-airplane <plane> <to>))
     (del (at-airplane <plane> <from>)))))
            (b)
```

Figure 12. (a) Control rule created by HAMLET; (b) The operator FLY-AIRPLANE. The rule
controls the selection of the bindings for instantiating the operator's variables.

After PRODIGY solves the problem, HAMLET learns the rule shown in Figure
12, which would be the one that a standard EBL system would learn. The rule
says that the planner should fly an airplane, *plane1*, from *airport1* to *airport3*
if the goal is to have the airplane at *airport3*, it is initially in *airport2*, and
it has another goal of having a package, *package1*, at the same destination
airport, *airport3*. This rule is erroneous, since it does not capture why it should
fly from *airport1*, instead of flying from *airport2*, which is where *plane1* is
in the current state. What is missing is the location of *package1* in the state.
If *package1* is at *airport1*, then everything is explained correctly, as it is
captured by the rule in Figure 13. However, if *package1* is at *airport2* in the
state of another similar problem, then this rule would fire incorrectly, leading

to a nonoptimal solution, as shown in Subsection 4.3. While traditional EBL systems could not recover from this erroneous rule, HAMLET's refinement approach specializes the rule, correcting it, as explained in Section 4.

```
(control-rule select-bind-fly-airplane-2
    (if (and (current-operator fly-airplane)
             (current-goal (at-airplane <plane1> <airport3>))
             (true-in-state (at-airplane <plane1> <airport2>))
             (true-in-state (at-object <package1> <airport1>))
             (other-goals ((at-object <package1> <airport3>)))))
    (then select bindings ((<plane> . <plane1>)
                           (<from> . <airport1>)
                           (<to> . <airport3>)))))
```

Figure 13. Rule learned by HAMLET after specializing the overly general rule in Figure 12.

4. Refinement. Generalization and Specialization

The rules generated by the Bounded Explanation module may be overly specific, as also noticed by (Etzioni and Minton 1992), or overly general, as we showed in Section 3. To address this problem, HAMLET uses the Refinement module, which generalizes the learned rules by analyzing new examples of situations where the rules are applicable, and specializes the overly general rules when it finds new negative examples. We have devised methods for generalizing and specializing four aspects of the learned knowledge:

- *Current state:* The predicates from the state are the first ones to be removed, since their presence in the antecedents of the control rules is the reason why most of the rules are overly specific.
- *Subgoaling structure:* We may relax the subgoaling links, for example as captured by the *prior-goal* predicate, since the same goal can be generated as a subgoal of many different goals.
- *Interacting goals:* Another way of relaxing the preconditions of rules consists of identifying the correct subset of the set of pending goals that affect a particular decision.
- *Object hierarchy:* Finally, it is also important to find the generalization level to which the variables in the control rules belong, considering the ontological type hierarchy that is available in the nonlinear version of PRODIGY.

HAMLET's refinement component behaves lazily in that it delays generalizing until new examples are found, and when these examples are found, the

---

Function **Refinement** (ST, ST_C, C, C')

ST is the search tree of solving a problem P with $C = \emptyset$
ST_C is the search tree of solving a problem P with control knowledge C
C is the set of learned control rules
C' is the set of new control rules without refinement
$\mathcal{T}$ is the set of target concepts for which there is at least one new negative example
R is a new learned control rule of the set C'

Forall $R \in C'$ do $C \leftarrow$**Generalize**(R, C)
$\mathcal{T} \leftarrow$ find-negative-examples(ST, ST_C)
Forall $T \in \mathcal{T}$ do $C \leftarrow$**Specialize**(T, C)
Return C

Figure 14. A high-level description of the Refinement algorithm.

generalization does not consider all previously seen examples, but only the ones that are being used at that time for their corresponding target concepts. This can be considered similar to other lazy learning systems that only keep prototypes of the different classes (Porter et al. 1990). However, a major difference with these approaches is that HAMLET still keeps all examples seen that are not subsumed by others.[9] This is needed for refinement purposes, as explained later in this section. A future research direction would study the possibility of only keeping some of them by computing the set of predicates that most probably will correctly refine an overly general control rule.

Figure 14 shows the top-level description of the Refinement module algorithm. It first calls the generalization phase (in case new positive examples were found, that is, new rules), followed by the specialization phase (in case any negative example was found). The function find-negative-examples returns the list of target concepts for which there is at least one new negative example. Negative examples are found by analyzing the differences between the search trees generated using the learned control rules (ST_C) and when not using them (ST). The following subsections describe the refinement algorithms. Subsection 4.1 discusses the generalization process, Subsection 4.2 presents the specialization process, and Subsection 4.3 presents an example of specialization.

---

[9] We use a similar concept to ILP's θ-subsumption (Muggleton 1992).

4.1. *Inductive Generalization of Control Knowledge*

Figure 15 presents the generalization algorithm. Upon generating a new control rule for a target concept, HAMLET tries to generalize it with previously learned control rules of the same target concept. If there were none, then the rule is stored as the only one of its target concept. If there were rules, the function `generalize-rule` will try to apply the generalization operators to combine all the rules of the same target concept. If it succeeds, it will create a new rule and delete the old ones. Also, it will recursively call itself with the new induced rule. If it fails to generalize the rule with any other rule, the rule is simply added to the set of rules of the target concept.

Function **Generalize** (R, C)

R is a new learned control rule
C is the set of learned control rules
T is the target concept of rule R
$\mathcal{R}$ is the old set of rules for target concept T
$\mathcal{R}'$ is the new set of rules for target concept T

If $\mathcal{R} = \emptyset$
Then `target-concept-rules`$(T) \leftarrow \{R\}$
Else $C \leftarrow C - \mathcal{R}$
    $\mathcal{R}' \leftarrow$ `generalize-rule`$(R, \mathcal{R}, T)$
    If $\mathcal{R}' = \emptyset$
    Then `target-concept-rules`$(T) \leftarrow$ `target-concept-rules`$(T) \cup \{R\}$
    Else `target-concept-rules`$(T) \leftarrow \mathcal{R}'$
Return $C \cup$ `target-concept-rules`(T)

Figure 15. Algorithm for the generalization of control rules.

A graphical example of the generalization process within a target concept is shown in Figure 16. "*WSP_i*" stands for *Whole Set of Preconditions* for *rule_i* and refers to the complete description of the current state and all available information about the meta-level decision on a certain search node.

4.2. *Specialization of Overly General Control Rules*

HAMLET may generate overly general rules, either by *goal regression* when generating the rules, or by applying the generalization step. The overly general rules need to be specialized. There are two main issues to be addressed: how to detect a negative example, and how to refine the learned knowledge according to it, shown in Figure 17.

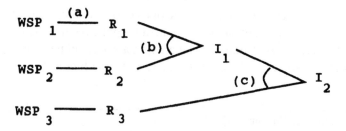

Figure 16. Three learning episodes of HAMLET within the same target concept. (a) shows the initial step of bounding the explanation from the *Whole Set of Preconditions* to R_1. (b) shows a generalization step from another rule R_2, generating induced rule I_1. (c) shows a second generalization step, generating I_2 from I_1 and R_3.

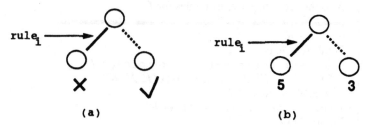

Figure 17. Two cases of negative examples (i.e., situations in which a rule applies incorrectly): (a) The rule selects a node that leads to a failure path; (b) The rule selects a node that leads to a node with a longer solution (five operators) than the best one (only three).

Definition: A negative example for HAMLET is a situation in which a control rule was applied, and the resulting decision led to either a failure (i.e., instead of the expected success), or a nonoptimal solution for that decision.

Negative examples are also represented as rules with their whole set of preconditions, WSP. They are stored in their corresponding target concept, and serve two purposes: refine an overly general rule, and establish an upper limit of generalization for future applications of the generalization module. Every time a rule is generated by either the Bounded Explanation or when applying the generalization module, it is checked against the negative examples of its target concept to determine whether it covers any of them. If so, the rule is refined. This is a *lazy* aspect in the sense that it does not try to obtain complete descriptions from all examples of the target concepts. Instead, it refines on demand the representative examples of each target concept, when new positive or negative examples are found.

4.2.1. *The specialization algorithm*
Since there are two kinds of rules (bounded and induced), there are two kinds of recovering methods. The bounded rules are refined by adding literals from their corresponding WSP set. The induced rules come from two generating

rules, so HAMLET tests whether each one of its corresponding generating rules also covers the negative example. If so, then HAMLET recursively refines that rule. If not, the induced rule is refined using a set of refinement operators. The top-level specialization algorithm is described in Figure 18.

Function **Specialize** (T, C)

T is an erroneous target concept (a negative example was found)
C is the set of learned control rules
$\mathcal{R}$ is the old set of rules for target concept T
$\mathcal{R}'$ is the new set of rules for target concept T, initially $\emptyset$
$\mathcal{N}$ is the set of negative examples for T

$C \leftarrow C - \mathcal{R}$
Forall $R \in \mathcal{R}$ do
  If describes-negative-examples($R, \mathcal{N}$)
  Then $\mathcal{R}' \leftarrow \mathcal{R}' \cup$ refine-rule($R, \mathcal{N}, \mathcal{R}'$)
  Else $\mathcal{R}' \leftarrow \mathcal{R}' \cup \{R\}$
target-concept-rules(T)$\leftarrow \mathcal{R}'$
Return $C \cup \mathcal{R}'$

Figure 18. HAMLET's specialization algorithm.

Figure 19 shows the case in which, while refining an overly general rule I_2,[10] one of its generating rules, I_1, was also overly general. In this case, it backtracks, and refines I_1 and I_2 with the rules that generated them, R_1, R_2, and R_3. R_1 was also overly general, so it had to backtrack to consider WSP_1, generating a refined version of R_1, RF_1. It generates RF_1 by finding one or two preconditions of the set $preconds(WSP_1) - preconds(R_1)$ that added to the set $preconds(R_1)$ do not cover the negative examples. Then, HAMLET deletes R_1. R_2 was not overly general, so it created a rule RF_2 from R_2 and I_1, then deleted I_1. Finally, R_3 was not overly general, so it generated a new rule RF_3, and deleted I_2. The dotted lines represent deleted links, the dotted boxes deleted rules, and the solid boxes the active rules after refinement.

4.2.2. *Choosing the right precondition to add*
HAMLET first tries to add preconditions from a set called *preferred-preconds*. We have found that the reason why most control rules were overly general was that they did not consider the needed preconditions (goal regression) for the other goals present in the decision. Instead of *eagerly* adding those

---

[10] R_i means a directly learned rule, I_i a generalized rule, and RF_i a specialized rule.

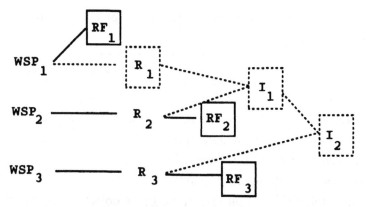

Figure 19. Graphical representation of the refinement of an overly general control rule I_2.

preconditions when the rule is created, the refinement algorithm incrementally adds the ones that it finds necessary for solving the over generality. When trying to add a precondition, HAMLET creates a pool of preconditions that can be added to the antecedent of the control rule,[11] it sorts the pool, and then it tests each one's coverage of negative examples. If a rule was directly learned by the Bounded Explanation module (i.e., it has no previous rules), then the tests are taken from its corresponding WSP. If it was an induced or refined rule, the tests are taken from the preconditions of its corresponding generating rules. The preconditions are always sorted according to an ordering function that prefers the preconditions that:

- refer to more variables that already appear in preconditions of the control rule – in this way, we keep the locality heuristic that was proposed in earlier work (Muggleton 1992; Borrajo et al. 1992a, b; Borrajo and Veloso 1994), and that empirical results show was effective-;
- refer to literals that have appeared more times in the preconditions of control rules of the same target concept; and
- refer to tests over the state rather than to prior goals, since computing a precondition referring to the prior goals is frequently more expensive than computing a precondition referring to the state.

4.3. *Example*

Suppose that PRODIGY solves a new problem in which *package1* and *plane1* also have to go to *airport3*, but this time they are initially in the same airport, *airport2*. When solving this problem using the overly general rule in Figure

---

[11] HAMLET creates this pool from the rest of preconditions that were not introduced directly into the rule when it was created.

12, PRODIGY yields a nonoptimal solution in the path that applies the rule, such as:

Plan	Achieved goals
fly-airplane(plane1,airport2,airport1) fly-airplane(plane1,airport1,airport3) fly-airplane(plane1,airport3,airport2) load-airplane(object1,plane1,airport2) fly-airplane(plane1,airport2,airport3) unload-airplane(object1,plane1,airport3)	(at plane1 airport3) (at-object object1 airport3)

In order to solve this problem, the specialization algorithm selects a test on the location of the object, since it is part of the goal regression of the other pending goals. Then, it creates the new control rule that was shown in Figure 13.

5. Empirical Results

We conducted extensive empirical tests to study the performance of HAMLET's learning algorithms in several experimental domains and problems within domains. We report in this article the results we obtained in two domains, the blocksworld and the logistics transportation domain.[12] The experiments are mainly of three kinds to test the behavior of the system along the following dimensions:

- **Lazy versus eager learning.** We compare the performance of HAMLET when it learns form the training problems with different eagerness, namely lazily and eagerly. Following a "lazy" learning bias, HAMLET learns control knowledge only from choices that contradict the default PRODIGY's heuristic behavior. Using an "eager" learning bias, HAMLET learns from every successful choice. The experiments interestingly show that HAMLET performs better with lazy than with eager learning.
- **Improvement of plan-generation efficiency and plan quality.** We show how HAMLET's *lazy* mode improves the search efficiency of the Base-Level PRODIGY planner.[13] More importantly, the experiments show that HAMLET learns knowledge capable of improving the quality of the generated plans.

---

[12] We have gathered results from other domains that will not be presented in this paper.

[13] All future references to Base-Level PRODIGY will refer to the planner using only its default heuristics and no control rule.

- **Convergence towards the correct learned knowledge.** These experiments illustrate the effect from incrementally refining the learned knowledge. The results show that HAMLET in *lazy* mode converges to the correct set of control rules, as a function of the number of training problems seen.

The following subsections describe the experiments and discuss the results. In all experiments, all problems were randomly generated, different sets of problems were used for learning and testing, and the distributions used for both sets of problems were the same. Also, the *optimality parameter* was always set to `true`, quality is measured as the number of operators in the resulting plan, and every training phase began with no control rules, $C = \phi$.

5.1. *Lazy vs. Eager Learning*

This experiment compares HAMLET's performance in *lazy* and *eager* learning modes. To show the difference between the two learning modes, we carried out the following experiment in the logistics domain. We trained HAMLET with the same 400 randomly-generated problems in *eager* and in *lazy* modes.[14] The learning problems were 200 one-goal problems involving up to four packages, and 200 two-goal problems involving up to five packages. In *lazy* mode, 19 rules were learned, while in *eager* mode, it learned 98 rules.

Then we tested the performance of the learned rules on 475 randomly generated problems from the same distribution as the learning set. The testing problems were of increasing complexity, generated by varying the number of goals in the problems from 1 to 10, and the maximum number of packages from 5 up to 20. The time bound given for all experiments reported in this article is $150 \times (1+\mathrm{mod}(\text{number-goals}, 10))$ seconds.[15] The results are shown in Tables 1, 2 and 3. In Table 1 the first column shows the number of problems solved by Base-Level PRODIGY (281), and using the learned control rules (239). The second column shows the total time spent, where the time of the unsolved problems is the time bound. The rest of the columns show the comparison using only the problems that were solved by both configurations. For instance, the third column shows the number of problems in which the solutions provided by Base-Level PRODIGY were better (i.e., according the the quality measure used) than using the learned control rules (eight cases) compared to the number of problems in which using the rules achieved better solutions than Base-Level PRODIGY (31 cases). The same applies for the other two columns. Table 2 shows the results using the rules learned in *lazy* mode

---

[14] *Eager* mode means calling HAMLET'algorithm (Figure 4) with the parameter $L =eager$, while *lazy* mode means calling HAMLET with $L =lazy$.

[15] We also tested using several time bounds, and the results were similar to the ones presented here.

using the same set of problems, and Table 3 shows the comparison between the two learning modes.

Table 1. Comparison of performance between Base-Level PRODIGY4.0 and PRODIGY4.0 using HAMLET's learned rules in *eager* mode for the logistics domain.

Rules Used	Solved Problems	Time (seconds)	Solved by both (197 problems)		
			Better solutions	Solution length	Nodes explored
no rules	281	58900	8	1208	7699
eager (98 rules)	239	72699	31	1164	5560

Table 2. Comparison of performance between Base-Level PRODIGY4.0 and PRODIGY4.0 using HAMLET's learned rules in *lazy* mode for the logistics domain.

Rules Used	Solved problems	Time (seconds)	Solved by both (278 problems)		
			Better solutions	Solution length	Nodes explored
no rules	281	58900	2	2995	16366
lazy (19 rules)	334	44091	89	2763	13030

Table 3. Comparison of performance between PRODIGY4.0 using HAMLET's learned rules in *lazy* and *eager* modes for the logistics domain.

Rules Used	Solved problems	Time (seconds)	Solved by both (228 problems)		
			Better solutions	Solution length	Nodes explored
eager (98 rules)	239	72699	12	1593	7810
lazy (19 rules)	334	44091	44	1474	6802

Discussion. In *lazy* learning mode, HAMLET performs more efficiently and yields higher quality solutions. With respect to efficiency, the number of solved problems increases from 50% up to 70%, while the time spent on solving the problems also decreases. In addition, the solutions provided are much better. More specifically, in *eager* mode, it performs worse for eight problems and better for 31. In *lazy* mode, it performs worse in only two problems, and better in 89! We believe HAMLET's lazy behavior is responsible for such good results, given that it learns only when it seems clear that a decision was the best one in any node in the search tree, and was not chosen by the default problem solver. That is, the goal of HAMLET is to provide the problem solver with a learned way of controlling when not to follow the default procedure, thus letting the problem solver decide when the default decision is correct.

There is also an important difference in the behavior of both modes: the number of learned rules. Since the *eager* mode learns from every decision, it learns many more rules, and many more types of rules. For instance, suppose that operator O_1 appears in the domain description before operator O_2, and both are relevant to the same goal g. Then the default behavior of PRODIGY4.0 is that, when it does not have control knowledge to know which operator to use, it uses the first operator that appears in the domain description. Thus, it will always try O_1 before O_2. If O_1 is always the best operator to achieve the goal g, then the lazy mode of HAMLET will never learn a control rule for that decision, while the eager mode will learn a rule each time that it uses O_1 and succeeds in achieving a solution. Therefore, eager mode suffers more from the utility problem than the lazy mode as can be observed in these tables in the time columns.

With respect to learning time, learning in *lazy* mode is a relatively fast process, since it generates fewer rules, and, therefore, spends a short time learning. The time spent on learning after every PRODIGY4.0 run on a problem is between two and ten times less than PRODIGY's search time. In contrast, learning eagerly can be very slow, since the refinement procedure needs to match many more rules against each other. It might take up to 20 times PRODIGY's search time.

We have been working on many experiments to find additional evidence of these two slow down phenomena (i.e., number of rules and learning time), and we have found that the eager mode does not work for most domains. It overloads the system with control rules, not allowing HAMLET to finish the learning phase due to memory problems. A potential advantage of *eager* mode over *lazy* mode might be that the *lazy* mode requires the whole search tree to be expanded for learning control rules, while *eager* mode can learn as soon as any solution has been found. Therefore, *lazy* mode should be used for domains for which learning in easy problems scales well to complex problems. We have found empirically that this is true for most of our planning domains.

Finally, if we compare the solution length and the number of nodes of both modes against not using the rules, we see that in *eager* mode it saves 3.6% in solution length and 27.8% in number of nodes, while in *lazy* mode it saves 7.7% in solution length and 20.4% in number of nodes. The performance is almost doubled for *lazy* mode in solution length, and better for *eager* mode in number of nodes. The reason why the savings in number of nodes is bigger for *eager* mode is due to the number of control rules it has, which prune more of the search space.

5.2. *Improving Efficiency and Solution Quality*

To show that HAMLET improves not only the efficiency of the base-level problem solver, PRODIGY4.0, but also improves the quality of the solutions provided by PRODIGY4.0 with the learned knowledge, we have carried out experiments in the logistics transportation domain, described in Subsection 3.4, and in blocksworld. We use the blocksworld to show a domain in which HAMLET improves mostly the efficiency of the problem solver, and logistics as a domain in which it also greatly improves the quality of the solutions provided by the problem solver. In this last domain the quality of the solutions is an important aspect, due to the possible unnecessary movements of the carriers. HAMLET learns knowledge that allows the planner to generate effective solutions for transporting packages.

Blocksworld results. We trained HAMLET with 200 simple randomly generated problems of one and two goals, and up to ten blocks. HAMLET generated 11 control rules. Then, we randomly generated 375 testing problems of increasing complexity. Table 4 shows the results of those tests. We varied the number of goals in the problems from one up to ten, and the maximum number of blocks from five up to 50.

Table 4. Results on increasingly complex problems in the blocksworld domain.

Test sets		Solved problems		Solved by both (174 problems, 46.4%)					
				Better solutions		Solution length		Nodes explored	
Goals	Problems	without rules	with rules	without rules	with rules	without rules	with rules	without rules	with rules
1	100	68	100	0	0	245	245	9227	1187
2	100	56	92	1	2	196	193	3924	1258
5	100	45	80	1	3	188	180	4085	1895
10	75	13	34	0	1	76	72	11048	313
Totals	375	182	306	2	6	705	690	28284	4653
%		48.5%	81.6%	1.1%	3.4%			Ratio	6.1

Discussion. The results show a remarkable improvement on the Base-Level PRODIGY solver performance when using the learned control rules. As an example, it increases the number of solved problems from 48.5% up to

81.6%, and expands six times fewer number of nodes.[16] It also generates better solutions using the rules in six occasions, while Base-Level PRODIGY only generates better solutions in two occasions. These results on solution quality are not as impressive as in the logistics domain (detailed below) due to the fact that, in the blocksworld task, most problems have the same number of operators in all possible solutions to the same problem.

Logistics results. We trained HAMLET in *lazy* mode with 400 simple randomly generated problems of one and two goals, and up to three cities and five packages. HAMLET generated 26 control rules. Then, we randomly generated 525 testing problems of increasing complexity. Table 5 shows the results of those tests. We varied the number of goals in the problems from one up to 50, and the maximum number of packages from five up to 50. Problems with 20 and 50 goals pose very complex problems to find good or optimal solutions, even for humans.

Table 5. Results on increasingly complex problems in the logistics domain.

Test sets		Solved problems		Solved by both (279 problems, 53.14%)					
				Better solutions		Solution length		Nodes explored	
Goals	Problems	without rules	with rules	without rules	with rules	without rules	with rules	without rules	with rules
1	100	95	100	0	11	327	307	2097	1569
2	100	85	94	0	25	528	479	3401	2308
5	100	56	82	1	33	865	777	5170	3463
10	100	32	68	1	24	770	668	3482	2941
20	75	13	39	0	10	505	455	2216	1924
50	50	1	10	0	0	34	34	143	141
Totals	525	282	393	2	103	3029	2720	16509	12346
%		53.7%	74.9%	0.7%	36.9%			Ratio	1.3

Discussion. The results show again a remarkable increase in the number of solved problems using the learned rules, as well as a large number of problems (103) in which the solution generated using the rules is of better quality, compared to the two problems in which Base-Level PRODIGY produced a

---

[16] In 10 goal problems using the learned rules, it expands 35 times fewer number of nodes in the search tree.

solution of better quality. The running times decreased using the rules, but not significantly.

Learning control knowledge to improve problem solving performance is a potential source of innefficiency due to the tradeoff between the savings obtained and the cost of using the learned knowledge. This is generally known as the *utility problem* in speedup learning (Minton 1988). Interestingly, HAMLET does not suffer substantially from the utility problem even with no special organization of the learned knowledge.[17] Due to its inductive step over the control rules of the same type, HAMLET keeps a small number of control rules, instead of retaining many variations of each rule type. This is one of the sources of power of the induction step applied to the bounded explained control rules. Nevertheless, we are currently developing efficient methods for organizing and matching the learned control rules. We consider this organization essential to the overall learning process to avoid a potential utility problem due to inefficient matching (Doorenbos and Veloso 1993).

After analyzing why some problems were not solved, we concluded that some rules were not correct after the training phase. This fact led us to carry on the next set of experiments towards testing the convergence of the learning approach.

5.3. *Convergence to the Correct Control Knowledge*

The previous results are important in the sense that they show that the learned rules after 400 training problems perform well. But someone could ask if the learned knowledge improves over time when more training problems are given, or it begins to oscillate in a local maximum, adding and removing the preconditions of the control rules. This is an important issue for any machine learning system, especially for a *lazy* system as HAMLET, since HAMLET relies on incremental refinement to correctly characterize the learned control rules. Therefore, it needs to converge as it sees more training examples.

To show that HAMLET improves with the number of training problems, we performed the following experiment: we trained HAMLET in *lazy* mode with 75 problems, 150 problems, and 400 problems in the logistics domain. Then, we tested the respective learned control rules on the same test set as before (525 problems of increasing complexity). Table 6 shows results that clearly illustrate the rules converge towards the correct behavior.

Discussion. After analyzing these results and the previous ones, we noted that there were problems in which HAMLET did not learn anything. These

---

[17] This is true even for *eager* mode that learns many more rules than *lazy* mode.

Table 6. Results on convergence in the logistics domain.

Training problems	Solved problems		Solved by both				
			Better solutions		Ratio Solution Length	Ratio Time	Ratio Nodes
	without rules	with rules	without rules	with rules	without/ with rules	without/ with rules	without/ with rules
75	53.71%	63.62%	0.35%	25.89%	1.11	0.49	1
150	53.71%	65.71%	0.72%	31.9%	1.06	0.33	1.25
400	53.71%	74.86%	0.72%	36.92%	1.08	0.32	1.34

problems belong to two different groups. The first group are problems that were too easy. They were solved by PRODIGY with no search, or the default strategy made the right decisions in the first place. The second group of problems were too complicated, so PRODIGY could not expand the whole search tree in the given time bound (usually 100 seconds), and, therefore, HAMLET could not learn any control rule. Here, there is some underlying assumption (bias) that influences HAMLET's behavior: HAMLET **will learn better from medium difficulty problems**. Having this bias in mind, the training problems were randomly generated so that: they were not too easy, such as problems in which the goals are true in the initial state; and they were not too complicated, such as problems with more than two goals. We believe that this is not an over simplifying assumption: control knowledge learned from them will still be applicable to easier or more difficult problems. As we have shown, the learned knowledge, even coming from a "biased" training phase, transfers well to more complicated problems, and does not interfere in the default PRODIGY behavior with simpler problems.

Since training can benefit from well-suited training problems, we are currently developing a better training schema in which problems are not generated randomly, but are biased towards the kinds of problems from which HAMLET learns better. This domain-independent biased generation of training problems should improve the convergence of HAMLET, and also reduce the training effort. We also plan to analyze, for each domain, the number of training problems that will be needed to obtain a certain degree of accuracy, based on research from computational learning theory (Valiant 1984).

6. Related Work

Most previous lazy learning approaches have been inductive approaches, such as the work in instance-based (Aha et al. 1991), memory-based (Stanfill and

Waltz 1986), or exemplar-based learning (Porter et al. 1990). Only some of the work has been applied to planning, usually in the context of analogy or case-based reasoning (Hammond 1989; Hanks and Weld 1995; Kambhampati 1989; Kettler et al. 1994; Veloso 1994a, b). Most of this work concerns domain-specific algorithms. Also, although these approaches demonstrated some useful lazy learning behavior, they did not, as we have, compare lazy and eager learning modes. The two main differences with these approaches are: control rules represent knowledge to control individual decisions, while cases chain multiple decisions together allowing therefore a global control of the planning process; and control rules fire only if their antecedents fully match, while cases allow partial matching.

Many of the inductive systems require many examples for learning complex definitions, since they do not use prior knowledge that can guide the search of generalized hypothesis. Some new techniques have been developed that use prior knowledge, but they are still mainly used for learning domain theories (e.g., (Quinlan 1990; Muggleton 1992)), instead of learning control knowledge.

Similar work on lazy learning includes Lazy Explanation-Based Learning, LEBL (Tadepalli 1989) and Lazy Partial Evaluation, LPE (Clark and Holte 1992). While LEBL refines the knowledge by introducing exceptions, HAMLET modifies the control rules themselves by adding or removing their applicability conditions. Also, LEBL applies to games, while we use HAMLET for general task planning. Finally, LEBL does not consider plan quality. In turn, LPE learns from all search paths, following a more *eager* approach than HAMLET's *lazy* mode, and has been used in a linear problem solver (Prolog) to solve constraint satisfaction problems, instead of applying it to nonlinear planning.

Most of the planners that learn follow an eager deductive approach. They try to eagerly and correctly explain the problem solving choices from a single episode or from a static analysis of the domain definition. These speedup learning systems are usually applied to problem solvers with the linearity assumption, such as the ones applied to logic programming problem solvers (Quinlan 1990; Zelle and Mooney 1993; Muggleton 1992), special-purpose problem solvers (Langley 1983; Mitchell et al. 1983), or other general-purpose linear problem solvers (Etzioni 1993; Fikes et al. 1972; Leckie and Zukerman 1991; Minton 1988; Pérez and Etzioni 1992). These problem solvers are known to be incomplete and incapable of finding optimal solutions (Rich 1983; Veloso 1989).

If we remove the linearity assumption, we are dealing with nonlinear problem solvers. In this article we show that nonlinear problem solving offers new learning opportunities where domain-dependent control knowledge can be used to further improve not only the problem solver's performance but also the quality of the solutions produced. Moreover, eagerly constructing correct explanations of the nonlinear problem solver's successes and failures *from a single example* is computationally expensive, since it is difficult to define the right language for describing the relations among goals when making decisions. Also, even if those needed predicates are kept, goal regression leads in nonlinear planning to control knowledge that is either overly general or overly specific. Some approaches to learning in nonlinear planning are (Estlin and Mooney 1995; Bhatnagar 1992; Laird et al. 1986; Leckie and Zukerman 1991; Kambhampati and Kedar 1991; Pérez and Carbonell 1994; Ruby and Kibler 1992; Veloso 1994b; Veloso et al. 1995). The main difference with our approach is the lazy aspects of HAMLET, and the way in which learned knowledge is represented. While improving problem solving efficiency has been studied frequently, learning to improve solution quality has only been recently pursued by some researchers, including (Pérez and Carbonell 1994; Ruby and Kibler 1992). We differ from Pérez and Carbonell's work in that HAMLET performs inductive refinement of the control rules, and in the way positive examples are generated. Ruby and Kibler's approach differs in the knowledge representation of the learned control knowledge, since it is a case-based learner.

7. Conclusions

We have described a learning approach, HAMLET, that lazily acquires successful and failure control patterns for a nonlinear problem solver. Within HAMLET, *lazily* means the combination of three lazy aspects:

- It learns rules that are not provenly correct by bounding the explanation of the problem solving successes to a reduced set of features that explain why a certain decision is the best one. The explanation does not consider the whole search tree, nor does it try to prove that it is correct. Hence, this is a *lazy* learning approach.
- It incrementally refines learned control rules. Since the rules might not be correct, they might fail to (optimally) solve future problems. HAMLET does not eagerly try to find those erroneous applications of the control rules, but lazily waits until it finds a negative example. Also, it refines on demand the descriptions of the target concepts, using only a subset of the examples found.
- These rules are learned only at the decision points that override the default behavior of the problem solver, instead of at all the decision points (i.e., as is done by other learning mechanisms). This is again a *lazy* learning approach for determining which rules should be learned.

The combination of these first two *lazy* aspects results in a system that can solve problems more efficiently, achieving better solutions than the heuristic-based problem solver.[18] Also, this lazy aspect allows HAMLET to learn useful control rules in nonlinear planning, which is a complex task to perform by *eager* approaches: it is difficult to describe the complete extra domain theory that *eager* approaches require in nonlinear planning (Minton 1988; Katukam and Kambhampati 1994). Furthermore, the results show that the third *lazy* aspect has several advantages over an *eager* learner since it achieves *better* solutions *more efficiently*, requires fewer learning resources (i.e., learning time and memory), and it suffers less from the utility problem.

Finally, HAMLET has been tested in a variety of experiments involving complex planning problems. The empirical results support the effectiveness of HAMLET's learning approach, in terms of improvement in planning efficiency, in the quality of plans generated, and in its incremental convergence towards the correct knowledge. In summary, HAMLET's learning power comes most directly from its overall lazy learning approach.

Acknowledgements

This research for the first author was sponsored by Ministerio de Educación y Ciencia and Comunidad de Madrid. This research for the second author is sponsored by the Wright Laboratory, Aeronautical Systems Center, Air Force Materiel Command, USAF, and the Advanced Research Projects Agency (ARPA) under grant number F33615-93-1-1330. The views and conclusions contained in this document are those of the authors and should not be interpreted as necessarily representing the official policies or endorsements, either expressed or implied, of Wright Laboratory or the U.S. Government. The authors would like to thank David Aha and the anonymous reviewers for their many useful comments.

References

Aha, D. W., Kibler, D. & Albert, M. K. (1991). Instance-based learning algorithms. *Machine Learning* 6(1): 37–66.
Bhatnagar, N. (1992). Learning by incomplete explanations of failures in recursive domains. In *Proceedings of the Ninth International Conference on Machine Learning*, pp. 30–36, Aberdeen, Scotland: Morgan Kaufmann.

[18] As stated in Section 2, the base problem solver already incorporates many useful domain-independent heuristics. It would be easier to outperform a system that performs completely uninformed search.

Borrajo, D., Caraça-Valente, J. P. & Morant, J. L. (1992a). Learning heuristics in planning. In *Proceedings of the Sixth International Conference on Systems Research, Informatics and Cybernetics*, pp. 43–49, Baden-Baden, Germany: The International Institute for Advanced Studies in Systems Research and Cybernetics.

Borrajo, D., Caraça-Valente, J. P. & Pazos, J. (1992b). A knowledge compilation model for learning heuristics. In *Proceedings of the First Workshop on Knowledge Compilation*, Aberdeen, Scotland.

Borrajo, D. & Veloso, M. (1994). Incremental learning of control knowledge for nonlinear problem solving. In *Proceedings of the European Conference on Machine Learning*, pp. 64–82. Catania, Italy: Springer Verlag.

Carbonell, J. G., Blythe, J., Etzioni, O., Gil, Y., Joseph, R., Kahn, D., Knoblock, C., Minton, S., Pérez, A., Reilly, S., Veloso, M. & Wang, X. (1992). PRODIGY4.0: The manual and tutorial. Technical Report CMU-CS-92-150, SCS, Carnegie Mellon University.

Carbonell, J. G., Knoblock, C. A. & Minton, S. (1990). Prodigy: An integrated architecture for planning and learning. In VanLehn, K. (ed.), *Architectures for Intelligence*, Erlbaum, Hillsdale, NJ. Also Technical Report CMU-CS-89-189.

Clark, P. & Holte, R. (1992). Lazy partial evaluation: An integration of explanation-based generalisation and partial evaluation. In *Proceedings of the Ninth International Conference on Machine Learning*, pp. 82–91, Aberdeen, Scotland: Morgan Kaufmann.

Cohen, W. W. (1990). Learning approximate control rules of high utility. In *Proceedings of the Seventh International Conference on Machine Learning*, pp. 268–276, Austin, TX: Morgan Kaufmann.

DeJong, G. F. & Mooney, R. (1986). Explanation-based learning: An alternative view. *Machine Learning* 1(2): 145–176.

Doorenbos, R. B. & Veloso, M. M. (1993). Knowledge organization and the utility problem. In *Proceedings of the Third International Workshop on Knowledge Compilation and Speedup Learning*, pp. 28–34, Amherst, MA.

Estlin, T. A. & Mooney, R. (1995). Hybrid learning of search control for partial order planning. In *New Directions in AI Planning*, pp. 115–128. IOS Press.

Etzioni, O. (1993). Acquiring search-control knowledge via static analysis. *Artificial Intelligence* 62(2): 255–301.

Etzioni, O. & Minton, S. (1992). Why EBL produces overly-specific knowledge: A critique of the Prodigy approaches. In *Proceedings of the Ninth International Conference on Machine Learning*, pp. 137–143. Aberdeen, Scotland. Morgan Kaufmann.

Fikes, R. E., Hart, P. E. & Nilsson, N. J. (1972). Learning and executing generalized robot plans. *Artificial Intelligence* 3: 251–288.

Hammond, K. J. (1989). *Case-based Planning: Viewing Planning as a Memory Task*. New York, NY: Academic Press.

Hanks, S. & Weld, D. (1995). A domain-independent algorithm for plan adaptation. *Journal of Artificial Intelligence Research* 2: 319–360.

Kambhampati, S. (1989). *Flexible Reuse and Modification in Hierarchical Planning: A Validation Structure Based Approach*. PhD thesis, Computer Vision Laboratory, Center for Automation Research, College Park, MD: University of Maryland.

Kambhampati, S. & Kedar, S. (1991). Explanation based generalization of partially ordered plans. In *Proceedings of the Ninth National Conference on Artificial Intelligence*, pp. 679–685. Anaheim, CA: AAAI Press.

Katukam, S. & Kambhampati, S. (1994). Learning explanation-based search control rules for partial order planning. In *Proceedings of the Twelfth National Conference on Artificial Intelligence*, pp. 582–587. Seattle, WA: AAAI Press.

Kettler, B. P., Hendler, J. A., Andersen, A. W. & Evett, M. P. (1994). Massively parallel support for case-based planning. *IEEE Expert* 2: 8–14.

Laird, J. E., Rosenbloom, P. S. & Newell, A. (1986). Chunking in SOAR: The anatomy of a general learning mechanism. *Machine Learning* 1: 11–46.

Langley, P. (1983). Learning effective search heuristics. In *Proceedings of the Eighth International Joint Conference on Artificial Intelligence*, pp. 419–421, Los Altos, CA: Morgan Kaufmann.

Leckie, C. & Zukerman, I. (1991). Learning search control rules for planning: An inductive approach. In *Proceedings of the Eighth International Workshop on Machine Learning*, pp. 422–426, Evanston, IL: Morgan Kaufmann.

Minton, S. (1988). *Learning Effective Search Control Knowledge: An Explanation-Based Approach*. Boston, MA: Kluwer Academic Publishers.

Minton, S., Knoblock, C. A., Kuokka, D. R., Gil, Y., Joseph, R. L. & Carbonell, J. G. (1989). PRODIGY 2.0: The manual and tutorial. Technical Report CMU-CS-89-146, School of Computer Science, Carnegie Mellon University.

Mitchell, T. M., Keller, R. M. & Kedar-Cabelli, S. T. (1986). Explanation-based generalization: A unifying view. *Machine Learning* 1: 47–80.

Mitchell, T. M., Utgoff, P. E. & Banerji, R. B. (1983). Learning by experimentation: Acquiring and refining problem-solving heuristics. In R. S. Michalski, J. G. Carbonell & T. Mitchell (eds.), *Machine Learning, An Artificial Intelligence Approach*. Palo Alto, CA: Tioga Press.

Muggleton, S. (1992). *Inductive Logic Programming*. London: Academic Press Limited.

Pérez, M. A. & Carbonell, J. G. (1994). Control knowledge to improve plan quality. In *Proceedings of the Second International Conference on AI Planning Systems*, pp. 323–328, Chicago, IL: AAAI Press.

Pérez, M. A. & Etzioni, O. (1992). DYNAMIC: A new role for training problems in EBL. In *Proceedings of the Ninth International Conference on Machine Learning*, pp. 367–372, Aberdeen, Scotland: Morgan Kaufmann.

Porter, B. W., Bareiss, R. & Holte, R. (1990). Knowledge acquisition and heuristic classification in weak-theory domains. *Artificial Intelligence* 45: 229–263.

Quinlan, J. R. (1990). Learning logic definitions from relations. *Machine Learning* 5: 239–266.

Rich, E. (1983). *Artificial Intelligence*. McGraw-Hill, Inc.

Ruby, D. & Kibler, D. (1992). Learning episodes for optimization. In *Proceedings of the Ninth International Conference on Machine Learning*, pp. 379–384, Aberdeen, Scotland: Morgan Kaufmann.

Stanfill, C. & Waltz, D. (1986). Toward memory-based reasoning. *Communications of the Association for Computing Machinery* 29: 1213–1228.

Stone, P., Veloso, M. & Blythe, J. (1994). The need for different domain-independent heuristics. In *Proceedings of the Second International Conference on AI Planning Systems*, pp. 164–169, Chicago, IL: AAAI Press.

Tadepalli, P. (1989). Lazy explanation-based learning: A solution to the intractable theory problem. In *Proceedings of the Eleventh International Joint Conference on Artificial Intelligence*, pp. 694–700, San Mateo, CA: Morgan Kaufmann.

Valiant, L. (1984). A theory of the learnable. *Communications of the ACM* 27(11): 1134–1142.

Veloso, M. & Blythe, J. (1994). Linkability: Examining causal link commitments in partial-order planning. In *Proceedings of the Second International Conference on AI Planning Systems*, pp. 170–175, Chicago, IL: AAAI Press.

Veloso, M. & Borrajo, D. (1994). Learning strategy knowledge incrementally. In *Proceedings of the Sixth IEEE International Conference on Tools with Artificial Intelligence*, pp. 484–490, New Orleans, LO: IEEE Computer Society Press.

Veloso, M., Carbonell, J., Pérez, A., Borrajo, D., Fink, E. & Blythe, J. (1995). Integrating planning and learning: The PRODIGY architecture. *Journal of Experimental and Theoretical AI* 7: 81–120.

Veloso, M. M. (1989). Nonlinear problem solving using intelligent causal-commitment. Technical Report CMU-CS-89-210, School of Computer Science, Carnegie Mellon University.

Veloso, M. M. (1994a). Flexible strategy learning: Analogical replay of problem solving episodes. In *Proceedings of the Twelfth National Conference on Artificial Intelligence*, Seattle, WA: AAAI Press.

Veloso, M. M. (1994b). *Planning and Learning by Analogical Reasoning*. Springer Verlag.

Waldinger, R. (1981). Achieving several goals simultaneously. In Nilsson, N. J. & Webber, B. (eds.), *Readings in Artificial Intelligence*, pp. 250–271. Los Altos, CA: Morgan Kaufmann.

Zelle, J. & Mooney, R. (1993). Combining FOIL and EBG to speed-up logic programs. In *Proceedings of the Thirteenth International Joint Conference on Artificial Intelligence*, pp. 1106–1113, Chambery, France: Morgan Kaufmann.

Artificial Intelligence Review **11**: 407–423, 1997.

IGTree: Using Trees for Compression and Classification in Lazy Learning Algorithms

WALTER DAELEMANS[1], ANTAL VAN DEN BOSCH[2] and
TON WEIJTERS[2]
[1]*Computational Linguistics, Tilburg University, The Netherlands*
E-mail: Walter.Daelemans@kub.nl
[2]*MATRIKS, Maastricht University, The Netherlands*
E-mail: {antal,weijters}@cs.unimaas.nl

Abstract. We describe the IGTree learning algorithm, which compresses an instance base into a tree structure. The concept of information gain is used as a heuristic function for performing this compression. IGTree produces trees that, compared to other lazy learning approaches, reduce storage requirements and the time required to compute classifications. Furthermore, we obtained similar or better generalization accuracy with IGTree when trained on two complex linguistic tasks, viz. letter–phoneme transliteration and part-of-speech-tagging, when compared to alternative lazy learning and decision tree approaches (viz., IB1, information-gain-weighted IB1, and C4.5). A third experiment, with the task of word hyphenation, demonstrates that when the mutual differences in information gain of features is too small, IGTree as well as information-gain-weighted IB1 perform worse than IB1. These results indicate that IGTree is a useful algorithm for problems characterized by the availability of a large number of training instances described by symbolic features with sufficiently differing information gain values.

Key words: lazy learning, eager learning, decision trees, information gain, data compression, instance base indexing

1. Introduction

In previous research, we have applied lazy learning techniques to a variety of problems in *language technology* (e.g., converting spelling to phonetic transcription, stress assignment, predicting morphological suffixes, and assigning syllable structure to words). See Daelemans (1995) for an overview, and Cardie (1993) for a similar case-based approach. This type of linguistic problem can be characterized by the following observations:

1. The problem can be described as finding a mapping from a pattern of *symbolic* (nominal and unordered) features (letters, phonemes, part-of-speech tags, etc.) to a *symbolic* class (phonemes, boundary symbols, affixes, tags, etc.).
2. The problem can be described as classification in context: given a target symbol and its immediate local context, produce one of a finite number

of possible classes for that symbol. For example, given a spelling symbol and its three left and three right neighbor letters, decide which phonetic symbol it corresponds to.

3. The instance features display an outspoken variation in their relevance to solving the task, and can be ordered according to this relevance. In general, the further away a feature (representing context) from the target, the less relevant it is.

4. The instance space is reasonably large (e.g., seven features with 27 possible values each, in the spelling-to-phonetic-transcription problem) and, typically, there are also many training instances available (on the order of 100,000 or more).

5. The problem is usually described (in terms of linguistic rules) as noisy and complex, with many subregularities and (pockets of) exceptions. In other words, apart from a core of generalizations, there is a relatively large periphery of irregularities.

In lazy learning (e.g., the IB1 algorithm in Aha, Kibler, and Albert 1991), similarity of a new instance to stored instances is used to find the nearest neighbors of the new instance. The classes associated with the nearest neighbor instances are then used to predict the class of the new instance. In IB1, all features are assigned the same relevance, which is undesirable for our linguistic problems. We noticed that IB1, when extended with a simple feature weighting similarity function, sometimes outperforms both connectionist approaches and knowledge-based "linguistic–engineering" approaches (Daelemans and Van den Bosch 1992, 1994; Van den Bosch and Daelemans 1993). The similarity function we introduced in lazy learning (Daelemans and Van den Bosch 1992) consisted simply of multiplying, when comparing two instances, the similarity between the values for each feature with the corresponding *information gain* for that feature (information gain is also implemented in C4.5 (Quinlan 1993) to guide decision tree building). We will call this version of lazy learning IB1-IG.

To compute similarity in IB1-IG, the similarity function sim in Equation 1 is used, in which X and Y are two instances of which the similarity must be computed, $G(fi)$ is the information gain of the ith feature, and $\sigma(x_i, y_i)$ is the overlap between the values of the ith feature in instances X and Y. Both instances contain n features.

$$sim(X, Y) = \sum_{i=1}^{n} G(f_i)\sigma(x_i, y_i) \qquad (1)$$

As we are only investigating the learning of instances with symbolic features, the overlap function proposed by Stanfill and Waltz (1986) is used (Equation 2).

$$\sigma(x_i, y_i) = 1 \ if \ x_i = y_i, \ else \ 0 \tag{2}$$

The main idea of *information gain weighting* is to interpret the training material as an information source capable of generating a number of messages (the classes associated with stored instances) with a certain probability. Data base information entropy is equal to the average number of bits of information needed to know the class given an instance. It is computed by Equation 3, where p_i (the probability of class i) is estimated by its relative frequency in the training set.

$$H(D) = -\sum_{i} p_i log_2 p_i \tag{3}$$

For each feature, its relative importance in the data base can be calculated by computing its information gain. To do this, we compute the average information entropy for this feature and subtract it from the information entropy of the data base. To compute the average information entropy for a feature (Equation 4), we take the average information entropy of the database restricted to each possible value for the feature. The expression $D_{[f=v]}$ refers to those instances in the database that have value v for feature f, where V is the set of possible values for feature f. Finally, $|D|$ is the number of instances in data base D.

$$H(D_{[f]}) = \sum_{v_i \in V} H(D_{[f=v_i]}) \frac{|D_{[f=v_i]}|}{|D|} \tag{4}$$

Information gain is then obtained by Equation 5.

$$G(f) = H(D) - H(D_{[f]}) \tag{5}$$

The classification function of IB1-IG computes the similarity between a new instance and all stored instances, and returns the class label of the most similar instance.

During experimentation, we noticed that accuracy (generalization performance) decreased considerably when instance memory was pruned in some way (e.g., using IB2, Aha et al. 1991, or by eliminating nontypical instances). Storing all training items by lazy learning (e.g., IB1) seems essential for achieving a high generalization performance in many linguistic tasks we investigated. The observation that the problems exhibit a lot of sub-regularity and exceptions may explain why full memory produces better results than an approach in which not all training items are kept in memory (cf. Aha 1992).

Unfortunately, as the prediction function in lazy learning has to compare a test instance to all stored instances, and our linguistic data sets typically contain hundreds of thousands of instances, processing of new instances is prohibitively slow. Hardware solutions to this problem have been proposed (e.g. data-level parallelism on massively parallel machines, Stanfill and Waltz 1986; or wafer-scale integration, Kitano 1993). We will not discuss these here as we focus on comparing implementations of different algorithms on serial machines. What we needed was an algorithmic variant of IB1-IG in which the instance base is reorganized (by compression rather than by pruning) in such a way that access to relevant instances is faster, and no generalization performance is lost.

We developed an algorithm, IGTree (a first version is described in Van den Bosch and Daelemans 1993), which uses the differences in information gain of features for ordering the instance base and optimizing access to the instance base. For the type of problem described above, IGTree produces a tree structure which is considerably smaller than the original data base; furthermore, tree retrieval is considerably faster than retrieval in IB1-IG.

In Section 2, we describe the IGTree model and its relationships to k-d trees and decision trees. Section 3 describes comparative experiments with IGTree, IB1, IB1-IG, and C4.5 on learning the linguistic tasks. We present our conclusions in Section 4.

2. IGTree

The positive effect of using information gain weights in the overlap function to define similarity in IB1 for our tasks, prompted us to develop an alternative approach in which the instance memory is reorganized, using information gain as a heuristic guide, in such a way that it contains the information essential for retrieval, but is compressed into a decision tree structure. In this Section, we will provide both an intuitive and algorithmic description of IGTree, discuss its relations to k-d trees and top down induced decision trees, and provide some analyses on complexity issues.

2.1. *The IGTree model*

IGTree combines two algorithms: one for constructing decision trees, and one for retrieving classification information from these trees. During the construction of IGTree decision trees, instances are stored as paths of connected nodes. All nodes contain a test (based on one of the features) and a class label (representing the default class at that node). Nodes are connected via arcs denoting the outcomes for the test (feature values). Information gain is used to determine the order in which instance features are used as tests in the tree. This order is fixed in advance, so the maximal depth of the tree is always equal to the number of features, and at the same level of the tree, all nodes have the same test. The reasoning behind this reorganization (which is in fact a compression) is that when the computation of information gain points to one feature clearly being the most important in classification, search can be restricted to matching a test instance to those stored instances that have the same feature value at that feature. Instead of restricting search to those memory instances that match only on this feature, the instance memory can then be optimized further by examining the second most important feature, followed by the third most important feature, etc. A considerable compression is obtained as similar instances share partial paths.

Instead of converting the instance base to a tree in which all instances are fully represented as paths, storing all feature values, we compress the tree even more by restricting the paths to those input feature values that disambiguate the classification from all other instances in the training material. The idea is that it is not necessary to fully store an instance as a path when only a few feature values of the instance make the instance classification unique. This implies that feature values that do not contribute to the disambiguation of the instance classification (i.e., the values of the features with lower information gain values than the the lowest information gain value of the disambiguating features) are *not* stored in the tree. Although one could opt for storing these features, not storing them does not affect the accuracy of IGTree's generalization performance.

Leaf nodes contain the unique class label corresponding to a path in the tree. Non-terminal nodes contain information about the *most probable* or *default* classification given the path thus far, according to the bookkeeping information on class occurrences maintained by the tree construction algorithm. This extra information is essential when using the tree for classification. Finding the classification of a new instance involves traversing the tree (i.e., matching all feature-values of the test instance with arcs in the order of the overall feature information gain), and either retrieving a classification when a leaf is reached, or using the default classification on the last matching non-terminal node if a feature-value match fails.

A final compression is obtained by pruning the derived tree. All leaf-node daughters of a mother node that have the same class as that node are removed from the tree, as their class information does not contradict the default class information already present at the mother node. Again, this compression does not affect the accuracy of IGTree's generalization performance.

In sum, in the trade-off between computation during learning and computation during classification, the IGTree approach chooses to invest more time in organizing the instance base using information gain and compression, at the gain of considerably simplified and faster processing during classification, as compared to lazy learning approaches that maintain instances in a flat file rather than using an reorganizing scheme.

A tree produced by the IGTree algorithm is *oblivious* because all nodes at a certain level in the tree test the same feature. The IGTree approach differs in two aspects from other oblivious decision tree (cf. Langley and Sage 1994) and oblivious decision graph (cf. Kohavi and Li 1995) approaches. First, in IGTree, information gain of features is used to determine the order in which they are expanded in the decision tree. The second difference is more fundamental, and is also related to the use of information gain as a guiding function in IGTree: in trees generated by IGTree, leaves are not necessarily stored at the same level. During tree building, expansion of the tree is stopped when all instances in the subset indexed by a node are of the same class. At that point, which may be at any level in the tree, all remaining features with a lower information gain value are ignored. Similarly, IGTree classifies a new instance by investigating a variable and often limited number of features, rather than a fixed number of (relevant) features, as in Kohavi and Li (1995).

The recursive algorithms for tree construction and retrieval are given in Figure 1.

2.2. *Asymptotic complexity*

As far as an asymptotic analysis of the complexity of storage, search and tree-building is concerned, it should be noted that only worst-case results are given. The actual compression (on which complexity of search, building, and storage depend) is completely task-dependent, and should be observed in empirical tests such as those in Section 3.

The worst-case complexity of searching an instance in the tree is proportional to $F * log(V)$, where F is the number of features (equal to the maximal depth of the tree), and V is the average number of values per feature (i.e., the average branching factor in the tree). This complexity presupposes alphabetic sorting of the values so that binary search and storage are possible. Retrieval by search in the tree is independent from the number of training instances, and therefore especially useful for large instance bases. In IB1, search complexity is $O(N * F)$ (with N the number of stored instances). In the grapheme–phoneme transliteration experiment described in Section 3, the average branching factor V is 2.3 (the number of possible values for each feature is 41).

The number of nodes necessary in the worst case to store the instances of the training set is N (maximal number of leaves) $+ (N - 1) * (V - 1)$ (number of non-terminal nodes). For each non-terminal node, a default class label and a pointer for each occurring value of the feature denoted by the node should be stored. This makes the storage requirements proportional to

Procedure **BUILD-IG-TREE**:

Input:

- A training set T of instances with their classes (start value: a full instance base),
- an information-gain-ordered list of features (tests) $F_i...F_n$ (start value: $F_1...F_n$).

Output: An IG subtree.

1. If T is unambiguous (all instances in T have the same class c), or $i = (n+1)$, create a leaf node with class label c.
2. Otherwise, until $i = n$ (the number of features)
   - Select the first feature (test) F_i in $F_i...F_n$, and construct a new node N for feature F_i, and as default class c (the class occurring most frequently in T).
   - Partition T into subsets $T_1...T_m$ according to the values $v_1...v_m$ which occur for F_i in T (instances with the same value for this feature in the same subset).
   - For each $j\epsilon\{1, ..., m\}$:
     if not all instances in T_j map to class c, BUILD-IG-TREE $(T_j, F_{i+1}...F_n)$, connect the root of this subtree to N and label the arc with v_j.

Procedure **SEARCH-IG-TREE**:

Input:

- The root node N of a subtree (start value: top node of a complete IGTree),
- an unlabeled instance I with information-gain-ordered feature values $f_i...f_n$ (start value: $f_1...f_n$).

Output: A class label.

1. If N is a leaf node, output default class c associated with this node.
2. Otherwise, if test F_i of the current node does not originate an arc labeled with f_i, output default class c associated with N.
3. Otherwise,
   - new node M is the end node of the arc originating from N with the label f_i.
   - SEARCH-IG-TREE $(M, f_{i+1}...f_n)$

Figure 1. Algorithms for building IGTrees ('BUILD-IG-TREE') and searching IGTrees ('SEARCH-IG-TREE')

N (compare $O(N * F)$ for IB1). In Section 3, we show that trained on the grapheme–phoneme transliteration problem, the IGTree decision trees use on the average 95% less memory than the IB1 instance bases.

Finally, the cost of building the tree on the basis of a set of instances is proportional to $N * log(V) * F$ in the worst case (compare $O(N)$ for training in IB1).

2.3. *Relation to k-d trees and induced decision trees*

The IGTree approach has strong similarities to both *decision tree learning* (Top Down Induction of Decision Trees, TDIDT, used for abstraction of knowledge from instances bases or indexing instance bases) and *k-d trees* (used for indexing instance bases).

A fundamental difference with decision trees concerns the purpose of IGTrees. The goal of Top Down Induction of Decision Trees, as in the state-of-the-art program C4.5 (Quinlan, 1993), is to *abstract* from the training examples. In contrast, we use decision trees for *lossless* compression of the training examples. Pruning of the resulting tree in order to derive understandable decision trees or rule sets is therefore not an issue in our approach. By *lossless*, we mean that the classifications of the training instances can be completely reconstructed, not that all feature-value information in the original training set can be reconstructed. Generalization is achieved by the defaults at each node, not by pruning. It should be noted here that IGTree decision trees can easily be expanded in such a way that compression is also lossless in terms of feature-value information, when node construction is not halted at the point where classification becomes unambiguous. However, we will refer in this paper only to the variant of IGTree in which features not relevant to classification are not stored.

A simplicification of IGTree as opposed to TDIDT approaches such as C4.5, is that IGTree generates oblivious decision trees, i.e., it computes information gain only once to determine a fixed *feature ordering*. TDIDT approaches, in contrast, recompute information gain (or similar feature selection functions) at each arc of the tree to guide selection of the next test. Finally, in IGTree, defaults are computed at each node of the tree (i.e., defaults are local), whereas in TDIDT, global defaults are used (although in C4.5, a similar local default assignment procedure is used).

In terms of high compression without generalisation performance loss, *C4.5rules* (Quinlan, 1993) appears a strong alternative to IGTree. However, C4.5rules, which extracts compact rule sets from trees generated by C4.5, becomes disproportionally slow when the C4.5-tree is large, as in our experiments: e.g., a C4.5-tree of >30,000 nodes, generated within about a half hour (which is similar to IGTree's processing time), takes several days to be processed by C4.5rules.

K-d trees (Friedman, Bentley, and Finkel 1977) are binary trees that have been proposed for indexing databases of instances (with ordered feature values, e.g., numeric values) for use in k-nearest neighbor approaches. The basic idea is to make use of the observed density of the instance space to structure it for efficient retrieval of the m nearest neighbors of a new (query) instance. To build the k-d tree, the original instance space is partitioned into disjoint subsets by selecting a feature (e.g., the one with the highest inter-quartile-distance) and a threshold value, and creating nodes for each of these subsets. Instances with values for that feature less than or equal to the threshold are stored in one daughter, the others in the other daughter. Nodes therefore represent subsets of the instances. This process is recursively repeated until the number of instances in a node becomes less than a parameter called *bucket size* (maximal allowed number of instances in a leaf node), in which case a leaf node is constructed. The leaf node does not contain class information, as in IGTree, but pointers to the instances in the original instance base that are captured in the bucket. During retrieval of nearest neighbors, given a query instance, the k-d tree is traversed as in decision trees and IGTrees, and at leaf nodes, a queue with the m nearest neighbors is updated. Two tests, based on the similarity of the most similar instance in the queue to the query, are used to determine whether it is necessary to inspect the sister of the current leaf node, and whether all nearest neighbors have been found (if not, backtracking is necessary). Recently, there has been renewed interest in k-d trees and related approaches for efficiently indexing instance bases in lazy learning (Omohundro 1991; Deng and Moore 1995; Wess, Althoff, and Derwand 1994; Wess 1995).

In contrast to k-d trees, the purpose of IGTrees is classification, not efficient nearest neighbor search. IGTrees cannot be used to find the nearest neighbors because the defaults on the leaf nodes do not contain information about the number nor the identity of instances on which they were based. Instances sharing the same subset of feature-value pairs and having the same class in the training set, are not differentiated. Another difference between k-d trees and IGTrees is that the former are restricted to ordered feature values, while the latter are restricted to unordered symbolic features.

Efforts are under way (Wess et al. 1994; Wess 1995) to extend k-d trees with symbolic values. However, extending the test determining whether backtracking is needed for the case of symbolic features significantly increases the computational cost of executing this test, and the test can perform poorly under certain circumstances. There is no gain in retrieval time because the test has to verify each dimension of the attribute space, which can be high for unordered symbolic attributes (Althoff, personal communication). No empirical studies addressing this issue have been published yet.

Although we developed IGTree to deal with the nominal, unordered features with which we describe our linguistic instances, IGTree can be extended to handle continuous features by means of discretization techniques (cf. Dougherty, Kohavi, and Sahami 1995).

Figure 2 graphically shows the differences between k-d trees, IGTrees and C4.5 decision trees on a small symbolic dataset. On the basis of size, shape, and number of holes, an object is to be classified as a nut, screw, key, pen, or scissors. The instance base contains 12 instances. It should be noted that (i) instances 5 and 10 are ambiguous (i.e., they have the same feature values but map to different classes); (ii) the information gain, computed over the full set of instances, of feature 'size' is 0.75, of 'shape' is 0.90, and of 'number of holes' is 1.10; (iii) in the case of k-d trees, 'size' and 'shape' are not treated as numeric features as their values in the instance base are not numeric; in Figure 2 the situation is shown for a k-d tree algorithm which tests a symbolic feature by expanding the tree for every occurring value of that feature. As can be seen in Figure 2, the tree generated by IGTree differs from the tree generated by C4.5 in the number of tests (i.e., IGTree performs fewer tests than C4.5), and in the number of nodes and leaves (e.g., the sum amount of nodes and leaves is smaller in the case of IGTree than in the case of C4.5). The difference between IGTree and the k-d tree is that the buckets in the k-d tree point to instances in the instance base, whereas the nodes and leaves in IGTree do not denote instances, but classifications.

Section 3 describes experiments illustrating the comparative performance (i.e., generalization accuracy and storage requirements) of IGTree, IB1, IB1-IG, and C4.5, for several linguistic tasks.

3. Experiments

In this Section we describe in detail empirical results achieved with IGTree on the letter–phoneme transliteration problem for Dutch. We compare the performance of IGTree in terms of generalization accuracy and storage to IB1, IB1-IG, and C4.5. We provide similar but less detailed results on two other tasks: part-of-speech tagging and hyphenation.

3.1. *Letter–phoneme transliteration*

Letter–phoneme transliteration is a well-known benchmark problem, first discussed in the context of Machine Learning by Sejnowski and Rosenberg (1987). They report on several experiments with the standard connectionist Back-propagation algorithm (Rumelhart et al. 1986) on the NETtalk data. In our experiments, we employ the same encoding scheme that Sejnowski and Rosenberg used to generate their instances (i.e., by moving a fixed-length window over a spelling word, and generating an instance by taking a snapshot of the word visible in the window). Each instance contains a target letter (in the middle) surrounded by left and right context letters. The class associated with the spelling input window is, in our case, the phonemic mapping of the target letter. As with Sejnowski and Rosenberg (1987), a class may be any of the phonemes in the phonemic alphabet, or a *phonemic null* inserted at points where a cluster of two or more spelling letters maps to one phoneme. An example of the generation of instances from a word-pronunciation pair, <boek> (book) – /buk/, is shown in Table 1.

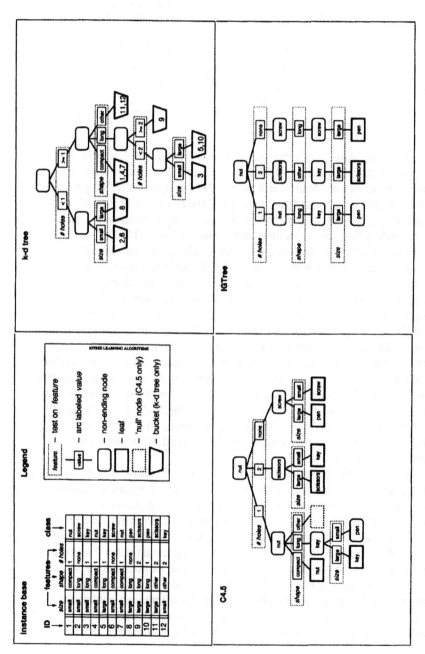

Figure 2. K-d tree, C4.5 decision tree, and IGTree decision tree constructed on the basis of a small instance base.

Table 1. Example generation of fixed-length window instances (3 left context characters, 3 right context characters) from the word-pronunciation pair <boek> – /buk/. Underscores depict word boundaries. The '–' is the phonemic null mapping to the <e>.

Letter in Context							Phoneme
_	_	_	b	o	e	k	b
_	_	b	o	e	k	_	u
_	b	o	e	k	_	_	–
b	o	e	k	_	_	_	k

Automatic learning of letter–phoneme transliteration of English (NETtalk, Sejnowski and Rosenberg 1987) has been claimed as a success story for Back-propagation (but see Stanfill and Waltz 1986; Wolpert 1990; Weijters 1991; and van den Bosch and Daelemans 1993 for examples of *k*-nn algorithms outperforming Back-propagation). The connectionist approach was replicated for Dutch in NetSpraak (Weijters and Hoppenbrouwers 1990).

From CELEX, a lexical data base of English, German, and Dutch, we derived a data base consisting of 20,000 Dutch word-pronunciation pairs. Words and phonemic transcriptions were made of equal length by inserting phonemic nulls ('–') in the phonemic transcriptions (by an alignment algorithm described in Daelemans and Van den Bosch 1994). By using the *windowing* technique described above, the 20,000 word set was converted into a data base containing 218,594 instances. Each instance thus contains seven feature values (each of which is one out of 41 values: the alphabet including letters with diacritics, and the space that occurs before and after words), and is associated with one out of 55 possible phonemes. In our experiments, we used a 10-fold CV setup: i.e., we trained and tested each algorithm on ten different partitions (90% training material, 10% testing material) of the full data base. All performance results reported below are averaged over these experiments.

In Table 2, the performance scores for correctly classified test instances (i.e., correctly transliterated phonemes) and their standard deviations are displayed. We report the scores of IG-Tree, IB1 with the overlap similarity function, IB1 with the information-gain-weighted similarity function (IB1-IG), C4.5 without pruning, and C4.5 with pruning (C4.5-p). It should be noted that C4.5 was run with (i) the information-gain-criterion rather than the gain-ratio-criterion (as our data does not contain value variance anomalies which would be handled by the gain-ratio-criterion, and as this is the same function as used in IG-Tree), (ii) when pruning, the default pruning confidence level of 10% is used, and (iii) a minimum number of instances on either side of a test is set at 1, which is similar to IGTree, rather than the default value of 2.

Table 2. Average generalization performance in terms of correctly transliterated phonemes of unseen Dutch word-pronunciation pairs, with standard deviation, and average memory usage in bytes needed to store the instance base or decision tree in memory, for IGTree, IB1, IB1 with an IG-weighted similarity function (IB1-IG), C4.5 without pruning, and C4.5 with pruning (C4.5-p).

Algorithm	Generalization accuracy on test phonemes	Standard deviation	Memory usage (bytes)
IGTree	97.07	0.11	77,749
IB1	92.11	0.15	1,573,885
IB1-IG	97.17	0.13	1,573,885
C4.5	97.03	0.14	992,047
C4.5-p	96.21	0.15	278,537

Table 3. Significance levels of the differences between the generalization performances of IGTree, IB1, IB1-IG, C4.5, and C4.5-p. One or two asterisks ('*') in a cell in this Table indicate that the algorithm in the row is significantly better than the algorithm in the column. '**' indicates a probability of a Type-I error of 0.001 ($t>3.61$); '*' indicates a Type I-error probability of 0.05 ($t>1.73$). A blank cell indicates that the difference is not significant.

	IB1	C4.5-p	C4.5	IGTree
IB1-IG	**	**	*	*
IGTree	**	**	–	–
C4.5	**	**	–	–
C4.5-p	**	–	–	–

Furthermore, Table 2 reports the average number of bytes needed to store the instance base or decision tree in memory. Given the fact that in our problem feature-values and classes are represented by one byte, the memory allocated by IB1 (and IB1-IG) can be computed by multiplying the number of instances with the number of features plus one (the class). In our implementation of IGTree, seven bytes per node are used: a 4-byte pointer, a feature-value, a (default) class, and one byte indicating the number of daughter nodes. If the same compact memory storage method would be implemented in C4.5, this algorithm would need eight bytes per node (including one byte to denote the feature number). However, in C4.5 (version 7), each feature is expanded for all its possible values, leading to a very large number of 'empty' end nodes that contain no feature-values. Needing only seven bytes per node in this case, the results in Table 2 are based on the numbers of nodes reported by C4.5.

Table 3 indicates the significance levels of the differences between the generalization accuracy scores reported in Table 2.

The performance results in Table 2 and Table 3 indicate that IB1 with the overlap distance similarity function and C4.5 with pruning are at a significant disadvantage as compared to IGTree, IB1-IG, and C4.5 without pruning. IB1-IG outperforms, with a slight but significant margin, both IGTree and C4.5.

The average memory usage displayed in Table 2 demonstrates the considerable compression (95.1%) obtained with IGTree as compared to IB1-IG, without losing much generalization performance. In comparison, with pruning, C4.5 obtains 82.3% compression.

As a second illustration of accuracy, we mention the results of a comparison between IGTree trained on a set of 70,000 Dutch word-pronunciation pairs, and Morpa-cum-Morphon (Nunn and Van Heuven, 1993), a state-of-the-art "linguistic–engineering" system for Dutch. Tested on an identical test set (provided by the developers of Morpa-cum-Morphon), IGTree produced 89.5% correctly transliterated words, whereas Morpa-cum-Morphon only converted 85.3% words correctly (Van den Bosch and Daelemans, 1993).

3.2. Hyphenation and part-of-speech tagging

In order to obtain a better insight into the properties of IGTree, we provide some additional results obtained with IGTree on different datasets.

Hyphenation
The problem of hyphenation (assigning syllable structure to the spelling of a word) is defined as a classification problem by using windowing as in grapheme–phoneme transliteration. For each target symbol (with a context of letters to the left and to the right of it), the class is either yes (start of a syllable at that position) or no (no start of syllable at that position). The experiment was based on 10-fold cross-validation on a dataset derived from 20,000 hyphenated English words.

The performance results indicate that IGTree (94.53%) performs significantly better than C4.5 (94.38%) and C4.5 with pruning (92.68%), but performs significantly worse than IB1 (95.30%) and IB1-IG (95.21%). Interestingly, there is no significant difference between IB1 and IB-IG. The information gain weights (reflecting feature accuracy) are insufficiently different in this case to make a difference.

The average memory usage again demonstrates the considerable compression (91.1%) obtained with IGTree as compared to IB1 and IB1-IG. In comparison, with pruning, C4.5 obtains 72.5% compression.

Part-of-speech tagging
In part-of-speech tagging, the task is to disambiguate the syntactic category of a word on the basis of preceding and following context. Again a windowing approach can be used to translate a corpus of tagged sentences into an instance

Table 4. Information gain values of the seven input features (the focus letter F surrounded by context letters) of the grapheme-phoneme-transliteration task and the hyphenation task, and the gain ratio values of the four input features of the part-of-speech-tagging task.

Task	F-3	F-2	F-1	F	F+1	F+2	F+3
Grapheme-phoneme transliteration	0.185	0.280	0.711	3.059	0.857	0.381	0.218
Hyphenation	0.040	0.093	0.083	0.047	0.081	0.035	0.013
Part-of-speech Tagging	–	0.06	0.23	0.69	0.21	–	–

base. The experiment was based on a single partitioning of a dataset into a training set of 100,000 instances, and a test set of 10,000 instances.

The performance results indicate that IGTree (95.1%) performs significantly better than IB1 (85.7%) and IB1-IG (94.7%). In this experiment we used Quinlan's (1993) gain ratio criterion rather than information gain, as not all features have an equal number of values in this problem. Memory compression with IGTree was 91.9% compared to IB1.

In Table 4, the information gain values of the seven input features of the grapheme-phoneme-transliteration task (cf. Section 3.1) and the hyphenation task (cf. Section 3.2) are displayed, as well as the gain ratio values of the four input features of the part-of-speech-tagging task (cf. Section 3.2).

4. Conclusions

We have shown that for two tasks, which are typical for a large class of real-world problems in natural language processing (cf. the characterisation of these problems in Section 1), IGTree performs only slightly worse or better in terms of generalization performance than IB1 augmented with an information-gain-weighted similarity function (IB1-IG), gaining considerably in memory resources needed for storage (91.9% and 95.1% compression in our experiments), and in search complexity ($O(F * log(V))$) rather than $O(F * N)$, which becomes especially favorable when N, the number of instances, is very large). Comparing IGTree with C4.5, which is aimed more at abstracting from training examples, we note that the current implementation of C4.5 (with pruning) generalizes less accurately than IGTree and IB1-IG, and uses more memory than IGTree. For a third task, viz. word hyphenation, in which there is no outspoken variation in the information gain values of the features, we have shown that both IGTree and IB1-IG generalise worse than IB1 with the overlap similarity function.

IGTree's tree building procedure is not aimed at indexing individual cases, as with k-d trees, but is aimed at compressed storage of those parts of training instances relevant to classification. Retrieval of class information from IGTree decision trees is speedy and deterministic, and does not involve backtracking. As the generalization accuracy of k-d trees (with symbolic values) can be assumed equal to that of IB1-IG, and since IB1-IG does not significantly perform better than IGTree, we conclude that, for the type of problem we investigated, it is not necessary to put extra processing effort in finding the absolute nearest neighbor to a new instance.

Given the fact that for many tasks large numbers of instances are available (several orders of magnitude more than the 1,000 instances of typical benchmark problems), the IGTree approach appears interesting and useful, especially for the type of problem characterized in this paper.

Acknowledgements

We gratefully recognize Jakub Zavrel, Stephen Omohundro, Klaus-Dieter Althoff, Andrew Moore, David Aha and the AI Review referees for valuable comments, discussions and analyses, and thank Fred Wan for his help with the significance tests.

References

Aha, D. W., Kibler, D., & Albert, M. (1991). Instance-Based Learning Algorithms. *Machine Learning* 7: 37–66.

Aha, D. W. (1992). Generalizing from Case Studies: A Case Study. In *Proceedings of the Ninth International Conference on Machine Learning*, 1–10. Aberdeen, Scotland: Morgan Kaufmann.

Cardie, C. (1993). A Case-Based Approach to Knowledge Acquisition for Domain-Specific Sentence Analysis. In *Proceedings of the Eleventh National Conference on Artificial Intelligence*, pp. 798–803, San Jose, CA: AAAI Press.

Daelemans, W. (1995). Memory-based Lexical Acquisition and Processing. In Steffens, P. (ed.) *Machine Translation and the Lexicon*, Lecture Notes in Artificial Intelligence, 898. Springer: Berlin.

Daelemans, W. & Van den Bosch, A. (1992). Generalisation Performance of Backpropagation Learning on a Syllabification Task. In Drossaers, M. & Nijholt, A. (eds.) *TWLT3: Connectionism and Natural Language Processing*. Enschede: Twente University.

Daelemans, W. & Van den Bosch, A. (1994). A Language-Independent, Data-Oriented Architecture for Grapheme-to-Phoneme Conversion. In *Proceedings of ESCA-IEEE Speech Synthesis Conference '94*. New York.

Deng, K. & Moore, A. W. (1995). Multiresolution Instance-Based Learning. In *Proceedings of the Fourteenth International Joint Conference on Artificial Intelligence*. Montreal: Morgan Kaufmann.

Dougherty, J., Kohavi, R. & Sahami, M. (1995). Supervised and Unsupervised Discretization of Continuous Features. In *Proceedings of the Twelfth International Conference on Machine Learning*, pp. 194–202, Tahoe City, CA: Morgan Kaufmann.

Friedman, J., Bentley, J. & Ari Finkel, R. (1977). An Algorithm for Finding Best Matches in Logarithmic Expected Time. *ACM Transactions on Mathematical Software* 3(3).

Kitano, H. (1993). Challenges of Massive Parallelism. In *Proceedings of the Thirteenth International Conference on Artificial Intelligence*, pp. 813–834, Chembery, France: Morgan Kaufmann.

Kohavi, R. & Li, C-H. (1995). Oblivious Decision Trees, Graphs, and Top-Down Pruning. *Proceedings of the Fourteenth International Joint Conference on Artificial Intelligence*, 1071–1077. Montreal: Morgan Kaufmann.

Langley, P. & Sage, S. (1994). Oblivious Decision Trees and Abstract Cases. In Aha, D. W. (ed.) *Case-Based Reasoning: Papers from the 1994 Workshop* (Technical Report WS-94-01). Menlo Park, CA: AAAI Press.

Nunn, A. & van Heuven, V. J. (1993). Morphon, Lexicon-Based Text-to-Phoneme Conversion and Phonological Rules. In van Heuven, V. J. & Pols, L. C. (eds.) *Analysis and Synthesis of Speech: Strategic Research Towards High-Quality Text-to-Speech Generation*. Berlin: Mouton de Gruyter.

Omohundro, S. M. (1991). Bumptrees for Efficient Function, Constraint, and Classification Learning. In Lippmann, R. P., Moody J. E. & Touretzky, D. S. (eds.) *Advances in Neural Information Processing Systems 3*. San Mateo, CA: Morgan Kaufmann.

Quinlan, J. (1993). *C4.5: Programs for Machine Learning*. San Mateo, CA: Morgan Kaufmann.

Rumelhart, D. E., Hinton, G. E. & Williams, R. J. (1986). Learning Internal Representations by Error Propagation. In Rumelhart, D. E. & McClelland, J. L. (eds.) *Parallel Distributed Processing: Explorations in the Microstructure of Cognition*, volume 1: Foundations. Cambridge, MA: The MIT Press.

Sejnowski, T. J. & Rosenberg, C. S. (1987). Parallel Networks that Learn to Pronounce English Text. *Complex Systems* 1: 145–168.

Stanfill, C. & Waltz, D. (1986). Toward Memory-Based Reasoning. *Communications of the ACM* 29: 1212–1228.

Van den Bosch, A. & Daelemans, W. (1993). Data-Oriented Methods for Grapheme-to-Phoneme Conversion. In *Proceedings of the 6th Conference of the EACL*, 45–53. Utrecht: OTS.

Weijters, A. & Hoppenbrouwers, G. (1990). NetSpraak: een neuraal netwerk voor grafeem-foneem-omzetting. *Tabu* 20(1): 1–25.

Weijters, A. (1991). A Simple Look-Up Procedure Superior to NETtalk? In *Proceedings of the International Conference on Artificial Neural Networks*. Finland: Espoo.

Wess, S., Althoff, K. D. & Derwand, G. (1994). Using k-d Trees to Improve the Retrieval Step in Case-Based Reasoning. In Wess, S., Althoff K. D. & Richter, M. M. (eds.) *Topics in Case-Based Reasoning*. Berlin: Springer Verlag.

Wess, S. (1995). *Fallbasiertes Problemlösen in wissensbasierten Systemen zur Entscheidungsunterstützung und Diagnostik*. Doctoral Dissertation, University of Kaiserslautern.

Wolpert, D. H. (1990). Constructing a Generalizer Superior to NETtalk via a Mathematical Theory of Generalization. *Neural Networks* 3: 445–452.